Risk Assessment for Object Conservation

Risk Assessment for Object Conservation

Jonathan Ashley-Smith

BUTTERWORTH HEINEMANN

OXFORD AUCKLAND BOSTON JOHANNESBURG MELBOURNE NEW DELHI

Butterworth-Heinemann
Linacre House, Jordan Hill, Oxford OX2 8DP
225 Wildwood Avenue, Woburn, MA 01801-2041
A division of Reed Educational and Professional Publishing Ltd

A member of the Reed Elsevier plc group

First published 1999

British Library Cataloguing in Publication Data
A catalogue record for this book is available from the British Library

ISBN 07506 2853 7

Library of Congress Cataloguing in Publication Data
A catalogue record for this book is available from the Library of Congress

Composition by Genesis Typesetting, Rochester, Kent

Contents

Health and safety warning

This book is about the effect of use and environment on objects in museum collections. It contains no information about hazards to health and safety posed by treatment of the collections or by the collections themselves.

Preface

> 'And she's dying to hear my explanation. And believe me I'd tell her, but I'm stumbling down various avenues of thought. Nothing coherent is coming out, 'cause there's so much to say, so many different words, so many millions of options to reverse and regret within each sentence, man. All the choices seem so seductive, so appealing, man. I just want to explain it all to her, bit by bit, no matter how long it takes,' (*Name the Baby*, Mark Cirino, 1997)

This book is the product of a year's research leave taken between October 1994 and October 1995. The majority of the reading and thinking, and some of the writing, was done in that 12-month period. Once back at the V&A I found it difficult to continue with the composition, but many of the ideas continued to surface in my mind. I continued to accumulate books and photocopies. I read some of them. A year later a further three months' leave was granted to enable me to complete the manuscript. As things turned out the three months were spread over a period of nine, so that the whole project took nearly three years.

The preparation for the concentrated period of study and creativity consisted of six years of academic research in chemistry, five years as a conservator of metalwork and 17 years as a senior manager in a major national museum.

It is probably the last 10 years in the senior management of a large museum that shaped the main direction of the book. During this time there was a steady decrease in direct support from central government. At the same time there was a steady increase in the demand for greater public access to the collections and for measures of value for money. Strategic planning and public accountability are now so much a part of museum thinking that it is impossible to believe that museums were created and run for many decades without any consideration of either. Attitudes change with time. It is possible that anyone chancing to read this book in 10 years' time will wonder why so much emphasis is placed on value, costs and financial benefits.

Although the attitudes expressed in this book may have developed over 30 years, nearly all the information used has only entered my head during the past three. There are many disadvantages in having a limited period in which to gather information, evaluate and represent it. The avenues I explored were always the easiest and most interesting rather than the most necessary. The books and articles I read were those that came to hand most readily, the people I spoke to were those that happened to be there on the day. I have not found time to correct the imbalance caused by this random selection.

Because much of what I was learning was new to me, my attitude to how true or how useful it was changed frequently. Like Lewis Caroll's Red Queen I believed several impossible things before breakfast. Deadlines can be shifted only so many times and eventually I had to declare 'This is what I believe right now'. Yet after that point I may have reinterpreted the evidence that I had available then or I may have come across new evidence in a reference that had eluded me previously. I recommend that you question everything you read.

Where I have had to deal with topics that are really beyond my comprehension, such as economic theory, I have used and presented them in a superficial manner that would make any specialist cringe. I have exercised the right of any human being to discuss both philosophy and psychology without anything more than a passing knowledge of the huge body of academic study in these areas.

Because it deals with value, cost and benefit this book is slightly, and for the most part unintentionally, political. The amount of money that is available for the conservation of the cultural heritage is directly and indirectly controlled by government. Through their allocations and taxation policies politicians show their personal valuation of heritage. By adopting short-term policies they appear to be making untrue assumptions about the values that their constituents place on the preservation of historic works.

In order to control deterioration through overuse it is necessary to impose some sort of rationing. The views of some groups of people must be considered more important than others. No matter how this is achieved it will inevitably create an élite, which is a political act.

This is a personal book. I have personal interests and personal views in areas such as materials science, the ethics of restoration, the costs of conservation and the philosophy of museums. Attempting to draw these disparate subjects into a coherent whole was for my personal satisfaction. Indeed it may satisfy no one but myself. Because the subject areas are disparate it is possible that the reader may be a specialist in one area but have no knowledge of any others. For this reason I have allowed myself the use of the first person in the text; in the singular to describe the author, and in the plural to describe the combination of author and reader discovering new ideas together. It is likely that many readers will have no scientific or mathematical interest. For this reason I have sometimes gone into laborious detail about the interpretation of scientific information which will be insufferable for the scientific reader but I trust will be welcomed by those from other backgrounds.

Shortly before the beginning of my research year, Robert Waller, a pioneer in the use of risk assessment for collections management, told me he didn't think that the profession was ready for a monograph on the subject. He is probably right. However, the book I have written served as a primer for my own expedition into this area. It may well serve the same purpose for you.

Jonathan Ashley-Smith

Reference

Cirino, Mark (1997) *Name the Baby.* Phoenix House, London. ISBN 1-86159-065-2, p. 100.

Acknowledgements

It took three years to persuade me to take research leave. Thanks for their persistence must go to John Murdoch and Elizabeth Esteve-Coll. Elizabeth also arranged for me to be a visiting scholar at Wolfson College, Cambridge.

During the year of my research leave the burden of managing the Conservation Department at the V&A Museum was shared, at great cost to their own work, by Graham Martin, Helen Shenton, Nick Umney, Agnes Holden and Timothy Stevens. After my official return all of them gave me encouragement and support so that I could complete the task.

The monetary costs of the research were covered by grants from the V&A Research Committee and the Leverhulme Trust. Special thanks go to the Leverhulme Trust for their sensible approach to financial accountability. I received backing for my Leverhulme application from Anna Plowden and Professor, the Lord, 'Jack' Lewis. I regret that I broke my promise to Anna, who demanded that the book should be simple enough for her to understand. I received support for my Research Committee application from Gerhard Banik, who also arranged for me to stay at the Schloss Solitude, a delightful and inspiring experience. He also forced me to give my first public lecture on this subject, an event that greatly focused my mind.

Within the V&A, everyone in the department suffered to some extent, but there were a few members of staff who had some idea of what I was trying to do and were able to offer assistance. They sent me press cuttings, photocopies, warned me of forthcoming meetings and looked things up for me. Notable among these were Elizabeth Martin, Dorothy Rogers, Lynda Hillyer and Alison Richmond.

Outside the museum I was made welcome in a great many homes and institutions. I have been lent books and photocopy cards, sent e-mails and faxes, been given ideas, photographs and journals. I have been driven places, plied with food and drink and offered places to sleep. Among many others, thanks to: Andreas Burmester, Emer Bell, Jim Druzik, David Erhardt, Alan Farancz, Gerald FitzGerald, David Howell, Johanna Leissner, Richard Lindo, Paul Marcon, Mark McCormick-Goodhart, Marion Mecklenburg, Lisa Mibach, Stefan Michalski, Ginny Naudé, Jerry

Podany, Derek Priest, Hannelore Römich, David Scott, David Tremain, Charles Tumosa, Dianne Van der Reyden and Robert Waller.

Finally, many thanks to my wife Diane and my children Joseph and Zoë. They tolerated my absences, brought me tea and coffee when I was present, and provided me with endless diversions that prevented me from getting obsessively engrossed in this work.

1 The conservation connection

In this chapter the study of risk in conservation is placed in the broad context of the politics and philosophy of the preservation of cultural heritage. The structure of the book, and its attempt at a logical progression through tools, concepts, information and examples, is described. There is encouragement to experience the excitement and beauty of using graphs, equations and mathematical modelling. There are warnings about a rigid reliance on quantification. Attitudes to risk and regulation are discussed. Finally, there is a stipulation about the dangers of anthropomorphism and an invitation to learn the skills of thinking logarithmically.

The big picture

'The urban sprawl of Cairo – whose population has risen from two million to seventeen million in the past forty years – has reached the Pyramids and the paws of the Sphinx, bringing with it cars, sewage, polluted air, and fast food culture.' (Article in *The New Yorker*, 1997)

'We will reduce the number of rooms open to the public. Next, we will switch over to the nineteenth century system, under which it will be possible to visit the museum only as long as it is light. Phase three really does put us on a "war" footing. That's when we won't be able to pay any of the security staff and will have to guard the valuables ourselves. And the last phase is when the only way to see the museum will be on the Internet, because, when it comes down to it, the main function of a museum is to preserve its works of art, rather than show them regardless of the consequences.' (Mikhail Piotrovsky, Director of the Hermitage, 1996)

'. . . we cannot simply be backward looking. Knowledge of the past can enhance our understanding of the present, but national well-being demands that our respect for the past is tempered by an impatience to improve upon it . . . the taxpayer should be seen as a

> critical partner – keen to join with others to achieve our policy but unwilling to act as the guarantor of projects for which there is inadequate support.' (Stephen Dorrell, Secretary of State for the National Heritage, 1994)

The Pyramids and the Sphinx have been around for a very long time. Their present state does not resemble the state they were in when they were created. They are deteriorating. Yet they exist in a form that can still inspire wonder, interest and enjoyment in those that visit them. The causes of deterioration are of concern to magazine readers in countries far from Egypt, people who may never have seen these monuments and have no plans to visit. The benefits and by-products of the modern civilization enjoyed by these remote readers are perceived as agents of destruction that will damage these ancient relics.

The preservation of cultural objects is not a simple subject. There are no simple solutions and there will never be universal agreement. It is dangerous to assume that there could be. If you start with a discussion about rates of deterioration or the effects of different methods of protection, you will find yourself relentlessly drawn into areas of philosophy, politics and economics. Part of the beauty of the Pyramids is that they have already been damaged. The people who 'own' these imperfect monuments feel obliged to slow the rate of damage. This requires money, which can best be derived from income gained from tourism. The visitors cause further damage to the objects and to the local culture. To preserve the physical reality, potential visitors could be offered virtual reality. Surprisingly, the people with the money and the determination to interfere with the state of the monuments, and to fund alternative realities, are neither the owners nor the visitors. Nor do they always care greatly for the rights or feelings of either of these groups.

Some of the artifacts of human civilization such as the Pyramids and the contents of the Pharaohs' tombs have lasted for thousands of years. Physical evidence of early life on this planet has lasted for millions of years. Yet many of the material traces of recent history have completely disappeared. The museum is a comparatively recent, and possibly short-lived, invention whose function is to stop this loss. In museums, objects are collected together for ease of study, to create an enjoyable experience and to enhance their chances of preservation. Yet objects that survived for millennia before entering a museum have rapidly changed for the worse once they have been acquired. A vocal global profession has been built on the premise that objects in museums are decaying, and that they need special environments and specialized treatment to make them last longer. Industries have been developed for the supply of equipment for storage of museum objects and the control of their environment.

The prevention of damage costs money. Provision of access to the objects in museums costs money. Access can be made to generate income, but only as long as the objects survive. Choices must be made about the need for revenue and the balance of expenditure between preservation and exploitation. Choices must be made about how much from the past can be preserved – surely not everything?

Yet the majority of museums continue to take on responsibility for more and more material. The majority of large holdings of cultural material rely on external funding, a large element of which is controlled by central government. When, for political, economic or philosophical reasons, governments feel unable to provide this money, further difficult decisions must be taken. These choices will be made in the light of opinions about the purpose of the museum, feelings about the benefits that access provides and the costs of maintaining the objects in an accessible state. Modern technology offers both opportunities and threats. Once collections are available 'on the Internet' it is debatable whether the real, expensive-to-keep and expensive-to-visit, object has any lasting purpose.

In the past two decades economics and dogma have forced governments to take increasingly short-term views about the provision of funds. This is alien to the traditional understanding of the long-term role of museums but encouraging to commercial exploitation.

Whether they admit it or not, this is the wider context within which curators and conservators are currently working. The following chapters explore ways of evaluating the consequences of decisions about the use and preservation of objects in museum collections, keeping in mind the world beyond the museum walls.

The purpose of the book

If you work within a museum-like organization, you will be familiar with five sorts of situation that arise regularly:

- those that result from decisions you made
- those that result from decisions made by someone who asked for your advice
- those that result from decisions made by someone who never listens to your advice
- those that result from lack of decision
- those that result from events outside the normal decision-making process, such as high winds or torrential rain

The discussions in this book should make you more able to influence those decisions where you have input, and may make you feel more comfortable with those where you do not. To that extent it is an answer to the traditional prayer: 'God grant me the serenity to accept the things I cannot change, the courage to change the things I can; and the wisdom to know the difference.'

The author's authority

My experience of this subject has been gained solely in one museum, but what I say should be relevant to any museum, gallery, archive, library, historic house or private collection. Whenever I use the word 'museum' I mean any or all of these.

My experience is principally with movable objects; books, archives and examples of fine and decorative arts. What I shall be talking about will derive from this experience but should apply to some extent to industrial collections, natural history collections and the built heritage. Whenever I use the word 'object' it is intended to cover anything smaller than a cathedral. When I use the word 'collection' it means any group of objects that for better management or easier comprehension is considered as one set, unified by some common factor such as location, material, date, manufacturer, culture or collector.

The conservation department in which I work is involved with environmental monitoring, passive and interventive conservation, preservation, restoration, training, research and technical examination. I shall use the word 'conservator' to mean someone whose main efforts are spent in one or more of these activities.

The use of models and mathematics

The book begins by providing the tools, such as the vocabulary and theoretical models, for assessing risk. It goes on to provide information about the way objects, and the materials from which they are made, react to the way they are used and to the environments to which they are subjected. By combining concepts and information we can begin to assess the risks to objects in museums.

In the following chapter you will begin to notice graphs. The graph is the simplest kind of model that will be used to present information and ideas. I am constantly disappointed to find that people who have chosen to work with historic objects, and claim to think in a very visual way, find graphs a great turn-off. At one level, if you are prejudiced against science, you could dismiss them as 'scientific'. A graph is a two-dimensional analogue of quantities that have been measured. It can be used as a database from which individual measurements can be retrieved. However, a graph can be much more elegant than that. It can be a striking visual representation of a relationship. The beautiful shape of the curve is a direct route to the understanding of a process. Looking at a graph you can instantly appreciate the similarities between disparate phenomena. Indeed, at this level, the graph becomes elegant because of its sheer simplicity. You will soon learn that nearly all observed relationships can be conveyed using a vocabulary of fewer than a dozen simple shapes of curve.

Having learned the basic jargon associated with risk we move on to consider decisions. Conservators and curators are not alone in the world in having to make decisions. There is a great deal to learn from other professions. Stefan Michalski, a name that will crop up frequently throughout the book, has written an eloquent entreaty to share responsibility for conservation decisions (Michalski, 1994). There are other philosophies and sciences that can be adopted as role models by the willing student.

Conservation is supposedly about making things last longer. There are many things that impinge on our daily life where other people have made decisions about how long things will last. We must be able to learn something from them. Engineers use the concept of 'reliability' to determine how often a missile will fail in the reality of battle, or how long it will be before your personal stereo just stops working. How *do* food packagers determine the 'eat by' date?

Yet unless great care is taken, the translation of one set of ideas into another discipline can provide, at best, disappointment and, at worst, misleading directions. Most of the words and methods used in this book come from management science. There are sound reasons for believing that the unthinking injection of pure managerialism into museums is not helpful (Brockley, 1997).

The principal model for decision-making used in this book is the decision tree. This is a graphic representation which shows the number of possible outcomes of a single decision. At that stage we begin to consider the probability that an outcome will not be one that we want. The name Bayes and the adjective Bayesian occur frequently in the literature on probabilities and decision-making (e.g. Morgan and Henrion, 1990). Thomas Bayes is responsible for a theorem, formulated in 1760, that mathematically relates our prior assessment of the probabilty of an event with our later prediction of future events. In essence the theorem indicates that it is *theoretically* possible to learn from experience. The degree to which this actually happens is debatable. As an example, the failure of a dam is one of many possible causes of the loss of heritage material. The earliest record of a dam failure dates from 1219 when a structure near Grenoble, France, failed after 28 years of service. Yet dams have continued to be built and have continued to fail. Out of a total of 1764 dams built in the US before 1959, nearly 90 failed (Levy and Salvadori, 1992).

Of course, the reason why people continue to build dams is that they serve a purpose. They provide benefits that are deemed to outweigh the risks. This is why the automobile has not been banned, even though it is responsible for death, injury and illness on a large scale. This is why conservators continue to apply solvents to the delicate surfaces of objects, and curators continue to expose those objects to shock and vibration by sending them out on loan. This is why the assessment and reduction of risk should be seen in the larger context of the museum business rather than as an obsessive end in itself.

In Chapter 4 an attempt is made to model the museum business from the perspective of the collections. It is a model that points to important relationships without describing them in any detail or attempting to quantify them. It qualifies as a 'metamodel' (van Gigch, 1991). It is a model of concepts that can aid strategic thinking but which does not provide usable information on demand. This particular 'metamodel' places the museum collections in the context of the greater environment. One where people have other concerns such as the conservation of the built heritage or the ecology of the planet. Blinkered concern for the objects alone has led to conflicts with those with other obsessions such as the integrity of historic buildings. A sign that a wider sharing attitude is developing is The New Orleans Charter (APT/AIC, 1992) which affirms that the care of historic structures and the care of their contents must be considered as one integrated whole rather than two conflicting ideals.

In later chapters a different sort of model is introduced, one in which numbers are put in at one end and different numbers come out at the other. The use of numbers can appear to give a misleading certainty. Like graphs, mathematical models *can* be used to deliver verifiable quantitative information. But we should not be afraid of using numbers merely as the fuel that makes the model work. Models may provide a way of clarifying and confirming what we already know. They may challenge our understanding of the causes and effects of changes that occur within the system we are studying. If we try to quantify the relationships that the model reveals, we are made much more aware of our current lack of understanding and information. Using a computer to generate models often accelerates this demonstration of weak areas of knowledge or reasoning. The computer dislikes incomplete information and usually requires quantitative data. In the simple computer programs that I used to help me understand relationships between decay, risks, costs and benefits, I was obliged to enter numbers with no notion of how close they were to a measurable reality. This in itself was a learning experience. Models that are used in this exploratory way are called 'toys'. I have found playing with them as powerfully addictive as I used to find the mysterious world explored through the eyepieces of a binocular microscope when I was a bench conservator.

Chapter 8 is littered with equations. The equation is seen as a 'scientific' tool and again is perceived as difficult, boring and exact. It is of course none of these. An equation is an exquisitely concise way of describing relationships. If neccesary it can be used exactly, but it also can be used creatively to explore concepts and connectivities.

There is a certain touching faith in the view that, because they are inhumanly logical, scientists, equations and computers must be purveyors of truth. However, all of them are vehicles of assumptions. The computer is more than a box of components that carries out arithmetic very fast. It is a social artifact that acts as a medium for social interactions. These relationships are built into a model using a set of encoded instructions. This means that one person's common sense can still come out the other end as someone else's garbage. In many cases where I mention models in this book I was the individual that concieved the problem, selected the equations and programmed the instructions. Until you started to read this book I was the only person reacting to the output. Yet I may have been deceived by the results because I wanted to believe the conclusion. The conclusion was a result of the personal biases I had used in the model.

Many risk analysis problems involve a great number of interlinked variables and need complex computer programs to evaluate them. In most cases the person that initially conceives and articulates the problem will not be the person that compiles the computer code. The person who uses the computer to gain advice on a particular problem may have no connection with either of these two.

There is an interesting example of risk assessment that resulted in tragedy because of the assumptions built into a computer program. Thirty-seven sailors died when the frigate USS *Stark* was hit by Iraqi-fired missiles in 1989. The sophisticated defence system ranked incoming missiles in terms of 'hostility' rather than proximity. The fact that the Iraqi missiles never showed on the monitor has been attributed to the fact that they had been manufactured in France, a NATO ally, and were therefore not 'hostile' at all (Chapman, 1994).

Quantification

Chapters 9–11 deal with observed and measured phenomena. They describe changes in the environment that may cause changes in museum objects whether they are being used, displayed, or left neglected in a cellar. The more we can understand the mechanisms of change, the more we will feel able to predict the outcome of similar changes in the future. The more we understand the relationships between the many agents of change, the easier it will be to devise methods of reducing the risk. Most of the descriptions in these chapters are qualitative, rather than quantitative, as is the case with a great deal of useful science.

However, one of the reasons for studying risk is in order to gain a sense of proportion. If we want to know which are the big risks that we should pay attention to, and which are so trivial they can be ignored, we need to begin to quantify. We need to measure, or to rely on other people's measurements. We need to have approximate numbers for probabilities of accidents and for the rates of progress of decay. If the figures are relevant and accurate then we will be able to predict with accuracy, and we will make accurate asessments of risk. If the figures are relevant but not really that acurate we will still be able to make useful comparisons and be able to rank the hazards in order of risk.

It is the relevance of the figures that causes the biggest problem. Physics has been defined as the science devoted to discovering, developing and refining those aspects of reality that are amenable to mathematical analysis (Ziman, 1978). We need to be sure that the reality with which we are concerned bears some relationship to that particular portion of reality that happens to be amenable to numeric manipulation.

Costs, benefits and attitudes to risk

A very simple view of cost–benefit analysis is given in Chapter 5. It is a considerably more subtle technique than I have been able to describe in a brief introduction. This blunt description does, however, lead to the idea of risks being probable costs. It points to the link between present estimates of value and a future stream of benefits. It leads in Chapters 6 and 7 to a definition of value that rests on utility, the potential to be useful.

These ideas are developed more fully in Chapters 12–15 which deal with the effects of access and use on the collections. It is at this point that comparisons between risk and benefit come to the fore. It is also at this stage that your individual attitude to risk will be formed or discovered. In museums risk information can be used solely to limit access to collections, because it is use that causes damage. Alternatively, risk information can be used to limit risk while allowing use, if not encouraging it. Developing an understanding of the benefits of access tends towards a greater acceptance of risk. A thorough understanding of risk can allow more adventurous behaviour which does not actually increase the danger of damage.

Margaret Thatcher, an English politician who bears considerable responsibility for shaping the world in which museums must now operate, excused capitalism on the grounds that only those that accept risks should be allowed to receive the benefits. In the context of museums this should be modified to say that risks should only be taken if the benefits warrant it. Accepting risks is an obvious admission of the concept of 'acceptable risk', which also implies that there must be some level of damage that is acceptable. These ideas are pursued in Chapter 11 through discussions of light-sensitive objects which, by definition, may be damaged every time they are seen.

A name that you cannot escape if you read any literature about risk in environmental health is Joseph Rodricks. He has written a very readable book called *Calculated Risks* in which he argues for a *relative* description of safety (Rodricks, 1992). Zero risk is a meaningless expression and to set standards that imply zero risk is mendacious not to mention costly.

The loss of benefits caused by too cautious an approach to risk was of concern to Mrs Thatcher's successor as prime minister in the UK, John Major:

> 'Over-regulation stifles the innovation and dynamism needed for a successful and growing economy, that is why all proposals for new regulation must now be accompanied on publication by an assessment of the cost to business of complying with them. However, regulation must also be proportionate to the problem. New regulation will be justified where there is a clear risk of death or serious harm, but it is a mistake to try and regulate against all risks. Balanced risk assessment should be an integral part of the policy-making process. This is just as important when regulations are being re-examined following specific incidents as in the day-to-day process of reviewing and improving regulation' (Major, 1993)

There is no reason why there cannot be innovation and dynamism in museums, and no reason why conservators and curators should not be a part of the process. They just need to appreciate the benefits and the risks. They do not need the polarized propaganda typical of campaigns against drug abuse, or blanket regulations that allow no exceptions and no expert interpretations. Just as not everyone who tries cocaine becomes an addict and not everyone who eats unpasteurized cheese dies of listeria, so not every piece of art on paper is damaged by light and not every piece of furniture is destroyed by fluctuations in humidity. Observation and investigation allow you to discriminate.

We can share our attitudes as well as our responsibilities with other professions. For instance with architects and engineers:

> 'Daring and Prudence, when used together, lead to new *and* safe structures. Today we can be more confident than ever of our designs and hence more innovative, but if wise we are also perpetually more vigilant.' (Levy and Salvadori, 1992)

If you know the limits of safe behaviour you can move away from them, as fast and as far as you possibly can, to get to an imaginary land where there is no apparent risk at all. Or you can stay a prudent distance away from the limits, erring on the side of safety. Or you can 'test the envelope', looking for the real threshold between safety and danger. My own attitude to risk in conservation is noticeably more 'reckless' now than it was 20 years ago. This may be a consequence of growing old, or of being in management too long. But maybe it is the result of a proper appreciation of the balance between benefit and risk.

In the last two chapters of the book the extent to which risk information has actually been used is described. The research that needs to be done to make this information more effective and incisive is discussed. But before you actually start the book I would like to make one stipulation and offer one piece of advice.

One fundamental premise – only people bleed

A great deal of the available literature on risk analysis comes from studies on effects of particular environments on the health of human beings. In a number of the chapters of this book we will be looking at methods that have been successfully applied in the area of human health and mortality and seeing whether they can be applied in the case of museum objects. Throughout those discussions it is very important to bear in mind that *objects are not living beings*. There are fundamental differences between people and objects. For instance, death is an inevitability for all humans, but it need only be an academic concept for museum objects.

There is a superficial resemblance between conservation and medicine. Confusion has been encouraged by the emotive interpretation of observed signs as symptoms of illness (bronze disease, sick glass). Objects are described as 'needing' a 'rest', needing to be 'fed' or needing to 'breathe'. We talk about objects 'suffering' through lack of treatment, or as a result of it. We talk about the 'welfare' and 'well-being' of objects. There is even a 'Collections Health Index'.

If you are trying to explain some material phenomenon, it can be a convenient shorthand to use metaphors that endow inanimate objects with need and volition. 'The molecule *wants* to be in a lower energy state'. 'The restrained panel *tries* to return to its original size'. We must recognize that these are metaphors to help understand difficult objective concepts about inanimate entities. As long as we bear this in mind, it can be reassuring to think of smiling molecules happy in their new energy state, or panels of wood panting and grunting as they try to cope with changes in humidity.

However, once we get into areas such as the values of objects and the ethics of actions we must be very clear where the emotions and attitudes are coming from. It is we, the human beings, that have the needs, desires, and rights, not the objects. It is we who create the values. It is only in terms of the actions and opinions of human beings that the success of any museum activity, preservation programme or conservation treatment can be judged.

In certain circumstances, decisions may be made based on beliefs in the spiritual powers of objects. I would still maintain that it is humans that hold those beliefs and that decide courses of action, not the artifacts.

A useful skill – talking powers of 10

The study of risk involves talking about objects and events in terms of numbers. Some of these will be very small numbers and some very large. Since we often only have an inexact knowledge of the quantities we are dealing with it is often convenient to talk about orders of magnitude rather than exact values. The probabilities of many unwanted events are very small. The probability that the cause of your death will be a dog bite is around one in a million. This could be expressed as 1 in 1 000 000 or as a decimal fraction 0.000 001. The probability that you will die in an air crash is more nearly 0.0001. Rather than sit and count the zeros every time it would be better to use a system that told you how many zeros there were.

If you were trained in the sciences, thinking in powers of 10 will probably come naturally to you. If the concept is unfamiliar you should consider learning the skill, as it has a number of advantages. The basis is simple: the number 100 which is 10×10 is called 10 to the power of two, written as 10^2. A thousand, which is $10 \times 10 \times 10$, is shown as 10^3. One-hundredth is written as 10^{-2}, one-thousandth as 10^{-3}, a millionth as 10^{-6}. The probability of winning the lottery jackpot is less than 10^{-7}, we will not be discussing many probabilities much smaller than that in this book! With a scale that has only 15 points on it, going from +7 to –7, we can encompass all the numbers from one up to 10 million and all the fractions down to one-ten-millionth. This scale is called logarithmic; you may remember from school maths that the logarithm of 10 was 1.0, 100 was 2.0 and so on. You may also remember that the use of logarithms was that they greatly eased the multiplication of big numbers. To multiply a million by a billion you only need to add the powers of 10; $10^6 \times 10^9 = 10^{15}$ (6 + 9 = 15).

It turns out that the relationship between the strength of a stimulus and its intensity as perceived by the human brain is approximately logarithmic. You need to switch on more than twice the number of lights to double the impression of brightness in a room. This physiological perception of a logarithmic scale carries into the psychological way humans have of handling the differences between very large numbers. It is impossible to grasp the enormity of astronomical distances, they seem only a few steps up the scale from the longest journey we could ever make in a plane. On a logarithmic scale they are.

At an early stage in the development of risk studies in medicine and mortality it was felt that lay people could more easily understand differences in risk if presented as a logarithmic scale. Often just the power of 10 is used as an indicator for magnitude of risk. An example is the SDU or Safety Degree Unit. An SDU of 2 is equivalent to an annual risk of death of 10^{-2}. The SDU for a road accident is 4, for murder 5 (BMA, 1987).

This logarithmic progression provides a convenient way of encompassing the vastly different timescales we must consider when contemplating the deterioration of the cultural heritage. From the fraction of a second it takes to smash a pot to the centuries of wear and tear on the Pyramids.

From Table 1.1 it can be seen that we are interested in rates of change that fall within the range 0–10 on this scale.

Table 1.1 *Time in powers of 10*

Time	*Seconds*	*Power*	*Human events*	*Deterioration events*
Split second	10^{-1}	–1		accident
Second	1	0		
Minute	6×10^{1}	2		
Hour	3.6×10^{3}	3		disaster
Day	8.64×10^{4}	5		
Month	2.59×10^{6}	6		
Year	3.11×10^{7}	7	war	pollution, creep erosion
Decade	3.11×10^{8}	8	career	
Century	3.11×10^{9}	9	museum	
Millennium	3.11×10^{10}	10	civilization	
Duration of homo-sapiens	10^{13}	13		
Duration of planet	10^{17}	17		

Table 1.2 *Shock scale as a function of the number of atoms (modified from Benarie and Druzik)*

Number of atoms (10^N)	*Degree (N/3 −1)*	*Mass ($10^N g$)*	*Measurement*	*Example*
3	0	−21		
6	1	−18		
9	2	−15		
12	3	−12		pollutant per
15	4	−9	nanogram	cubic metre
18	5	−6	microgram	of air
21	6	−3	milligram	
24	7	0	gram	sheet of paper
27	8	3	kilogram	furniture
30	9	6	tonne	monument
33	10	9	kilotonne	cathedral

Another logarithmic scale that has been proposed for use in risk analysis concerns the amount of matter displaced by a 'shock' of some sort (Table 1.2, Benarie and Druzik, 1992). This relates to the amount of energy needed to create such a shock, which enables predictions of the frequency of damaging events. This can be used to broadly predict the lifetime of classes of object.

Natural radioactivity causes slow damage to solid materials as the disintegration of each atom breaks chemical bonds in around 1000 adjacent molecules. This would be termed a degree 0 shock. At a few disintegrations a second it will take around 10^{20} seconds to cause an object to crumble (see Table 1.1 to work out what sort of threat this is). A degree 6 shock involves the sort of masses affected by acidic deterioration of paper or surface corrosion of metal, it takes only 10^8 seconds for the effect to be damaging. A major earthquake is a degree 10 shock on this scale, it causes massive damage in a short time.

Something to think about

(At the end of each chapter are a series of questions designed to test understanding and to encourage a sceptical attitude to the ideas presented.)

Who has the right to determine what should happen to the Pyramids?

Who has the right to say how the objects in a publicly owned museum should be treated? Is your view any different if you know that current taxation is not covering running costs?

Is it true that objects cannot have rights?

Measurements using logarithmic scales are found in some health and safety assessments and in some conservation treatment reports. Can you name them?

References

APT/AIC (1991) The New Orleans Charter for the Joint Preservation of Historic Structures and Artifacts. Adopted by the Boards of Directors of the American Institute for the Conservation of Historic and Artistic Works and the Association for Preservation Technology International.

Benarie, M. and Druzik, J.R. (1992) Entropy and Risk Assessment of Cultural Heritage Conservation. *European Cultural Heritage Newsletter*, Vol. 6, No. 4, October, pp. 14–17.

British Medical Association (1987) *Living with Risk – the BMA Guide*. John Wiley and Son, London. ISBN 0-471-91598-X.

Brockley, Marion (1997) Is the Cult of Managerialism Threatening Collection Care? *Museums Journal*, August, p. 35.

Chapman, Gary (1994) Making Sense Out of Nonsense: Rescuing Reality from Virtual Reality, in *Culture on the Brink: Ideologies of Technology*. Bay Press, Seattle. ISBN 0-941920-28-3, pp. 149–155.

Dorrell, Stephen (1994) Press Release. Department of National Heritage, London, 7 October.

Levy, Matthys and Savadori, Mario (1992) *Why Buildings Fall Down*. W.W. Norton and Co., New York, London. ISBN 0-393-31152-X.

Major, John (1993) Quoted in: G.C. Goats and D.J. Ball. The Management of Risks Posed by Food Chemical Contaminants: Scope for Rationalisation? Research Report No. 24. Environmental Risk Assessment Unit, University of East Anglia, Norwich. ISBN 1-873933-75-4, p. 7.

Michalski, Stefan (1994) Sharing Responsibility for Conservation Decisions, in *Durability and Change: The Science, Responsibility, and Cost of Sustaining Cultural Heritage*, edited by W.E. Krumbein, P. Brimblecombe, D.E. Cosgrove and S. Staniforth. John Wiley and Sons. ISBN 0-471-95221-4, pp. 241–258.

Morgan, M. Granger and Henrion, Max (1990) *Uncertainty: A Guide to Dealing with Uncertainty in Quantitative Risk and Policy Analysis*. Cambridge University Press. ISBN 0-521-42744-4.

Piorovsky, Mikhail (1996) Quoted in Elena Skvortsova, The Lights Are Going Out All Over Russia. *Art Newspaper*, Vol. VII, No. 63, October 1996.

Rodricks, Joseph V. (1992) *Calculated Risks: The Toxicity and Human Health Risks of Chemicals in Our Environment*. Cambridge University Press. ISBN 0-521-42331-7, pp. 202–223.

The New Yorker (1997) Alexander Stille. Perils of the Sphinx, *The New Yorker*, 10 February.

van Gigch, John P. (1991) *System Design Modeling and Metamodeling*. Plenum, New York, referred to in van Gigch, John P. Rosvall, Jan and Lagerqvist, Bosse, Setting A Strategic Framework for Conservation Standards. ASTM Symposium on Standards for Preservation and Rehabilitation, 10–11 October 1993. Fort Worth, Texas.

Ziman, John (1978) *Reliable Knowledge: An Exploration of the Grounds for Belief in Science*. Cambridge University Press. ISBN 0-521-40670-6.

2 A rough guide to risk

In this chapter the vocabulary associated with risk is defined. Hazards that may affect museum collections are listed and categorized. A graphical method of visualizing changes in objects affected by various types of hazard is introduced.

The vocabulary

Before we can use 'risk analysis' to help with the conservation of objects, or before we carry out a 'risk assessment', we need to understand the range of meanings that these expressions can have. To do this we need to see how 'risk' and a number of other associated words are used in everyday language and in the technical writings of specialists.

'Assessment' means using judgement to combine present observation with past experience to aid the prediction of future events or to guide future action. The word 'risk' also relates to the future. It concerns events that have not yet happened but that we have reason to believe will occur eventually.

The word 'risk' is not used to describe events that we look forward to with enjoyment and eager expectation. If we have planned a party outdoors, we talk about the risk of rain not the risk of sunshine. Only with sarcasm do we say of the proposed festivity 'there's a risk I might enjoy myself tomorrow'. Once we do start to enjoy ourselves we may seriously consider that there is a risk of being sick, getting fat or becoming pregnant. So 'risk' usually refers to something unpleasant or unwanted, though not unforeseen. The problem is not that we can't foresee it but that there is uncertainty about the exact timing or extent of the unpleasantness.

We can make an informed guess about the chance or probability that unwanted events will occur within the period of time with which we are concerned. There are various ways of doing this. We can use our own experience; we have some idea of the quantities and combinations of food and drink that have made us feel sick in the past. We could use tables of calorific value, body weight and energy expenditure to predict whether we will put on weight. Although we may have no personal experience, we can refer to the accumulated knowledge of cause and effect that relates to pregnancy. We can use the advice of experts by listening to the weather forecast. This weighing of evidence leading to an informed guess is called a 'risk assessment'.

We frequently use the words 'chance' and 'probability' interchangeably. Events are ranked in increasing likelihood with expressions like 'no chance', 'fair chance' and 'good chance', always stopping short of complete certainty. Or we sometimes apply numbers to appear more certain in the face of uncertainty; 'a fifty per cent chance'. In the area of risk the word 'probability' should strictly be applied to the numeric value given to the likelihood of a chance occurrence. Probability is usually given as a number between one and zero, that is, as a fraction. If there is no cheating, the probability of a tossed coin landing 'heads' up is $\frac{1}{2}$ or 0.5. Sometimes the fraction will be expressed as a percentage, in this case 50%. The probability of throwing a six with a die is $\frac{1}{6}$ or 0.16667. Or it may be expressed as betting odds, in this case 5:1.

The literature on uncertainty in decision-making abounds with games involving tossed coins or dice and the more surreal experience of drawing a ball of a particular colour from an urn in which there is a number of balls of different colours (Raiffa, 1968). The probabilities in such games follow simple mathematical rules. The mechanisms for arriving at an outcome, e.g. tossing a coin, are easily understood and the various options such as the six faces of a die, or the 36 combinations for the top faces of a pair of dice, are exactly known. To that extent the probability is directly mathematically calculated and can be used to predict the outcome of future experiments. If you toss a coin 100 times it will come up heads around 50 times. If you toss a die 6000 times the number of occasions when the number on the top face is a six will be very close, if not equal, to 1000. In such situations the 'uncertainty' of this result is very small.

The numbers that are applied to predictions such as weather forecasts, 'a 30% probability of rain', are of a different nature, as are those in horseracing; 'odds of 100:1'. They involve a human judgement based on current information of varying degrees of accuracy, relating to complex occurrences whose mechanisms are not fully understood. There is no possibility of a controlled series of identical experiments to verify the stated probability. This is known, perhaps misleadingly, as 'subjective' probability. It can be treated logically and mathematically in exactly the same way as 'mathematical' probability. Indeed mathematical probability can be thought of as a trivial case of subjective probability where anyone can quickly acquire the necessary knowledge to become an expert.

However, in complex situations there is uncertainty about the accuracy or reality of our estimated probabilities. 'Probability' is usually used to describe the number that we have derived and intend to use for our decision-making. 'Uncertainty' is the measure of confidence that we have in the accuracy of that number. In the fields of risk and conservation many of the probabilities we shall discuss are of this complex 'subjective' nature. Decisions have to be made in the face of large uncertainties.

Before refining our use of the word 'risk' we must look at another associated word, 'hazard'. Hazard refers to things that are known to be dangerous in some circumstances but which are not necessarily always unwanted or unpleasant. Rain, fire and alcohol are all hazards. In the right environment and at the right time, each can be pleasant if not positively beneficial. When experienced in different circumstances they are responsible for suffering and death.

In the context of undesirable outcomes, the word 'hazard' should be used to describe the agent or action that gives rise to the unwanted event. However, it is also loosely used to describe the manifestation of the event. Thus tobacco, cigarettes, cigarette smoke and cigarette smoking are all referred to as hazards because in some circumstances they may give rise to unwanted occurrences such as cancer or fire. Cancer and fire are also hazards because in some circumstances they may result in unwanted outcomes such as death and destruction. In the conservation literature the word 'agent' is frequently used to describe the basic element of a hazard. Pollutant gases, ultraviolet radiation and high humidities are all 'agents' of deterioration for organic objects.

The use of the word 'risk' should strictly be limited to descriptions, in quantitative terms, of the probability that exposure, of a specified intensity and duration to a particular hazard, will result in a particular outcome. The quantitative element may involve trying to put an accurate numerical value to the risk or it could be achieved by ranking the risks in order of relative magnitude with or without numbers. In many cases it may merely involve the application of descriptive words such as 'great', 'small' and 'negligible' to describe the relative risks. There is often little value in seeking extreme numerical accuracy. It is unlikely that the difference between a 5% and a 10% chance of rain would affect our decision to hold a party outdoors.

As we shall see in later chapters, the most useful definition of risk is one that includes not only the probability of an undesirable event but also a quantitative measure of the loss that would result. This loss may be directly measurable as loss of money or loss of material but may also be a measure of loss of enjoyment or expectation. Since probability is a pure number, the units of measurement of risk are those used to measure the loss. A game of poker may involve a risk of 10 pounds or 20 matchsticks. The measurement associated with death is the loss of one life. The life/death option has no in-between states. In cases where there is no subtle gradation between different states or, as in mortality studies, where death is the only result of interest, the risk is often quoted as if it were a pure number. The annual risk of a fatal lightning strike is 10^{-7}.

Needless to say, in the technical literature, as in everyday use, the word 'risk' is used with a broad range of meanings, often without stating the units of measurement. The words 'probability', 'uncertainty', 'hazard' and 'risk' are used loosely and with senses that overlap.

In many instances we are able to control our exposure to a particular hazard. In the case of the picnic we can, if we choose, take action to eliminate or minimize the risks from the recognized hazards by moderation, abstinence or suitable preventive precautions. This is 'risk management'. In the case of rainfall, where we are not in control of the hazard, we can go equipped with umbrellas, raincoats and awnings. Or we can have an emergency plan to rush to someone's house in the event of a downpour. These preparations are a particular aspect of risk management called 'risk mitigation'.

Depending on their education, experience and prejudices different people see the same activity as more or less risky. They have differing 'risk perceptions'. Arguments about risk perception often arise when the public express disquiet about something such as the building of a nuclear power station. The proponents of the scheme believe that the uninformed local residents are over-reacting, overestimating the risk, because of the emotive values of words and phrases such as 'radiation' and 'nuclear

Table 2.1 *First definitions*

Probability	A number between 0 and 1 (or a percentage between 0% and 100%) that indicates the likelihood of an event occurring within specified circumstances, e.g. within a certain time period or within a series of related events.
Uncertainty	The level of confidence in the probability stated.
Hazard	A material, agent or action that sometimes has an undesired effect.
Risk	Either the probability that a hazard will cause the undesired effect in specified conditions and within a specified time. Or: an indication of the probable loss due to that hazard in the specified circumstances.
Risk assessment	An informed judgement about particular risks.
Risk management	Control of exposure to hazards in order to minimize risk.
Risk mitigation	Minimizing the potential loss due to hazards that are difficult to control.
Risk perception	Some people's subjective assessment of risk may not be the same as that calculated by rigorous analysis.

waste'. The advocates and their experts have 'calculated' the risk and 'know' it to be very small. From our own experience we know that alarming experiences are not always actually damaging. Dirty and ill-kempt people who mumble or shout at us in the street may be frightening but very rarely cause physical harm.

In addition to the phrases summarized in Table 2.1 the word 'risk' is found combined with a variety of other words which are defined in later chapters, but are fairly self-explanatory anyway: risk aversion, risk-loving, risk-seeking, risk information, risk communication, risk map, risk register.

Given the range of uses for the word 'risk' it can be seen that the phrase 'risk assessment' will mean different things in different circumstances. It can be one person's rough guess based on long experience or it can be the synthesis of a number of well-organized attempts to quantify different aspects of the factors that combine to create unwanted outcomes. Frequently, researchers who are responsible for only one small part of this whole effort refer to their work as risk assessment.

Relationships in risk studies

The relationships between the various aspects of the studies and use of risk information can be shown schematically as in Figure 2.1 (Covello and Merkhofer, 1993).

Vincent J. Covello, one of the authors of the book from which the chart was derived, is another name that you will find cited in a great many publications dealing with environmental risk. Risk management is seen as the useful end product of risk analysis. Risk analysis consists of three stages: hazard identification, risk assessment and risk evaluation. Hazard identification is sometimes seen as an essential stage of risk assessment. As far as the cultural heritage is concerned no fundamentally new group of hazards has been discovered for 50 years, and most were recognized centuries ago. As the list of hazards is well known, the identification of new ones would only be an integral part of a very specialized assessment. 'Identification' merely means specifying the hazard being studied.

Risk assessment consists of four conceptually distinct steps.

1. Release assessment. This is an attempt to describe and quantify the potential of materials, activities or events to introduce risk agents into the environment of objects. This could also include an indication of how we can modify this potential. For example, a study of the release of organic acids from showcase materials could also include an assessment of the lower rate due to application of a barrier layer. Although it is semantically uncomfortable, we also talk about the

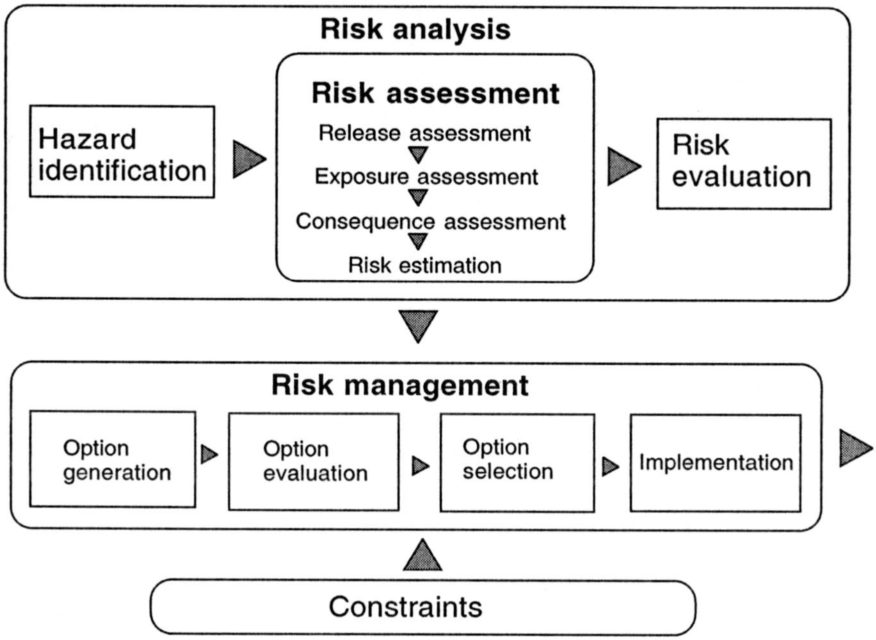

Figure 2.1 *Relationship between risk assessment and risk management (after Covello and Merkhofer)*

'release' of kinetic energy experienced in a plane crash, or the 'release' of radiation when we switch on a spot-light.

2. Exposure assessment. A description and quantification of intensity, frequency and duration of exposure, including an estimate of the number and nature of the objects exposed.
3. Consequence assessment. This involves describing and quantifying the observed effects on materials and objects given specified exposure conditions. In studies of museum objects this must include not only measures of physical and chemical changes but also the degree to which such changes are actually perceived as damage.
4. Risk estimation. This is the integration of the first three steps, giving rise to a quantitative measure of risk to a certain group of objects given a particular exposure experience. This would include an estimate of the distribution and severity of effects and an indication of the uncertainties inherent in the estimate. This is roughly equivalent to the stage of 'risk characterization' used in other schemes.

Before the information from the risk assessment can be fed into the risk management process the risks should be evaluated. A judgement needs to be made about the significance of the risk in comparison with others. A sense of proportion and priority must be established. The traditional museum example is that there is no point spending money to reduce the risk of damage due to fluctuating humidity if there is no lock on the door. If the evaluation stage is left out there can be an unnecessary burden of effort and expense.

The risk management decision-making process consists of four stages.

1. All the possible courses of action, including doing nothing, are listed.
2. Each of the options is evaluated in the light of the risk information *and* information about constraints such as budgets, political attitudes and technical feasibility.
3. One or more options are selected.
4. The selected options are introduced and monitored.

Stage two is very important as it is a second point at which a sense of the real world is introduced. Decisions in the real world do not always conform to the expectations of the analyst, especially if there are politicians or museum directors involved.

Risk management

Risk management is not solely about the immediate reduction of risk. The range of options is shown in Figure 2.2 which is taken from a useful paper by Norbert Baer, who should be credited with the introduction of risk assessment to the field of conservation (Baer, 1991).

The management decision could be to accept the risk and do nothing about it. This is not irresponsible if the risk is small. A second option is to 'share' the risk. You make your loss certain but spread it out over time by paying insurance premiums. In theory at least, the insurance company suffers a loss when you eventually suffer damage to property. The risk can be changed or reduced by regulating the release of hazards or exposure to them. This may involve causing changes in attitude and behaviour. Zero risk can be approached through avoidance which involves a moratorium or the total prohibition of the hazardous activity.

It is important to understand that risk information alone is not sufficient to enable risk management. Every proposal to minimize or eliminate a specific risk will have effects on other sources of risk, on other groups of objects, and on the allocation of resources to other museum activities. All of these consequences have to be considered before the most suitable option can be selected. It must also be remembered that risk

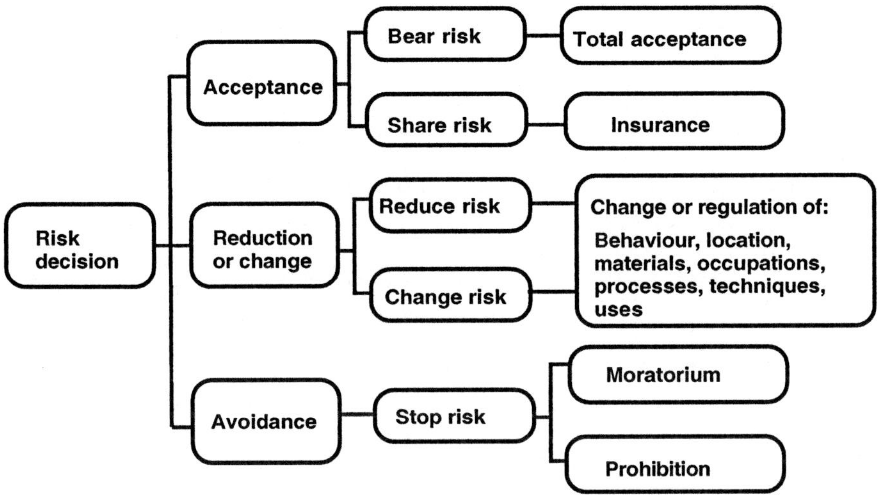

Figure 2.2 *The options of risk management*

management is only that – the management of risk. It is not the management of business. The management of business must take into account the generation of favourable outcomes not just the avoidance of the undesirable.

Risks in conservation

For the moment we must take it as given that collections of objects in museums are there to be looked at and enjoyed, and that records are held in archives to be consulted. If this is truly the case, the most obvious undesirable occurrence would be that the object could no longer be found when it was needed for examination. Or that not all of a collection could be found. Only slightly less annoying would be that parts were so discoloured, disfigured or distorted that the objects no longer gave the expected pleasure or the records no longer yielded the desired information.

Without defining the word, we can describe these undesirable occurrences as changes of 'state' with time. We can also see that in some way these are changes in 'value' with time. Rough numbers can be applied to these changes and the process can be visualized in an abstract way with the use of a graph (Figure 2.3).

The horizontal axis shows the passing of time. The point where the vertical axis meets the horizontal axis (called the origin) marks the beginning of the period of interest. If we define this starting point as the

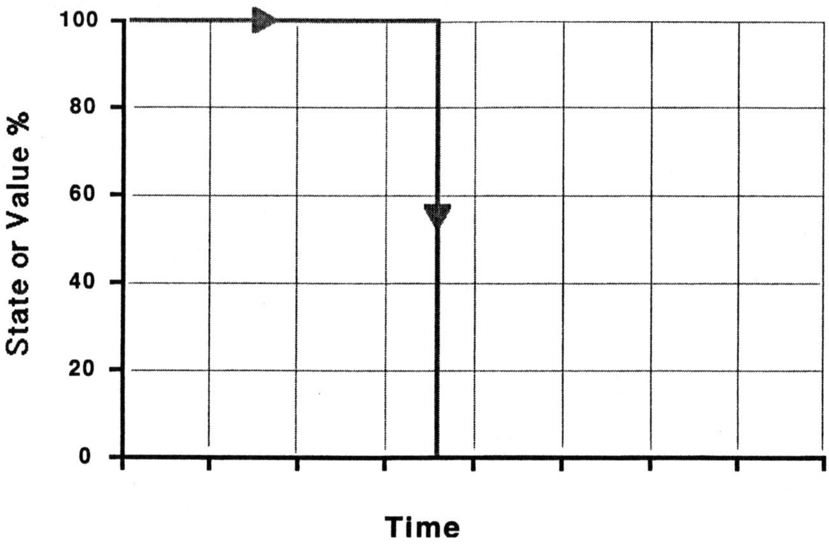

Figure 2.3 *Graphical representation of total catastrophic loss of state or value*

present moment, any position on the line to the right of this first point represents an exact moment in the future. In this instance no units of measurement for time have been specified. In museum planning and decision-making we are likely to be talking about units from days to decades rather than microseconds or millennia.

The vertical axis gives a measure of the state of the object or collection. At the time 'now' its state can be given an arbitrary number such as 100. Any state which we consider worse than this can be given a number less than 100. When the object ceases to exist, its state can be defined as zero. Any state of the object can be defined as a number between zero and 100 which will be represented as a point on the vertical axis. That is, future 'worse' states are represented as percentages of the initial state. (We will not consider just yet the possibility that the condition of the object could improve from its initial state.)

On the graph the progress of the object through time is plotted as a grey line. At the point in time 'now' the state is 100%. As we move across toward the right the state remains at 100 until, at some time in the future, the state instantaneously plummets to zero. The grey line stops at this point because nothing further can possibly happen to an object that has ceased to exist.

The complete disappearance of the object shown in Figure 2.3 is the extreme case of the more typical example where the object suddenly goes from one state to a worse state and then continues in this poorer condition for some time (Figure 2.4).

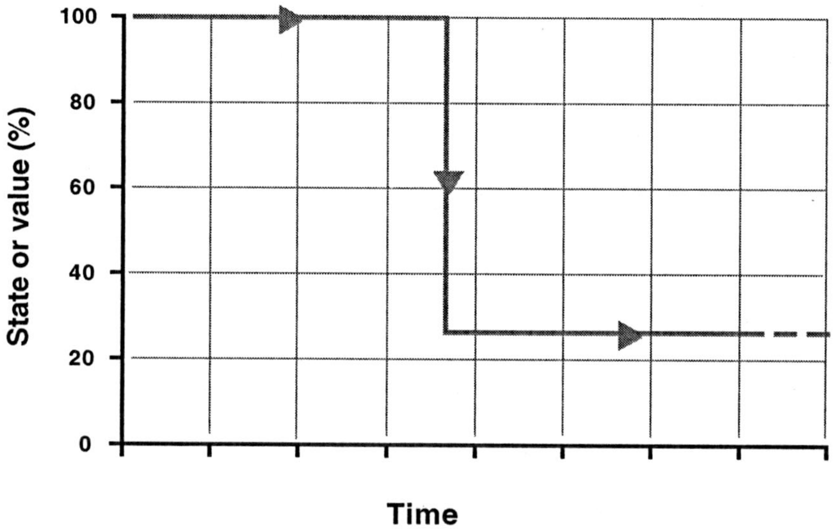

Figure 2.4 *Graphical representation of partial (75%) loss of state or value*

The state of an object is not the same as its value. For the time being we will assume that there is a direct relationship between state and value. When the object is in its initial state we can ascribe to it a value of 100%. When an object ceases to exist its value becomes zero. There are a range of possible values between 100% and 0%. Assuming a simple proportional relationship, when the *state* of the object at any future time is represented as a percentage of its initial state, the new *value* will be represented by the same percentage. A drop of 75% to a worse state will result in a new value of 25% of the initial value. By considering *percentage* changes of value we avoid specifying the units of measurement. This means that we can put off for the time being the worry that we are assigning monetary values to priceless or worthless objects.

So once again following the progress of the object through time as shown in Figures 2.3 and 2.4, the object maintains its initial value for a while and then it suddenly has a much lower value. What sort of event can have taken place? What types of hazard could possibly lead to such a large and sudden loss in value? Table 2.2 gives a list of possible hazards. You may be able to think of others.

The type of event shown in the graphs, immediate loss of value or existence, is known as 'rapid onset' or 'catastrophic'. The word 'disaster' is usually reserved for a large loss resulting from a rapid onset event. All of the items in the Table 2.2 have effects that can be rapid and catastrophic, although some hazards, such as war and custodial neglect, may continue over protracted periods. Although the relationship between

Table 2.2 *Rapid onset hazards*

• War	• Tornado	• Failure of support
• Terrorism	• Tidal wave	• Power failure
• Vandalism	• Landslide	• Conservation treatment
• Fire	• Plane crash	• Custodial neglect
• Flood	• Building collapse	• Theft
• Earthquake	• Dropped packing case	• Repatriation

the hazard and a sudden loss in value may be obvious in most cases, some of the entries in the table may need some explanation.

An example of failure of support would be a poorly designed showcase shelf that collapses when an object is placed on it, or the failure of adhesive or some other means of fixing for display.

The power failure could cause a number of different disasters. Objects kept in cold storage or as frozen specimens could reach the wrong temperature. The lights could go out in the middle of a difficult handling manoeuvre.

Conservation treatment is supposed to improve the state *and* the value of an object. This is not always the case, even when it is the honest belief of the conservator that this is what has been achieved. Twenty years ago a long-serving member of my department defined a good conservator (restorer) as someone who had nearly 'lost' an object during treatment, but who had the nerve and practical skill to retrieve it from the edge of disaster. Twenty-five years ago, as an incompetent trainee conservator, I was responsible for the total loss of one complete (very small) object and the loss of part of another.

Custodial neglect can take many forms and is not restricted to negligence of security or ignorance of environmental control. In extreme cases the custodian (the governing authority rather than a curator) may abandon the object or collection to save money or to make money by developing the site. A collection whose value consists in being kept as a single group may be broken up into smaller units and dispersed. The curator may mislay the documentation that gives value to an object or that confirms the museum's right to ownership. With large collections the custodian may just not know where a particular object is.

Theft, repatriation and aspects of custodial neglect such as the loss of the object location or the loss of the associated documentation may not immediately seem to be examples of catastrophic loss. This is a first indication that we must be very careful to understand the particular framework within which we choose to carry out an analysis. After theft or repatriation the state of the object may be still be 100% but those who used to derive benefit no longer can. For this group of people there has been a loss in value even if there is no net loss when we consider the whole world. After theft, or the loss of object location, the object *may* have suffered no change of state but there is no way of testing or verifying this. As far as the institution is concerned the object has ceased to exist and so ceased to have any value.

The different hazards in Table 2.2 could be subdivided into various sets united by common features or they could be arranged in various hierarchies. Many are not mutually exclusive and some may be considered as subsets of another. One obvious classification is into those that are caused by nature such as earthquakes and those that are the responsibility of human beings (anthropogenic) such as plane crashes. There will always be some overlap; a flood could be the result of sudden torrential rain, but the fault could be in a badly constructed dam or in guttering and downpipes that have not been properly maintained.

In pursuing links and subgroups it could be pointed out that fire, theft, vandalism, custodial neglect and building collapse are all consequences of war. Flood may well follow fire, as the fire brigade pump water into the burning building. And so on.

The hazards might profitably be classified by the degree to which their mechanisms are understood, by the degree to which the time of onset can be predicted and the degree to which the probability of onset can be minimized by management.

Another form of analysis consists in trying to identify the basic elements of each hazard. The hazard of fire could be broken down into constituent elements; high temperature, smoke, loss of structure, and the effects of the fire brigade with their big boots, axes and hoses. In turn, smoke could be seen as a mixture of particulates and corrosive gases. If you analyse the nature of each hazard until you find the basic agents that directly interact with the object, you find that rapid onset events share a relatively small number of common elements.

When viewed like this they become parts of the studies of chemistry, physics and engineering. They are, at least theoretically, susceptible to analysis by controlled experiment and subject to numerical manipulation and computer modelling.

Table 2.3

- High temperature
- Large tensile, compressive or shear forces
- Rapid application of such forces (shock)
- Chemical and physical interaction with a liquid (usually water)
- Interaction with airborne substances (gases and particulates)

The components that are not subject to this analysis are failures of security which could be seen as outcomes of poor management.

Uncertainty about timing

The graphs in Figures 2.3 and 2.4 had no units of measurement for time along the horizontal axis. The unfortunate event is shown as occurring at an exact moment in the future, but until it happens we do not know what that exact moment is. All we can do is say that there is certain probability that it will occur within a specified period of time. Trying to determine the probability that an event will occur within a specified time period in the future should not be confused with an attempt to predict the exact moment of the event.

Suppose we want to know whether a hurricane will occur at a specific location within a specified period in the future. Beyond a period of about 10 days we can only make predictions in a 'probabilistic' fashion, based on the recorded frequency of occurrences in the past. There may be early warning signs, as conditions that lead to the formation of hurricanes are observed. Although we are now talking about cause and effect we can still only talk in terms of probabilities, though by now these may be quite large. However, once the path of a developing storm pattern has been plotted by satellite, the occurrence of a hurricane at a particular location can be predicted in a 'deterministic' way with a high degree of certainty.

Impact and frequency

If a museum were affected by serious damaging events with great frequency there would be no collections left. If the collections still exist we can assume that major disasters occur only infrequently. However, small accidents can occur quite often. The probability of a leaking radiator is very much higher than the probability of a major flood. The probability that a packing case will be dropped a short distance is very much higher than the probability that the plane carrying the case will crash into the sea. However carefully the packing case is handled it will suffer some small shocks as it is lifted or set down.

This relationship between the impact of an event and its frequency is shown in Figure 2.5 (Waller, 1994). When trying to assess the risk posed by a particular agent, for instance physical forces, it may be sensible to consider the 'dramatic but infrequent' as a separate category from the 'slight but continuous'.

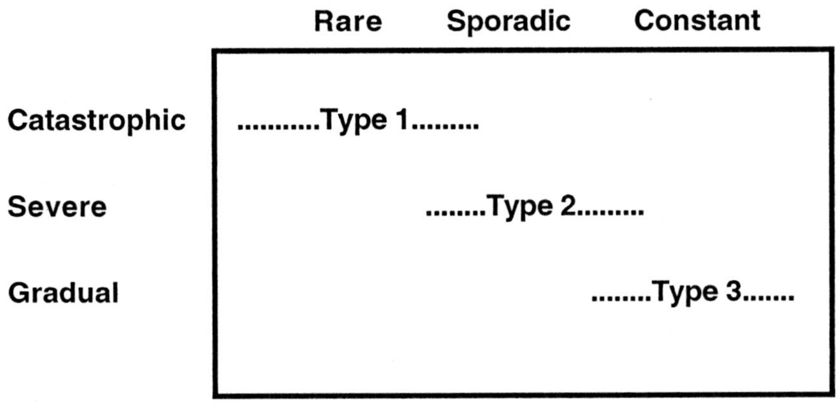

Figure 2.5 *Three types of risk categorized by their frequency and severity (after Waller)*

If we want to assess risks with any accuracy the relationship between seriousness and frequency must be known. This relationship will be discussed further in Chapter 8.

Slow acting hazards

Much of the deterioration observed in museums does not take place in the sudden catastrophic manner suggested by Figures 2.3 and 2.4. Instead the changes that take place are gradual. The change to a worse state or lower value is slow but continuous. This type of behaviour is shown in Figure 2.6 where the grey line slopes down from 100% at the beginning of the time period, taking lower and lower values as time progresses. Where the slope is steep there is a high rate of damage. Where the line levels off, the rate of damage is smaller. **Note that the point at which time is zero and the state is 100% is not necessarily the point at which the object was created or the point of acquisition. Although we have called it 100%, this may not be the very best state the object has ever been in.**

Some of the hazards responsible for this type of damage are listed in Table 2.4. Most of these are familiar or self-explanatory, but some may require some elucidation. Conservation treatment may initiate gradual decay if it removes some element that was protective to the material (sizing in paper) or adds some material that is unstable (poly(vinyl acetate)). External pollution refers to gases and particulate matter generated outside the museum and transported in by various means.

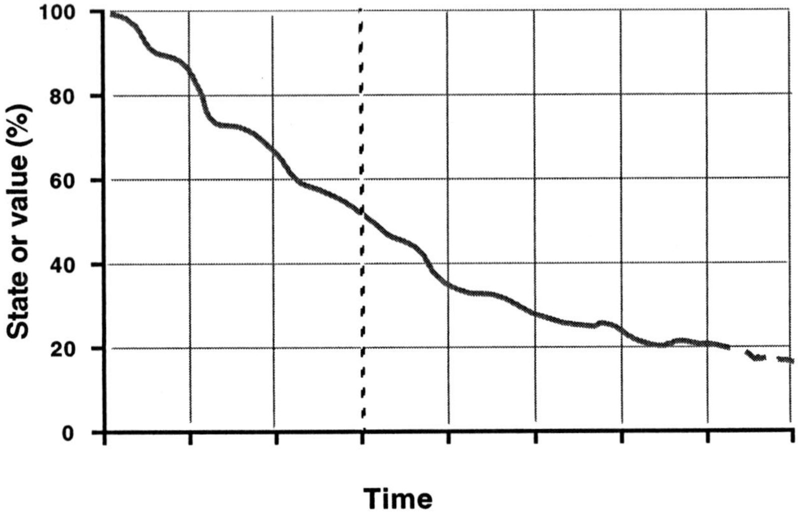

Figure 2.6 *Graphical representation of gradual loss of state or value with time*

Internal pollution refers to gases and articulates that are generated by materials and processes within the museum or within the immediate environment of the object. The word 'ageing' is used to include any process that causes change that is not the result of interaction of the material with agents in the environment (changes in the crystallinity of polymers).

Once again the suggested hazards are not independent or mutually exclusive. They could be grouped or classified in a variety of ways. They vary in the degree to which local management can reduce the risk. For instance, it is not within the power of museum staff to directly decrease emissions from power stations or to control rainfall. It is, however, possible to select showcase materials that do not emit formaldehyde.

Table 2.4

• High temperature	• Light	• External pollution
• High humidity	• Exhibitions	• Internal pollution
• Fluctuating humidity	• Handling	• Dust
• Mould	• Conservation treatment	• Rain
• Insects	• Use	• Ageing
• Rodents	• Wear	• Vibration

Table 2.5

- Interaction with radiation (light)
- Interaction with water vapour
- Chemical and physical interaction with a liquid (usually water)
- Interaction with airborne substances (gases and particulates)
- Abrasion
- Chewing

There are two common features. In general, if there is a constant level of the hazard we would expect a fairly steady continuing process of decay. If the amount of the hazard increases we would expect to see an increase in the rate of change. The extent to which this is true is explored in Chapter 10.

If we tabulate the basic elements of the hazards we can again see that they can be reduced to a small number of classes. Once more this analysis suggests that the decay processes should be amenable to systematic study.

The risk attached to gradual onset hazards is calculated in a slightly different way to that used for rapid onset events. The progress of the change of state or value is deterministic rather than probabilistic. The question is not 'how probable is it that this will happen within this period of time?' but 'to what extent will this have happened by the end of the period?'

Thus in Figure 2.6, at the time marked by the vertical dashed line the state of the object has declined until it is only 50% of what it was to begin with. If there is a simple direct relationship between the state of the object and its value then the value will also have dropped to 50%.

A useful classification

After several years of experience, staff at the Canadian Museum of Nature have found that the classification of hazard types shown in Table 2.6 is suitable for evaluating risks in their collections (Waller, 1994).

They have also used it to train staff responsible for other types of collection. The analysis of the agents of deterioration is taken to a point where it still relates to a known experience. The actions of fire, pests and criminals are not broken down into further subcategories although they easily could be. Some agents are further categorized by considering differences in frequency and severity, following the scheme in Figure 2.5.

Table 2.6

Agent type	*Example of hazard or effect*
Physical forces – Type 1	Earthquake, building structure collapse, etc.
Physical forces – Type 2	Dropping specimens, etc.
Physical forces – Type 3	Poor support, constant vibration, etc.
Fire	
Water – Type 1	Flood
Water – Type 2	Roof and plumbing leaks
Water – Type 3	Rising damp
Criminals – Type 1	Major theft
Criminals – Type 2	Isolated instances of theft or vandalism
Criminals – Type 3	Embezzlement by staff or frequent users
Pests	Pest infestation
Contaminants – Type 1	Fallout from industrial or transport accident
Contaminants – Type 2	Construction dust, use of corrosive cleaner
Contaminants – Type 3	Gases from storage hardware
Light and UV radiation	Fading colours, structural damage
Incorrect temperature – Type 1	Thawing of frozen tissue sample
Incorrect temperature – Type 2	Thermal shock
Incorrect temperature – Type 3	Higher than ideal
Incorrect rel. humidity – Type 2	Mould outbreak
Incorrect rel. humidity – Type 3	Splitting shells, transitions in minerals
Custodial neglect – Type 1	Collection abandoned
Custodial neglect – Type 2	Loss of specimens, specimen data, etc.
Custodial neglect – Type 3	Ongoing failure to ensure ownership, etc.

Something to think about

How easy do you think it would be to find out the frequency of damaging events in museums?

Do you think it is reasonable to equate the state of an object with its value?

Do objects 'die' (achieve zero value) in museums?

References

Baer, N.S. (1991) Assessment and Management of Risks to Cultural Property. Science, Technology and European Cultural Heritage. Proceedings of the European Symposium, Bologna, Italy, 13–16 June 1989. Butterworth-Heinemann for the Commission of the European Communities. ISBN 0-7506-0237-6, p. 27.

Covello, Vincent T. and Merkhofer, Miley W. (1993) *Risk Assessment Methods: Approaches for Assessing Health and Environmental Risks*. Plenum Press. ISBN 0-306-44382-1.

Raiffa, Howard (1968) *Decision Analysis – Introductory Lectures on Choices under Uncertainty*. McGraw-Hill. ISBN 0-07-554866-6.

Waller, Robert (1994) Conservation Risk Assessment: A Strategy for Managing Resources for Preventive Conservation. Preventive Conservation: Practice, Theory and Research. Preprints to the Ottawa Congress, 12–16 September. IIC, pp. 12–16.

3 Tricky decisions

We make decisions everyday, but we don't usually think about the processes of decision-making. By trying to create formal models of the decision process we become aware of the types of information that are needed to solve our problems. Decisions are based on comparisons of the relative values of different possible outcomes. These estimated values are a combination of assessments of probability and evaluations of possible gains or losses. By breaking a complex subject down into simpler parts it becomes easier to study, but there is the danger of losing sight of the essential interconnectivity between components.

Planning and decisions

The purpose of studying risk analysis is either to manage the risks in our business or to manage our business while understanding the risks. Whichever our task is, the essential element of management is taking decisions, that is, choosing one course of action from a number of possible options.

Decisions are notoriously difficult to make. In museums it often seems that decisions are hardly ever made and, when they are, they are wrong. There is a sound reason for this.

There is no single, simple way of measuring success in the greater part of museum business. The values that are used to compare the outcomes of different courses of action are not simple units like pounds or dollars. Outcomes are measured in increases in understanding and enjoyment, not in growth of income.

There is no single, simple way of defining success in a museum. Indeed there seem to be directly opposed objectives – to preserve the collections and to give greater access to the collections. Preservation is best achieved by locking the doors and switching off the lights. Access implies the reverse of this.

In the technical jargon of decision analysts this would be called decision-making in the context of conflicting objectives which would involve constructing a multi-attribute utility function. This is the most complex type of decision-making to analyse, which suggests that it will always be difficult to make consistently good decisions about the use and welfare of museum collections.

Decision-making sounds very much a part of the world of industry and finance and so not a lot to do with conservation of collections. Until recently, it seemed that museums attracted and nurtured staff who rejected the methods and motivations of the business world. In the first few chapters of this book you will come across a vocabulary that derives from the study of business-like organizations. These 'management' concepts, and the jargon associated with them, often seem far removed from anything in the real world. Yet they are only formal and systematic ways of looking at things that we all do quite naturally everyday in an informal and unsystematic way.

From the time that you decide whether to pay attention to your alarm clock in the morning, to the time that you decide when and with whom you will go to bed at night, every day presents a relentless stream of decisions to be made.

Much of the time we are not aware of the processes we use to make routine decisions and we probably would not consider, and certainly would never admit, that we were using management techniques such as risk assessment or cost–benefit analysis. But the patterns of thought associated with deciding what to eat for breakfast, or where to go on holiday, are the same as those used to decide whether to invest in a new production line or whether to open another airport for London. These patterns of thought are certainly appropriate for deciding which collection should have its environment improved first or which object should be treated next and in what way.

A few minutes' reflection will show that all the decisions we make in our everyday lives consist of most if not all of the following stages:

- A rough formulation of what we want to achieve and by when
- The comparison of a number of courses of action, their immediate benefits and drawbacks and their likely long-term outcomes
- A consideration of available funds, materials and time
- The choice of the course of action most likely to have the desired outcome

An everyday story of decision-making

Consider choosing what to eat in a restaurant. The menu provides a list of options and the cost to you of choosing each one. This information alone is not necessarily sufficient to help make a selection. You have to construct a multi-attribute utility function: the price of each dish is not a simple reflection of how delicious it will be, and gives you no indication of which wine will complement the dish. You may be working with conflicting objectives: having a good time and trying to impress someone.

Your choice of dishes will to some extent be determined by who is going to pay and what their ability to pay is. Even if resources are somewhat limited it may be possible to consider several combinations of more or less expensive dishes and remain within budget. If the desired outcome is the experience of a delicious meal you may use a variety of sources of information to help rank the options and minimize the risk of an unfortunate choice.

1. Make observations. What have other diners chosen? Are they enjoying it?
2. Make deductions. Study the descriptions in the menu. Is the stated combination of ingredients and method of preparation likely to produce a dish to your taste?
3. Study the literature. Have food journalists or restaurant critics praised any of the dishes?
4. Consult an expert. The chef, the waiter or your partner may make recommendations that rely on their own experience of the process or the product or on observation of other peoples' experience.
5. Consider your own experience. Have you eaten the same dish in another restaurant or a similar dish in the same restaurant.

An individual piece of information does not guarantee a successful choice but the combination of different approaches and the use of a number of different sources will greatly increase the probability of a desirable outcome.

Eating in restaurants would be a very banal experience if the correct answer could always be found by looking up a chart in a single, standard reference book.

Whatever the preparation, the outcome is usually not one hundred per cent certain. You may discover a fly in your soup or the waiter may trip and drop the soup in your partner's lap.

The probability of an outcome should not be confused with its impact. If the restaurant meal is part of a grand seduction, the probable choice of an inappropriate wine will have much less impact on the final outcome than the unlikely lap-full of soup.

Decision trees

We are not usually faced with one isolated decision but a series of decisions, the second decision depending on the outcome of the first and so on. To assess the probability that the final result will be the one we desire we need to estimate the likelihood of different outcomes after each decision. If we were to plot this on paper or a computer screen we would have a tree-like structure, starting from the first decision and fanning out as different possible outcomes follow successive decisions. On the right-hand side will be a column of possible final results, each with its probability of happening. Some will coincide with our original definition of success, others will not.

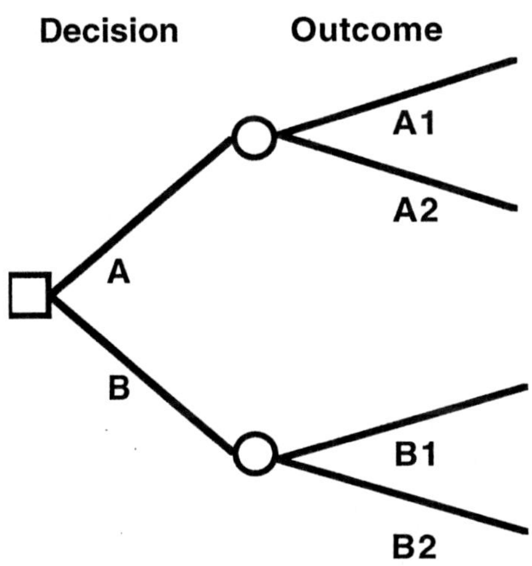

Figure 3.1 *Decision tree showing a choice between two options, each of which has two possible outcomes*

Figure 3.1 shows a simple form of decision tree. The square indicates a point at which a decision must be made. The two lines that spread out from the side of the square represent two possible options; decide to do A, or decide to do B. This could be something like A, decide to treat the object or B, decide to leave it alone.

It is important to remember that continuing to do what we always have done constitutes making a decision. Even continuing to do *nothing* constitutes a decision.

Although in this example only two options are shown, there might be many more. However, it could be argued that a large number of options can always be broken down into a series of two-option decisions.

The circles represent the point at which we examine the situations that may possibly arise from each decision. Often these will be determined by circumstances beyond our immediate control. In this case only two possible outcomes are shown for each decision but there could be many more.

Suppose that the object is discoloured and the proposed treatment is to clean it. Imagine examining the object a year later when four outcomes might be:

A1 Object appears clean and stable
A2 Object appears newly discoloured
B1 Object appears just as it did a year ago
B2 Object appears more discoloured than it did a year ago

So, not yet knowing how things will be in a year's time, should we choose A or B?

It is obvious that we cannot choose unless we have a way of predicting how likely the possible changes are and how far they may have progressed in a year. We also need a way of comparing the changes described in A2 and B2. Is *this* discoloration worse than *that* one? Can such a comparison be made objectively or will it always be a matter of opinion?

It is not until we develop ways of assessing the probability of certain outcomes and until we can assign comparable values to them that we can construct mechanisms for making sensible decisions.

The use of decision trees is clearly described in books such as *Decision Synthesis* (Watson and Buede, 1987) and *The Anatomy of Decisions* (Moore and Thomas, 1988). I am not advocating the use of the decision tree as a mechanism for decision-making. It takes a very particular type of person to want, and to be able, to analyse and quantify every possibility and commit this to a diagram on a piece of paper or on a computer screen. It is probably better to develop a more intuitive approach to decision-making while realizing that the steps that are taken, rapidly and almost subconsciously, *could* be analysed in the form of a decision tree. The decision tree is a descriptive model of the decision process. The value of such a model is not how we can use it but what we can learn from it.

The simple model in Figure 3.1 immediately demonstrates one point. A single decision can have many outcomes. This divergence is very much greater when we have a succession of decisions. Figure 3.2 shows the effect of a second decision consequent on the outcome of the first.

A chain of only two decisions causes us to consider 16 possible outcomes. Such a succession of events would occur if, for instance, we were trying to decide whether to re-treat an object if the first treatment fails or whether to institute a programme of regular treatment to maintain a decaying object.

Figure 3.3 shows a simple tree for a problem that we will be examining in greater detail in later chapters. We can learn two things from it. First,

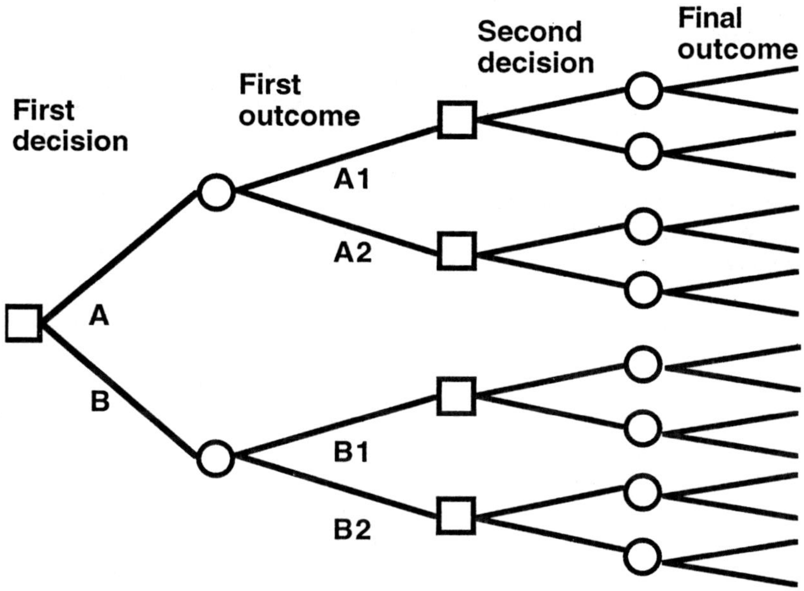

Figure 3.2 *Decision tree for two successive decisions leading to 16 possible outcomes*

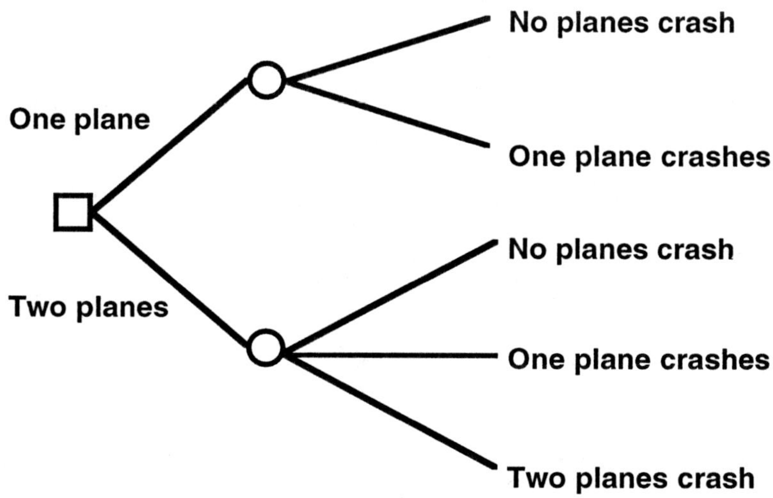

Figure 3.3 *Decision tree for choosing whether to send a valuable air freight consignment in one or two shipments*

that we must be careful to note whose viewpoint we are considering and second we need to consider a *combination* of probabilities and values of the different outcomes.

Imagine you are planning to send all the paintings in your collection by air to an exhibition several thousand miles away. There has been a recent television documentary about falling safety standards and poor maintenance in major airlines. The trustees become worried. You are advised that it would be better to send the loan as two consignments in separate planes. Would this be a wise decision?

The major concern is that a plane will crash and destroy the valuable, indeed irreplaceable, paintings. Figure 3.3 shows the five possible outcomes of the two options under consideration. If all of the possible outcomes have equal weight then it would seem that the 'two plane' option is the worse because it is the only one that leads to the loss of two planes rather than one or none. But Figure 3.3 shows the losses to the airline not the losses to your museum. A more helpful decision tree would be Figure 3.4.

This shows the losses suffered in terms of the collection of paintings rather than the number of planes. It also includes a qualitative estimate of the probability of each loss. Both options have high probabilities that nothing will happen. If the two plane alternative is chosen, the probability of losing everything is reduced from very low to so-low-as-to-be-negligible. The two plane option is also the only one that offers the

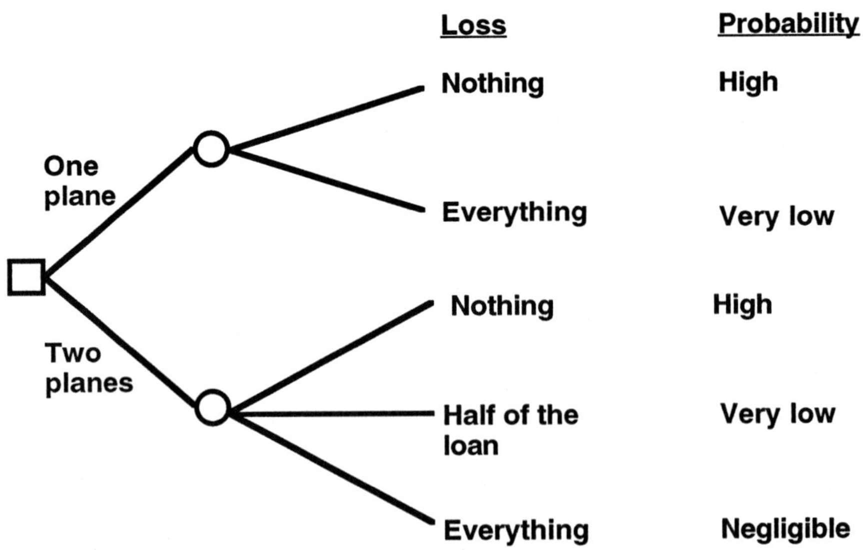

Figure 3.4 *Decision tree with qualitative estimates of the probabilities and impacts of different outcomes*

chance of losing only half the consignment. With half the paintings remaining it would still be possible to continue business as a museum.

If the decision were being made for a business whose sole purpose was to make money, and if the consignment were of replaceable commodities, then the single plane option would be the best choice. Separating the shipments would increase administration and transport costs, yet the risks of loss are very small. This choice would be seen as aiming to maximize profit by minimizing costs and accepting the small risk of total loss (which could be insured against anyway). This type of behaviour is typical of entrepreneurial activity which tends towards the acceptance, or even love, of risks if the potential return is high enough.

For a museum, the costs of separating the shipments is likely to be higher still, as the travel and subsistence costs of an additional courier will have to be found. However, curators and trustees cannot accept an option that involves the possibility, however small, that the whole consignment could be lost, even if it is more costly in the short term. Insuring against loss is possible but not totally meaningful. Future visitors to the paintings gallery are unlikely to be impressed by a framed cheque for a large sum of money. One of the purposes of a museum is to hold objects in trust for future generations. This trust would be negated if the whole collection were to be lost. This attitude to decision-making is called 'risk aversion' and by definition the trustees and staff of museums should be risk averse.

Comparing the values of different outcomes

Figure 3.5 shows another example of the branches of a decision tree. Option A might represent the decision by a manufacturer to invest in more machinery, option B might be the alternative of running the present machines for longer hours each day. The wiseness of the decision will be judged in the light of outcomes that the manufacturer has little control over, whether the actual demand for the commodity increases or decreases.

The manufacturer guesses that the probability that demand will fall is some fraction P. In that case the probability that demand will rise or stay the same must be $1 - P$ (one minus the probability). It is $1 - P$ because the sum of all related but mutually exclusive probabilities must be unity, that is, absolute certainty. The two options will have different costs and the different outcomes will produce different returns depending on whether demand rises or falls. Thus each of the four possible outcomes will have a different net return or 'payoff', N_1, N_2, N_3 or N_4. But the choice is not between the four possible payoffs but between the two options. Outcomes must be combined in some way to provide a single predicted

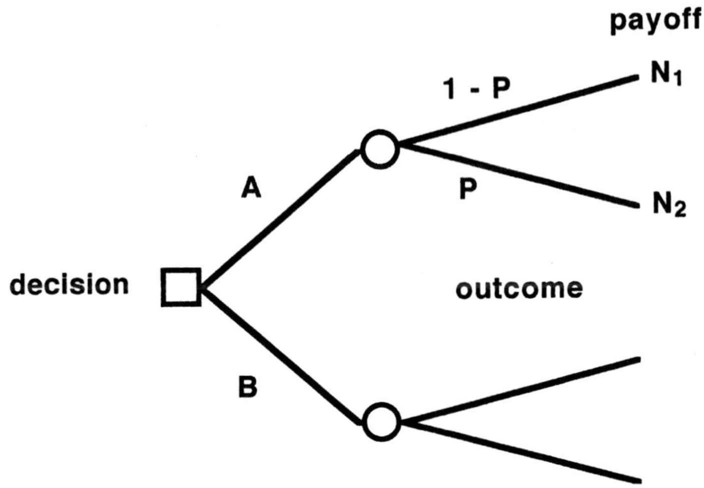

Figure 3.5 *Basis for calculating expected value (EV) using a decision tree*

future value for each option. These two values can then be compared and the most sensible (profitable?) option selected.

In decision analysis this value is called the Expected Monetary Value (EMV). It combines two payoffs in proportion to their relative probabilities, giving an answer in monetary units such as pounds or dollars. The first payoff N_1 is multiplied by the probability of it happening P. This product is added to the product of payoff N_2 and its probability $1 - P$. For decision-making in museums we will not always be able to make direct comparisons with monetary amounts so I shall use EV, Expected Value, without specifying units[1]. The EV of option A is given by the following equation[2]:

$$\mathrm{EV_A} = N_1P + N_2(1 - P) \tag{3.1}$$

[1] In other texts the abbreviation EV is used to represent another quantity, the Equivalent Variation. As this quantity is not referred to in this book and as the initials E and V have the meanings Expected and Value in a variety of other economic abbreviations, e.g. EMV, EMVUC, EUV, EVPI, EVSI, I feel justified in using them to represent Expected Value in this context.

[2] Some of the quantities such as EV consist of two initials; however, I shall also be using the mathematical convention of omitting the multiplication sign between two variables as in N_1P. To avoid confusion I shall explain in the text when a set of initials represents the product of two variables. As far as possible I will keep double initials to the left side of the equation and combinations of single initials to the right-hand side.

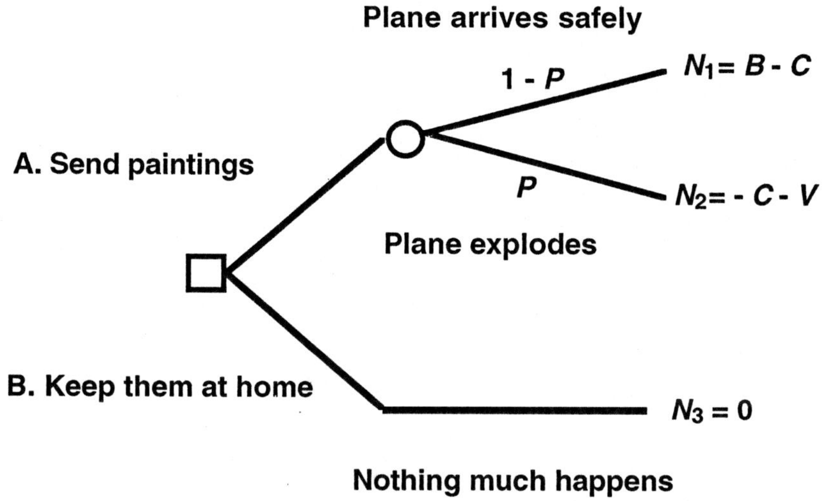

Figure 3.6 *Decision tree for an exhibition involving air travel*

similarly for option B:

$$\mathrm{EV_B} = N_3P + N_4(1 - P) \qquad (3.2)$$

Expanding on the use of these equations we could look at a very simplified tree for a decision on whether to send all our paintings in one air shipment to an exhibition for a fee (Figure 3.6).

If we do not send the paintings to the exhibition then life goes on much as usual and we can assume there are no new benefits or costs in doing this. In comparison to any other option this can be considered as having a payoff of zero (with a probability of one).

If we do send the paintings there are costs C associated with preparation and transport. There are new benefits B in the form of an exhibition fee. The net payoff is the difference between benefits and costs, $N_1 = B - C$.

There is a very small probability P that, on the way to the exhibition, the plane will explode, scattering flaming fragments of the world-famous collection of paintings into the ocean. We have already paid the costs C but we have also lost paintings with value V. The net payoff is the negative amount $N_2 = - C - V$.

If we substitute these expressions for N_1 and N_2 into equation (3.1) we arrive at an equation for the EV of a decision to send the paintings.

$$\mathrm{EV} = B - C - PB - PV \qquad (3.3)$$

The first part of this equation $B - C$ is the net benefit. The next element $-PB$ has a minus sign in front, suggesting a loss. It is the probability P of losing the benefit B. This is an expression of the loss of opportunity. The final part $-PV$ is the probability P of losing the value of the objects V. This is an expression which combines probability with loss of value which we can now see as an exact mathematical representation of the *risk* attached to this decision. The element $-PV$ is the risk to the collection. The two elements containing a probability can be combined as $-P(B+V)$, this is the risk to the enterprise. Equation (3.3) places risk in its proper environment as just one of several pieces of information necessary for making a decision.

Since, in this simple example, the EV of doing nothing is zero, any EV for the alternative option that is positive, greater than zero, will represent an option worth considering. You may care to put in amounts for fees, costs and values with which you are familiar to see how big P (the probability of an exploding plane) has to become before the option looks unfavourable.

In a more complex example there would be many more factors to consider and more than one stage of decision-making. This would result in a range of EVs. A risk-loving entrepreneur might automatically choose the option with the highest EV. A risk averse person would not. In the simple example shown in Figure 3.6, and expressed in equation (3.3), a risk-loving person would go for the option if EV was positive. A risk averse decision-maker would want to know that the probability of total loss was considerably smaller than the critical value of P (call it P_C) that makes the EV greater than zero. At the moment we don't have the figures to advise what such a margin might be, but I think it would be reasonable to suggest that the actual value for P should be at least a hundred times smaller than the critical value P_C, preferably a thousand times.

$$P_C > 1000P \tag{3.4}$$

Equation (3.3) can be used for any object-related decision that can be reduced to a case where the two options are: continuing as usual, and doing one thing different. You must know what the probability of something going wrong is and what the loss in value would be if it did. The loss of value could be partial, something may be rescued from the wreckage.

Analysis of object-related decisions

The care of museum collections poses a wide variety of problems. Each problem requires a choice between several options and each option can have several outcomes. To clarify this multiplicity of possible outcomes we can look at object-based decisions in museums to see if any simplifying patterns emerge.

Unassociated decisions with indirect consequences

Things happen outside museums which eventually have some effect on the objects inside them. There are events such as a storm or an aircraft crash where there is little that can be done to influence the occurrence but something to be done before or after the event to minimize its effect. Some aspects of government politics, such as the decision to wage war with a neighbouring country, are probably also beyond the influence of individual museums. Yet those responsible must make decisions about the most valuable and vulnerable parts of their collections in order to protect them.

Over a period of time, museum staff might be able to influence change in political attitudes to the heritage which in turn might alter the decision to reduce funding or be critical in fighting the proposal to build a motorway next to a monument.

Museum staff make decisions that are intended to improve the possibility or the pleasure of gaining access to the collections but which may indirectly affect the individual objects adversely. To raise funds the museum may organize banquets and balls. To cheer the place up the galleries may be repainted and plants and flower arrangements installed. To make more display and storage space, partitions may be erected. To return to the architectural purity of the original building, partitions may be removed and vistas opened up. More visitors will be encouraged which will include large groups, possibly of gum-chewing children.

The good intentions and the potential benefits of such decisions are obvious. It is less easy to determine whether they will result in increased damage to the objects.

Object-associated decisions with direct consequences

Lastly there is a group of decisions that are made by museum staff that directly affect the objects. These constitute the core business of the museum's collections staff. To acquire, to display, to store, to lend, to treat and occasionally to dispose. These activities have been going on for many decades, if not centuries, and there is a great deal of accumulated knowledge about the effect that they have on objects. However, there is a continuing debate about the interpretation of the accumulated data. People still take sides in the preservation versus access debate which can lead to very partial and polarized interpretation. In the past such lop-sided views have been inherited by new students and junior staff who then concentrate on selecting information to help win the debate rather than seek agreement or compromise.

At first sight there is such a great number of museum activities that may directly or indirectly affect the condition of the collections that it may appear that there can be no simple general rules. Each case will have to be judged on an individual basis. Fortunately many of the diverse activities have common components. The effects of most of these basic factors are reasonably well known and there is a fair degree of consensus. Fortunately for museum decision-makers a great many sensible generalizations can be made.

In Table 3.1 a variety of museum activities is analysed into component parts.

Some of the recurrent activities can be separated into more basic components (Table 3.2).

The activity 'handle' can in turn be analysed as possible combinations of the hazards, pressure, abrasion and transfer of chemicals, which brings

Table 3.1

Activity	*Possible components*
Direct	
Acquire	handle, pack, move, analyse, photograph, change environment
Dispose	handle, pack, move, change environment
Display	mount, enclose, make function, illuminate, invite people, leave alone
Store	mount, enclose, leave alone
Study	move, unpack, handle, make function, illuminate, analyse, reformat, photograph
Loan	move, handle, pack, photograph, change environment, mount, enclose, treat, make function, illuminate, invite people, leave alone
Preserve	mount, enclose, change environment, reformat treat
Treat	handle, move, analyse, photograph, illuminate, change environment, add material, remove material, release volatile substances.
Action following disaster	move, handle, change environment, treat
Indirect	
Party	invite people, cook, serve drink, arrange flowers, play music
Build	create dust, change environment
Decorate	create dust, release volatile substances

Table 3.2

Pack	handle, enclose, change stress patterns
Analyse	handle, move, illuminate, irradiate, remove material
Photograph	handle, move, mount, illuminate
Mount	handle, change stress patterns, add material, remove material
Reformat	handle, move, illuminate, add material

it close to the lower levels of analysis of risk agents discussed in the last chapter.

It is not easy to devise categories that are totally mutually exclusive. Nor is it possible to break each down into components that have exactly equal weight. For instance 'leave alone' is a very simple activity but is associated with a multitude of possible outcomes such as creep, oxidation, acid hydrolysis, fire, theft, insect attack and fluctuating humidity.

But at this stage it is possible to make a few observations:

- Some words such as 'handle' occur very frequently. If we can reduce the risk from components that appear frequently we will have gone a long way to reducing the total risk.
- Some activities are more complex than others. The activity 'loan' which is generally considered more risky than the activity 'store' has a far greater complexity, that is, it has more components. Using that criterion, 'treat' is among the most complex, risky activities.
- It is possible to consider probabilities and outcomes without considering the motive behind the decision. At this level of analysis there is very little difference between acquisition and disposal. Actions such as treat, preserve and reformat which are all motivated by a desire to help the object can be seen as a collection of activities that have potential to cause harm.
- The activities imposed by undesirable outside events such as war or disaster are identical to those imposed by benign events such as rebuilding a gallery or acquiring a new object. Only the timescale is altered. The same decisions must be taken but more quickly.

The central part of this book deals with what is known about the possible outcomes of the activities shown in Table 3.3.

Although it is possible to break down the subject to a level where we can make objective observations which are independent of subjective evaluation we should resist thinking that scientific or objective observations are more valid or more useful in decision-making. The act of

Table 3.3

• Leave alone
• Enclose
• Change environment
• Invite people
• Illuminate
• Handle
• Move
• Make function
• Add material
• Remove material

collecting objects and putting them into museums involves subjective judgements. Visiting a museum and enjoying the objects on display involves subjective judgments. The objective information discussed in Chapters 9 to 14 can be used to help predict the outcomes of certain decisions but cannot be used to say which is the best decision.

The objective information that we need to use to help our estimates of probability and to help predict the consequences of decisions is subject to considerable limitations. To simplify the process of scientific experiment and observation, the number of interacting factors has to be severely reduced. It is then easy to quantify the relationship between one factor and another and to begin to understand the mechanisms of cause and effect in this simplified system. To that extent scientific data can be compared to the visual intellectual model. They are not of the real world but their study can lead to insights about the real world.

Analysis can appear to simplify decision-making, but ignoring the complex interactivity of the whole system could merely lead to simplistic decisions.

Something to think about

The cost of a lottery ticket is greater than its EV. Why do people buy them?

The cost of insurance is greater than the risk of loss. Why does anyone buy insurance?

What would the form of equation (3.3) be if the plane exploded on the way home?

Only monetary benefits were considered in the derivation of the equation but it would be equally valid to consider other benefits. What might these be?

In Table 3.1 all of the components of the activity 'party' could be further analysed. What hazards could these components be reduced to?

References

Moore, P.G. and Thomas, H. (1988) *The Anatomy of Decisions* (2nd edn). Penguin Books. ISBN 0-14-009120-3.

Watson, Stephen R. and Buede, Dennis M. (1987) *Decision Synthesis: the Principles and Practice of Decision Analysis.* Cambrige University Press. ISBN 0-521-31078-4.

4 The model museum

Twenty-five years ago it would have been quite easy for a conservator or curator to believe that their decisions and actions were not connected with anything beyond their studio or office. The work that goes on inside the museum is both resourced and judged from outside. In this chapter a model is developed that identifies the inputs and outputs of the museum, the points of decision-making within the museum, and the effects of those decisions on the collections.

The purpose of museums

In order to judge whether isolated object-related decisions are good or bad, or to decide how risk-averse museum professionals can afford to be, there must be some agreement about the long-term aims of museums. Without this agreement it is impossible to judge whether an institution is treating its collections recklessly or whether it is being unsociably cautious. Without this agreement it is difficult to determine whether an institution is providing its funders with value for money or indeed to derive any of the values that are needed in the assessment of risk.

A recent comprehensive discussion of the purposes of museums appears in Suzanne Keene's *Managing Conservation in Museums* (Keene, 1996). The professional view of the purpose of museums is incorporated in the statutes of the International Council of Museums. A museum is an institution that 'acquires, conserves, researches, communicates and exhibits, for the purposes of study, education and enjoyment, material evidence of people and their environment' (ICOM 1990). These primary aims are repeated in other documents, such as the National Heritage Act in the UK, which are designed to establish the purpose of individual institutions (HMSO, 1983). These definitions suggest a number of aims, some of which relate to the preservation of the collections and others to their display and interpretation. There is an implicit assumption that these aims carry equal weight and there is no suggestion that they conflict. Yet most people assume that the aims of preservation and access are in conflict and that some sort of agreement is needed about the correct balance.

Under pressure from government, museums in the United Kingdom have over the past 15 years become more concerned about accountability to the taxpayer, who is still the major funder of their activities. This has resulted in a number of changes, among which has been the preparation and publication of 'mission statements'. These represent the aspirations of the current senior management and indicate the current ethos in a way that the dispassionate definitions of an Act of Parliament never can.

The mission statement for the Victoria and Albert Museum states that the purpose of the museum is to 'increase the understanding and enjoyment of art, craft and design through its collections'. This is a clear statement that preservation is not an end in itself. The objects in the collections are to be used, or exploited, to engender changes in the mental and emotional states of human beings. Such a mission statement was formulated at a time that standards of preservation in English national museums were under attack. However, the criticism was not about the decline in condition of objects, but the lack of availability for use (National Audit Office, 1988).

Twenty-five years ago it was quite usual and quite acceptable for a conservator to make a decision to treat an object in a particular way because preservation or restoration was something that began and ended within the museum if not within the confines of the studio. Its purpose was not questioned and did not need to be justified or compared with other museum activities. At the end of the twentieth century it is inconceivable that decisions about the objects inside a museum can be made without consideration of the connections to the world outside.

This viewpoint is the basis of a conceptual model for object-related activities in a museum. This model will be used to try to work out more precisely what relationships must be better understood and what information is necessary before we can evaluate risk.

Inputs and outcomes

The most basic level of the model is shown in Figure 4.1.

Nearly all collections rely on external resources for their maintenance. Even among private collections and independent museums there are no instances where the resources for preservation derive solely from income that is generated by the collection. In the absence of grants some form of external trading is necessary. All the inputs are treated together under the heading 'resources'.

Not all the inputs are in the form of cash. A museum consumes vast quantities of energy, usually in the form of electricity. Decisions about the welfare of collections must be made with a view to economy of energy as well as of money.

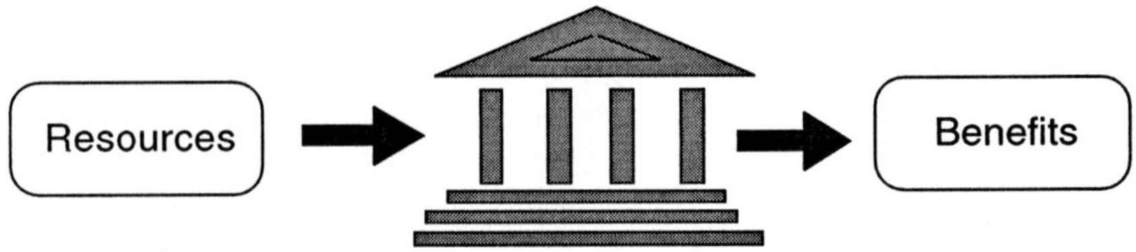

Figure 4.1 *The museum in the real world, making use of external resources and providing benefits outside its walls*

Museum objects exist to stimulate a response in an audience. The audience that derives benefit from a museum collection comes mainly from outside the organization that maintains the collection. This is true whether the collection is small and privately owned or large and on display in a national museum. The effects that museums have on the world outside are best considered as long-term outcomes rather than short-term outputs. The outcomes of the presence of museum collections are assumed to be universally beneficial and are considered under the heading 'benefit'.

This is a 'net' benefit because not all the outputs of a museum are beneficial. There are quantities of waste products which may be adding to the greenhouse effect or depleting the ozone layer, polluting water or providing additional stuffing for landfill. Decisions relating to preservation or access to the objects must also consider the effects of those decisions on the welfare of the whole planet.

It is representatives of society, usually the government, but also volunteers, enthusiasts and rich philanthropists, that provide resources. And it is society, or at least certain classes and colours within society, that gain benefit from the efficient allocation and application of these

Table 4.1

- Buildings management
- Cleaning
- Conservation
- Curators
- Education
- Exhibitions
- Finance
- Loans
- Object movement
- Personnel
- Research
- Security
- Special events

resources within the museum. Table 4.1 shows some of the groups or functions to which the resources can be allocated. If more goes to one group then automatically less is available to the others.

Think about a collection or organization with which you are familiar. Go down the list and imagine what would change, in relation to the objects, if the amount of money allocated to each of these were to be doubled or were halved.

There are a number of administrative functions which can be considered neutral in this respect. Increasing or decreasing the allocation would alter the amounts available to other functions but have no direct effect on the collections. There are some functions, such as buildings management, for which altering the allocation would have a direct bearing on the environment of the objects. There are some, for instance education, that would have an effect on the amount of direct access to the objects, the amount of use they would get. There are one or two, notably conservation, that would affect the amount of interventive treatment to which the objects were subjected.

Environment treatment and use

Decisions that alter the nature of the environment, the use of the objects or their physical treatment are the key types of decisions that will have a detectable effect on the objects themselves. These three areas represent points of control over attributes of the individual objects or collections.

- Environment. This covers all those activities that ensure freedom from floods, earthquakes, thieves and arsonists. Making sure that the roof doesn't leak, the bugs don't bite and there is control over quantities of heat, light, moisture, dirt and air.
- Use. This includes all forms of access to the objects obtained directly through display, reference collections, handling collections, exhibitions, loans, replicas, research, and indirectly through photographs, books, CD-ROMs and on-line databases.
- Treatment. This covers all forms of direct intervention with the objects whether for preservation or restoration.

Conservation treatment does not usually command a large proportion of resources, usually considerably less than 10% for most organizations. However, all major collections spend some money on interventive treatment each year. Treatment can have a dramatic effect on individual objects. It affects how long they will last and how easy they are to use. For some large groups of objects, e.g. limestone buildings and nineteenth-century books, interventive treatment is likely to be the only route to continued existence.

These three factors – environment, treatment and use – have effects on the collections and their individual constituents. I have separated these effects into two. Effects on the state of the object or collection, and effects on the value of the object or collection.

State and value

The words were introduced in Chapter 2 and were used without definition. Although both are apparently short and simple, the two words 'state' and 'value' have complex connotations.

Briefly, 'state' is what physically defines an object at any moment in time. All those physical attributes such as material, dimensions, decoration and evidence of manufacture that might appear in a curatorial catalogue entry are combined with what the conservator would recognize as descriptions of condition.

'Value' is a controversial and elusive subject. The various approaches to it are explored in Chapter 6. Paul Greenhalgh, Head of the Research Department at the V&A, warned me that 'value is something to be discussed in the pub'.

'Value' is not only what the owners or trustees were, or would be, willing to pay for the object, it also reflects the return on that investment, in the number of visitors that choose to see it, the number of students that wish to refer to it, the number of images that are sold or licensed throughout the world. It is a measure of demand for that particular work. It also contains an element of what economists call Net Present Value (this will be discussed further in Chapter 5). This is the value for us today, of net benefits that are predicted to accrue in the future. Thinking about the long-term benefits does something to eliminate the temporary fluctuations in value due to fashion. It also reminds us that there *is* current value in preserving *some* objects for extended periods.

In Chapter 2 the words 'state' and 'value' were used interchangeably as the attributes that could be altered by various agents. Although the two words are strongly connected, it is easy to show that they are distinct. A change in relative humidity will alter the weight, dimensions and flexibility of a panel painting but will have no effect on its value. The retribution of a painting can have a dramatic effect on its monetary and interest value without any change in its state.

The unconnected model

To summarize, we have three areas as shown in Figure 4.2.

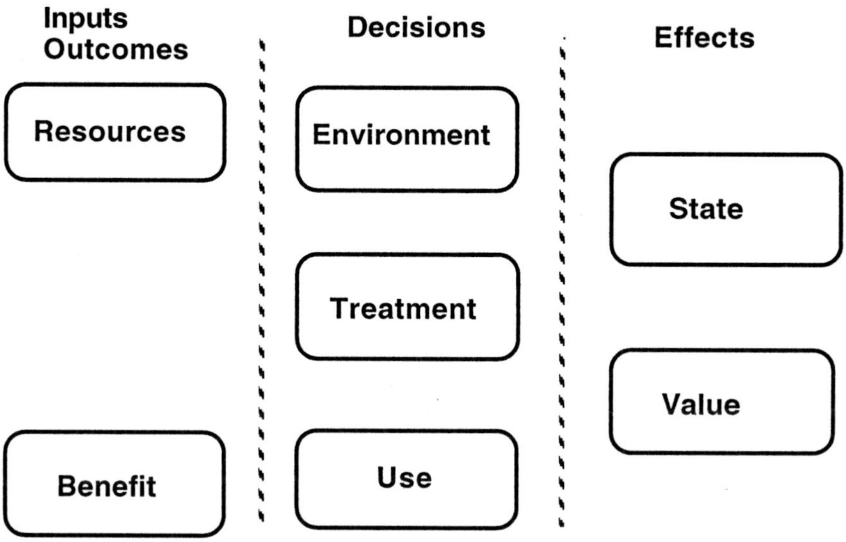

Figure 4.2 *The three divisions: inputs and outcomes, areas of control and effects on the objects*

- The area of inputs and outcomes, which exists largely outside the museum.
- The area of control, where through policy, resource allocation and daily practice we decide how we use and abuse the collections.
- The area where we observe the effects of our decisions on the objects.

To make this a *working* model we have to examine all the possible relationships between these seven elements. If we alter one of these elements, what effect does this have on any of the others? There are some 32 possible interactions in this model.

The interactions can be of several sorts. For simplicity these will be restricted to two sets of two: those that are strong and those that are weak, those that are of equal strength in both directions and those that are not. Changing an aspect of one entity may have an obvious effect on another, this is shown by a thick arrow. The reaction of one entity to change in another may only be slight or may not be consistent, in which case this relationship is represented as a thin arrow. Where the interaction is equally strong in both directions this is shown by a double headed arrow. Quite frequently, however, although change in entity A may promote change in entity B, an attempt to alter entity B by some other means has no effect on any aspect of A.

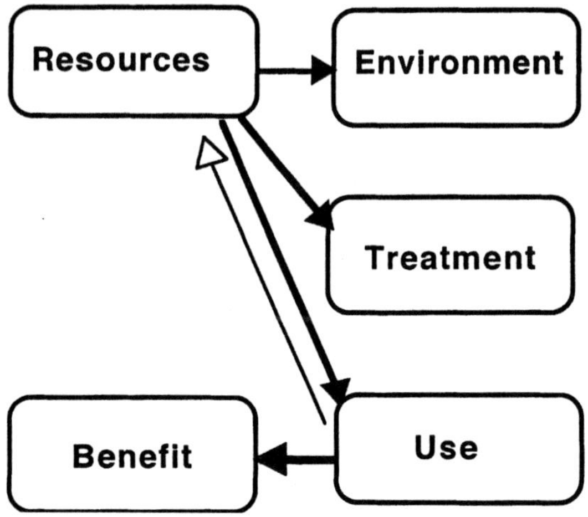

Figure 4.3 *Relationships at the world/museum interface*

The museum/world interface

As shown in Figure 4.3 a change in the available resources can have a direct effect on the three areas of control. The reverse is not true. Altering the environment does not have a strong effect on the resources, neither does altering the amount or nature of treatment. It is possible to charge for use but in the majority of organizations this contributes only a small amount (usually much less than 20%) to the available resources. This is shown as a weak interaction.

It is the use of the collections that leads to the long-term benefits experienced outside the museum. In the long term those benefits are so diffused that they do not have a direct effect on the amount or type of use to which objects are put. This one-way connection is shown by a thick arrow.

The state and value of the collections do not have direct effects on inputs and outputs, but interact through the medium of the areas of control.

Interaction between areas of control

There are some weak interactions between the different areas of control that do not directly affect the objects themselves. This is shown in Figure 4.4.

The amount of use can alter the environment. People need light. A large number of people will have some effect on levels of temperature, humidity,

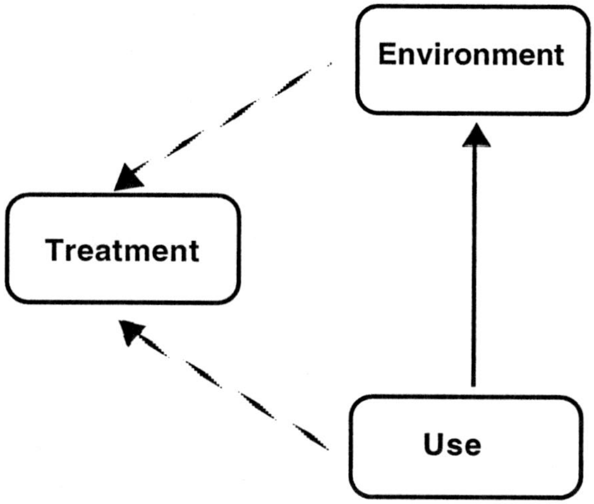

Figure 4.4 *Relationships within the areas of decision-making*

dust and certain pollutants. The presence of a large number of people may reduce security and increase the risk of fire. This interaction will be dealt with in Chapter 13. The reverse interaction is not significant. Although it has been proposed that more people will come to an air-conditioned gallery than one without control because it is more pleasant, this effect has not been proven and, given the huge number of uncontrolled environments in libraries, museums and historic houses, is insignificant.

A change to the environment may promote a change in the proposals that are made for treatment even if there is no resulting change in the objects. This is, however, a very weak link and will not be used in the final model. A change in proposed treatment is unlikely to have an effect on specification for environment that are actually realized.

At first sight it may appear that there are connections between use and treatment. Proposals to increase use may lead to proposals to treat in a different way. For instance, there may be a need to disbind an album or to bind together a series of loose leaves. This is another very weak link. Treatment may allow greater use, e.g. by easing the opening of a book that has been bound too tightly, but this is not a direct interaction as it only takes place by altering the state of an object.

Interactions between state and value

There is a strong one-way relationship between state and value as shown in Figure 4.5.

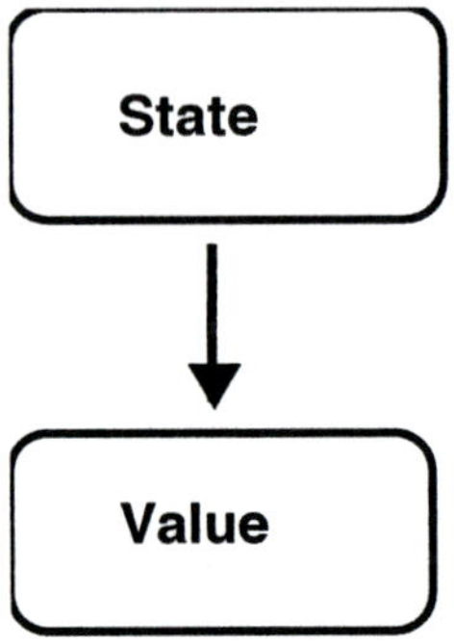

Figure 4.5 *The one-way relationship between state and value*

As the state of an object is altered by restoration or by deterioration, so its value will change. This relationship is by no means simple and will be discussed in Chapter 7 and again in Chapter 15. The value of an object can be altered by a number of means, including research and publication, none of which has any physical effect on the object.

Interaction between areas of control and attributes of the object or collection

Environment, treatment and use all have obvious effects on the state of objects, as is shown in Figure 4.6.

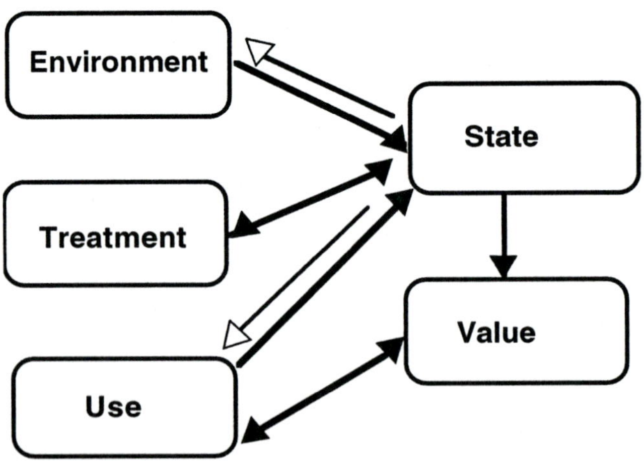

Figure 4.6 *Interactions between the areas of control and the attributes of the objects*

Chapters 9–14 deal with attempts to clarify and quantify those effects. The state of an object determines the nature of treatment, and will have an effect on its cost and likelihood of success. The treatment–state relationship is shown as strongly two-way.

The state of some objects can affect the immediate environment. Hygroscopic materials such as wood and textiles exchange moisture with the atmosphere. Some degrading objects, e.g. cellulose nitrate film, release gases into the environment that, in turn, can alter the state of other objects. As this is only true of a limited number of objects, this is shown as a weak interaction.

The state of an object will determine the demand for use and suitability for use. A book may be withdrawn from public access if it cannot be handled safely. One of the reasons for disposal from the collections allowed by the National Heritage Act is if the object 'has become useless for the purposes of their collections by reason of damage, physical deterioration, or infestation by destructive organisms'.

There is a strong two-way relationship between use and value. As we shall see in Chapter 6 one way of estimating value is by measuring use. Research may increase the value of an object. It does this through the intermediary of documented information as shown in Figure 4.7. Information about the object that has little or nothing to do with its physical state may be very important in determining value. A photograph of a person or a geographic location has very little value unless the identities of sitter and location are documented along with the date that the photograph was taken. None of this valuable information may be discovered by examining the object.

There is, however, a great deal of information locked up in the state of an object which can be interrogated and interpreted in a variety of ways, often involving complex analytical equipment. This physical and

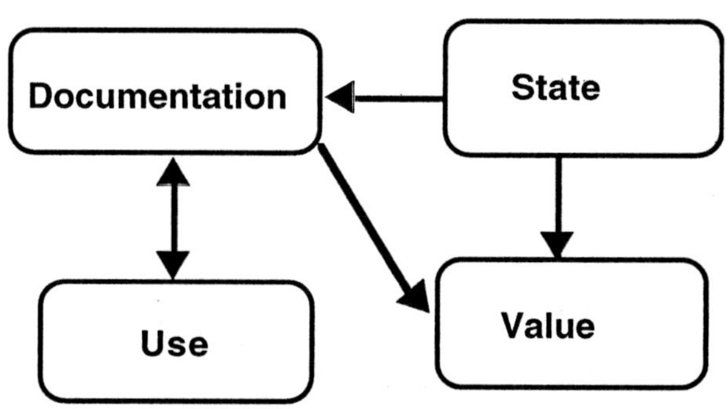

Figure 4.7 *The involvement of documentation in the use/value relationship*

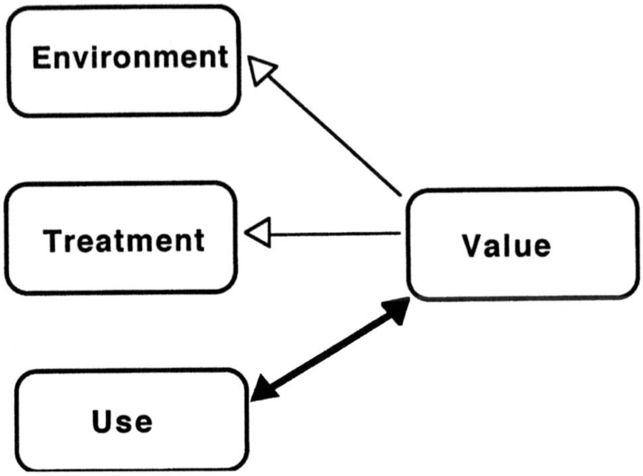

Figure 4.8 *The effect of value on areas of decision-making*

chemical information can be translated into documented information about authenticity or attribution which is then separate from the object.

As documented information is only one of the determinants of value it is not shown as a separate entity in the complete model (it is reinstated in the more detailed discussion in Chapter 15).

There are some tenuous relationships between value and treatment and value and environment (Figure 4.8). The more someone values an object the more they are willing to pay for it to be looked after. Although it is not very satisfactory, looking at the amount of money or time allocated to a particular object or collection may be the only way of estimating its value. However, the relationship is not necessary or direct and is left out of the main model.

Nice picture – but so what?

Figure 4.9 shows the completed model. Does it have any use? I have used the model to organize the structure of this book so that some sections deal with the relationship between use and value, others with value and state and so on. I have tried to use it as a basis for computer spreadsheets that relate changes of state of the object to changes in Net Present Value, as costs of treatment or costs of maintaining specific environments are altered. The output of these attempts gave me a greater feeling for some of the economic and philosophical concepts dealt with in the next few chapters.

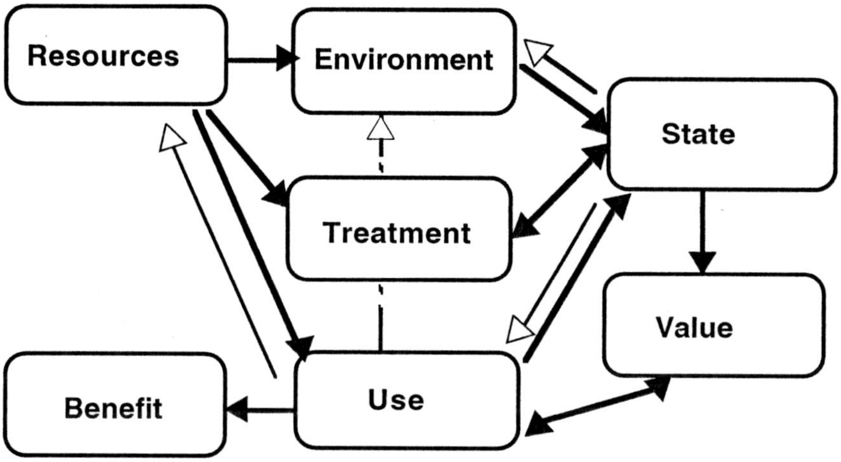

Figure 4.9 *The complete model*

When I was discussing these experiments with a professional computer modeller he told me that what I had was a VHD – a Valuable Heuristic Device. He said they had a bin in the middle of the room into which they threw all their VHDs. It is something that cannot (yet) be used to unerringly provide quantitative answers but whose study can produce useful insights.

The value of this model is that it demonstrates that there is not a simple route to carrying out a cost–benefit or risk–benefit analysis because there are so many connections between elements that can affect one another. The model causes the modeller and the reader to consider what are the important relationships in decision-making. It isolates specific relationships that need to be quantified and creates a desire for this quantification. These interactions can each be studied in isolation but the model shows that they cannot be used in an isolated way. If you alter one part it may have effects elsewhere in the organization that you would not otherwise predict.

Political and social changes outside the museum have an effect on the state of the collections. The state of the collections will have an effect on the benefits that museums bestow on society.

Something to think about

Do you agree that the benefits that museums provide to society have little or no direct effect on the level of use of collections?

The model was created by someone who identifies himself as a conservator. How different would the model be if it had been developed by someone from a museum education department?

The chapter title suggests that this is a model for a museum. Could it be used for a single object or a small part of a collection?

References

HMSO (1983) National Heritage Act 1983. Chapter 47. Her Majesty's Stationery Office, London.

ICOM (1990) Statutes: Code of Professional Ethics. International Council of Museums, Paris.

Keene, Suzanne (1996) *Managing Conservation in Museums.* Butterworth-Heinemann in Association with Science Museum, London. ISBN 0-7506-2384-5.

National Audit Office (1988) Management of the Collections of the English National Museums and Galleries. Report by the Comptroller and Auditor General. National Audit Office. Her Majesty's Stationery Office, London.

5 Costs and benefits

In trying to decide whether a proposed course of action is sensible, all the costs and all the benefits must be considered. Some of the effects of a decision may spill over into areas beyond the immediate concern of the decision-maker. In this chapter a list of the stages in a cost–benefit analysis is provided and the concept of Net Present Value is introduced. Museum activities are seen as attempts to increase or maintain value. Risk is shown to be a component in the evaluation of a proposal to do something to maintain or raise value.

Cost–benefit analysis and decision-making

There are times when we just can't make up our minds about something, such as whether to move, to change jobs, or to commit to a permanent relationship. Helpful friends often suggest drawing up two lists, one setting out all the good things and another listing all the bad things about the subject of our indecision. This is another example of a model that doesn't actually give the answer, but prompts us to think and evaluate, which may lead to a decision. Possibly one we are happy with. The decision would not be driven by the fact that one list was slightly longer than the other, as some of the points we listed might be very much more important than others. The different points would have different values. However, if there were considerably more points in favour of one course of action then we might be swayed.

In Chapter 3 we looked at a simple decision and said that, subject to certain reservations, we would choose the option with the highest positive Expected Value. For that example the Expected Value was given by the equation:

$$\mathrm{EV} = B - C - PB - PV \tag{3.3}$$

We can simplify this by (rashly) assuming that nothing will go wrong (probability of misfortune is zero, $P = 0$) in which case the equation becomes:

$$\mathrm{EV} = B - C \tag{5.1}$$

The Expected Value is the net benefit, that is the sum of all the benefits *B*, minus the sum of all the costs *C*. So all we have to do is make a list of all the bad things (the costs) and a list of all the good things (the benefits) and compare them. If the benefits far outweigh the costs then this is an option we might choose.

The trouble is that we can only perform the simple subtraction in the equation if we use the same units of measurement for both benefits and costs. (My school algebra teacher used to say 'You can't take oranges from apples!'.) The unit of measurement associated with most of the costs is money. Many people have a strong objection to using this same unit to measure abstract entities such as happiness or learning, even if it were possible. In previous chapters we have discussed that it is important to know the viewpoint from which degree of risk or change in value is assessed. One person's cost will be another person's benefit. A decision made in one place may have both costs and benefits, in other places and at other times, that were not the immediate concern of the decision-maker.

A thorough analysis of costs and benefits will consist of listing all the benefits and all the costs across all the areas where there will be a noticeable effect. The analyst will have to quantify the effects of a proposal in a way that makes comparisons between options possible and yet does not offend those who reject crass quantification of intangible and emotional values.

This area of study is called, logically enough, Cost–Benefit Analysis (CBA). To give emphasis to the more complex part of the study it is sometimes called Benefit–Cost Analysis, particularly in the US. Where the cost that is of most concern is the possible loss of something really valuable, life or health, it is called Risk–Benefit Analysis. It has been described as '. . . an art that, to be done well, requires an appreciation of a substantial amount of economics as well as sensitivity to ethical and philosophical issues' (Zerbe and Dively, 1994). Entrepreneurs and investors have always used a simple version based on profit and loss. Their decision-making is egocentric and does not consider effects beyond the local concern of income generation and personal wealth creation. By contrast, governments that consider investments of public money in large schemes such as building dams or bridges have to be aware of the effects of their proposals on a wide range of people and their activities.

The basic concepts of CBA relating to public works originated with the French engineer Dupuit in the mid-nineteenth century but were not developed further until in 1936 the US Flood Control Act required that projects be undertaken only '. . . if the benefits to whomsoever they may accrue are in excess of the estimated costs . . .' (Gilpin, 1995). The technique of CBA developed further as the environmental movement developed. During the 1970s the fields of environmental economics and natural resource economics gained recognition. In the late 1980s and early 1990s studies of the economics of health care expenditure began to use CBA methodology.

This is a large and complex subject and we will only be using a small and simple part. The basic principles are well covered in general texts (Mishan, 1975; Zerbe and Dively, 1994). The areas with most parallels to conservation and museums are those dealing with ecological impact and health care and there are now fairly readable books dealing with CBA applied to these specialist subjects (Hanley and Spash, 1993; Johansson, 1995).

It is desirable to think that decisions taken in boardrooms and conservation laboratories within museums will have long-term outcomes beneficial to members of society outside the museum. CBA is therefore an appropriate, but by no means simple, adjunct to conservation decision-making.

A simple museum example

In its simplest form the analysis consists of basic accountancy and arithmetic which can be used to compare two courses of action to show which of them is more economically sensible. In many instances one course of action involves making some sort of investment while the alternative is maintaining the status quo. The aim is to decide whether, over a given period of time, the investment will produce the desired effect, usually that of increasing income or reducing costs, or both.

Imagine a museum with a large number of small pieces of sculpture and ceramics on open display. The museum is an old building situated at a busy crossroads in the centre of town and is visited by a consistent number of people every day. Dust from the traffic outside comes in through the sash windows and more comes through the door every time a visitor arrives. Unknown to them, each visitor distributes small samples of clothing fibres and flakes of dead skin as they walk round the galleries, in addition to the dirt that falls off their shoes. The objects become dusty very quickly and a keen young arts graduate is hired to carefully dust each object and keep the displays looking clean and cared for. However, one year the city council announce that next year their grant to the museum will be cut and will probably have to be further cut in the following year. The curator in charge wonders whether the objects could be put in some kind of showcase to prevent them getting dusty, thus saving the salary of the object cleaner.

The cost of each showcase can be found in the supplier's catalogue. The annual cost of dusting can be calculated from the length of the treatment, its frequency, the number of objects treated and the rate of pay of the person doing the dusting. If cleaning each object takes 5 minutes and is done once a week by someone costing £6 an hour, the annual cost per object is £26. There are nearly 500 objects, the object cleaner attends to each one weekly at an annual cost of £13 000. The curator finds that even a tacky showcase which will house 10 objects will cost £1500 and 50 are needed. Is the investment worth it? The annual cost of cleaning each group of 10 objects is £260 so there is no clear, immediate saving. If the Council Finance Officer would allow the curator to think long term, it could be argued that the investment would pay for itself in six years. In the first year the EV of the decision to replace the object cleaner is the cost, £1500 per case, less the benefit, the saving of £260, that is –£1240. A negative EV suggests a bad decision. At the end of six years the EV is +£60, which suggests a reasonable decision. The further into the future the EV is projected the more sound the decision seems. Based on this analysis the curator and the finance officer agree to release the object cleaner.

A more thorough analysis

A complete cost–benefit analysis consists of the nine stages shown in Figure 5.1 (Gilpin, 1995, p. 37). We can examine the example above to see in more detail how it fails, bearing in mind that although the analysis may be incomplete or misguided the decision might still have been right.

Step 1. Determine scope and objectives
The decision-makers have chosen the objectives which are:

- Save money
- Keep the objects clean

They have limited the scope of the analysis to the finances of the museum.

Step 2. Consider constraints
We have not been made aware of any considerations such as contracts of employment, redundancy pay, limits to financial discretion of the decision-makers or the terms under which the museum was established.

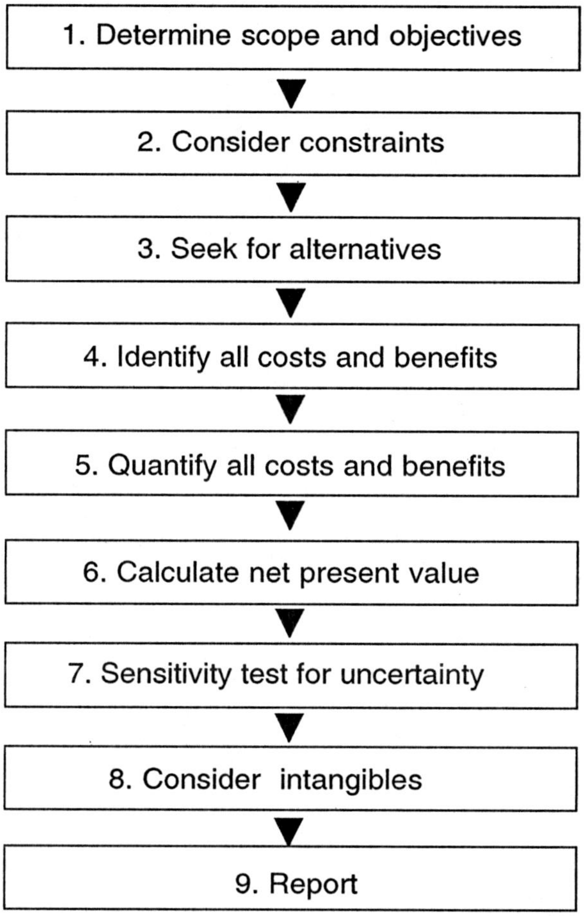

Figure 5.1 *The nine stages of a complete cost–benefit analysis (after Gilpin)*

Step 3. Seek for alternatives
Only two options were considered. Retaining the status quo or casing the objects. Given the two objectives, and the limited scope, there are alternative approaches to solving the problem, some of which might be more acceptable:

- Save money
  - reduce cleaner's hours with or without increased efficiency
  - reduce curator's hours
  - other savings – heating, lighting, security
  - shut the museum permanently

- Clean objects
  - seal windows
  - ropes to distance the visitors from the objects
  - mechanical air flow management with or without filtration
  - review definition of 'clean'
  - shut the museum permanently

Each of these alternatives should be subjected to the next five steps of the analysis.

Step 4. Identify all costs and benefits

A very limited number of the costs and benefits involved have been included in the calculation. This could well be because the person driving the decision has particular obsessions which limit the overview. The curator in this story may be driven by a personal dislike of the object cleaner, by a good lunch provided by the showcase salesman or a general disregard for the visiting public. The following are some of the factors that have been ignored:

- The showcases need to be cleaned as the dust is still uncontrolled.
- The showcases will leak and the objects will still have to be cleaned.
- Installation of the cases involves object movement and dust creation.
- Installing cases may mean altering the lighting.
- The tackier the showcase the more frequently it will need maintenance.
- And the sooner it will need to be replaced.
- Cases increase security and decrease accidental damage.
- Cases may reduce rates of deterioration.
- Dusting increases risk of damage and causes wear.
- Dust may increase deterioration.
- Showcases restrict freedom of gallery design.
- Showcases limit public appreciation of objects.
- The presence of someone in the gallery makes it seem more alive.
- The activity of cleaning makes it seem that the museum cares.
- The cleaner, now quite knowledgeable, chats to the public about the collection.
- The change might create bad publicity.

Depending on which option is being considered, each of these is either a cost (negative benefit) or a benefit (negative cost). The factors that affect public enjoyment have an effect outside the museum, they could be considered as 'societal' costs or benefits. The loss of a benefit is an opportunity cost.

Some of the costs are one-off, or only repeated infrequently. Some are continuous. The longer the timespan we consider, the more important the continuous costs become.

Step 5. Quantify all costs and benefits

The only costs identified, purchase price and salary, were easily quantified. This may have been the reason they came so readily to mind in the first place.

A few of the others are easy to estimate, for instance the need for and the cost of a new lighting system. Most of them are very difficult to quantify or give a value to.

First, because we don't know whether they actually have any real effect, e.g. the presence of a chatty cleaner. Second, because we don't know enough to quantify the outcome, e.g. how much slower is the rate of deterioration inside a showcase (assuming it *is* slower)? Third, it is difficult to place a value on a change of state. What is the difference between a dusty sculpture and a clean one, a bronze that is patinated and one that is corroded? However, some attempt should be made to put money values against as many of these as possible. Attempts to answer these questions occur later in this book.

Step 6. Calculate Net Present Value

After the quantification of benefits the most contentious part of CBA is 'discounting'. Earlier in this example we calculated EV at various stages in the future until we arrived at a point in time at which it was positive. Because it became positive, and did so within an acceptable time period, the decision was declared a sound one to make at this point in time. In the calculation we used the same value for the cost of cleaning year after year. Economists would insist that this is not reasonable because money in the future does not have the same value right now. The further in the future the money is, the less value it is to you at this moment.

To demonstrate this, suppose I give you a choice of £100 now, or £100 in a year's time. You are likely to accept the cash immediately. Money now is more useful, has greater 'utility', than the promise of money, so the 'present value' of next year's £100 is less than this year's. Looked at another way, if £100 is invested now, in a year's time it will have become a larger amount, say £105. The *present* value of next year's £105 is only £100. The economist might argue that, at least theoretically, the £75 000 investment in showcases should be examined to see what it would yield if invested in some other way. All the other sums of money, whether one-off payments or continuous outgoings, should be treated in this way. For this reason, future flows of income and expenditure are discounted at a rate that relates to the current rate of interest for investment of money.

Inflation also has an effect on the future of value. Its effects are often deliberately left out in simple financial projections and results are quoted in terms of this year's pound or dollar. Alternatively the rate of inflation can be incorporated into the discount rate. For simplicity throughout this book the effect of inflation is ignored but, as far as the arithmetic is concerned, it is very easy to incorporate it if you wish.

If all the future flows of benefits and all the future flows of costs are discounted, and the discounted costs subtracted from the discounted benefits, we get a number that represents the present value of the net benefit of a proposal. This is called the Net Present Value or NPV:

$$\text{NPV} = B(\text{discounted}) - C(\text{discounted}) \tag{5.2}$$

The larger the NPV the more favourable the option seems. If the NPV is negative the proposal is probably not sound, but a less negative NPV still indicates a better option. Remember that the status quo is not always a favourable option.

Each of the terms in equation (5.2) is derived from a relationship which states that any quantity Q, dealt with at a certain number of years in the future t, discounted at the rate r, has a present value of:

$$\frac{Q}{(1 + r)^t}$$

This makes the full equation for Net Present Value:

$$\text{NPV} = \sum_{t=0}^{n} \frac{B_t}{(1 + r)^t} - \sum_{t=0}^{n} \frac{C_t}{(1 + r)^t} \tag{5.3}$$

This may look very daunting to anyone not familiar with mathematical notation. The Σ symbol is shorthand for the sum of all the discounted quantities from now (year $t = 0$) to a certain time n years in the future (year $t = n$). It may look more complicated than equation (5.2) but says more or less the same thing. Most computer speadsheets will have a financial function that carries out discounting or calculates NPV without having to memorize or understand the equations. Arguments surrounding the selection of an appropriate discount rate are discussed in Chapter 15.

Step 7. Sensitivity test for uncertainty

In Step 5 we noticed a great deal of uncertainty about the likelihood of effects and their quantification. If we ignore the fact that the numbers we derive are uncertain, and then incorporate these values into the equation, we will end up with an NPV that is used to make a decision but which may in fact be meaningless. If we try out some alternative values for different factors, and see what the effect on the NPV is, we will get an idea of how much our ignorance actually affects the answer. This is a test of sensitivity. This exercise helps determine how realistic the NPV is. It may also have the beneficial effect of teaching us that we don't have to achieve complete accuracy in quantifying things that we find difficult to value.

Step 8. Consider intangibles

It has been argued that monetization of values merely exposes the analyst's prejudices and can be used to lead to any desired conclusion (Stern, 1976). If, at Step 5, we conclude that we really cannot give quantitative values to some of the costs such as damage, or to some of the benefits such as enjoyment, then we need to declare them as intangibles. These will be described and reported qualitatively. They will be considered at the same time as the NPVs for different options and, depending on the audience, will have more or less effect in swaying a decision.

Michel Benarie, who deserves to be considered as one of the great philosophers of conservation, says '. . . there is no (correct mathematical) way to compare non-comensurable entities. It seems paradoxical that while mathematically the comparison, or its outcome, the decision, is not possible, in our everyday life at almost every step we rather easily accomplish analogous choices.'

A balanced approach to quantitative and qualitative information is called Multi-Criteria Analysis (MCA).

In many cases it is possible to have a clear idea that we *feel* that this damage is much worse than that damage, or that this enjoyment is more intense than that enjoyment. This relative ranking of feelings is often a sufficient degree of quantification to help make a sensible decision. After all, our goal is not to quantify but to distinguish between options.

Step 9. Report

The final stage of the analysis is reporting the arguments and the conclusions. The fact that this is considered an important stage implies that the conclusions are to be reported to other people, not only the decision-makers. There will probably be a large number of stakeholders in any proposal that merits a full analysis. You might also infer that a full analysis is best carried out by an impartial expert who consults and reports to everyone with an interest. In the example under consideration the analysis of the problem was carried out by two people with strong interests and did not involve consultation with major stakeholders, the visiting public and the object cleaner.

As far as analysis is concerned this is the final stage. As a part of good management we would, however, continue to monitor and evaluate. As our uncertainties about the future became more certain we could put better numbers into the equation. As world circumstances changed we could review whether our conclusions, and therefore our decisions, were still sound.

Cost–benefit and risk

It is arguable that the purpose of preventive conservation (passive or interventive) is to maintain the value of an object and that the purpose of restoration is to restore value (add value to a devalued object). It is also arguable that the purpose of new galleries, exhibitions and loans is to increase the value of collections and to increase the flow of benefits from them. This will be discussed in more detail in the next chapter. If those views can be accepted for the time being it could also be argued that once the value of an object or collection has been increased it will from then on provide a higher rate of return. The words 'value', 'return' and 'investment' do not have to be interpreted in money terms. For instance, once an object has been made more famous by an exhibition more people will want to see it in the future. Its 'cultural' value is increased.

Adding value

Figure 5.2 shows a simple decision tree used to decide whether to go ahead with a treatment or event that is designed to raise the value of an object or collection.

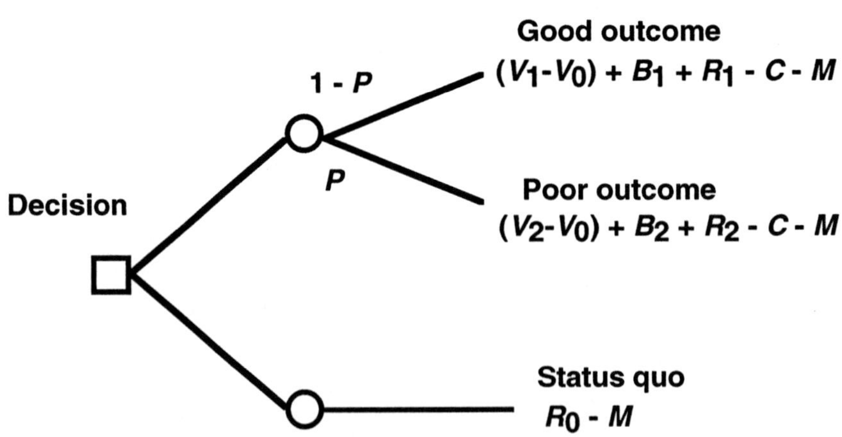

Figure 5.2 *Decision tree comparing the status quo with the effect of a treatment or event designed to increase value*

This could be a decision to send a group of ceramics to an exhibition in Japan, to restore a painting or mass-deacidify a library-full of brittle books. As with Figure 3.6 in Chapter 3 this compares the option of doing one thing with the option of doing nothing. At the present time the object or collection has a value V_0. The benefits of doing nothing are R_0, which is the current return on investment. The costs of doing nothing are the continuing costs of maintenance M (elements of heating, lighting, security, etc.).

Assume that the treatment or enterprise is as successful as we plan. The benefits of a good outcome will be the increase in value $V_1 - V_0$, plus any immediate benefits B_1 (such as a loan fee or entrance charges for an exhibition), plus the long-term return R_1 over a specified number of years. The costs are the immediate costs of the treatment or event C and the continuing maintenance M.

There is a probability P that the operation will not be as successful as intended. In that case there will be a new lower value V_2. This could be lower than V_0, it could even be zero if something goes disastrously wrong. Figure 5.3 shows diagrammatically the intended change in value and the possible failure of the attempt.

Because the value has decreased we should expect a lower rate of return R_2. If an object is totally destroyed its value is zero and it is unable to give anyone any continuing benefit, so R_2 is zero. It is reasonable to

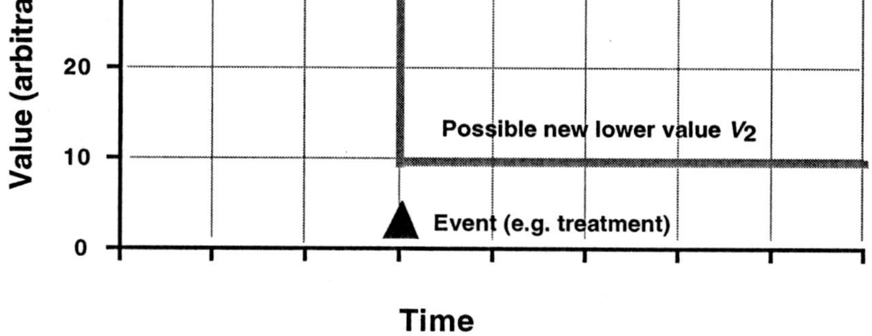

Figure 5.3 *Diagrammatic representation of changes of value resulting from successful and unsuccessful treatment*

assume that if the new value V_2 is somewhere between the initial value and zero then the new flow of benefits will be somewhere between the initial return and zero.

If we discount all the future flows of return and maintenance we can calculate the NPV for going ahead with the proposal and we can calculate the NPV for the status quo. If we subtract one from another we end up with the net benefit of actually doing something. This might be termed the Relative Present Value, RPV[1]. A positive RPV indicates that the option to do something new is a good one. When the RPV is calculated it is seen to be composed of two parts:

$$\begin{aligned} \mathrm{RPV} = {} & (V - V_0) + (R_1 - R_0) + B_1 - C \\ & \underline{- P(V_1 - V_2) - P(R_1 - R_2) - P(B_1 - B_2)} \end{aligned} \qquad (5.4)$$

The first part is the net benefit, that is the increase in value, plus the increase in return, plus the immediate benefit less the immediate cost. The second part (underlined) consists of a number of terms that relate to possible losses of value and opportunity. These terms represent the risk. The risk is the probability of failure multiplied by the losses of value and return that would be caused by that failure.

Maintaining value

In Chapter 2 we saw that some objects slowly deteriorate over time. This can be considered as a slow decrease in value (recall Figure 2.5). Although it is inevitable (P=1), this future loss of value is still termed a 'risk'. Preventive measures such as environmental control will ideally stop the decay, that is, change the rate of deterioration to zero. This can be seen as an attempt to reduce or eliminate the risk. The introduction of air-conditioning or the supply of storage cabinets involves a cost. The benefit is the slower rate of loss in value (merely stopping decay cannot increase the value).

In Figure 5.4 the value of the object or collection is initially V_0 and slowly decreases at a rate k_0, so that after t units of time the new value V_t is equal to $V_0 - k_0 t$. For the moment we are assuming that the rate of deterioration is linear with time (see Chapter 10). Equation (5.5) relates

[1] In CBA it is conventional to calculate the NPV for each of the options including that of doing nothing. The values, whether positive or negative, can be compared and the most appropriate option chosen. RPV in which the NPV of the status quo is subtracted from the NPV of each of the positive actions will not be found in other textbooks. It has the benefit of caution, always reminding you that doing nothing *might* be a sensible option. A negative RPV always indicates a bad decision.

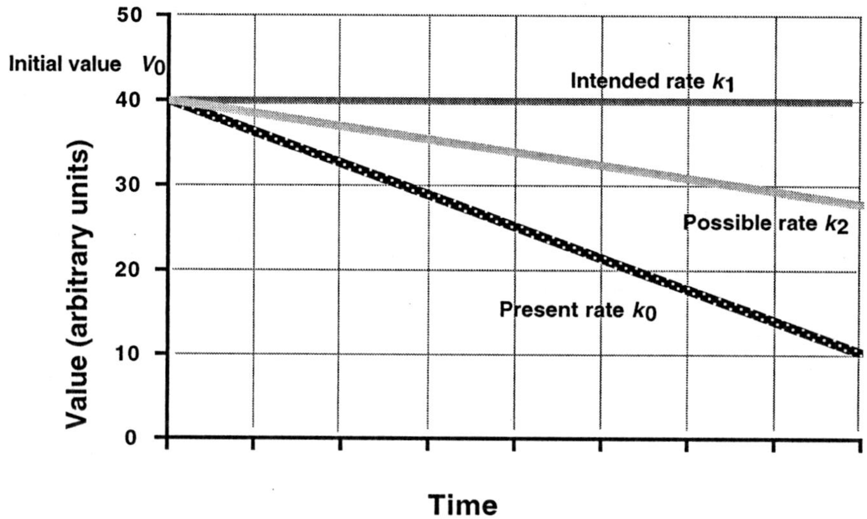

Figure 5.4 *Diagrammatic representation of rates of deterioration before and after investment in plant*

how damage increases with time and could be considered as a simple 'damage function':

$$V_t = V_0 - kt \qquad (5.5)$$

Investing a certain amount of money C will hopefully have an effect on the rate of deterioration. In the example shown the new rate k_1 is zero, the value of the object no longer decreases with time. There is a probability P that the investment will only slow the rate down to k_2. The investment in plant may involve a new running cost M_1. For simplicity we assume this will be the same whether or not the scheme works as planned. The situation is summarized in Figure 5.5.

The RPV consists of two parts:

$$\text{RPV} = t\,(k_0 - k_1) - C - (M_0 - M_1) - \underline{Pt(k_1 - k_2)} \qquad (5.6)$$

The first is the net benefit for a successful outcome which consists of the long-term saving in value less the investment cost and the change in running costs. The second part (underlined) indicates the probability that not as much value has been saved as was anticipated. This is the risk of making an uninformed decision and is related to the uncertainty of the relationships involved. It is not the risk to the collection.

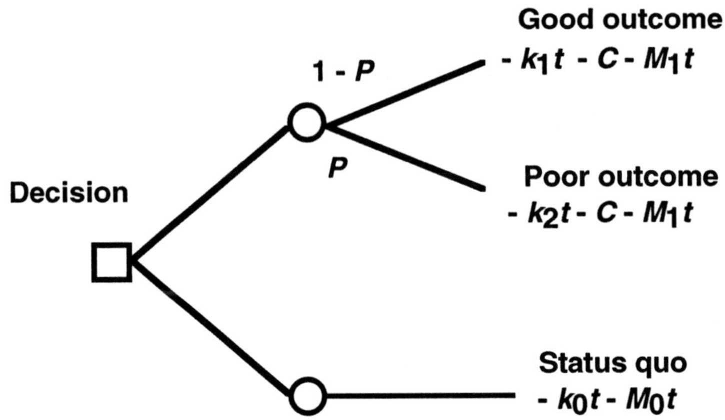

Figure 5.5 *Decision tree comparing the status quo with the investment in plant designed to slow down deterioration*

The change in risk to the collection, if all goes well, is $t(k_1 - k_0)$ which is negative, a decrease. If things do not go well the change in risk to the collection is $t(k_2 - k_0)$ which may or may not be negative. If k_2 is larger than k_0 then the risk to the collection has been increased. An example of this would be the installation of cases which emitted acid gases that accelerated rather than slowed the rate of decay.

Real examples

At the moment there are very few examples of complete cost–benefit analyses in the field of conservation. Most are related to attempts to cost the effect of air pollution, especially acid rain, on the built heritage. A reduction of this damage is seen as a benefit brought about by investment in industrial pollution reduction. The methodology used in NAPAP (National Acid Precipitation Assessment Program) is summarized in Figure 5.6 (Lareau, 1986).

A sample tract of buildings is studied to make an inventory of the different materials, this is extrapolated to a much larger area such as a city. Air quality data for that area is fed into a damage function for each material to give a rate of damage. The cost of damage is computed as a change in replacement and maintenance costs. These are then aggregated for all the materials. No account is taken of loss in value. Similar methodologies have been adopted in other countries, e.g. BERG (The Building Effects Review Group) in the United Kingdom.

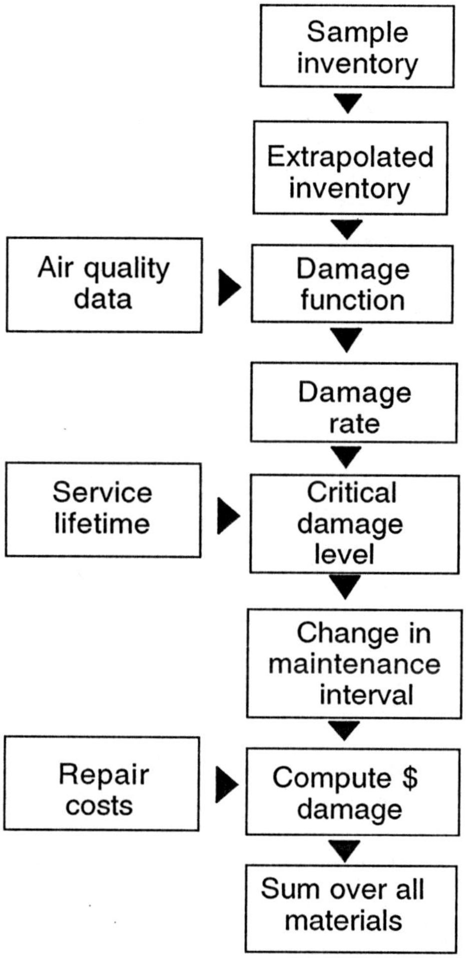

Figure 5.6 *Flow chart for calculating costs of damage to buildings caused by air pollution (after Lareau)*

Other related studies have linked changes in air quality to levels of public enjoyment. Air pollution has an effect on the visibility of distant objects such as mountains. People are less likely to visit famous sites if they can't enjoy the view (Rowe and Chestnut, 1982).

More recently it has been suggested that the benefits of different proposals can be given scores depending on their contribution to the institution's mission. This allows the benefits to be ranked and the most beneficial option chosen, subject to costs (Cassar, 1998).

Comparing costs with benefits

Rather than subtracting the costs from the benefits to achieve the net benefit, the ratio between costs and benefits can be calculated. A ratio of benefits to costs of greater than 1:1 suggests a good option, the greater the ratio the better the option. A ratio gives you no indication of the actual size of the different options. However, if you are able to quantify the benefits, but not using the same units of measurement as for the costs, you can still compare cost–benefit ratios for different options.

If it turns out to be impossible to use any unit of measurement for benefit, things become more difficult. What if the difference in costs, measured in money, tells you one thing and the qualitative ranking of benefits leads you to the opposite conclusion?

Suppose you are comparing two options, A and B. If the costs of A are very much lower than for B, and if the benefits for A are very much greater than for B, the decision is easy. Option A wins on both counts. However, there is theoretically an equal chance that the benefits of B will be greater than those of A, in which case you will not be able to decide. You will have to make an arbitrary decision to be driven by either costs or benefits. If you are considering three options, then only one-third of the possible results will give an unequivocal answer. If you have four options only a quarter will be unequivocal and so on.

To avoid this difficulty comparisons are often made of costs alone. The benefits are assumed to be about the same for a range of options of different cost. This approach is more correctly termed Cost Efficiency Analysis (CEA), since what are being compared are the economic efficiencies of achieving the same goal. This has been used to determine whether cold storage of acetate film negatives is a better option than duplication of originals, to preserve the inherent information (Puglia, 1985).

It turns out that the answer is dependent on the size of the collection, duplication is more economic for small collections, preservation for large ones. The analysis involved the use of damage functions to calculate the rate of deterioration. Full details of all the sources of cost are given. In other studies, the sources of costs for maintenance of a natural history collection have been listed (FitzGerald *et al.*, 1997) and the range of costs of interventive treatments in fine and decorative arts have been determined (Farancz *et al.*, 1984).

CEA has been used to show that continuing low level maintenance of monuments is more cost effective than occasional restoration (Nardi, 1994). It has also been used to suggest the economic value of different types of environmental control (Ayres *et al.*, 1989; Staniforth, 1990).

Something to think about

The studies of environmental economics began at a time of world prosperity, the studies of health economics during a time of recession. What are the implications of this for conservation?

Can we always think of a cost as a negative benefit and vice versa?

In Figure 5.3 only one possible undesirable outcome is considered, how can we include other possible outcomes with different impacts and different probabilities?

If the Pyramids or the Mona Lisa ceased to exist physically, could they still continue to provide benefits?

References

Ayres, J.M., Druzik, J. *et al.* (1989) Energy Conservation and Climate Control in Museums. *Int. J. of Museum Management and Curatorship*, **8**, pp. 299–312.

Benarie, M. (1990) Decision-Making in Environmental Matters. *Atmospheric Environment*, **24A**, No. 6, p. 1585.

Cassar, M. (1998) *Costs/Benefits Appraisals for Collections Care: A Practical Guide.* Museums and Galleries Commission, London ISBN 0-94863-64-7.

Farancz, Alan, Hutchins, Jane, Moon, Thomas P., Preusser, Frank D. and Roberts, Barbara O. (1985) Cost Parameters in the Conservation of Works of Art in both Museum and Private Sectors in the USA in 1984–85. AIC. Preprints 13th Annual Meeting, Washington DC, 22–26 May–1985.

FitzGerald, Gerald R., Whiting, Peter and Shepherd, Kieran (1997) A Comparison of Methodologies Used for Valuation of the Fish Collection at the Canadian Museum of Nature. International Conference on the Value and Valuation of Natural Science Collections, Manchester, April 1995, edited by J.R. Nudds and C.W. Petitt. Geological Society, London, ISBN 1-897799-76-4, pp. 110–117.

Gilpin, Alan (1995) *Environmental Impact Assessment: Cutting Edge for the Twenty First Century.* Cambridge University Press, ISBN 0-521-42967-6, p. 36.

Hanley, N. and Spash, C.L. (1993) *Cost–Benefit Analysis and the Environment.* Edward Elgar Publishing. ISBN 1-85278-947-6.

Johansson, Per-Olov (1995) *Evaluating Health Risks – an Economic Approach.* Cambridge University Press. ISBN 0-521-47878-2.

Lareau, Thomas J., Horst Jr., Robert L., Manuel Jr., Ernest H. and Lipfert, Frederick W. (1986) Model for Economic Assessment of Acid Damage to Building Materials. Materials Degradation Caused by Acid Rain. ACS Symposium Series, edited by Robert Baboian, pp. 397–410.

Mishan, E.J. (1975) *Cost–Benefit Analysis* (2nd edn). George Allen and Unwin. ISBN 0-04-338080-8.

Nardi, Roberto and La Rocca, Eugenio (1994) Preventive Conservation and Restoration: a Matter of Costs. Preventive Conservation: Practice, Theory and Research. Preprints to the Ottawa Congress, 12–16 September. IIC, pp. 24–31.

Puglia, Steven (1995) The Preservation of Acetate Film Materials. A Cost Benefit Analysis for Duplication and Cool/Cold Storage. *Topics in Photographic Preservation*, Vol. 6, American Institute for Conservation, Washington DC.

Rowe, Robert D. and Chestnut, Lauraine G. (1982) *The Value of Visibility: Economic Theory and Applications for Air Pollution Control*. Abt Books, Cambridge, Massachusetts. ISBN 0-89011-472-9.

Staniforth, S. (1990) *Benefits Versus Costs in Environmental Control. Managing Conservation*. UKIC, London. ISBN 1-871656-10-9, pp. 28–30.

Stern, George J.A. (1976) SOSIPing, or Sophistical Obfuscation of Self-Interest and Prejudice. *Operational Research Quarterly*, Vol. 27, pp. 915–929.

Waller, Robert (1995) Risk Management Applied to Preventive Conservation, in *Storage of Natural History Collections: A Preventive Conservation Approach*, edited by C.L. Rose, C.A. Hawks and H.H. Genoways. Society for the Preservation of Natural History Collections.

Zerbe Jr, R.O. and Dively, D.D. (1994) *Benefit–Cost Analysis in Theory and Practice*. Harper Collins, New York, ISBN 0-673-18066-2, p. 1.

6 Value

The reasons why it is necessary to study value, and desirable to quantify it, are introduced in this chapter. Different contributions to value are listed and different ways of calculating and combining these factors are discussed. The study of willingness to pay for objects, or the benefits that come from them, is illuminating even if the results are unsatisfyingly elusive.

Value – too difficult to be bothered with

In Chapter 4 it was proposed that there were relationships between the value of an object, its use and its state. In this chapter we will investigate some of these relationships and attempt to quantify them. Many people would say that there are so many different sorts of value, some of them transitory or subjective, that attempts to quantify are doomed. There is no doubt that the study of the value of museum collections is full of paradoxes and circular arguments. This is no excuse for taking the easy way out and using only information that is easy to comprehend to make difficult decisions.

Value is a social construct dependent on social relationships. This is why it is connected to 'Use' by a big black arrow in Figure 4.9. There is no value without some involvement of people.

Value is bound to change through time and between cultures. It is not always possible to get close agreement on value. We cannot know exactly how values will change in the future. These are not reasons to abandon value as a factor in museum decision-making. In Chapter 11 we will be talking about relative humidity (RH) and its relationship to objects. Relative humidity is changing all the time, it is very context dependent. It poses different problems in different countries and no two measuring techniques give the same answer. None of these difficulties prevents conservators from discussing RH or trying to use it as a lever to change museum expenditure. They are the factors that make its study worthwhile.

Value is a property used to describe objects and actions. It is an extrinsic property that cannot be directly detected by the senses, it does not exist without a social context. The value of an object can only be derived by comparison with the values of other objects or actions. This comparison is often achieved by exchange, where the values of the exchanged objects are considered to be the same. In many modern social groups a common reference standard, money, is used to facilitate comparisons. If, on exchange, there is an obvious difference in monetary value, this is usually acknowledged by positive or negative emotions in the people involved in the transaction. These feelings have value, they have an impact that cannot be ignored. Arjun Appadurai has written a stimulating essay on the 'political lives' of objects in their capacity to act as goods to be exchanged and thus to carry value (Appadurai, 1994).

There are many types of value, some of which come from comparisons of objects, some of which come from comparisons of feelings. Most people have no difficulty in aggregating a number of value types and using this aggregate as a single tool to group objects together and to discriminate between groups. For instance: this collection of drawings has greater value than this collection of bus tickets; this drawing has greater value than this photocopy of the drawing; any drawing by Leonardo da Vinci has greater value than any drawing by Jonathan Ashley-Smith.

Why we need to consider value

The study of risk is concerned not only with probability but also with impact. If there is an equal probability of two unfortunate events occurring, they can be distinguished by the different impacts they will have. The impact will be detected as damage, that is, a loss in usefulness, a loss in value or a loss in the stream of benefits. There are understandable relationships between value, utility and benefit. To that extent they can be considered together as manifestations of the same thing. If we can determine relative values we can rank them. We can say that because this loss in value is greater, then this impact is greater and so this risk is greater. This allows us to prioritize our risk management options.

If we can go one stage further and quantify the probable change in value, we can evaluate the risks. We may possibly conclude that at least one of the risks is so small that it can safely be ignored. At the V&A a curator is allowed to give permission for the loan of an object if its value is less than £500 000. Above this value permission to travel must be granted by the Board of Trustees. This is an example of a primitive risk assessment where objects are grouped by value and the two groups are treated differently.

Consistency in decision-making is a desirable goal, especially when resources are restricted. If a certain sum of money is spent to reduce the risk to one part of a museum collection this implies a certain value for those objects. Given reasonable estimates of other variables this value could be derived from, for example, equation (5.6) in the last chapter. This first decision sets a standard. It would be reasonable to question any later decision that denied money to objects at a higher risk or lavished greater sums of money on reducing a smaller risk.

Some codes of ethics for conservators suggest that all objects have equal value. This has been a block to the development of the conservation profession (Drysdale, 1988). Rejecting the notion of relative values does not allow prioritization and it inhibits analysis of the decisions and actions of conservators. When considering the ethics of conservation treatment it is important to know which of the various contributions to value are being affected by the intervention (see Chapter 15). Lisa Mibach, a great contributor to lateral thinking in conservation, has included monetary value as well as changes in aesthetic and information value in an analysis of the ethics of mass treatment (Mibach, 1989).

Benarie has given as the primary reasons for valuation of the cultural heritage the need for cost–benefit analyses and the need to assign priorities:

> 'In a world of limited resources and almost limitless needs, one must have guidelines for deciding what to do first and how much money should be used in the best possible way.' (Benarie, 1989)

There have been suggestions for prioritizing library conservation needs by determining which were 'most valued' (Shenton, 1992) and by a combination of economic value and demand for use (Atkinson, 1986). Standards of care in collections have recently been developed which justify directing differing amounts of effort and expenditure to classes of object with different values, national relevance and importance being key factors (Parks Canada, 1994; Museums and Galleries Commission, 1994).

For many applications we do not need to have an absolute value, we are primarily interested in *changes* of value. The growth of my children is recorded in dated pencil marks on their bedroom door frames. I can use a 15 centimetre ruler to measure how much their height changed in any one year. I don't need to get out the 2 metre tape and measure how tall they were on each occasion.

We may be able to ignore some of the more difficult contributions to value if we are convinced that they will not change in the circumstances we are considering. For instance, a historical association that adds value will not be altered by deterioration of the object. In many cases we do not need to give an absolute value to the change but can be content with an assessment of the proportional or percentage change in value. Even where it is desirable to determine absolute values, the degree of accuracy need not be great. All that is needed is some means of classifying objects so that we can distinguish one group from another and treat them in different ways.

Types of value

'Value' is a word that is used with a variety of meanings in everyday speech and this variety extends into the texts of writers who are trying to treat value as a single subject. It is a word so abused in the history and philosophy of politics and art that post-modernists have declared 'the end of value' along with 'the end of history'.

Many writers, from Marx to Baudrillard to O'Rourke, have expressed views on the way that the value of objects is derived (Horrocks, 1996; Ashley-Smith, 1995). Many different suggestions for categories of value associated with cultural artifacts have been published (Riegl, 1903; Fielden, 1993; Leigh, 1994; Michalski, 1994). The categories they use are not all of the same type, some are obviously subclasses of another. As the words associated with value are themselves heavily value laden the meanings of some published category titles are not always clear. They can be roughly sorted into two groups: those that a sufficient number of people would say could not be aggregated and treated as a single entity, and those that can be treated as factors that contribute to a single concept of 'value'.

Table 6.1 lists five broad categories of value which many people might try to separate. Along side each type is a list of some other words that have been used to describe value. These may help you understand what I mean by each grouping (or disclose something of my own value system).

Economic values are those defined by transactions that are easily described in terms of monetary units, or of utility, which can be related to money. The greater the demand to use a collection, the greater its value.

Table 6.1

Economic	use, exchange, monetary
Informational	documentary, scientific, perceptual
Cultural	symbolic, spiritual, social, political
Emotional	aesthetic, personal narrative
Existence	–

Informational values are those that arise from hidden or exposed information that can be gleaned from an object or its associated documentation (see Chapter 4). Peter Cannon-Brookes claims that, above all, a museum object is a vehicle which embodies information and ensures the transmission of that information through extended periods of time (Cannon-Brookes, 1990). Cultural values are very dependent on time and place. They are heavily influenced by the spirit of the time (*Zeitgeist*), but often have to be learned through understanding of religious iconography or philosophical vocabulary. Emotional values can only be distinguished from cultural values by the fact that they are more personal and probably more difficult to articulate. These are the gut reactions experienced when attending a Metallica concert or listening to Beethoven's 9th.

Existence value is a concept that developed in the mid-1980s in CBA studies of the environment. It reflects the view that you may care very much that dolphins or rain forests are threatened, even though you have never seen one and don't intend to seek one out (Kopp, 1992). The economic argument has been developed for urban architecture (Crocker, 1986).

Based on the view that every person can be bought at some price, hard-hearted economists would say that all of these values could be 'monetized', equated with a sum of money.

Table 6.2 lists various factors that might contribute to a single concept of value. These are factors that most people would accept had contributed to the asking price of a historic object. They might contribute to a sense of loss if evidence of these factors was destroyed by decay or vandalism.

The fact that an object is old or shows sign of age, even decay, contributes to age value (Riegl, 1903; Lowenthal, 1994). The older the object the more likely that other examples have not survived, which

Table 6.2

- Age
- Rarity
- Material
- Complexity
- Quality
- History
- Identity
- Information
- Context
- Potential
- Condition

contributes to its rarity value. Uniqueness is the high point of rarity although it doesn't guarantee high monetary value or universal acclaim. Every one of my 11-year-old daughter's drawings is unique.

If an object is made of gold encrusted with diamonds it has a head start in value over something made of paper or plastic. If an object is of complex construction it will probably have a greater cost associated with its manufacture which could affect its value. Complexity is among the reasons that paintings have achieved greater value than many other art forms.

Most people would accept that the quality of execution of a design would affect the value, although in a small number of cases a rough primitive finish is prized. The appreciation of 'quality' can be learned, but requires a strong subjective input.

Values arise from association. The object's history may be linked with other historical events that have achieved importance. Identity gives a specific description or name to the object; *a* Leonardo drawing, *the* Mona Lisa. A standard issue cavalry sabre has greater value if it was used in the Charge of the Light Brigade. A walking stick becomes more valuable if it was known to have belonged to Charles Dickens. A drawing by Leonardo da Vinci will always be more valuable than a drawing by Jonathan Ashley-Smith, no matter how skilful or famous the latter becomes. History and identity contribute to what Michalski refers to as the Impersonal Narrative Value, things gaining value in a 'world view' rather than from a personal viewpoint. The relationship to me will increase an object's value to me – strong Personal Narrative Value. This 'sentimental' valuation is not shared by others.

Information about an object concerning its history, identity and associations can have an effect on the value, as can information implicit in the object itself. The information that the object provides can be interpreted in terms of information theory, where the basic units of a message survive transmission and are successfully interpreted despite the noise (Pierce, 1980). Complexity and rarity of information are powerful factors. They are further determining elements in the apparent art-historical supremacy of paintings.

The context of an object can affect its worth. If removed from its context, or treated in such a way that it no longer seems to belong, it loses value. Insurance valuations may include a pairs and sets clause whereby damage to one object in a set could result in a claim being settled for the value of the whole set (McBride, 1995).

The potential of an object can contribute to its current value. In the same way that an object that has survived a long time has increased in value, so the longer an object is expected to survive into the future the greater its Net Present Value. An archaeological site can have value based on what may be uncovered at a later date.

The state of an object obviously has an effect on its value. The relationship between condition and value will be dealt with more fully in the next chapter.

Changes in value with time

The value of an object can change dramatically with time. In his classic book on the creation and destruction of value, *Rubbish Theory,* Michael Thompson describes the three phases of an object's life that lead to three very different values (Thompson, 1979). In the first or 'transient' phase the object is new and available to anyone. It is exchanged for a reasonable price determined by supply and demand. As it drops out of use its value declines. There then follows a much longer phase when the object ceases to be fashionable or even desirable. It is not exchanged for anything and ceases to have value. This is the 'rubbish' phase. Eventually the merits of the class of object are recognized again. The object becomes desirable again and its price begins to rise. What may once have been a common object gains a certain class value, its price rises dramatically and continues to stay high. This final phase is when the object becomes 'durable'. The main thrust of Rubbish Theory appears in an extract from the book *Interpreting Objects and Collections* edited by Susan Pearce which contains a number of essays that are more or less relevant to the discussion of value in museum objects (Pearce, 1994).

One example Thompson gives is of the commemorative woven silk pictures called Stevengraphs. He follows the fate of the image of Dick Turpin. When they were first created in the 1870s the pictures cost five pence each. Production stopped in 1881 and until the 1950s there was no second-hand trade, during this period they had no value. In 1963 revival of interest stimulated an exhibition at which typical examples of scenic Stevengraphs were priced at eight guineas. By the 1970s individual examples were being valued at £100.

The same pattern is observed for Victorian working class dwellings which fell into disrepair, declined in value, and passed through a long rubbish phase. Eventually they underwent 'gentrification', that is, they became the fashionable dwellings of young professionals with considerably greater incomes than the original inhabitants.

This pattern of initial decline of value followed by a later rise has been shown graphically by a number of authors. Benarie describes the shape of the curve as a catenary, the shape of a freely hanging rope or chain suspended at both ends (Benarie, 1989). This is a symmetrical shape, whereas in Thompson's examples the final durable value is very much greater than the initial transient value. Figure 6.1 shows the initial decline or 'devalorization', followed by an indistinct 'critical phase'. A second

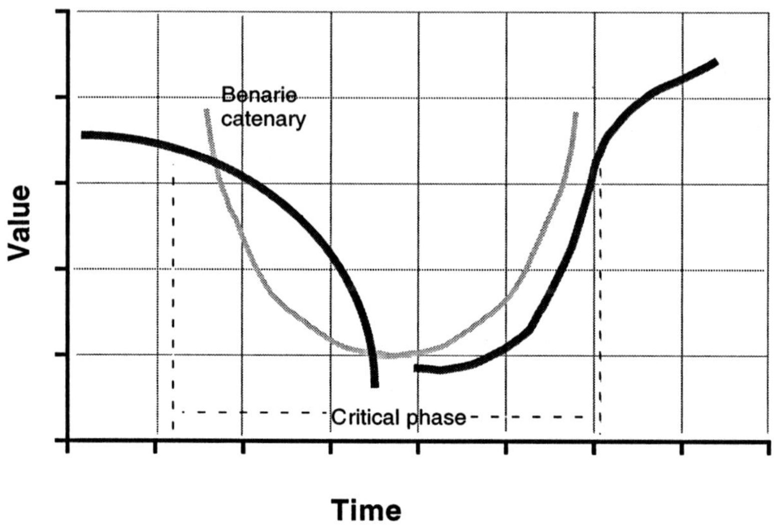

Figure 6.1 *Separate curves showing the initial decline and later rise in value (after van Gigch, Rosvall and Lagerqvist). Benarie's catenary curve for change in value with time is superimposed*

curve shows a rise to a value greater than the original, showing 'added value' (van Gigch, Rosvall and Lagerquist, 1993).

In Rubbish Theory the transfer from transient to rubbish to durable is irreversible and is subject to class control (Figure 6.2). The people who own and control goods of durable value enjoy more power and prestige than those who inhabit the world of transient value or the world of rubbish. In both the transient and durable categories there are established views of what an appropriate value is, the 'world view' determines the appropriate action. However, between these there is an area of flexibility where action can influence the world view. An article in a reputable journal or a museum exhibition can suggest that previously unvalued objects should in fact be considered valuable. Museums are in the business of creating value and maintaining it.

Multivariate values

To combine the many different contributions into one overall 'value' we would want some mathematical function that weighted each factor, added or subtracted it, and accounted for all the interactions. This would be the multivariate utility function mentioned in Chapter 3. It would be easy enough to show it as a set of mathematical symbols, but

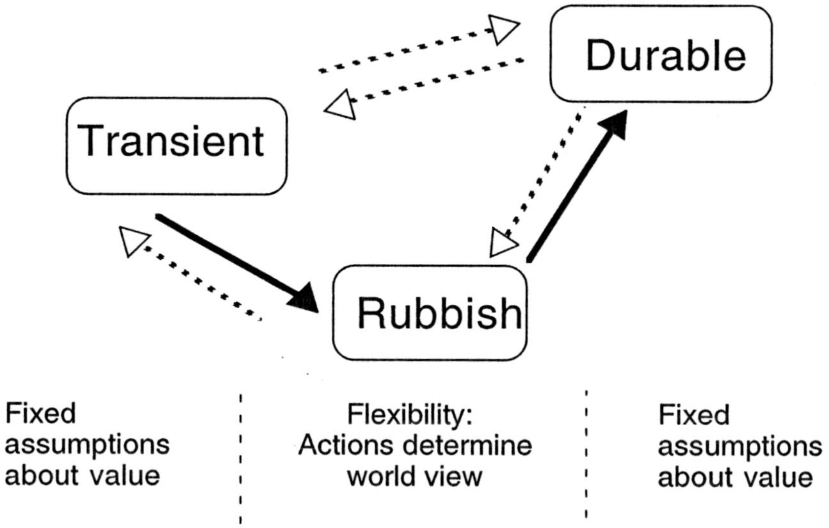

Figure 6.2 *Transfers between object categories in Rubbish Theory (after Thompson). The heavy arrows show transfers that are observed. The dotted arrows show possible transfers that never happen*

substantially more difficult to calculate. However, there is an approach to combining different value factors which helps to distinguish groups with different overall value.

If each of two value factors is quantified in some way, the two elements can be combined as coordinates on a graph. In Figure 6.3 the vertical axis shows increasing quality, that is, success of execution. The horizontal axis shows some measure of age. The units of measurement for each axis are obviously different. A drawing by Leonardo da Vinci has both high quality and old age. A drawing by my daughter has little age and at the moment her ability to draw does not match her ambition. A poor photocopy of either drawing will be more recent and have lower quality.

The further away from the origin, a point which represents no age and no quality, the greater is the value. The highest values represented by the combination of these two factors will lie on the diagonal.

Michalski has combined three value factors in a three-dimensional graph (Figure 6.4) (Michalski, 1994). The Mona Lisa is not as important to *me* as a my mum's picture, but in an impersonal way is considered more valuable. An X-radiograph of the Mona Lisa has the same scientific value as my X-ray but it is not so important to me. The X-radiograph of the painting is not as valuable as the painting itself.

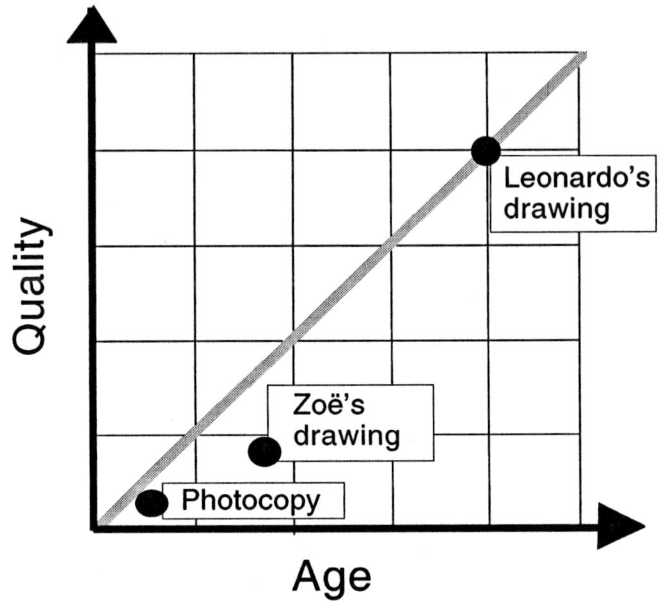

Figure 6.3 *Two-dimensional representation of contributions to value*

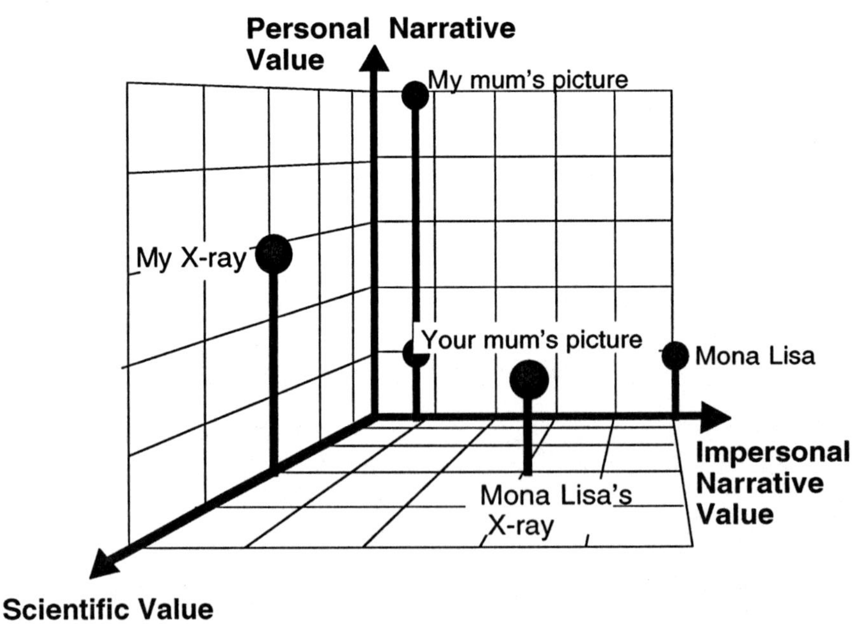

Figure 6.4 *Three-dimensional representation of contributions to value (after Michalski)*

Beyond three dimensions it becomes difficult to visualize, but mathematically it is quite possible to think of a point in multidimensional space whose coordinates record the various contributions to value. Distance from the origin would be a measure of total value. The more accurately the contributions could be quantified (preferably using the same unit of measurement) the easier it would be to ascribe relative rank or absolute value.

Valuation

A word obviously related to value is 'valuation'. Whereas value is variable with time and differs with viewpoint, a valuation is fixed at a particular time and agreed for a particular purpose. It may not bear any relation to the value that the 'world view' would suggest or which might be calculated by one of the methods suggested in the next section of this chapter.

Different valuations would be arrived at for sale, purchase, insurance, probate or auction. A valuation may include costs other than the original asking price. An insurance valuation might involve all the costs of searching for and acquiring a replacement. Even though the value of an object had been lowered by damage, the insurance valuation would remain higher to reflect the replacement costs. An insurance 'write-off' may still have considerable exchange value and may have lost none of its sentimental value.

Sometimes a valuation is merely a statutory requirement and has little or no logic in relation to value. In the UK, the historic property belonging to local governments is given a valuation of the historic cost of each object, regardless of how market values may have altered since acquisition. If there is no record of the original cost, the object or collection is given a valuation of zero (Evans, 1997). This is obviously not a sound basis from which to calculate risk.

A valuation may be sought for political purposes. The collections of the Canadian Museum of Nature were declared to be of 'Scientific Value Only' and given a book valuation of $1000 in the museum's financial statements. This low valuation prejudiced the possibility of government investment in new storage facilities. A valuation based on replacement cost was calculated.

> 'Government authorities who in the past could not understand why they should authorize an expenditure in the order of $30,000,000 to preserve collections with a declared asset value of $1,000 changed their perspective for the same collections with an estimated replacement cost in excess of $1 billion.' (Fitzgerald, Whiting and Shepherd, 1997)

Different methods of calculating value

Methods of quantifying benefits or values rely on determining a Willingness To Pay (WTP). What is it that people are willing to exchange, or give up, in order to own an object or gain a benefit? An alternative approach is Willingness To Accept (WTA). How much does someone have to be given to compensate for the loss of an object or a benefit? WTP and WTA are examples of what are known as Contingent Valuation Methods (CVM) which enable values to be estimated for a wide variety of commodities not traded in markets. Many of them rely on calculating or estimating the Consumer Surplus (CS). This is the difference between what a consumer seems prepared to pay and what they actually have to pay. Free entrance to museums probably involves a consumer surplus.

There are two approaches to assessing willingness to pay. You can observe behaviour to see how people allocate their money, time and effort. How many people visit museums and what do they do when they are there? How much do they spend? Alternatively you can ask them directly what they would do if given a choice. Would you rather have £5 or visit a museum?

Objects reside in museums for a variety of reasons. Keene has distinguished three main purposes, which distinguish three main types of museum. Broadly speaking art museums own objects for display, technology museums hold objects to demonstrate function, archaeological and natural history museums hold objects to be used as evidence (Keene, 1996).

Art museums hold objects with high value but in relatively small numbers. One aspect of value is tested periodically, when similar objects are sold at auction or new objects are acquired at great expense. The market price is likely to be a good start in assessing value because it is a direct measure of someone's WTP. Supporting evidence of value comes from the fact that people are willing to pay to travel to see the art objects and can be obliged to part with money to enter the museum.

The situation is less clear for the evidential museum or archive. Very large numbers of objects are housed, many of which have little or no market value. There is an acceptance that the institutions provide benefits because governments and philanthropists continue to fund their existence. This willingness to pay for the continued benefits must be a measure of the value of the collection.

Measurements of WTP for museums will not give values for individual objects and can only give very approximate answers for the value of collections. However, investigating the different aspects of WTP can give a new perspective to those who work with museum collections.

Issues of public ownership, and rights of public access will cloud the assessment of WTP, but observing recent changes in these influences can be illuminating.

Collections as capital

There are strong similarities between attempts to value items of art and heritage and attempts to value human life. Similarities between the value of human injury and the value of object condition will be explored in the next chapter. Excellent reviews of attempts to derive a Value Of Life (VOL) are to be found in the reports of the Environmental Risk Assessment Unit at the University of East Anglia in Norwich, England (e.g. Soby and Ball, 1991). Statistical valuations of life and limb are necessary to determine whether the expense of risk reduction measures is justified.

In later chapters we will see that it is desirable to estimate the value of a collection to within one order of magnitude. We want to be able to say that it is worth between a hundred thousand pounds and a million pounds, rather than vaguely suggest that it is somewhere between ten thousand and ten million pounds. Estimates of a VOL which use assessments based on observed behaviour, or views volunteered about what would entice someone to risk their life, are accurate within one order of magnitude. So we can hope that the same methods will help us assess the value of collections, a task which ought to be slightly less distasteful.

Studies based on legal compensation for loss of life give values well below those derived from other studies. This will come as no surprise to anyone who has tried to claim on UK government indemnity for the loss of an object. So we must look beyond examples of compensation and beyond insurance valuations.

One method of determining the value of a life is called the Human Capital approach. A human being is assumed to be capable of continuing to generate income into the foreseeable future. If this person dies then society has been deprived of the capital and of the future return on investment. A Net Present Value can be calculated for each person by summing the discounted flow of expected future benefits:

$$\text{NPV} = \sum_{t=0}^{\infty} (B - C)P(1 + r)^{-t} \tag{6.1}$$

This equation is very similar to equation (5.3) but it includes the symbol P which is the probability that the person will be alive in any one year between now (t=0) and the distant future (t=infinity). These probabilities can be found from actuarial tables.

There are strong moral and philosophical objections to applying the Human Capital approach to humans, as it discriminates against women, the unwaged and the elderly. These objections are not valid if it is applied to inanimate objects.

First, we have to make an arbitrary decision about an appropriate discount rate (see Chapter 15). Then, if we know the value of a collection we can derive an estimate of the annual benefits that should result. This was the assumption made in the CBA models described in the last chapter. Conversely, if we can estimate the flow of benefits, we can put a value on the collection.

As discussed in the last chapter it is easier to estimate costs than benefits. A value for a collection can be derived from studying just the costs, assuming that they represent a WTP for the collection's maintenance. This capitalized cost approach was one of the methods used by the Canadian Museum of Nature. It gave a valuation of the same order as that found by calculating how much it would cost to replace the collection.

We need to assess the flow of benefits that are derived from the collection. There will be a hierarchy of benefits. Direct users will gain benefits but they in turn will pass benefits on to others who do not have direct contact with the collection. The benefit gained by the first level of user (visitor, scholar, educator) should be related to their willingness to pay.

Willingness to pay

WTP to see the objects

Over the past 20 years the subject of free access to national museums in the UK has been a subject of debate. Published attendance figures showed that when some museums introduced admission charges, attendance dropped by as much as 40%. This appears to indicate a low WTP and therefore a low public valuation of the museum experience. However, when in 1996 the V&A moved from a voluntary donation on admission to a compulsory charge, the number of visitors increased slightly. In the 1980s the argument was that the taxpayer did not want to pay twice, once in taxes and again at the door. By the late 1990s it was widely understood that not much tax money was going to support museums and so the museum visitor had to express their WTP directly.

If, over a prolonged period, a million people a year each pay £5 to enter a museum this suggests an NPV for the *objects that they see* of around £80 million. In an art museum, where the market price of one object may be of this order, this may be a low valuation.

WTP to travel to the objects

One of the indirect methods of assessing the value of a resource is to find out how much individuals are willing to spend in order to get there. For a historic site this could be estimated from a visitor survey, finding out how far visitors had come, by what means of transport, and compensating for the fact that they may have visited other sites on the same trip. Many museums are in metropolitan locations where there are many other attractions. Details about access to transport and journey times of museum visitors have been published (Merriman, 1991; Davies, 1994). The calculation and evaluation of the Travel Cost Method is explained in texts on cost–benefit analysis (e.g. Hanley and Spash, 1993).

Half of overseas visitors to the United Kingdom give museums and galleries as a major reason for visiting the country. Half of the visitors to London's main museums and galleries are from abroad. Foreign visitors are likely to have substantially greater travel costs than residents. If only a small proportion, say 5%, of the total travel costs are attributed as WTP to visit one particular museum this still adds up to a large sum of money. The money is spent outside the museum but as a result of the wish to visit the museum. This could be seen as a social economic benefit that results from the value of the collections. Calculations show that for a large museum it is of the same order as the running costs of the museum, in the order of £10^7 a year.

One difficulty in using these methods is determining how important actual objects are as a part of a museum visit. Cultural tourism is not about leisurely contemplation of the collections. A sizeable minority of museum visitors avoid seeing the collections altogether (Kelly, 1994).

WTP to preserve the objects

In the UK the amount of revenue funding for museums from central and local governments has been decreasing in real terms over a long period. If the amount paid to preserve collections is a measure of the social benefits derived from museums then it is also a measure of the way the collections are valued. The elected members seem to be suggesting that the electorate is placing less value on the existence of collections.

Shifting the emphasis onto the direct users' willingness to pay at the door ignores another large contribution to value. This is the 'existence value' of historic collections. Surveys of people who are *not* museum visitors show that more people think museums are important than actually visit them. In one survey 82% agreed that museums do an invaluable job in protecting the heritage (Davies, 1995, p. 79). By lowering the contribution of taxes to museums the government is denying the electorate the expression of WTP for the continuing existence of museums.

Where museums are willing to pay for interventive treatment, the amount of time lavished on the restoration of one object would supply some evidence of value.

Something to think about

Access to the Lascaux caves is severely restricted on conservation grounds. If no one ever gets to see them, surely they cease to have any value.

A document in an archive will not be touched for the next 50 years. When it is consulted the benefit to that user will be equivalent to £50. What is the present value of the forsaken object? Is this of the same order as the cost of maintaining it?

What actually happens to values in museums over a long period, surely there are 'rubbish' phases there too?

Can you 'damage' an object in the rubbish phase?

References

Appadurai, Arjun (1994) Commodities and the Politics of Value, in *Interpreting Objects and Collections*, edited by Susan M. Pearce. Leicester Readers in Museum Studies. Routledge, London. ISBN 0-415-11288-3, pp. 76–91.

Ashley-Smith, J. (1995) *IIC Bulletin*, April.

Atkinson, Ross W. (1986) Selection for Preservation: a Materialistic Approach, *Library Resources and Technical Services*, Vol. 3, pp. 341–353.

Benarie, M. (1989) Valuation of Cultural Heritage, *European Cultural Heritage Newsletter on Research*, Vol. 3(4), pp. 7–9.

Benarie, M. (1987) Probability of Conservation of Cultural Heritage. *European Cultural Heritage Newsletter on Research*, Vol. 1(4), pp. 9–13.

Cannon-Brookes, Peter (1990) Editorial. *International Journal of Museum Management and Curatorship*, **9**, pp. 235–239.

Crocker, Thomas D. (1986) Economic Features of Materials Degradation. Materials Degradation Caused by Acid Rain. ACS Symposium Series, edited by Robert Baboian, pp. 369–383.

Davies, Stuart (1994) By Popular Demand. A Strategic Analysis of the Market Potential for Museums and Art Galleries in the UK. Museums and Galleries Commission, London. ISBN 0-948-63030-2.

Drysdale, Laura (1988) The Eternal Triangle: Relationships Between Conservators, Their Clients and Objects. Conservation Today. UKIC 30th Anniversary Conference, London. ISBN 1-871656-01-X, pp. 18–20.

Evans, Martin (1997) Accounting for Local Authorities' Museum Collections. International Conference on the Value and Valuation of Natural Science Collections, Manchester, April, edited by J.R. Nudds and C.W. Petitt. Geological Society, London. ISBN 1-897799-76-4, pp. 191–195.

Fielden, Bernard M. (1993) Is Conservation of Cultural Heritage Relevant to South Asia? *Journal of the Society for South Asian Studies*, London, Vol 9, pp. 1–10.

FitzGerald, Gerald R., Whiting, Peter and Shepherd, Kieran (1997) A Comparison of Methodologies Used for Valuation of the Fish Collection at the Canadian Museum of Nature. International Conference on the Value and Valuation of Natural Science Collections, Manchester, April, edited by J.R. Nudds and C.W. Petitt. Geological Society, London. ISBN 1-897799-76-4, pp. 110–117.

Hanley, N. and Spash, C.L. (1993) *Cost–Benefit Analysis and the Environment*. Edward Elgar Publishing. ISBN 1-85278-947-6.

Horrocks, Chris (1996) *Baudrillard for Beginners*. Icon Books, ISBN 1-874166-36-6.

Keene, Suzanne (1996) *Managing Conservation in Museums*. Butterworth-Heinemann in Association with Science Museum, London. ISBN 0-7506-2384-5, p. 16.

Kelly, Robert F. (1994) The Museum as a Pilgrimage Destination, Paper presented to the American Association of Museums, Seattle. A similar paper is published as: Cultural Tourists and Cultural Tourism, 3rd International Conference on Arts Management, London, July 1995.

Kopp, Raymond J. (1992) Why Existence Value Should Be Used in Cost–Benefit Analysis. *Journal of Policy Analysis and Management*, **11**(1), pp. 123–130.

Leigh, D. (1994) Group Report: What are the Responsibilities for Cultural Heritage and Where Do They Lie?, in *Durability and Change: The Science, Responsibility, and Cost of Sustaining Cultural Heritage*, edited by W.E. Krumbein, P. Brimblecombe, D.E. Cosgrove and S. Staniforth. John Wiley and Sons. ISBN–0–471–95221–4, pp. 269–286.

Lowenthal, D. (1994) The Value of Age and Decay, in *Durability and Change: The Science, Responsibility, and Cost of Sustaining Cultural Heritage*, edited by W.E. Krumbein, P. Brimblecombe, D.E. Cosgrove and S. Staniforth. John Wiley and Sons, ISBN–0–471–95221–4, pp. 39–50.

McBride, Colin (1997) Insurance Implications of Display of Collections Made up of Unique Items With Little or No Commercial Market Interest. International Conference on the Value and Valuation of Natural Science Collections, Manchester, April 1995, edited by J.R. Nudds and C.W. Petitt. Geological Society, London. ISBN 1-897799-76-4, pp. 180–182.

Merriman (1991) *Beyond the Glass Case: The Past, the Heritage and the Public in Britain*. Leicester University Press. ISBN 0-7185-1349-5.

Mibach, Lisa (1989) Personal communication. Ethical Issues in Mass Treatment. Script for a lecture presented at the 15th Annual Art Conservation Training Programs Conference, Harvard University Art Museums, 27–29 April.

Michalski, S. (1994) Sharing Responsibility for Conservation Decisions, in *Durability and Change: The Science, Responsibility, and Cost of Sustaining*

Cultural Heritage, edited by W.E. Krumbein, P. Brimblecombe, D.E. Cosgrove and S. Staniforth. John Wiley and Sons. ISBN 0-471-95221-4, pp. 241–258.

Museums and Galleries Commission (1994) *Standards in the Museum Care of Larger and Working Objects*. London, ISBN 0-948630-26-4.

Parks Canada (1994) *Guiding Principles and Operational Policies*. ISBN 0-662-21559-1.

Pearce, Susan M. (ed.) (1994) *Interpreting Objects and Collections*. Leicester Readers in Museum Studies. Routledge, London. ISBN 0-415-11288-3.

Pierce, John R. (1980) *An Introduction to Information Theory: Symbols, Signals and Noise* (2nd rev. edn from 1960). Dover. ISBN 0-486-24061-4.

Riegl, Alois (1903) The Modern Cult of Monuments: Its Essence and Its Development, in *Historical and Philosophical Issues in the Conservation of Cultural Heritage*. The J. Paul Getty Trust. ISBN 0-89236-250-2, pp. 69–83.

Shenton, Helen (1992) *A Conservation Strategy for Books at the Victoria and Albert Museum*. Institute of Paper Conservation. Conference Papers. Manchester. ISBN 0-9507268-3-4, pp. 133–140.

Soby, B.A. and Ball, D.J. (1991) *Consumer Safety and the Valuation of Life and Injury*. Environmental Risk Assessment Unit. School of Environmental Sciences, Norwich. ISBN 1-873933-00-2.

Thomson, Michael (1979) *Rubbish Theory. The Creation and Destruction of Value*. Oxford University Press. ISBN 0-19-217658-7.

van Gigch, John P., Rosvall, Jan and Lagerqvist, Bosse (1993) Setting a Strategic Framework for Conservation Standards. ASTMS Symposium on Standards for Preservation and Rehabilitation, Fort Worth, Texas, 10–11 October.

7 Definitions of damage

One of the key factors in risk analysis is the ability to assess what change in value will result from a particular event or from a particular continuing set of circumstances.

Damage is usually associated with a loss of material, a loss of well-being or a loss of expectation. Not everything that people consider as damage results in a change of value. Not every change in physical or chemical properties results in loss. The relationships between state, value and use are examined in an attempt to arrive at definitions of damage. The most useful definition is related to changes in utility.

Definitions of state

In Chapter 4 the term 'state' was used to construct a model of a museum without any rigorous definition. A definition is necessary because we are about to discuss *changes* of state. Without a reference there is no measure of the importance of these changes.

The word 'state' is intended as a description of everything that can be defined or discovered about an object by observation, measurement or analysis. It is an attempt to define properties that are intrinsic, objective, impersonal, and in distinct contrast to the properties of 'value'. Table 7.1 gives a list of properties, starting at the internal, atomic and molecular level and working up to the gross, external appearance of the object.

Little subjective interpretation is involved so far. There are further levels of description which, although they imply some judgement, can usefully be added to a definition of state before it begins to overlap with a definition of value. These are basic descriptive terms such as 'costume' or 'furniture' and subcategories such as 'dish', 'dress', 'table', or 'chair'.

Changes of state that entailed changes in these gross descriptions would be far from subtle. A curtain becomes a dress or a bench becomes a chair only after deliberate human intervention. Permanent changes at the level of shape or dimension are usually conspicuous but could be either deliberate or accidental. A square table might become

Table 7.1

Composition	– Major, minor and trace components – Elements, compounds, minerals
Microstructure	– Crystal structure, cell structure, heterogeneity, dislocations
Substructure	– Fibre blend, weave structure, grain, cracks
Construction	– Joints, seams, welds, dowels – Layer structure, glaze, veneer, paint
Surface features	– Image, inscription, engraving, abrasion, dirt
Dimensions	– Mass, density, height
Shape	– Form, outline

round, the arms might fall off the Venus de Milo. At the surface level the change in appearance can be obtrusive or subtle, accidental or deliberate. A painted wardrobe becomes stripped pine, a fine patina develops on a bronze.

The more microscopic the level of description, the less likely it is that any change will alter the object's use as an item of display. However, changes at the level of construction or even substructure may alter the object's ability to demonstrate function. Signs of provenance, date, method of manufacture or relationship with other species can reside at the microstructural and molecular levels. Any alteration at these levels will affect an object's ability to function as a source of evidence.

When considering risk and changes of state we must ask not only how important the changes could be, but also how likely they are. Very few things in the routine of museum life – except drastic conservation treatment – will alter molecular state or microstructure. Very few things will alter gross description or shape – except catastrophic disaster or curatorial vandalism.

Wear and tear from use, and deterioration caused by reaction with the environment, can cause a range of changes in the intermediate levels of description such as dimension, surface features and construction. These changes are quite likely to happen and likely to be noticed. The most probable changes are in surface appearance. The surface is the interface between the object and the environment, and between the object and its users. It is liable to change. For most museum objects, the value for the main user (the visitor) rests in all the information to be gained from surface features. Changes in colour, texture, decoration or image can have a dramatic impact.

Change is not damage

Noticeable change does not automatically lead to any permanent sense of loss.

Change can be:

- Beneficial – damaging stresses relieved. Sample removed for scientific analysis.
- Reversible – original dimensions return when environmental conditions revert.
- Beautiful – copper roofs turn green, weathering adds dignity to a building.
- Evidential – dirt hidden under paint layers betrays later restoration or faking (see Figure 7.1).

Changes that were originally associated with loss can gain historic value, such as a hole in Nelson's jacket caused by musket fire. What was once damage can achieve the status of a memorial (see Figure 7.2). In general, the term 'damage' should be used where there is a permanent and noticeable loss in value or potential. Some changes, caused by the environment or by use may be either too inconsequential to worry about or just not have any effect on value.

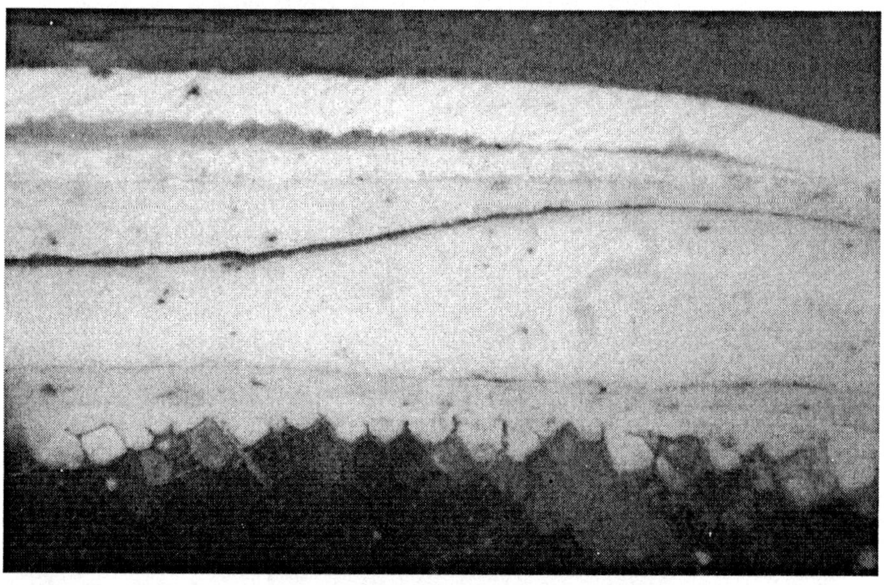

Figure 7.1 *Dirt is not damage if it proves that two paint layers were applied at different times. Photomicrograph of two layers of decorative paint from Apsley House, London (×500)*

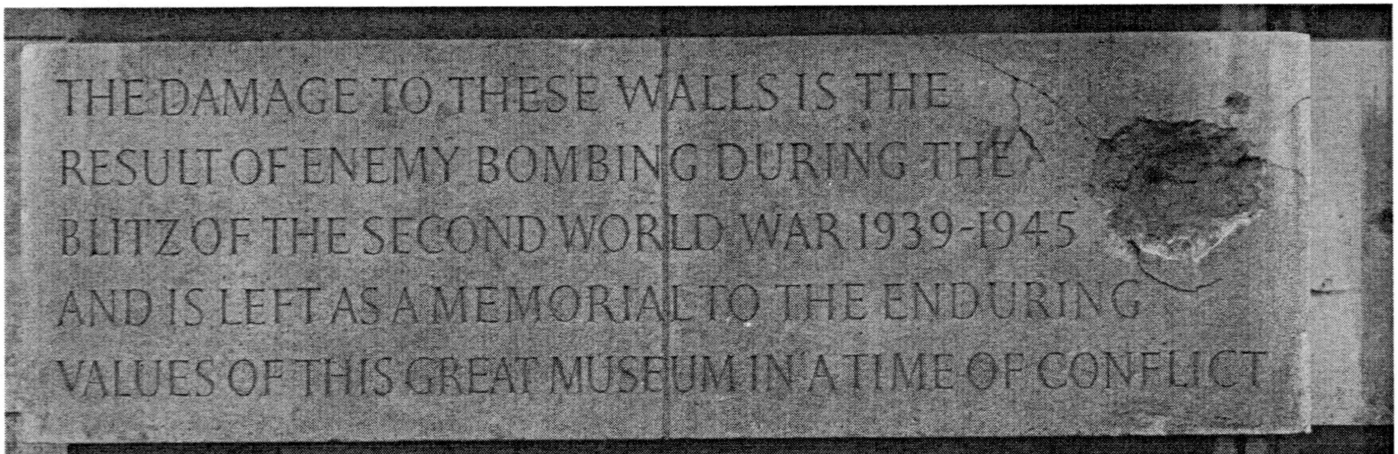

Figure 7.2 *Physical damage gains value as a memorial. The west façade of the Victoria and Albert Museum in London*

Changes of value with changes of state

In the last chapter we saw that there were a number of different contributions to an assessment of value. Some of these were so divergent that they might be considered as separate types of value. Which of these elements of value are likely to be altered by changes in state? I have grouped the descriptors of value, that appeared in Tables 6.1 and 6.2, according to my estimation of whether physical change is likely to result in monetary or emotional loss (Table 7.2).

Table 7.2 *Will a change of state cause a change in value?*

Value	Likelihood
Exchange, monetary Use Potential Complexity Documentary Scientific Aesthetic	highly likely
Personal narrative Social, political Symbolic, spiritual Existence Quality Rarity	unlikely
Material Age Context History Identity	impossible

Changes of state with strong correlation to changes in value

Where there is a market for objects that exist in large numbers, which were all originally in the same state, there are agreed relationships between condition and exchange value. Coins and medals at auction are catalogued in certain categories of condition such as 'mint'. Books dealing with the prices of second-hand cars give ranges of value depending on the state of the automobile compared to a standard expected for one of that age. Perhaps the most clearly expressed correlation between value

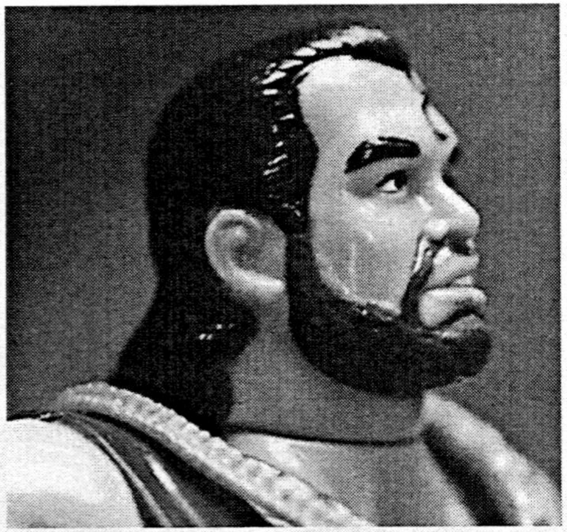

Above: **Razor Ramon at C-8. One (1) barely noticeable scratch (in this case a scratch can just barely be seen at the beard line). Estimate price at 10% less than Book Value.**

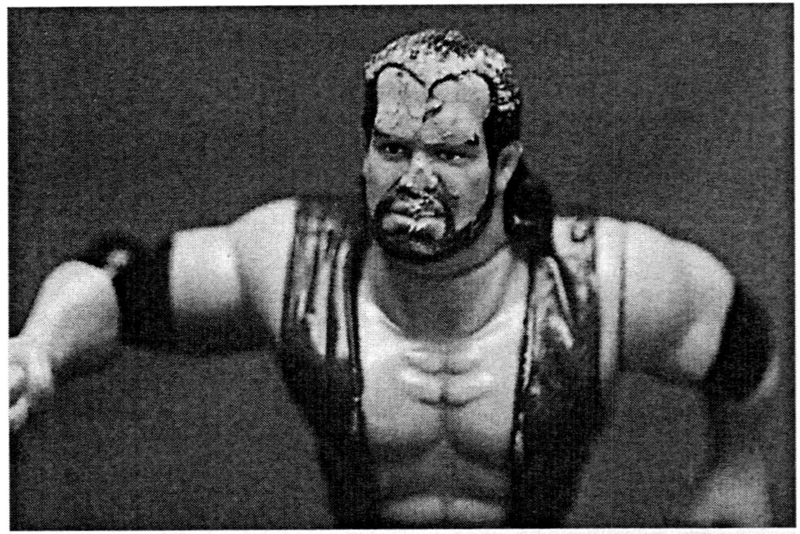

Razor Ramon at C-1. Gouges and paint wear that are so disfiguring that distinguishing features have been all but obliterated. Figure may be missing a limb, or limbs. This is a "customizer's dream". This type of figure is only of interest to a customizer searching for useable body parts. Estimate *total* value at between $1.00 to $0.10.

Figure 7.3 *Photographic guide to relationship between condition and value of figures of Razor Ramon (courtesey of AFN & TR)*

Table 7.3 *Grading guide for plastic action figures*

Grade	*Description*	*Percentage value*
10–9	Near mint without observable damage or flaws	100
8	Barely noticeable scratch	90
7	One pronounced scratch	80–85
6	Two or more pronounced scratches on painted surface. Exposed area no more than 0.25 in square	60–70
5	Excessive paint wear, fading or discoloration of paint/plastic	40–50
4	Excessive paint wear and noticeable gouge in plastic especially if in a distinguishing feature, i.e. nose, eye	20–30
3–2	Heavy damage. Multiple disfiguring gouges. Excessive paint wear	10
1	Gouges and paint wear so disfiguring that distinguishing features are all but obliterated. Customizer's dream	0

and condition that I have come across is the guidance given to would-be traders in plastic action figures, such as the models of *Star Wars* characters (*Action Figure News*, 1995).

Condition is graded on a 10-point scale. Figures are valued on a percentage scale that corresponds to this grade. The grading guide comes with clear photographs of damage types (see Figure 7.3). A summary of the valuations is given in Table 7.3.

This information is shown in idealized form in Figure 7.4. It appears that the very first signs of damage have little effect on value. It also appears that once the object has been damaged, there comes a point where a bit more damage has little effect on the remaining value. The S-shaped curve can be seen as an amalgamation of two curves that reflect different phenomena.

Imagine a pristine piece of white porcelain or plain silver. The very first chip or scratch is the one that will cause most distress. The difference between the ninety-ninth and the hundredth scratch is not going to be noticed. Figure 7.5 shows this as a concave curve where, after a while, the increasing physical change has no effect on value. In some cases, where each contribution to damage is slight and is evenly distributed, the appearance of age and use may actually add value. There are other instances where small changes are unusually disturbing (Michalski, 1994). Because the eye uses lines and corners as 'feature detectors', and because human artifacts have a certain regularity, loss of line and edge are often seen as serious defects.

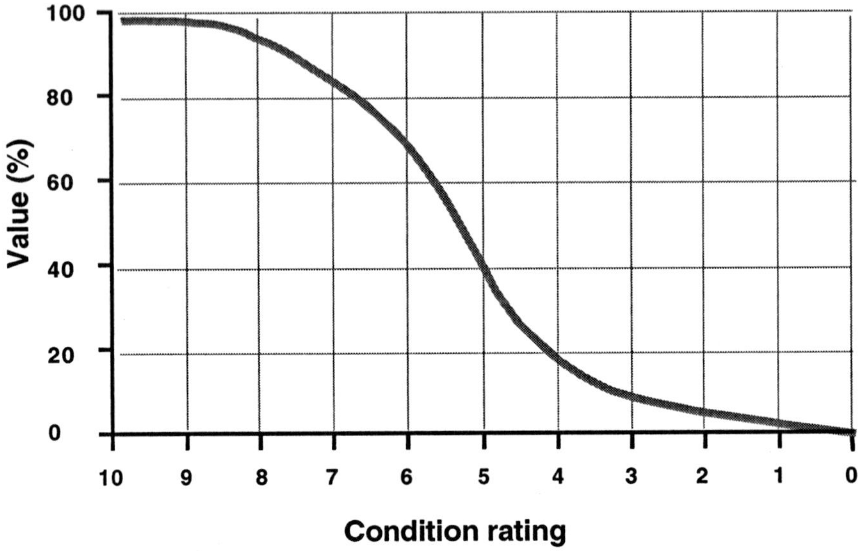

Figure 7.4 *Idealized curve derived from the change in book value predicted for different condition ratings of plastic action figures*

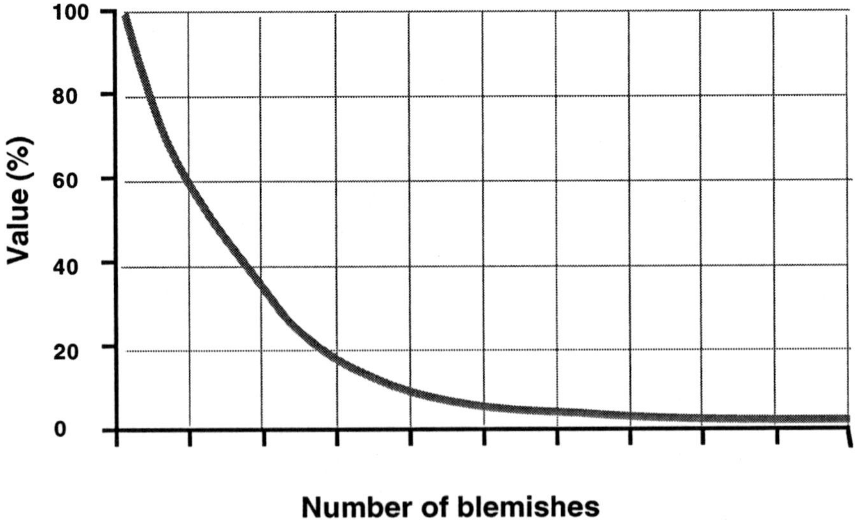

Figure 7.5 *Graphical representation of loss in value with increasing number of chips or scratches on a plain background*

Imagine a large object with a complex asymmetric design in a variety of colours, say an oil painting of people in a landscape. One small surface loss or crack is not going to alter the message of the image. As long as the losses are small and randomly distributed the overall value of the object will not be diminished. At some point the random losses may begin to occur next to one another and discernible chunks of the design will be lost. These losses will be more important if they remove key parts of the message or purpose of the piece. In paintings, as in action figures (and indeed in human injuries), loss of facial features is considered very disturbing. This sudden loss of value after a long accumulation of damage is shown as a convex curve in Figure 7.6.

The S-shaped curve in Figure 7.4 is formed by the aggregation of Figures 7.5 and 7.6. Although the two curves appear to show opposing relationships they are in fact both examples of Fechner's law, which is the generalization about human perception of sensory events such as light and colour changes mentioned in Chapter 1 (Baird and Noma, 1979). It states that the strength of a just noticeable increment in a sensation is proportional to the logarithm of its stimulus (see Figure 7.10 for a logarithmic plot).

For the action figures the agreement about the loss associated with damage relates to their current use as items of display and investment. One of the original purposes of the figures was for children to play with (although the notion of investment 'buy the complete series and the

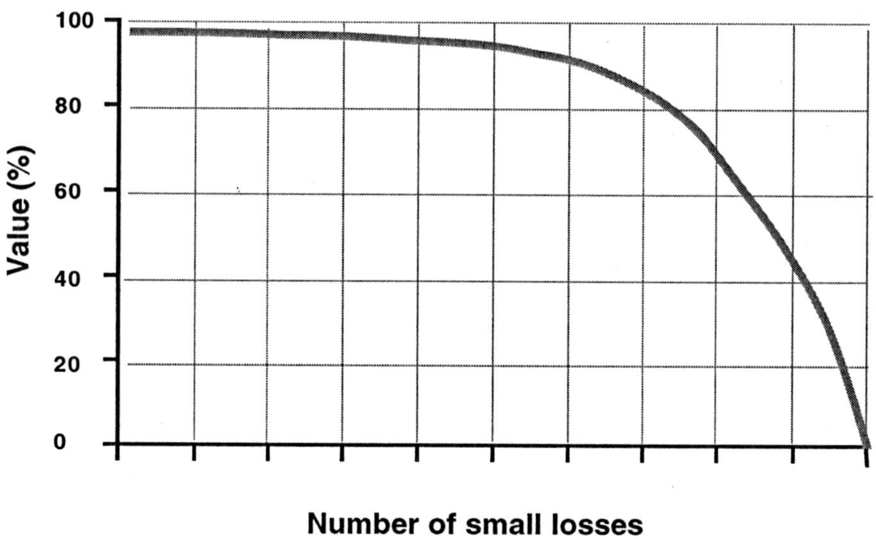

Figure 7.6 *Graphical representation of loss in value with increasing number of small random losses from a complex design*

display cabinet' was always there). For figures that were played with, damage would occur through use and have little effect on the play value until the figure no longer resembled the character it was modelled on (convex curve). Similarly a museum display of toys of the 1970s and 1980s might deliberately show figures that had been played with. Damage accumulated on display would have little effect on the message intended (tail end of concave curve). Thus changes of state have differing effects on use value depending on what the use is.

My assertion that the use of a painting is not affected by small random changes of state is either an aesthetic judgement dressed up as science, or more probably a scientific simplification dressed up as aesthetic certainty. Kirby Talley warns against scientific interpretations of matters that are predominantly aesthetic (Talley, 1996).

Figure 7.6 could be interpreted as a graph of loss against complexity. Large losses reduce the complexity of a painting. The accumulation of surface dirt or the yellowing of varnish reduce the number of potential units of information being perceived by the viewer. The message received is less complex. There is an implication that physical change will always reduce complexity and so will always result in lower value. For two-dimensional objects this is probably true. Three-dimensional objects which are predominantly monochrome and rely on abrupt changes in contour to give their message may benefit from a bit of 'damage' to accentuate their form. Dirt and tarnish remaining in the lines of engraving on silver are a good example.

Soiling of buildings may emphasize architectural detail. Architecture in northern cities in Europe has borrowed elements that originated in countries where the climate assured sharp, well-defined shadows. Slight soiling supplies the desirable contrast in the absence of sunshine. Chris Andrew has proposed an aesthetic theory of building soiling. Initial deposition of dirt increases complexity and aesthetic value (Andrew, 1992). Increasing deposition leads to loss of complexity and stronger perception of soiling as the building becomes more uniformly black. An initial slow increase turns to a rapid dive into negative aesthetic vales (Figure 7.7).

Aesthetic value comes from complex human reactions to information that derives from the form, outline and surface features of an object. The documentary value of the object may lie primarily in its surface but there may be documentary or scientific evidence in the materials and construction. Much of this information is evenly distributed throughout the object, e.g. trace elements, inclusions, metallographic microstructure. There is great redundancy of information as the message is repeated again and again throughout the object. Where this is the case, quite large material losses can be suffered without any important loss of information. Think of a pile of evening papers at the news stand. The essential

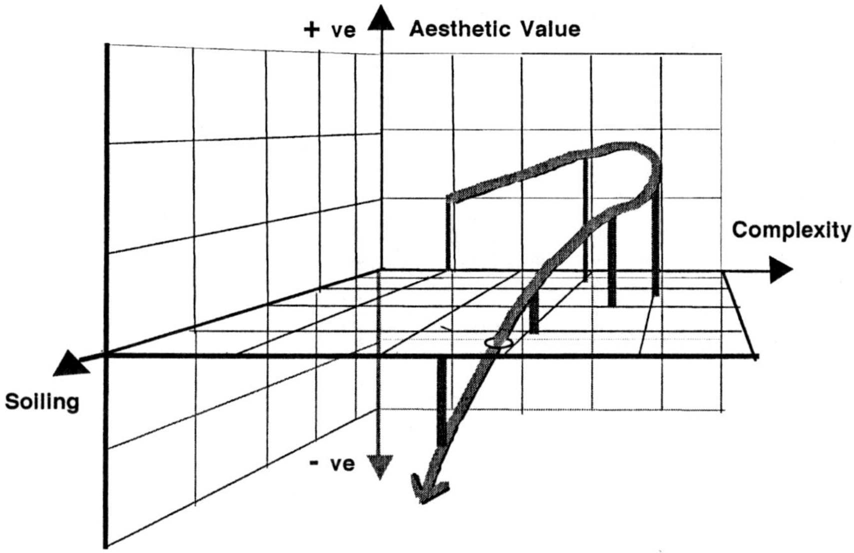

Figure 7.7 *Soiling of a building initially adds complexity which raises aesthetic value. With further soiling complexity decreases and negative aesthetic values are reached (after Andrew)*

information is not diminished every time a newspaper is sold. All the information you need is where you want it, until the last copy is removed.

However, there are some hazards that can completely remove certain kinds of information from the whole object without obvious material loss. High temperatures and strong radiation will alter microstructures and thermoluminescence characteristics which give information about methods of manufacture and authenticity.

No correlation

Some of the contributions to value remain unchanged by changes of state.

The contribution of the nature of the material to the value of the object can only be altered if the nature of the material is completely changed by chemical reaction. In general the most highly valued materials are the most stable: gold, platinum, diamond. So such a change is incredibly rare and would not take place in a museum. Only in particular geological or archaeological conditions is the material of original construction completely replaced. No amount of damage can turn a piece of mahogany into beech. It is true that physical loss of matter will lower the total value by removal of valuable material, but the proportional contribution to value will remain the same.

Age, context, history and identity are not actual properties of the object. They are properties of its relationship to other narratives, other histories, other conventions. Deterioration or loss of material will not alter the contributions to value of these factors. An object remains the same age whether it deteriorates or not. Charles Dickens' walking stick is his regardless of whether it is falling apart or has recently been repainted. A decaying fragment of a drawing by Leonardo da Vinci will still be more valuable than a pristine drawing by Jonathan Ashley-Smith.

Uncertain correlation

Strong correlation between state and value exists where the value is a measure of information derived directly from the object. There is no correlation when the value is imposed on the object by information derived from other sources. In either case the estimation of value is strongly dependent on common understanding of the sources of value. It needs a common education and a common vocabulary.

There are a number of value factors which are not necessarily driven by universal views. They relate to the beliefs of individuals or groups with their own experiences and their own vocabularies. This is the area of spiritual and political values. I would say that, in general, these individuals or groups imposed value on to objects rather than derived value from them. For instance, I would say that a statue of Lenin was a potent political symbol whether or not it was covered in bird droppings. I would say that a crumbling Hindu temple was still a place for religious veneration.

However, I have noticed that some personal objects ceased to have sentimental value when they had decayed or been physically damaged. It is possible that the spirits of ancestors may feel the same way. There is a similarity to the flexible phase in Rubbish Theory (Chapter 6). In the absence of a fixed worldview, a strong enough assertion that spiritual values have been affected by physical change stands a good chance of becoming accepted as the truth.

Ways of assessing damage

Various methods of assessing damage in museum collections have developed over the past decade. They depend on viewpoints that do not fully subscribe to the definitions of damage implied by the discussion in this chapter and the last. I have termed the two major viewpoints as that of the conservator and that of the scientist, although either view could be held by any museum professional.

The conservator's view

When conservators write condition reports they have a wide vocabulary for signs of change of state. There are all sorts of words for things that, in the conservator's opinion, shouldn't have been allowed to happen. Wrinkle, cockle, tent, dent, fade, stain, accretion, loss. But when it comes to comparing one object with another or looking at the same object at different points of time the vocabulary becomes relational and poorly descriptive. Very scratched, considerably faded, more wrinkled. It is because of this lack of a quantitative vocabulary that increasing use is made of photographs in condition reports.

Surveys of the state of whole collections involve an assessor, usually a conservator, placing the observed condition of individual objects into one of several categories.

Table 7.4 shows the categories in most common use (Keene, 1996).

The choice of an even number of categories forces the assessor to place the condition on one or other side of a central dividing line. Above this line objects are stable, no action needed. Below the line we have unstable objects, action needed. Above the line there is nothing for the conservator to do, below the line the assessor has justified the continued existence of conservators. The majority of judgements are about the state of the objects. It is above the line that we see judgements about value, words like 'disfigured', phrases like 'in context'. Below the line there is a reference to use.

The assessments are all about *changes* of state. Unstable means moving from one state to another. Conservators believe that they can make a holistic appraisal of a dynamic process by making a *single* observation.

Table 7.4 *Conservation condition*

1. GOOD	Good condition in context. Stable
2. FAIR	Disfigured or damaged but stable. No immediate action needed
3. POOR	Restricted use, probably unstable. Action desirable
4. UNACCEPTABLE	Severely weakened, highly unstable, actively deteriorating, affecting other objects. Immediate action

Table 7.5 *Main damage types*

- Major structural damage
- Minor structural damage
- Surface damage
- Disfigurement
- Chemical deterioration
- Biological attack
- Bad old repairs
- Accretions

This follows the tradition of the medical profession but is at odds with strict scientific method. The concentration on the change rather than on the remaining value of the object is apparent from Keene's observation that the worse the condition of the object the more description is needed (Keene, 1996, p. 145).

In a thorough survey, categories of damage are noted. These are believed to fall into eight major damage types (Table 7.5).

These are partly descriptions of different mechanisms of damage. They imply a successful attack by a known hazard and so could be part of a risk assessment (after the event). They imply some judgements about aesthetic value, but as they concentrate on stability are predominantly judgements about potential changes of an undiscussed range of values.

The scientist's view

The scientist will choose one physical or chemical property of one of the materials the object is made of and measure it. The property chosen is one that could reasonably be expected to change with time. The act of measurement is a comparison with a standard, something that is not expected to change.

After a period of natural or accelerated ageing the scientist will take another measurement and record a new value (yet another use of the word). This process will be repeated at regular intervals so that a graph can be drawn of the change in that attribute with time. The measurement is rarely of the whole object, normally it is of a small sample area or even of a detached sample. Or for convenience it may be of a standard token that is believed to be representative of this particular aspect of the behaviour of the real object. A minimum of three measurements is necessary to establish a trend. For example, timber which is exposed outdoors initially darkens then turns lighter again (Feist, 1990). If only two observations were made, the process could be wrongly interpreted in three different ways.

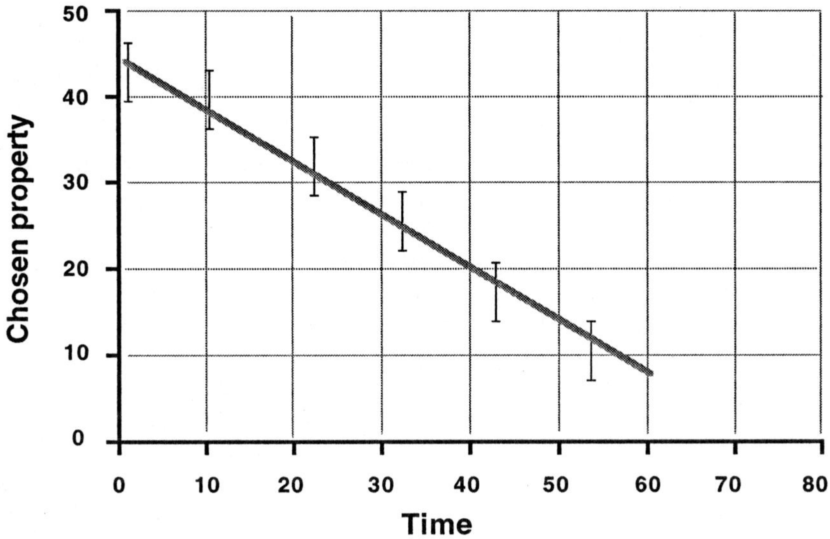

Figure 7.8 *Data from instrumental analysis is plotted against time. The length of the vertical bars shows the uncertainty of each measurement. A line can be drawn which passes through or close to most points*

A typical set of results is shown in Figure 7.8. The measurement of the chosen property is shown by the height of the data point above the baseline. A line can be drawn which joins the points and suggests a trend. In this case the line slopes downwards from left to right as the numerical value of the observed property decreases with time. This would be the case if the measured characteristic were the tear strength of a piece of paper. It would slope upward if the measurement were of the number of carboxylate groups in degrading cellulose. Although in this case the scientist has chosen to draw a straight line through the data points there is sufficient uncertainty about each measurement (shown by the length of the vertical bars) that a slightly convex curve could also be drawn.

As a definition of state a measurement made by instrumental analysis has the advantage that it can be compared to other measurements using the same methods of analysis. The numbers can be subjected to mathematical and graphical analysis. For instance, we can extrapolate and predict that the property in Figure 7.8 will have a value of zero when time equals between 60 and 80 units.

It has the disadvantage that it can only be applied to properties that are subject to quantitative measurement. That is, the attributes are chosen for their relative ease of measurement rather than by their relevance to the way the object is used or valued. The impartiality of science is also a handicap. A measurement of 10.2 units may be accurate and reproducible but is it good or is it bad? Is a downward trend good or bad? The hardness of a paint film may increase with age. Is that good or bad? The paint film is less susceptible to scratching and dirt pick-up and also less prone to damage during cleaning. But the concomitant change in stiffness may make it susceptible to cracking due to shock or environmental change.

Moreover the strength of the scientific method is also its weakness. Each set of measurements applies to a separate property *in isolation*. For instance, with a suitable instrument we can take colour measurements of small areas on the surface of a watercolour painting. However, the appreciation of a watercolour may not just be a function of the reflected colours of small patches of pigment, but of the uniformity of larger patches of that colour, the contrast of colour or density between adjacent areas, or the distribution of different densities across the whole painting. So even though a number of the colours may change quite noticeably, the holistic appreciation of the object may hardly alter. The measurement of state when applied in the real world of people turns out to be an inappropriate measurement of value.

It is fairly common for chemical signs of change to have little or no relationship to mechanical properties. Alterations in colour, brightness or acidity can be independent of changes such as decreased tensile strength or increased brittleness (e.g. Abadie-Maumert, 1994; Leary and Zou, 1994; Whitemore and Colaluca, 1995). It is necessary to have some idea of the importance of the property to the way that the object is used, before extrapolating measurements to determine permanence or expected life-span of an object.

This difficulty is alleviated if we choose a measurable property that relates to the way that the object is going to be used. For example, measurements of the fold endurance of paper are more relevant to an archive of printed material than measurements of the rate of yellowing. It is quite easy to read black type on yellow paper but very difficult if the pages keep crumbling in your hands. However, the exact colour of a textile sample in a pattern book may be the sole reason for its being preserved. If steps are taken to see that it is not handled directly, its folding endurance is irrelevant.

Utility

The word 'utility' has been used several times so far without definition. It has the general meaning of usefulness or ability to serve a purpose. In philosophy it has the more specific meaning of the ability to satisfy the needs of the majority or indeed the whole human race. In economics it is interpreted as the personal convenience of profit. Utility is the value to an individual of additional increments of income or wealth. An extra £100 has more utility to an impoverished student than it does to the chairman of a privatized industry. Utility is therefore a measure of an individual's satisfaction and as such it is also a measure of an individual's risk preference (Figure 7.9). The Italian economist Vilfredo Pareto, whose name is cited frequently in texts on CBA, is responsible for theories that allow the ranking of the utilities perceived by different people.

In connection with museum collections the word can be used with shades of all three meanings. The collections are there to be used, to serve a purpose. The trustees of the V&A are permitted to '... do such things as they think necessary or expedient for preserving, and increasing the *utility* of, their collections ...' (HMSO, 1983). The relationship between value and benefit described in the last chapter implies that, the greater the number of people using a collection, the greater is its value. In that case utility implies both use and value. Different museum collections are used in different ways and so contribute to an individual's satisfaction to different degrees. Anything that lessens utility leads to a lower value. This is a loss that could be described as damage.

Methods of quantifying damage as change in value have been applied in the field of health studies (Soby and Ball, 1991; Ives, Soby, Ball and Kemp, 1992). Attempts to quantify damage to the health of a human being do not involve lists of bits and pieces lost, or accretions of sores and scabs. They relate to change in utility measured as decrease of mobility, self-care and social activity.

Table 7.6 *The EuroQol classification*

Mobility	1. No problems walking about 2. Unable to walk about without a stick, crutch or walking frame 3. Confined to bed
Self-care	1. No problems 2. Unable to dress self 3. Unable to feed self
Main activity	1. Able to perform main activity (e.g. work, study, housework) 2. Unable to perform main activity
Social relationships	1. Able to pursue family and leisure activities 2. Unable to pursue family and leisure activities
Pain	1. No pain or discomfort 2. Moderate pain or discomfort 3. Extreme pain or discomfort
Mood	1. Not anxious or depressed 2. Anxious or depressed

Table 7.6 gives one example of such a classification (EuroQol, 1990). The six categories are each divided into two or three levels giving a total number of 216 possible health states. Systems of classification have been proposed that result in millions of distinct, if not distinguishable, states of health.

Not all these qualities can be directly attributed to inanimate objects that cannot suffer from moods or pain. You have the choice of ignoring these categories or transferring them to the human beings associated with the object – visitors, curators, scholars, conservators. Does the condition of the object cause anyone to feel anxious or depressed? The main point is that this is not a description of state but a description of ability to function in a specified environment.

One of the ways of quantifying the change in utility caused by injury is called the Relative Utility Loss approach (RULA). Designated health states are given a utility score on a scale from zero to unity (or 0–100%). Unity represents full health and zero represents death (fates worse than death having a negative value). The value of the impairment is calculated from the relative utility loss (that is, unity minus the utility score) which is then multiplied by the Value of a Life. If the VOL had been calculated using the Human Capital approach the RUL would appear as:

$$\text{RUL} = \text{VOL} \times (1 - U) = \sum_{t=0}^{\infty} (1 - U)(B - C)P(1 + r)^{-t} \tag{7.1}$$

The utility score (U) is determined by asking different groups of people to rank different health states. One approach is to ask whether the respondent would rather have a specified low health state for a certain number of years (followed by death) or full health for a shorter number of years (also followed by death). Monetary value can be assessed to some extent by medical statistics on how much a particular (severe) injury reduces life expectancy or, as in the case of blindness, it might affect earnings.

In one study (Kind, Rosser and Williams, 1982) physicians, nurses, and medical and psychiatric patients were asked to rate health states in a matrix of eight levels of disability and four levels of distress. If we equate disability with condition and distress with value we end up with data that could be compared with Figures 7.5 and 7.6.

The evaluations of health state for the highest and lowest levels of distress are plotted against disability rating in Figure 7.10. The convex curve is the same as for the hypothetical case of an increasing number of random losses from an oil painting. From the point of view of sufferers, carers and curers, it seems that quite a large amount of disability can be suffered before there is a drop in utility (the quality of life). Interestingly the doctors put greater emphasis on the patients' subjective assessment of suffering than the patients themselves. At higher levels of overall distress

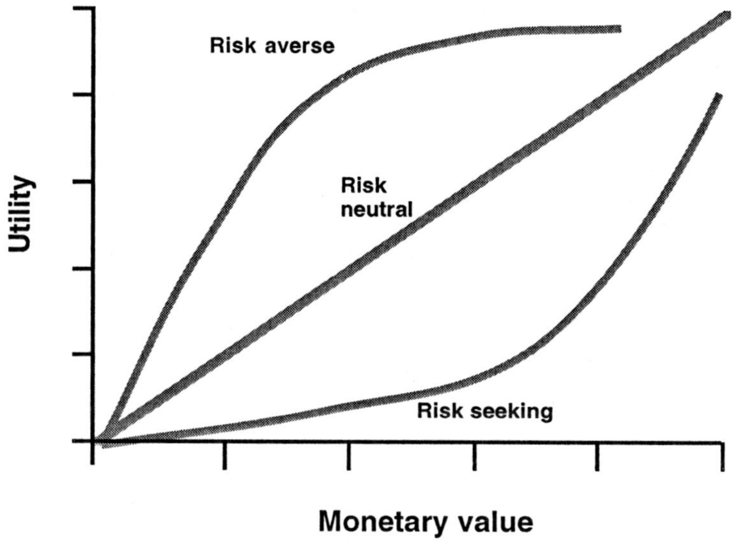

Figure 7.9 *A risk-averse person sees utility in objects of low value*

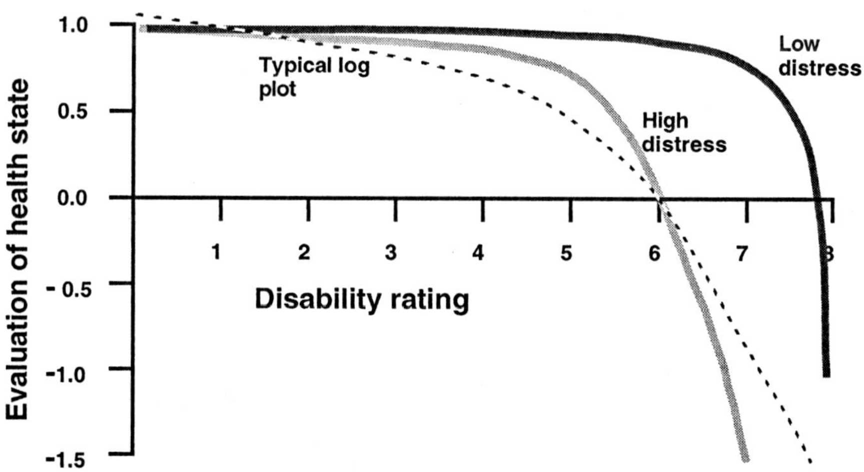

Figure 7.10 *Estimates of the utility of various human health states. The two grey curves show changes in utility for different degrees of disability associated with low and high levels of distress (using data from Rosser)*

zero utility is reached sooner but not dramatically so. It seems likely that for any complex subject, consecutive equal changes of state do not immediately lead to equivalent changes in a multivariate utility. The relationship does not have to be a simple mathematical one but it is probably approximately logarithmic.

But small changes do matter!

The implication of adopting a definition of damage based on utility is that in many instances small changes do not contribute to damage. Scientists, who can accurately detect changes at the molecular level, and conservators, who can see immense pits and cracks when they look down their binocular microscopes, might not agree.

The point is that there *may* come a time when there are enough small changes to be called damage. The purpose of conservation is to slow down and prevent that process. The small changes we detect *may* be signs of worse things to come. The purpose of risk studies is to find out whether it is worthwhile reacting, and, if so, when and how.

Something to think about

Is the change in value less for damage that took place before an object entered the museum than for the same amount of physical change after acquisition?

If small fragments of pigment fall off a painting on display, is this damage? If fragments of the same size are removed in the course of technical studies, is this damage?

Does it really matter whether value is lost rapidly first and slowly later, or slowly first and rapidly later? Surely the only thing that matters is where it eventually ends up after the maximum potential loss in value?

References

Abadie-Maumert, F.A. (1994) Stabilité au Viellissement Articiel des Papiers Contenant des Pâtes à Haut Rendement. Environnement et Conservation de l'Écrit, de l'image et du Son. *Actes des Journées Internationales d'Études de I'ARSAG*, Paris, ISSN 0765–0248.

Action Figure News (1995) The Action Figure News and Toy Review Guide to Collecting Loose Figures, Vol. 1. Lee Publications, US.

Andrew, Chris (1992) Towards an Aesthetic Theory of Building Soiling, in *Stone Cleaning: and the Nature, Soiling and Decay Mechanisms of Stone*, edited by Robin G.M. Webster. Donhead. ISBN 1-873394-09-8, pp. 63–42.

Baird, J.C. and Noma, E. (1979) *Fundamentals of Scaling and Psychophysics*. John Wiley and Sons, New York.

EuroQol Group (1990) EuroQuol – a new facility for the measurement of health related quality of life. *Health Policy*, **16**, pp. 199–208.

Feist, William C. (1990) *Outdoor Wood Weathering and Protection. Archaeological Wood*. American Chemical Society, pp. 264–297.

HMSO (1983) National Heritage Act 1983, Chapter 47. Her Majesty's Stationery Office, London.

Ives, D., Soby, B., Ball, D.J. and Kemp, R.V. (ed) (1992) Revaluation of Non-Fatal Road Traffic Casualty Costs: Relative Utility Loss Methodologies Report on Stage 2. Environmental Risk Assessment Unit, School of Environmental Sciences, Norwich. ISBN 1-873933-45-2.

Keene, Suzanne (1996) *Managing Conservation in Museums*. Butterworth-Heinemann in Association with Science Museum, London. ISBN 0-7506-2384-5, p. 141.

Kind, P., Rosser, R. and Williams, A. (1982) *Valuation of Quality of Life: Some Psychometric Evidence. The Value of Life and Safety.* Amsterdam: North Holland Publishing Company, pp. 159–170.

Leary, Gordon J. and Xuejun Zou (1994) The Optical Properties of Lignin-Containing Papers as they Relate to Paper Permanence. Workshop on the Effects of Aging On Printing and Writing Papers. ASTM Institute for Standards Research, Philadelphia.

Michalski, S. (1994) Sharing Responsibility for Conservation Decisions, in *Durability and Change: The Science, Responsibility, and Cost of Sustaining Cultural Heritage*, edited by W.E Krumbein, P. Brimblecombe, D.E. Cosgrove and S. Staniforth. John Wiley and Sons. ISBN-0-471-95221-4, pp. 241–258.

Soby, B.A. and Ball, D.J. (1991) Consumer Safety and the Valuation of Life and Injury. Environmental Risk Assessment Unit, School of Environmental Sciences, Norwich. ISBN 1-873933-00-2.

Talley, M. Kirby (1996) The Eye's Caress: Looking, Appreciation, and Connoiseurship. Introduction to Part 1 of *Historical and Philosophical Issues in the Conservation of Cultural Heritage*. The J. Paul Getty Trust. ISBN 0-89236-250-2.

Whitemore, Paul M. and Colaluca, Val G. (1995) The Natural and Accelerated Aging of an Acrylic Artist's Medium. *Studies in Conservation*, **40**, February, pp. 51–65.

8 Calculated risk

Although in many instances it is not necessary, it is possible to derive a numerical value for risk. There are a number of different equations that can be used for this calculation. They are all modifications of the simple relationship that risk is a combination of probability and potential loss. Probabilistic and deterministic risks can be treated in the same way. The relationships of the variables used in the equations are complex and certain simplifying assumptions must be made.

One simple relationship

Risk is a combination of probability and change in value. In Chapter 5 we used decision trees to derive present values for proposals that contained expressions such as $P(V_1 - V_2)$ which were described as representing risk. The probability P of an event is multiplied by the difference between an initial value V_1 and the value following that event V_2. If we use the symbol R to represent the Risk and the symbol L to represent the Loss in value[1], $(V_1 - V_2)$, we can construct an equation which shows how to calculate risk.

$$R = P \times L \quad \text{or simply} \quad R = PL \tag{8.1}$$

If all we are concerned about is total loss, then the loss L is the total value V and the equation is:

$$R = PV \tag{8.2}$$

[1] There is no agreed set of symbols for risk in conservation. Waller uses: MR for Magnitude of Risk instead of R, LV for maximum possible Loss in Value instead of L_{max} and FS for Fraction Susceptible instead of F_a. This makes for easy understanding but possible mathematical confusion between multiple initials and the algebraic convention of leaving out the multiplication sign. At the risk of insulting a pioneer in the field I have chosen to use single initials.

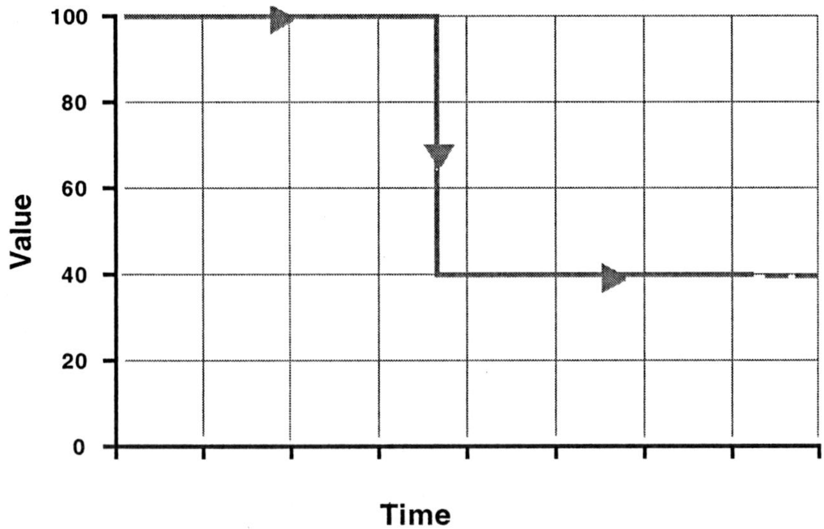

Figure 8.1 *Graphical representation of a catastrophic loss of 60% value*

These equations are the simplest mathematical expressions of risk. While they convey the essence of risk calculation they are probably too simple to help with meaningful risk assessment.

In Figure 8.1 we see a situation similar to one first encountered in Chapter 2. An object or collection has an initial value $V = 100$, in arbitrary units of measurement. At some point in time an event happens that causes the value to drop to $V = 40$. There are several ways of expressing this change. The loss could be described in absolute terms as $100 - 40 = 60$ units. Alternatively it could be described in terms of proportionate loss, as the fraction 0.6 or as the percentage 60%. There are merits in both the absolute and the proportionate approach but care must be taken not to mix the two together in comparisons of risk.

Although a probability can be described in terms of odds or as a percentage, it is simplest to stick to the convention of stating probability as a decimal number between 0 and 1, e.g. 0.5 for the chance of heads in a coin toss. This is a pure number without units of measurement. Risk is that number multiplied by the loss in value. Risk will have the same units as the loss in value. If the loss is measured in pounds or dollars then the risk will be calculated in the same units. However, when talking about a risk we are talking about a useful mathematical concept, not a real sum of money.

Figure 8.2 shows the two outcomes of a decision to toss a coin. Suppose I have a pound coin and will decide what to do with it depending on the result of the toss. The value of the decision to do nothing is zero since

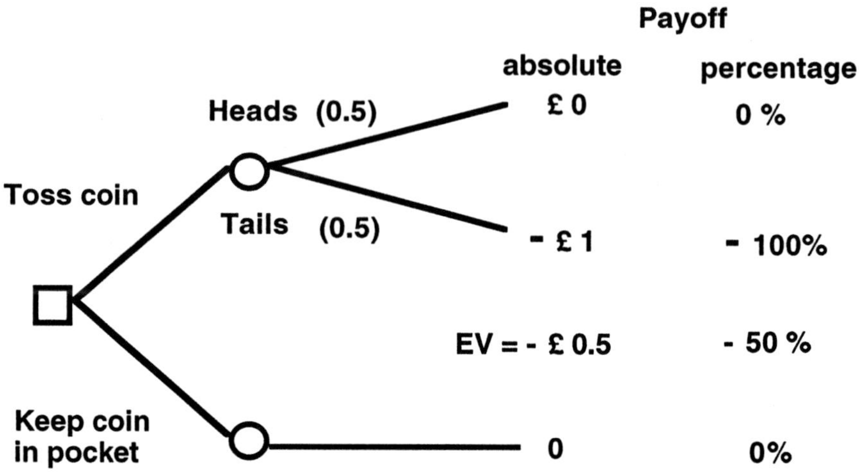

Figure 8.2 *Decision tree for a game based on tossing a coin. Although only a one pound coin is involved, the expected value and the risk of the game are both 50 pence. Percentage losses are shown for comparison*

there will be no change in my wealth. The game is that if the coin lands tails up I will give it to you: if it lands heads up I will hang on to it. The expected value to me is minus £0.5, it is a game where I can't win. The expected value for you is plus £0.5, it is a game where you can't lose. The only sum of money that exists or would change hands is a one pound coin. The risk is calculated as 50 pence, an imaginary sum, a mathematical convenience to describe the magnitude of risk. However, it is a figure that allows comparisons with gambles involving smaller or larger sums of money. If there were two wagers, one for £1 and one for £100 wagered were £100, and you had the option to take the first or the second gamble, you would know that a magnitude of risk of £50 was different from one of 50 pence. Yet the figure on its own doesn't give any information about the probabilities involved.

If we use proportionate change, the expected value of both the £1 and the £100 gamble is 50% to you (minus 50% to me). So you can't decide which gamble to go for based on this information. The risk is 50% which tells you what *sort* of risk it is. It tells you at once how chancy the deal is, but not what you stand to win or lose.

If we use the symbol L_{abs} for the real or absolute loss in value measured in units such as pounds or dollars, we can reserve the symbol L for proportionate loss. The two are connected by the relationship:

$$L_{abs} = VL \tag{8.3}$$

As long as we always remember to quote the units of measurement, £, $, %, we will know what sort of risk we are talking about. If risk is quoted as just a number without any units then we should assume that the loss in value is proportionate and has been measured as a number between 0 and 1, e.g. 0.6 in the case of Figure 8.1.

Suppose the vertical axis in Figure 8.1 represents value in $, and the probability of the damaging event occurring in any one year is 0.01 (probability of happening once in 100 years). The annual risk can be presented in three ways:

$$0.01 \times \$60 = \$0.6 \text{ or } 60 \text{ cents}$$

$$0.01 \times 60\% = 0.6\%$$

$$0.01 \times 0.6 = 0.006$$

This is the annual risk to a particular object for a particular hazard or hazardous event. As well as specifying the particular hazard or agent, it is important to specify the period of time that is being considered. It is impossible to make direct comparisons of risks that have been calculated for different time periods. For collections management issues, demanding a broad strategic approach, a period of 100 years seems about right. This fits in with common classifications such as 'storm of the century'. For issues that require tactical decision-making, such as transport of objects to exhibition venues, a much shorter time period, in days or months, must be specified. Adjustments will need to be made to be sure that calculated risks can be compared. An annual risk of 0.006 is a risk of 0.6 per century and 0.0005 per month.

More complex equations

For a particular type of object and a particular hazard, it may be possible to specify a maximum possible proportionate loss in value L_{max}. As we discussed in the last chapter, not all contributions to value are affected by changes of state. The pattern of small cracks on the surface of an oil painting is, among other things, a response to fluctuating relative humidity. There comes a point when the craquelure pattern ceases to develop even if humidity continues to fluctuate. This is the maximum amount of change that will happen. It does not amount to 100% loss in value, at most it might amount to 10% (Michalski, 1994).

This maximum may not be reached within the time period being discussed. The Extent to which the maximum is achieved by the hazard in the specified time can be defined by a fraction E:

$$L = L_{max} E \tag{8.4}$$

If we assume that P refers to the probability of an event that will effect all the objects in a collection at the same time, a flood or an earthquake, then the risk for a whole collection can be given by

$$R = P \sum_{i=1}^{n} L_{\max\ i} E_i \tag{8.5}$$

This notation means that all you have to do is examine every object, agree what the maximum possible loss for that object type is, and determine what the extent of change for that particular object might be given its individual state and location. This gives a proportionate loss L_i for each individual object. For a collection containing n objects all of the n losses are added together and then multiplied by P to obtain the total risk. Although it looks very neat mathematically, it obviously involves too much work and a great deal of guess work. A broader, simpler and no less accurate method is needed.

In a collection of n objects only a certain number n_a will be susceptible to the agent a. In a mixed collection of silver and ceramics only the silver will be tarnished by sulphur-containing pollutants. A moderate earthquake would probably cause more damage to the ceramic objects than to the silver ones. A more severe earthquake would probably cause more damage to tall, thin sculptures than to squat ones. A flood would probably affect objects in the basement more than those on the top floor. A thief is more likely to take a small, valuable object than a heavy, worthless one. And so on.

The Fraction susceptible is the number of objects susceptible to a particular hazard a divided by the total number of objects.

$$F_a = \frac{n_a}{n} \tag{8.6}$$

Extent and fraction susceptible can be seen as ways of moderating the magnitude of risk that would be calculated using a simple equation like (8.1).

The risk to a whole collection based on proportionate loss in value becomes:

$$R = \frac{n_a P L_{\max} E}{n} \tag{8.7}$$

In Waller's methodology, though not his notation (Canadian Museum of Nature, 1995), this would be written as:

$$R = F_a \times P \times L_{\max} \times E \tag{8.8}$$

In this case the loss in value and extent must be average figures for the collection. For a mixed collection in a museum with a variety of different storage and display methods these would be very rough global estimates. A compromise between viewing the collection as a single entity and inspecting every object would be to consider collection units of similar object types and similar environments. The risks for the collection units could then be aggregated if necessary.

The risk based on actual values would be:

$$R = P \sum_{i=1}^{n} V_i \, L_{\max\,i} E_i \quad \text{or} \quad R = \frac{V n_a \, P \, L_{\max} E}{n} \qquad (8.9)\ \&\ (8.10)$$

where V_i is the value of an individual object and V is the total value of the collection.

Using proportionate value loss you might conclude that the risks to a collection of bus tickets, a collection of drawings by Leonardo da Vinci and a collection of my drawings were at equal risk. If you were trying to decide which collection deserved most money spent on protective measures, or which ought to be rescued first, you might want to include the actual value.

To what extent?

The fraction susceptible is a number that can be verified by inspection. The probability is something that can be derived statistically or agreed independently of the collection. The maximum loss in value could be agreed for a particular type of object after discussion within an institution or throughout the museum profession. For rapid onset catastrophic events the extent of damage is very much dependent on local storage and display methods, work practices and standards of care.

Figure 8.3 shows a gradual progressive deterioration. For simplicity it is shown as a straight line. If the object or collection is exposed to a hazard to which it is susceptible then there is absolute certainty that some damage will take place, P=1. In this case, at the end of 60 years it is observed that there has been a loss in value of 60%. The annual rate of proportionate loss of value is 1% or 0.01. This rate can be used to determine the extent for any particular time period. Extent can be calculated from a rate k multiplied by a time of exposure t. For this simple linear model:

$$E = kt \qquad (8.11)$$

In Chapter 5 we used a simple decision tree to determine the expected value of investing in plant to arrest deterioration. The calculation yielded

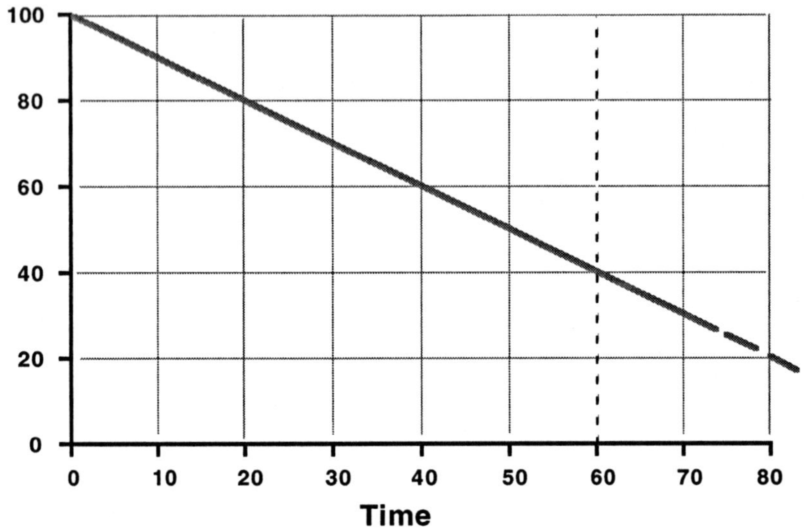

Figure 8.3 *Graphical representation of a gradual loss of 60% in value*

an expression $(k_1 - k_0)t$ for the change in risk to the collection, giving k_0t as the initial risk. If this is compared to equation (8.10) it can be seen to be the same expression for risk R, simplified by a number of assumptions. It was assumed that *all* the collection would be susceptible, $F = 1$, that *all* the value of the collection would be lost, $L_{max} = 1$ and that only one agent would affect the collection and do so in a uniform, deterministic way, $P = 1$. The rate of deterioration was assumed to be linear and was expressed as a rate of change of value, rather than a rate of change of state.

With those assumptions the risk reduces to value multiplied by extent:

$$R = Vkt \tag{8.12}$$

Risk calculated by proportionate loss of value reduces to simply a function of time. The time of exposure t might only be a small fraction of the actual time elapsed. For instance, only keeping a proportion of objects on display and only illuminating those during visiting hours will reduce the time objects are exposed to light.

If most of the simplifying assumptions are removed then the risk associated with a slow onset deterministic hazard is given by the equation:

$$R = \frac{Vn_aL_{max}kt}{n} \tag{8.13}$$

Table 8.1

	Type	*Risk*, R =	*Equation*
Probabilistic	partial loss, proportionate	PL	(8.1)
	partial loss, absolute	PL_{abs}	
	total loss	PV	(8.2)
	moderated, proportionate	$\frac{n_a P L_{max} E}{n}$	(8.7)
	alternative view	$F_a \times P \times L_{max} \times E$	(8.8)
	moderated, absolute	$\frac{V n_a P L_{max} E}{n}$	(8.10)
Progressive	moderated, proportionate	$\frac{n_a L_{max} E}{n}$	
	alternative view	$F_a \times L_{max} \times E$	
	rate constant, absolute	$\frac{V n_a L_{max} kt}{n}$	(8.13)

P Probability of event
V Value of object or collection
L proportionate Loss in value
L_{abs} Loss in measured units, e.g. pounds, dollars
L_{max} maximum possible proportionate Loss due to particular hazard
E Extent to which value is lost in a particular period
n number of objects in collection
n_a number of objects susceptible to hazard a
F_a Fraction of collection susceptible to hazard a
k rate constant for proportionate loss of value in one unit of time
t time of exposure

If the expression kt is read as meaning 'some function involving time' the objection that change in value is hardly ever linear is removed.

Table 8.1 summarizes the equations derived in this chapter.

Risk without gambling

It may seem odd to apply the term risk, which is about uncertainty, to something inevitable like steady deterioration. However, the similarity of the equations for calculating deterministic and probabilistic risk suggests that it is valid to use the same word for both types of process.

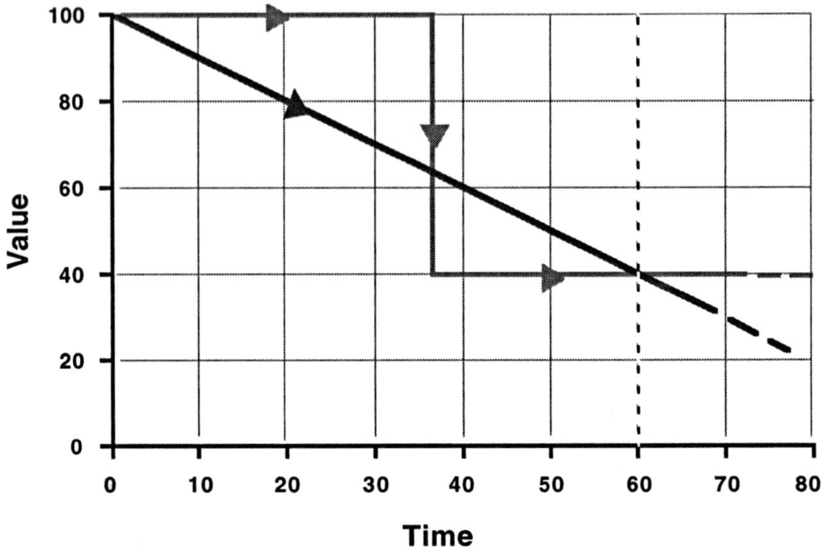

Figure 8.4 *At one point in time a particular gradual loss will have exactly the same effect as a catastrophic loss. Stochastic and deterministic risk can be modelled in the same way*

It is also easy to combine the graphs in Figures 8.1 and 8.3 to suggest that the different processes result in the same end-point (Figure 8.4). We cannot know at what point the rapid onset event will take place (vertical line). But we know that the horizontal line representing the second phase of constant lower value will eventually cross the sloping line that represents slow deterioration. At that point in time one particular probabilistic risk will be equivalent to the loss caused by a particular rate of decay.

It is possible to imagine that the steady deterioration is in fact made up of a long series of small probabilistic events. The two ways of expressing risk differ only in the scale of the events that are being studied.

Suppose you have a large collection and some random hazard is destroying the objects one by one. This is probably easier to imagine if you think really big and consider historic monuments around the whole world, rather than pots in your own collection. Initially you have n_0 objects, but after a while you have a smaller number n_1 and after that a still smaller number n_2. If the probability of this terrible event occurring in one unit of time is P, the rate of disappearance will initially be n_0P. As time progresses, although the probability remains the same, the number of objects will decrease, so the rate of disappearance decreases. After

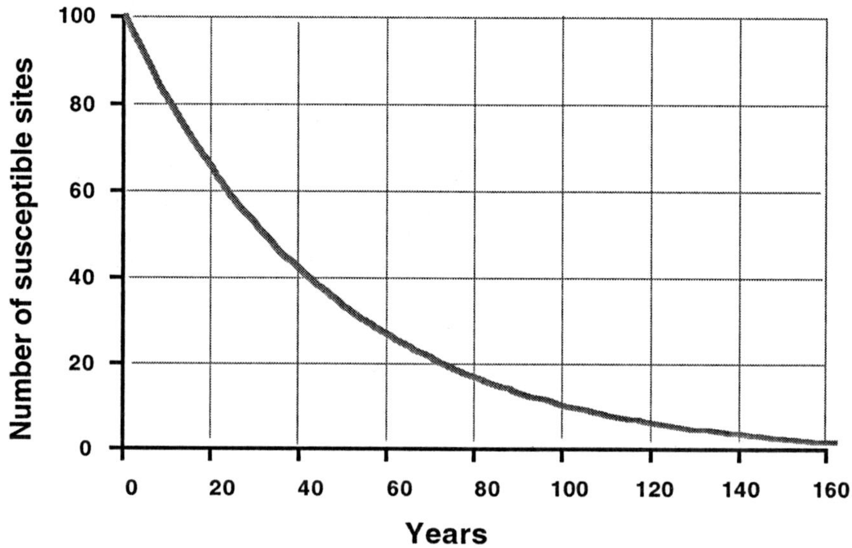

Figure 8.5 *Random loss of whole objects, or attack at random points on one object, both lead to a first order decay curve*

some time the rate of disappearance falls to n_1P and later to n_2P. This decreasing rate of loss with time is shown in Figure 8.5.

Instead of a collection of susceptible objects, we can consider a number of (hypothetical) susceptible sites on one single object. These could be sites where a pollutant might react or where photolytic attack can take place. As the number of available sites diminishes, the overall rate of reaction decreases and so we observe the same curve. However, instead of observing the probabilistic loss of individual objects from a collection we are now looking at the deterministic decay of one object (Benarie, 1991).

The form of the curve in Figure 8.4 is that found for first order deterioration reactions, which has properties that will be discussed in Chapter 10.

Comparison and aggregation of risks

The purpose of calculating risk is to use the result to aid decision-making. We may want answers to questions like: Which part of the collection is at greatest risk? Is it more dangerous to send an object by road, or by air?

What is the risk to this sculpture from exposure to light? What is the risk to this object from all hazards?

To answer these questions we have to be able to compare one risk with another and to be able to aggregate (add together) separate risks to see what the overall risk from a group of hazards might be.

There may be a high probability ($P = 1$) that a hazard such as rough handling will cause a small loss in value (say $L = 0.001\%$) to an art object. The magnitude of risk is $PL = 1 \times 0.001\% = 0.001\%$. Conversely there may be a low probability ($P = 0.00001$) that an earthquake will totally (100%) destroy the object. In this case the risk $PL = 0.00001 \times 100\% = 0.001\%$. So in this example the risk due to bad handling is identical to the risk of damage due to an earthquake. A comparison that might be useful in training object handlers.

The information that is available for calculating probability, extent and value is so imprecise that it would be wrong to base decisions on small differences in risk. The uncertainty is so great that a calculated risk would have to be at least one power of 10 greater than another before you could begin to feel confident about declaring it a worse risk.

In Chapter 2 we considered a proposal to send a collection of valuable paintings by air to an exhibition in another country. You have been told that the probability of a plane crash that would destroy the paintings is around one in a million (see also Chapter 14). The value of the collection is £100 million. The risk associated with the air flight is £$10^8 \times 10^{-6} =$ £100.

It is suggested that you should send the collection as two consignments, A and B, on separate flights. The probability that both flights will crash disastrously, $P_{(\text{A and B})}$, is found by multiplying the two separate probabilities, $P_A \times P_B$.

$$P_{(\text{A and B})} = P_A P_B \tag{8.14}$$

In this case $P_{(\text{A and B})} = 10^{-6} \times 10^{-6} = 10^{-12}$ which is an incredibly small number. The risk of total loss is £$10^8 \times 10^{-12} = 0.01$p.

The probability that just one of the two flights will crash, $P_{(\text{A or B})}$, is found by adding the separate probabilities and subtracting the probability that both planes will crash:

$$P_{(\text{A or B})} = P_A + P_B - P_{(\text{A and B})} \tag{8.15}$$

As we have seen, when P_A and P_B are small, $P_{(\text{A and B})}$ is a very small number and can usually be ignored, so that the equation becomes simply

$$P_{(\text{A or B})} = P_A + P_B \tag{8.16}$$

Thus by shipping the paintings on two separate flights we have doubled the probability that some part of the collection will be lost, but more or less eliminated the possibility that the loss will be total. The risk associated with the loss of one plane is the probability $P_{(\mathrm{A\ or\ B})}$ multiplied by the value of either of the two shipments V_A or V_B. If the shipments were equally divided, the risk is $(10^{-6} + 10^{-6}) \times £5 \times 10^7 = £100$.

We would get approximately the same result if we had added the risks rather than first adding the probabilities and then calculating the new risk (we get exactly the same result if the probabilities and values of both shipments are identical):

$$R_{(\mathrm{A\ or\ B})} = R_\mathrm{A} + R_\mathrm{B} = (P_\mathrm{A}\ V_\mathrm{A}) + (P_\mathrm{B}\ V_\mathrm{B}) \qquad (8.17)$$

The calculated maximum risk for the two plane option is the same figure as for a single consignment. So if we were to compare merely the two maximum risks we would be unable to make a clear choice between the two options. But by observing that the risk of total loss has been reduced to something so small as to be negligible, the risk averse manager is guided to choose the two plane option.

Table 8.2 summarizes the equations for aggregating probabilities and risks.

Strictly speaking, if risks have different probabilities, we can only add them together if the events are completely independent of one another. In

Table 8.2

Probability of both A and B happening	$P_\mathrm{A} P_\mathrm{B}$
Probability of one or other but not both	$P_\mathrm{A} + P_\mathrm{B} - (P_\mathrm{A}\ P_\mathrm{B})$
Approximate probability of one or other happening	$P_\mathrm{A} + P_\mathrm{B}$
Approximate risk from one or other happening	$R_\mathrm{A} + R_\mathrm{B}$
Risk for *n* objects involved in one event	$P \sum_{i=1}^{n} L_i$
Approximate risk for *n* objects in different events	$\sum_{i=1}^{n} R_i$

P_A Probability of event A
P_B Probability of independent event B
R_A Risk attached to event A
L_i Loss suffered by damage to object *i* (one of *n* objects)
R_i Risk to individual object *i* (by any equation from Table 8.1)

a museum many of the events that cause damage are inter-related and not strictly independent. However, most of the risks in a museum are very small. As long as the risks are small they can be added together to calculate a total risk to the collection that will be accurate enough to help with decision-making.

Frequency and severity

If we are going to calculate an overall risk for a number of objects that have different susceptibilities and different environments we are going to need ways of arriving at average figures for E, L_{max}, P and F for the whole of the collection unit that we are considering. To do this we must first understand the varying relationships between them.

Equation (8.6) for F assumes that the objects fall neatly into two categories, susceptible and not susceptible. With a mixed collection there will be many more categories. The susceptibility of an individual object is the same as the proportionate risk, $PL_{max}E$, where any of the three variables may be equal to unity. Susceptibility will be a number between 0 and 1 or between 0% and 100%. If we consider the theft of whole objects $L_{max} = E = 1$. So the susceptibility is the same as the probability of theft. This will be dictated by value, access and portability. For a collection of light-sensitive material on display P=1, susceptibility would be a combination of E and L_{max} depending on which materials were present (E is related to the rate of deterioration) and the way they were put together (the same degree of colour change could have differing effects on value for different designs).

Conservators' decisions are often governed by the most sensitive part of a mixed collection. If we make an assumption that all objects have the susceptibility of the highest we will overestimate the risk. Figure 8.6 shows a collection of 10 objects that have differing susceptibilities to a particular hazard. A convenient model, which might well come from a quick visual inspection of the collection, would suggest that F = 0.4 because objects 1–4 are noticeably different from the rest. They represent 85% of the total risk at an average susceptibility of about 70%. The remainder of the collection carries only 15% of the risk at an average susceptibility of 7%. This would imply a threshold of sensitivity at about 10% which is not unreasonable although it underestimates the total risk. Saying that 0.4 of the collection is 100% susceptible overestimates the risk. A simple model which accounts for the risk of the whole collection is to say that F = 0.4 with an average susceptibility of 80%.

The Extent, E, is the measure of impact or loss. There is a direct relationship between extent and loss shown by equation (8.4). For simplicity we can assume that the greatest possible proportionate loss

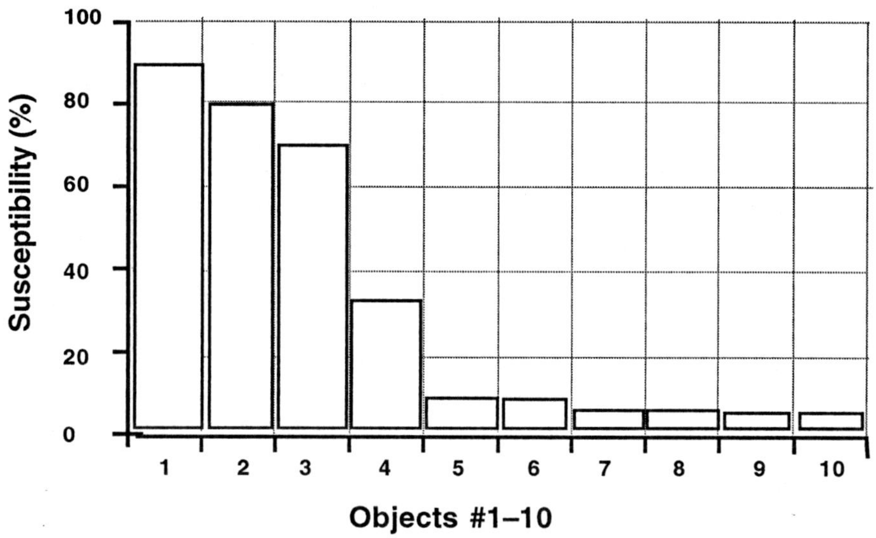

Figure 8.6 *A collection of 10 objects with differing susceptibilities. The total risk of the collection can be modelled by assuming that four objects* (F_a = *0.4) have an average susceptibility of 80%*

due to any one hazard L_{max} will be constant for any particular object type. However, we must recognize that it may change depending on the severity of the hazard. The maximum damage you could achieve with a sledge hammer is probably greater than the most you could manage with your bare hands, even though both would be categorized as 'physical force'.

The probability *P*, is a measure of the frequency with which damaging events occur. Not all events are of equal severity. You can have a big flood or a little flood, a car crash at 5 miles per hour or at 69 miles per hour, a packing case dropped 10 centimetres or 2 metres. The severity of events is usually a measure of the amount of energy involved. This could be kinetic, potential or chemical energy depending on whether we are discussing fast moving trucks, earthquakes, bright display lights or high concentrations of pollutant. Each of these different forms of severity has its own name and symbol, some of which will be introduced in later chapters. No single symbol for severity will be introduced at this stage. There is a relationship between the severity of events and their frequency. The more severe the event, the greater the extent. For simplicity it can be assumed that $E = 1$ for infrequent catastrophic events and that $P = 1$ for sporadic and constant occurrences that are less severe.

We need to establish thresholds of severity so that we can arrive at single figures for *P*, *E*, L_{max} and *F*. Waller gives an example where the severity of an earthquake that would displace unrestrained objects by 10 cm is taken as the threshold. The frequency of less severe earthquakes is not considered. The probability of an earthquake at least that severe is used to calculate the risk (Waller, 1994).

Data about frequency and severity of a variety of events such as fires, plane crashes and earthquakes is available for different countries. Mostly this data is collected because of statutory obligations or the interest of insurance companies. Large numbers of people die each year and huge sums of money change hands so there are many data points. The number of museum objects in a metropolis will far outnumber the human population but not many will change hands or cease to exist in any one year. The risks to museum objects that are internally generated are not subject to widespread data collection and what information does exist is not openly shared. The small amount of data, and the uncertainty about its completeness, mean that it is difficult to import data from outside your own institution to help derive probabilities. You will mostly be working with the anecdotal memories of the longest serving staff.

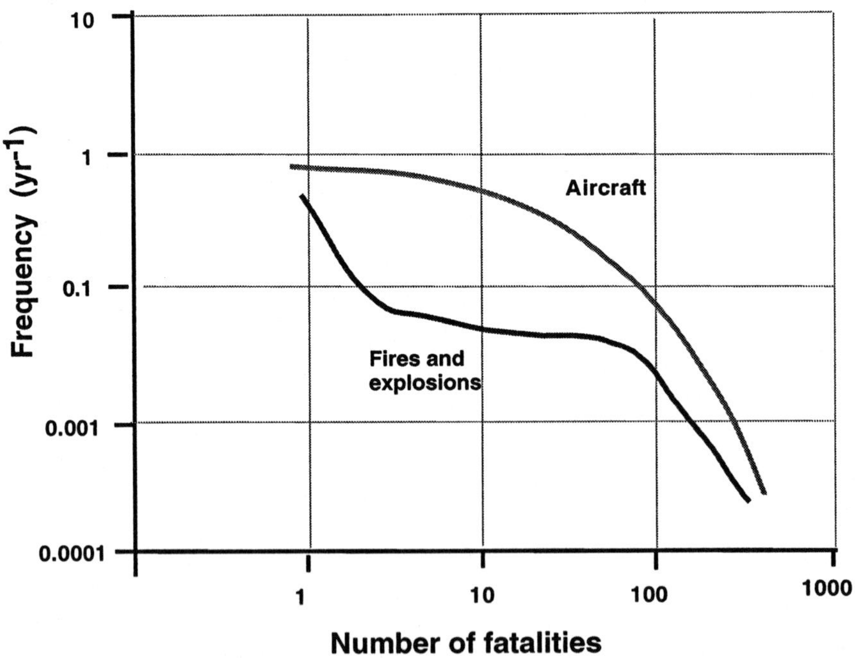

Figure 8.7 *Man-made accidents. A plot of severity versus frequency of events with at least this severity for two types of disaster. (Note that the measurements along the axes change in powers of 10)*

Although the relationship between frequency and severity follows general trends it is not always easy to make exact predictions even where there is a lot of data. Moreover since most data will be about people or money, an assessment will have to be made about the relationship with the fate of inanimate and individual historic objects. People in aircraft are not packed as carefully as art objects, fires kill people by asphyxiation as well as incineration. Figure 8.7 shows the relationship between the number of people killed in individual accidents (severity) and the frequency of accidents that caused in excess of that number of fatalities (Health and Safety Executive, 1989). Both curves slope downwards, which is reasonable since we might expect that accidents involving large numbers of people would happen less frequently than those involving smaller numbers. However, the two curves do not have the same shape and so we have to be careful about choosing a simple model to decide on average probabilities of catastrophic events.

Dealing with insufficient data

The probabilities of catastrophic incidents are revised every time a new one occurs. The next earthquake might be the record breaker. A giant meteor has not struck London recently. Where there have not been enough occurrences to build up a reasonable picture, there are several possible solutions.

The first, event tree analysis requires some knowledge of the mechanisms by which disasters happen. It is assumed that some chain of small events, each with its own probability, will eventually lead to what is recognized as a disaster. Fault tree and consequence analysis methods are variations on this simple model (Lieberman 1976). The system was developed to assess the safety of nuclear reactors at a time when there had been no disasters. The few problems that have happened since have helped to refine the data used in the model. With enough knowledge about mechanisms it can be used for any event, natural or man-made. In form it is identical to a multi-stage decision tree where each event has a probability of good or poor outcome (Figure 8.8). The probability of each stage is judged by experts in that particular field. The use of experts will be discussed in Chapter 17.

If some data is available, assumptions can be made about the distribution of further data points. In drug testing, where it may not be possible to study a large population over a number of years, until some undesirable side effect shows up, the 'rule of three' has been proposed (Urquhart, 1987). This states that if there are zero adverse events in n patient-years of treatment, one may have 95% confidence that the annual risk of an adverse event is less than 1 in $n/3$.

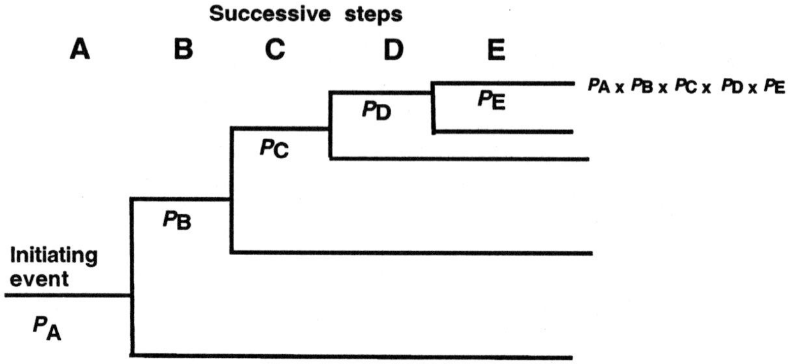

Figure 8.8 *Event tree for an accident resulting from five successive dependent steps. The probability of the final state is given by the product of the probabilities of each stage*

Extreme Value Theory (EVT) is a statistical discipline aimed at estimating the magnitude of the largest possible damaging event from a small data set that may not include this maximum (Matthews, 1996). Predictions that were previously thought to need billions of data points can be achieved with just a few hundred.

Something to think about

Is it easier to use proportionate loss or absolute loss for the one plane/two plane scenario?

What is the most extreme damaging incident that could happen to your collection? What chain of events would be necessary for this to occur? How likely is it?

References

Benarie, M. (1991) The Establishment and Use of Damage Functions. Science, Technology and European Cultural Heritage. Proceedings of the European Symposium, Bologna, Italy, 13–16 June 1989. Butterworth-Heinemann for the Commission of the European Communities, p. 214.

Canadian Museum of Nature (1995) Assessing and Managing Risks to Your Collections. UKIC Natural Sciences Section. Museums Association Annual Conference, Leicester.

Health and Safety Executive (1989) *Quantified Risk Assessment: Its Input into Decision Making*. HMSO, London. ISBN 0-11-885499-2.

Lieberman, Gerald J. (1976) Fault-Tree Analysis as an Example of Risk Methodology, in *Energy and the Environment: A Risk Benefit Approach*. Pergamon Press. ISBN 0-08-020873-8.

Matthews, Robert (1996) Far Out Forecasting. *New Scientist*, No. 2051, October, pp. 37–40.

Michalski, S. (1994) A Systematic Approach to Preservation: Description and Integration with Other Museum Activities. Preventive Conservation: Practice, Theory and Research. Preprints to the Ottawa Congress, 12–16 September. IIC, pp. 8–11.

Urquhart, J. (1987) Perception of Risk, in *Medicines and Risk/Benefit Decisions: Proceedings of Centre for Medicine Workshop* 1/10/85. MTP Press. ISBN 0-85200-978-X.

Waller, Robert (1994) Conservation Risk Assessment: A Strategy for Managing Resources for Preventive Conservation. Preventive Conservation: Practice, Theory and Research. Preprints to the Ottawa Congress, 12–16 September. IIC, pp. 12–17.

9 Big trouble

This is the first of three chapters dealing with the risks to objects that are just sitting still, waiting to be used. Events and activities outside the museum can have noticeable effects on the collections within. Apart from the immediate damage caused by the release of energy from explosions, earthquakes or torrential rain, there are secondary economic effects of disasters which may affect preservation in the long term. Although managers of collections may not be able to alter the probability of large-scale disasters, there are often simple ways of limiting the extent of damage. Although the probability of smaller internally generated occurrences such as floods and fires cannot be totally eliminated they can be minimized by preventive measures.

Disaster

When a great deal of property is suddenly damaged and large numbers of people are killed and injured, this is called a disaster. Where people and property are destroyed there is a strong chance that items of cultural heritage will also be lost. Statistics about disasters as they affect 'the world's most vulnerable people' are published by the International Federation of Red Cross and Red Crescent Societies (International Federation, 1997). Fires and floods, generated within museums and libraries can cause considerable loss of material without physical injury to humans.

The rapid onset of disaster is attractive to the news media because there is an opportunity to be first on the scene, to show the destruction and grief, and to reassure the viewers that it didn't happen to them. Then, if there is no one handy to blame, it's easy to move on to another story. There is no doubt that rapid onset damage is a bad thing, but it should always be borne in mind that quick and noticeable change may not reflect the greatest long-term risk. Slow attrition is not newsworthy. Ninety per cent of people die from common medical disorders, only 3% die in any sort of accident (Smith 1992, p. 3). Only large or local accidents make the news.

There has been growing conservation interest in disasters over the past 20 years. There are two main thrusts to this interest. The first is the need for thorough documentation (Thornes, 1995). This ensures that even if the object is lost, knowledge about its appearance and relevance may be preserved. There is also the hope that the information can be used to regroup objects that have been dispersed, or reconstruct objects that have been damaged. The process of documentation may also include some assessment of vulnerability and value, basic elements of a risk assessment (Fielden, 1987). The second theme is that the amount of damage can be substantially reduced if preventive measures are taken beforehand and procedures are in place for dealing with the aftermath. The documentation, the mitigation measures and the salvage planning all take time and money. This cost has to be weighed against the risk of the disaster and against the need for measures to prevent more reliable hazards.

Although disasters happen suddenly, their effects last for a much longer period. The true cost of the event may not be known for many years afterwards. Estimates of total cost are necessary for evaluation of risk. Figure 9.1 shows that following a catastrophe there may be up to four waves of activity before the affected location is back on its previous path of development. Each wave represents an input of time and money, and each new burst of effort takes considerably longer

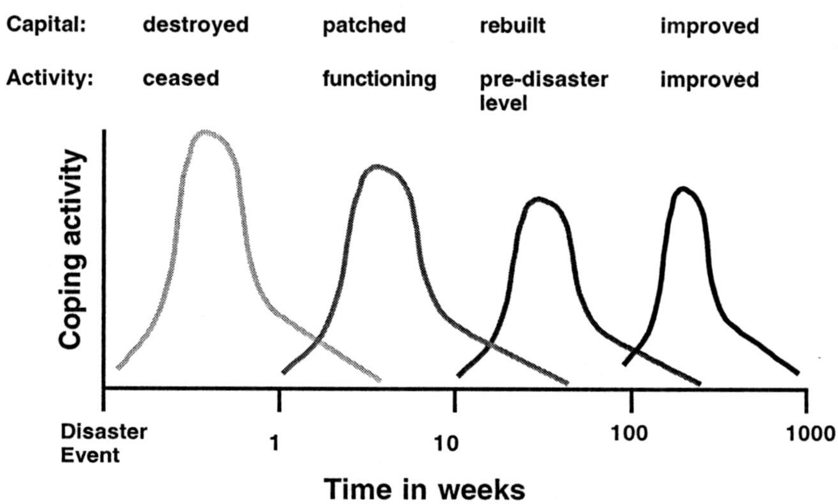

Figure 9.1 *Four stages of coping with the effects of a disaster. Note that the scale is logarithmic so each stage takes 10 times longer than the last (after Haas in Smith, 1992)*

than the last. Until the final phase there is the additional opportunity cost of not getting on with business (Smith, 1992, p. 71).

The effects of disasters are dependent on the economic ability to cope and to recover, especially if faced with repeat events. If you are still recovering from the first disaster you have no time or money to invest in preventive measures to limit the effects of the second. This means that the effects of disaster are far more devastating in less developed countries, which brings a political element to the study of disaster. For an excellent introduction to the political implications and interpretations of disaster you should read Keith Smith's *Environmental Hazards – Assessing Risk and Avoiding Disaster.* Many of the charts and statistics in this chapter are derived from it. These global observations about the relationships between wealth and ability to cope can be scaled down to the level of individual collections in individual countries.

Disasters that affect historic collections can be divided into two categories: those where the managers of the collection could not be expected to influence the probability of occurrence and those where they could (Table 9.1).

In all cases museum staff could be expected to limit the extent of the damage if the risk were thought to be severe enough.

Table 9.1

Management can't affect probability:

- War
- Terrorism
- Pollution
- Global warming
- Earthquakes
- Tidal waves
- Volcanic eruptions
- Hurricanes
- Tornadoes
- Bad weather
- Sea and river floods
- Nuclear meltdown
- Falling space junk

Management can affect probability:

- Fire
- Floods from roof and plumbing leaks
- Vandalism
- Theft
- Pest infestation

War, terrorism and political unrest

War can be seen as a continuing series of disasters. It therefore provides good examples of the secondary effects of catastrophic events. Even when the first phase of physical damage is over (Figure 9.2), there are economic considerations that may work against the preservation of historic objects. The breakdown of law and order will allow looting and the development of organized crime. The necessity to invest in rebuilding and economic recovery will draw central resources away from 'non-essential' activities. Many conflicts are aimed at eliminating the ruling élite. Preservation of the past is a minority interest with a strong relationship to the rich and powerful. With the dominant interest removed, other forces of dispersal and neglect will come into play.

The effects of the primary event, the conflict, are not random. There is a high probability that damage will occur to objects of high value. Historic buildings which are meant to be protected by international convention become the targets of war, because of the high value placed on them by the local populace. Museums that represent the national pride of one ethnic group may be destroyed as another group temporarily assumes power (Weill, 1995). Works that represent the religious values of one group may be defaced or destroyed in campaigns of 'cultural cleansing'. Museums, monasteries and religious shrines in Cambodia were deliberately destroyed by the Khmer Rouge. More than 60 churches were destroyed in the war between Croatia and Serbia. Nearly 1500 mosques were damaged during the conflict in Bosnia (Thornes, 1995, p. 9).

The international conventions that are supposed to regulate the effect of warring factions on the cultural heritage and their obvious limitations were discussed at a conference on risk preparedness held in Kobe, Japan (Clement, 1997; Phares, 1997).

Protecting historic artifacts in times of war has a high cost, at a time when political pressure may give higher priority to the war effort. Attempts at damage limitation may be foiled by those you thought were on your side if they feel their need for materials is greater than yours (Asmar, 1995).

There have been studies of the frequency of 'deadly quarrels' which indicate that half of all the revolts and civil wars between 1825 and 1945 broke out within 23.5 years of the establishment of a government that was intended to form a common bond of peace (Benarie and Druzik, 1992). This means that in some politically unstable areas the cycle of destruction and repair of monuments could be less than a quarter of a century. It is less than 60 years since London was under threat of annihilation by high-explosive ballistic missiles from another part of Europe. The dream of eternal peace based on the economic unity and central administration of Europe is not four decades old.

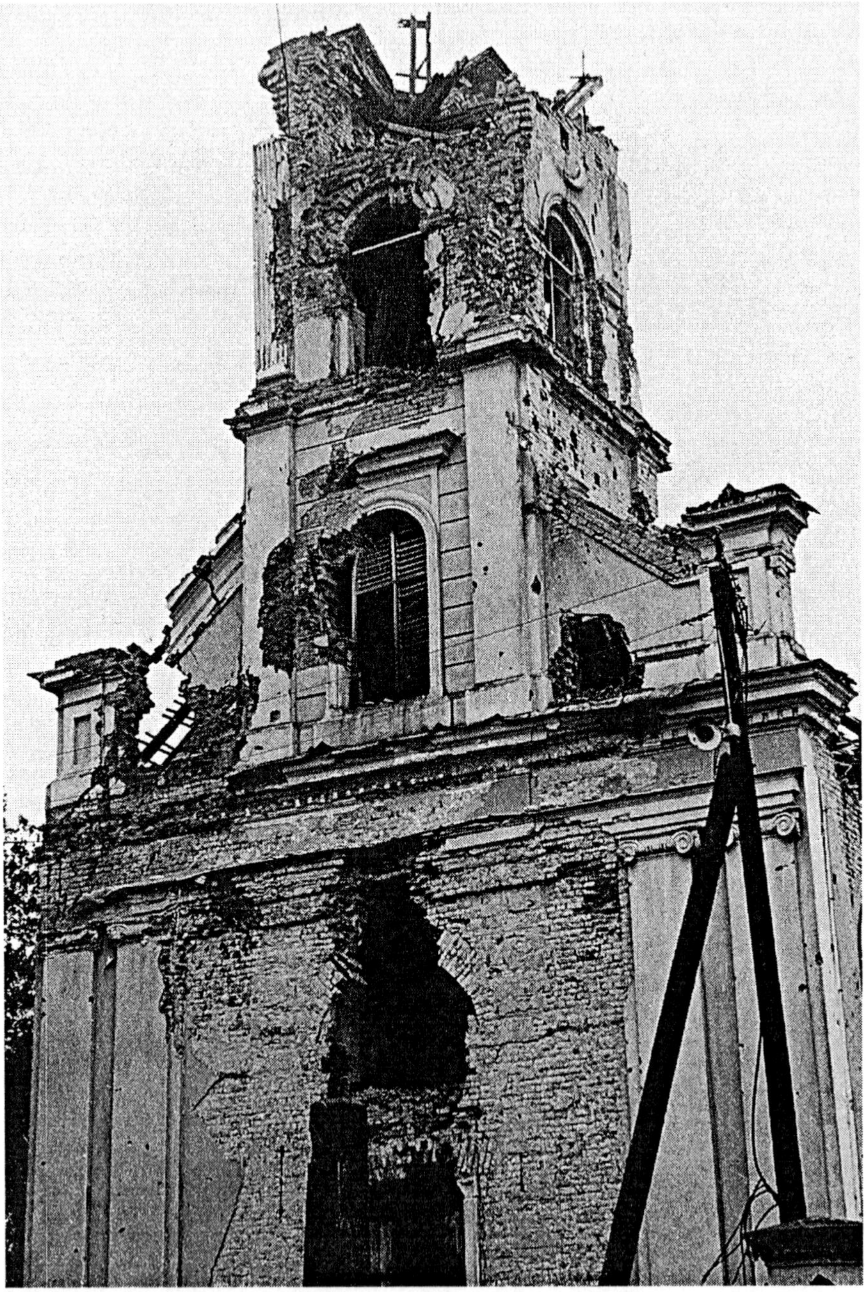

Figure 9.2 *Parish Church of St Vendelin the Monk, Jarmina, Croatia: Obvious physical damage caused by armed conflict in Croatia. The loss of a place of worship has more than immediate physical consequences (Courtesy: Agency for the Protection of Cultural Heritage, Ministry of Culture, Republic of Croatia)*

Table 9.2 *Number of major armed conflicts by type*

	1990		*1991*		*1992*		*1993*		*1994*		*1995*		*1996*	
	G	*T*	*G*	*T*	*G*	*T*	*G*	*T*	*G*	*T*	*G*	*T*	*G*	*T*
Europe	–	1	–	2	–	4	–	6	–	5	–	3	–	2
Middle East	1	4	2	5	2	3	2	4	2	4	2	4	2	4
Asia	5	10	3	8	4	9	4	7	4	7	4	8	4	7
Africa	8	3	8	3	6	1	6	1	6	1	5	1	5	1
Americas	4	–	4	–	3	–	3	–	3	–	3	–	3	–

G = attempt to change government system.
T = attempt to change control over territory.

The causes and effects of armed conflicts around the world are collated by the Department of Peace and Conflict Research of Uppsala University, Sweden, and published in its annual report 'States in Armed Conflict' (International Federation, 1997, p. 135). Data from these reports was used to compile Table 9.2.

Where the historic treasure is not destroyed it may be confiscated. UNESCO was notified of the loss of thousands of cultural objects from Kuwait during the Gulf War. Nazis carried out organized looting in occupied Europe and the Red Army took works of art from Germany to Russia. Political change without conflict may be enough to increase rates of theft. Figure 9.3 shows the increase in thefts from historic and cultural

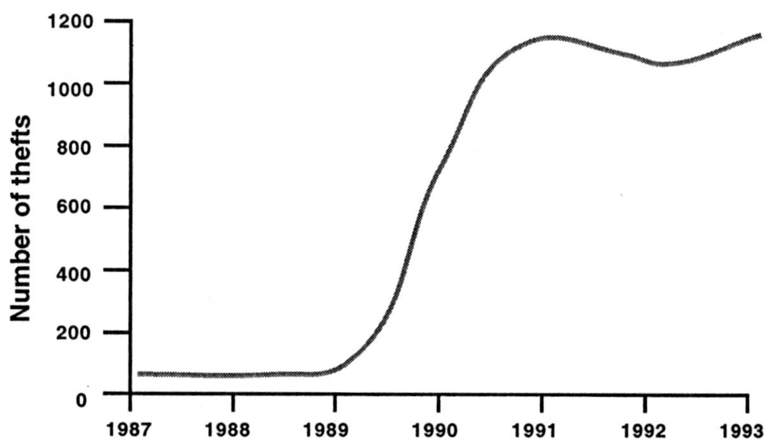

Figure 9.3 *Fewer border restrictions and the need for hard currency caused a dramatic increase in the number of thefts from Czech churches, castles and museums*

sites in Czechoslovakia over a period of six years of political upheaval in Eastern Europe (Jirásek, 1995).

Terrorism is a form of warfare. Because museums are linked to the minority establishment, they have become targets for terrorist attacks. In May 1993 a car bomb killed five people and destroyed several artworks in the Uffizi Gallery, Florence. Cultural property in London has been both the deliberate and the accidental victim of terrorist attacks. At the time of writing there is still a state of 'war' between republican factions in Eire and the government of Britain.

Man-made and natural disasters

Although there are some catalogues of the destruction to cultural property caused by recent conflicts in Eastern Europe (Informatica Museologica, 1993), I have not come across any systematic attempt to document and cost the effects of disasters on museum collections. A general overview with some dramatic examples is given by Robert Adams in his book *The Lost Museum* (Adams, 1980). And in an attempt to raise awareness about potential destruction from rapid onset events Norbert Baer gives a short selection of examples ranging from the flood at Corning Museum of Glass to the fire at the National Academy of Sciences Library in Russia (Baer and Siena, 1989). We are still left with trying to interpret information derived for other purposes. However, some of this can help get some sense of proportion about disaster.

Figures 9.4 and 9.5 show the severity of accidents/disasters in the US, measured as dead people or property damage in dollars, plotted against the annual frequency. The main message of these two graphs is that natural hazards are substantially more frequent and more damaging than those caused by man (Lieberman, 1979). Nature still has more energy at her disposal. Man-caused disasters frequently occur in relatively localized areas where there is a concentration of industrial plant. As a generalization such locations are less likely to have major holdings of historic artifacts. Some of the greater man-caused disasters such as the chemical leak at Bhopal in 1984, although devastating to humans, would have little effect on inanimate objects.

Which of the natural hazards is the most frequent or damaging can be judged from the list in Table 9.3. This shows the number of disasters that occurred globally between 1947 and 1981. In this instance disaster is defined as an incident that caused greater than 100 dead or greater than \$1 million damage (2.8 million in 1981 \$) (Thompson, 1982).

Not all of these would necessarily destroy historic objects or monuments but the top four, which account for nearly 80% of incidents, definitely have the power and occur in the right locations. Some further

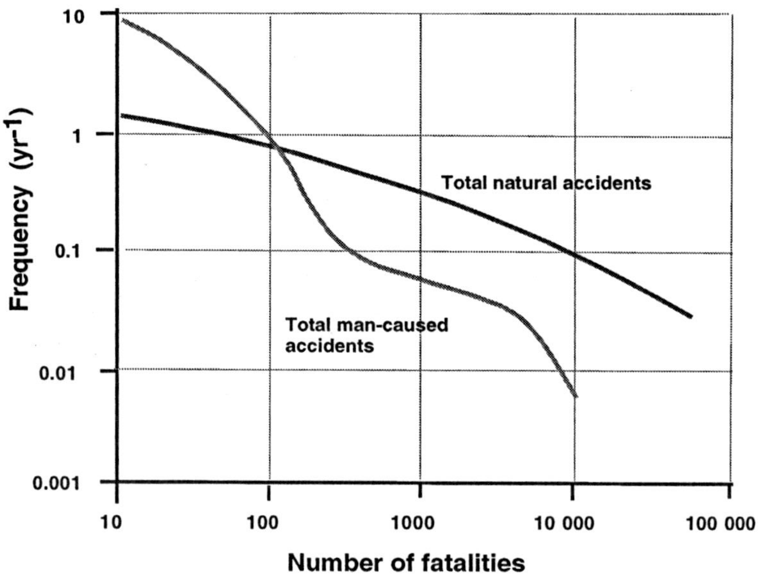

Figure 9.4 *Severity of natural and man-caused accidents, measured as number of deaths, plotted against the annual frequency of incidents in which this number or greater are killed (after Lieberman)*

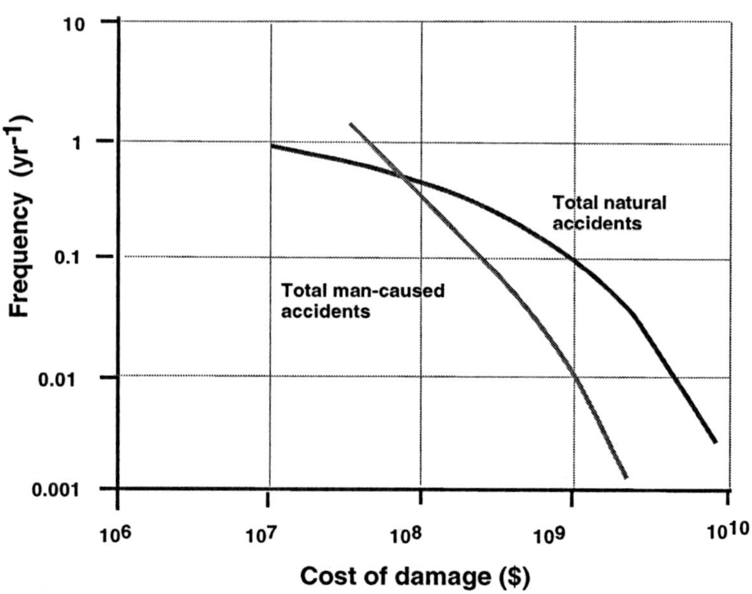

Figure 9.5 *Severity of natural and man-caused accidents, measured as damage to property in $, plotted against the annual frequency of incidents in which this cost is equalled or exceeded (after Lieberman)*

Table 9.3 *Global disasters 1947–81*

Agent	*Number*	*Percentage*
Flood	343	32
Hurricane	211	20
Earthquakes	161	15
Tornadoes	127	12
Snowstorms	40	
Thunderstorms	36	
Landslides	29	
Rainstorm	29	
Heatwave	22	
Volcano	18	
Coldwave	17	
Avalanche	12	
Tsunami	10	
Fog	3	
Frost	2	
Sandstorm	2	

Table 9.4

Hazard	*Annual rate per 1000 households*
Floods	3.4
Hurricanes/tropical storms	3.4
Tornadoes/windstorms	10.0
Earthquakes	1.8

evidence about the frequency of such events can be found in Table 9.4 which lists annual rates of selected natural hazards causing injury or property damage in US households in the period 1970–80.

There are different probabilities of the various hazards in different parts of the US: the annual death risk from earthquake in California is much the same as that for tornadoes in the Mid-West (1 in 500 000). However, the overall picture is that wind and water are more frequent causes of damage than earthquakes. The severities of hurricanes and earthquakes are of the same order. Tornadoes, although more frequent, are more localized and have severities one or two orders of magnitude lower.

A Canadian study has taken a more local look at disaster (Hewitt and Burton, 1971). In this instance disaster was defined as more than 10 dead or more than half a million dollars damage. Events occurring over a 10-year period were recorded for 57 cities each with around 200 000 inhabitants. There were 35 incidents, 18 man-made, 17 natural. This suggests that in a small city an incident severe enough to take out 0.005% of the population in a newsworthy fashion occurs every 16 years. At a rough guess this means that substantial damage to something of local historical or artistic interest in one of these cities might occur about once in 200 years.

Global warming and ozone depletion

Atmospheric pollution, one of the by-products of the civilized world, is responsible for destroying many of the symbols of civilization. The effect of acid gases on objects made of stone, metal and paper will be discussed in the next chapter. Although the attrition is very obvious it is too slow to make a good news story. However, it appears that civilization is responsible for altering the atmosphere in ways that may eventually cause damage in more catastrophic fashion. Global warming caused by the release of 'greenhouse gases' may affect weather patterns and sea-level in ways that could have devastating impact (Barrow, 1991). For a rational argument that dissociates the currently observed changes in climate with the postulated cause of 'the greenhouse effect' read Nigel Calder's *The Manic Sun* (Calder, 1997).

The average prediction for increase in temperature is that it will be about 2°C warmer in 30–40 years' time. Winters in high Northern latitudes could be 6°C warmer. It is predicted that northern summers will become drier and the winters wetter. Increased rainfall is predicted for India, the Middle East and both coasts of the US. Although the general effect would lead to less water flowing in most rivers, increased flow is predicted for the Blue Nile in Africa, the Mekong in Indochina and the Brahmaputra in India.

Predictions for rise in sea-level have varied between 30 cm and 3 m; an average of 65 cm by the year 2030 was widely accepted in the late 1980s. In the mid-1990s, despite vehement lobbying from the producers of fossil fuel and consistent reappraisal by scientists, the Intergovernmental Panel on Climate Change was still predicting between 20 cm and 1 m by the year 2100 (Schneider, 1997). The minimum of 20 cm relates to the agreed observation that the sea-level has been increasing by 2 mm a year for several decades. Table 9.5 lists regions that are vulnerable to a moderate rise (0.5–1.5 m). Any rise makes an area more susceptible to tidal surges or exceptional storms. One flood can do the necessary damage, you don't

Table 9.5 *Areas vulnerable to moderate sea-level change*

Coastal areas on North Sea: Netherlands, London, Hamburg
Lowlands around the Baltic
Lowlands around deltas in the Mediterranean: Nile, Po, Rhône and of course Venice
Ebro Estuary, Gulf of Cadiz in the Iberian Peninsula
Mississippi delta, Louisiana
Eastern Seaboard of the US: Boston at risk if only 50 cm
Parts of Florida
Bangladesh: Ganges–Brahmaputra–Meghna delta
Coastal lowlands of China
Huanghe delta

have to wait until you are permanently under the sea. Some land masses are sinking relative to a stationary sea level, the east coast of the US is sinking at a rate of 2 mm a year. If you are looking at the risk to your institution over the next century it doesn't matter what you believe about the cause of the present rise in sea-level, you just need to know whether it is likely to affect you.

Even where there are no historic monuments or artifacts in direct danger, the economic impact on the country would have secondary effects on the care of cultural property. In some areas such as Bangladesh and Egypt many tens of millions of people would have to be evacuated. It has been speculated that a sea-level rise of 1.4 m would have a devastating effect on food supplies to about one-fifth of the world's population. This could lead to political instability and possible armed conflict.

One really good war, especially one involving nuclear weapons, could throw enough dirt into the air to counter the effect of greenhouse gases for many decades.

The major effect of pollution on depletion of stratospheric ozone has been the appearance of a definite 'hole in the ozone layer' over the antarctic. However, reductions of up to 6% in ozone concentrations have been noticed in the northern hemisphere as far south as Nottingham in the UK. The major effect of stratospheric ozone depletion is the increase in UV radiation reaching the lower atmosphere. The possible results of this are greater concentrations of ground level ozone and other constituents of phototochemical smogs which may cause damage to art objects (Druzik, Stulik, Preusser and Cass, 1991). The increased UV radiation will also increase deterioration of outdoor structures using polymeric materials such as paint, plastics and wood.

Secondary effects will be pressure on the economy caused by reduced crop levels, increased cancers and increased greenhouse effect.

Rising water tables

The London *Evening Standard* of 13 August 1997 carried the headline 'London facing flood menace'. Despite a succession of dry summers London's water table is rising by about 3 metres a year. The stability of high-rise buildings is at risk, and underground carparks, the underground railway, and domestic basements are threatened. British Telecom's communication systems are also under threat.

Given the serious and powerful concerns who approached the Deputy Prime Minister with this news it must be taken seriously, but there is no simple way of predicting its effect on museum collections.

Earthquakes

Although bad weather may cause just as much damage as earthquakes there appears to be something more fascinating about the ground shaking than the skies opening. There are several reasons why this might be the case. Earthquakes don't move around like storms do and their magnitude is fairly easy to measure, so they are more easily subjected to statistical and scientific analysis. Everyone has suffered from bad weather at some stage, earthquakes are a bit more exotic. One of the world's major conservation research centres, and a notorious art museum of the same name, are in a seismically active zone. Whatever the reason there is considerable conservation interest in controlling the effects of earthquakes on museum collections. With increasing demands for objects to travel to the US and to Japan it is necessary for museum staff from seismically safe areas to understand the risks and some of the mitigation measures. Safe is a relative term; in 1990 there was a shock registering 5.2 on the Richter scale in Shropshire, the second earthquake of this magnitude in the UK this century (Stewart, 1990)!

The areas that are subject to earthquakes are well charted (Ganse and Nelson, 1981). In some areas the degree of knowledge is quite detailed and is available in the form of risk maps where areas of different predicted seismic intensity are superimposed on city street maps. Many of these are available on-line (ABAG, NCEDC). Most serious earthquakes occur on known faultlines which are near the boundaries of tectonic plates. About one in a thousand large earthquakes are some way from the major faultlines, e.g. Lisbon 1755, New Madrid, Missouri 1811 (Tazieff, 1989).

The intensity of earthquakes is measured in several ways. The scale most popularly recognized is the Richter scale which is continuous, theoretically running from plus infinity to minus infinity. Every 0.2 increase on the scale represents a doubling of the energy released at the source. Zero was the weakest tremor that could be measured at the time that the scale was proposed. Nothing above Magnitude 9 has been measured yet.

An alternative scale measures not the energy of the quake but its observable effect. The MSK (Medvedev, Shebalin and Karnik) scale or the Modified Mercali scale measure damage in discontinuous steps given the roman numerals from I to XII. Intensity VI is sufficient for books to fall from shelves, pictures to fall from walls and furniture to be overturned. Level IX is called 'highly destructive', strong enough for reinforced concrete structures to crack and underground pipes to burst. Several well-known earthquakes such as Agadir 1960, Mexico 1985, and Armenia 1989 where there was large loss of life were all rated IX on this scale. Level XI is termed 'disaster', where very few structures are left standing and XII, 'major disaster', where there are large-scale changes to ground structure, lakes burst their banks and rivers change course. Since the scale refers to observed effects and does not rely on measuring equipment it can be used to assess the magnitude of historic events. Although France and Switzerland are not noted for earthquakes, contemporary records suggest that the incidents in Basel in 1356 and Nice in 1564 were of scale X–XI.

The damaging effects are caused not only by shaking, falling or being struck but also from subsequent fires. In the 1906 San Francisco quake 80% of damage was caused by fire. In more recent incidents fires have been started from fractured gas pipes and have been more difficult to extinguish because water pipes were also broken. Other secondary hazards are soil liquefaction, landslides, avalanches and tidal waves. If tidal waves occur in the sea they are often referred to as tsunami, if they occur on lakes they are called seiches. A Richter scale 7 shock can generate a wave 1–1.5 m high. Scale 8 can cause waves 4–6 m in height, and magnitude 8.25 can cause 12 m waves.

Some feeling for the probability and severity of earthquakes can be gathered from Table 9.6.

The vulnerability of different building structures is well studied and is explained in highly technical texts (e.g. Koridze, 1988, 1990) or in more readable form (Levy and Salvadori, 1997). If the building that surrounds a collection of objects does not catch fire or collapse, then the risks are due to the objects moving or other loose items striking the objects. The effect of an earthquake is often measured in terms of the peak acceleration that

Table 9.6 *Frequency and effects of earthquakes*

Richter magnitude	*Global frequency number per year*	*US West Coast per 100 yrs*	*Period of ground shake (seconds)*	*Radius of strong shaking (km)*
8	1	1	30–90	80–160
7	15	12	20–50	50–120
6	140	80	10–30	20–80
5	900	400	10–30	20–80
4	8000	2000	0–5	0–15

the object suffers as the ground vibrates. There are vertical and horizontal components to the acceleration which are normally measured in multiples of the acceleration due to gravity, shown[1] by the symbol G. The horizontal acceleration necessary to cause an object to overturn (Barov, 1994) is given by the equation:

$$G = \frac{D}{2H_{cg}} \qquad (9.1)$$

where D is the diameter of the base of the object and H_{cg} is the height of its centre of gravity above the base.

The acceleration that will cause an object to slide horizontally is given by the equation:

$$G = \mu \qquad (9.2)$$

where μ is the conventional symbol for the coefficient of friction. For the materials of which shelves, floors and objects in museums are normally made of μ has values of 0.2–1.0.

Peak horizontal accelerations are quite small, 0.06 G for a scale VI event up to 0.6 G for scale X. However, there is no simple relationship and accelerations up to 0.8 G have been recorded for quite weak tremors.

For a theoretical object shaped like a uniform block or column, the height of the centre of gravity will be exactly half the height of the object. The acceleration needed to tip the object is the same as the ratio of the

[1] When discussing acceleration in the context of earthquakes and transport (Chapter 14) I shall use the symbol upper case G to represent multiples of the acceleration due to gravity. This avoids confusion with lower case g which is a measurement of mass in the SI system.

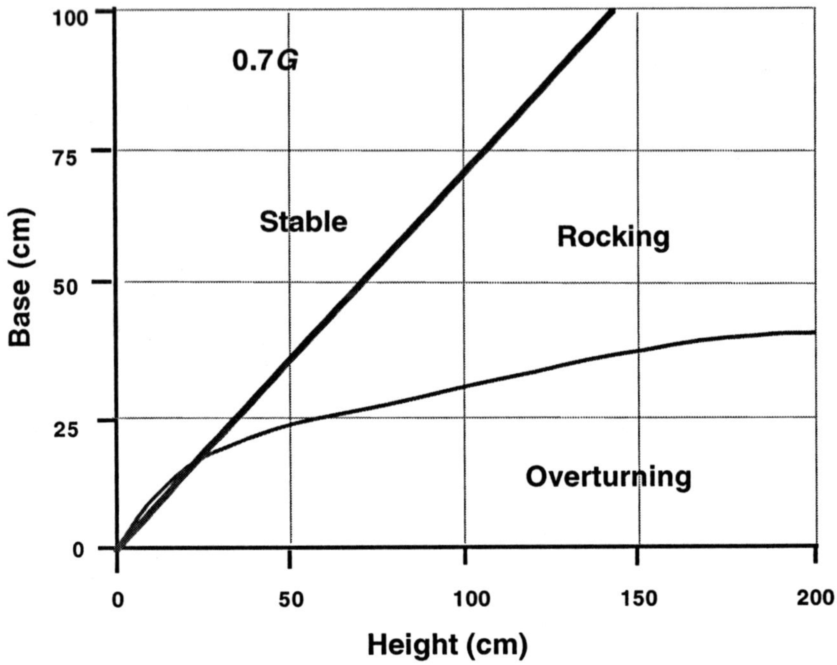

Figure 9.6 *Stability of a uniformly shaped object to a peak horizontal acceleration of 0.7*G *dictated by the ratio of base width to height. Objects with heights greater than 1.4 × the base width are not stable*

base to the height. If the height is twice the diameter of the base, an acceleration of 0.5 *G* could cause the object to topple. The object will certainly rock. Whether it will actually fall over will depend on other factors such as the duration and frequency of shaking. The stability of objects with different base/height ratios is shown graphically in Figure 9.6 (Podany, 1995).

More complex objects require more complex mathematics but the principles are the same. Podany gives several examples of calculations for different shapes of object which are treated as being constructed from a number of simple geometric shapes. The vulnerability of large structures can be studied using computer modelling techniques such as the Finite Element Method and the Distinct Element Method (Verdel, 1994).

Peak vertical accelerations may be as high as 2 *G*. At 1 *G* an unsecured object leaves the ground. Hanging fixtures must be strong enough to support an object that suddenly behaves as if it were twice its normal weight.

Mitigation measures can be simple and unobtrusive. There are two basic approaches. The first is to lower the centre of gravity by adding weight (lead shot in the base of a vessel) or by securing to a heavy plinth. The second, which is appropriate for tall, massive objects such as a sculpture, is to isolate the object from the ground, so that the ground moves back and forth leaving the object effectively unmoved until the shaking has stopped. A variety of isolation methods have been devised (Agabian, Ginell, Masri and Nigbor, 1991; Haak, 1994). Small amounts of wax or mastic under the base can prevent objects such as vases slipping, overturning or lifting (Barov, 1994). Unnecessary damage can be prevented by securing storage cupboards, and firmly fixing lighting and display fittings so that they do not fall on to objects. Although there is nothing that can be done to alter the probability of an earthquake, a considerable amount can be done to limit the extent to which it causes damage. To calculate risk as discussed in the last chapter you would need to know whether any of these simple steps had been taken if you wanted to avoid an overestimate.

Bad weather

The frequency of natural disasters appears to be increasing. This may be a question of detection or definition or it may be a real effect. Certainly the economic losses due to natural disasters were about three times greater in 1990 than in 1960 (Smith, 1992, p. 36). At the same time related deaths appear to be decreasing, which suggests that forecasting and preventive measures have improved.

According to the team of scientists at Colorado State University Atmospheric Science Department, who underestimated the number of Atlantic hurricanes by 25% in 1996. 'A new era of hurricane-spawned destruction appears to be approaching' (45-year averages for the American Atlantic coast are: 5.7 hurricanes, 9.3 named storms, 46 named storm days, 25 hurricane days (International Federation 1997, p. 83)).

It is now fashionable to blame bad weather anywhere in the world on El Niño. This phenomenon in the Pacific Ocean has caused storms in Santa Monica and failed monsoons across Asia. An equivalent but less romantically named phenomenon is observed in the Atlantic Ocean. Its title, the North Atlantic Oscillation, contains a reminder that, like El Niño, it is cyclic. Things may be getting worse at the moment but will not necessarily continue to do so (Morton, 1998).

Figure 9.7 shows how the number of deaths from tornadoes in the US has declined whereas the number of cases where the damage was above a certain monetary threshold has increased. The same pattern is seen for hurricane damage in the coastal states. However, deaths from floods appear to follow the trends of economic losses.

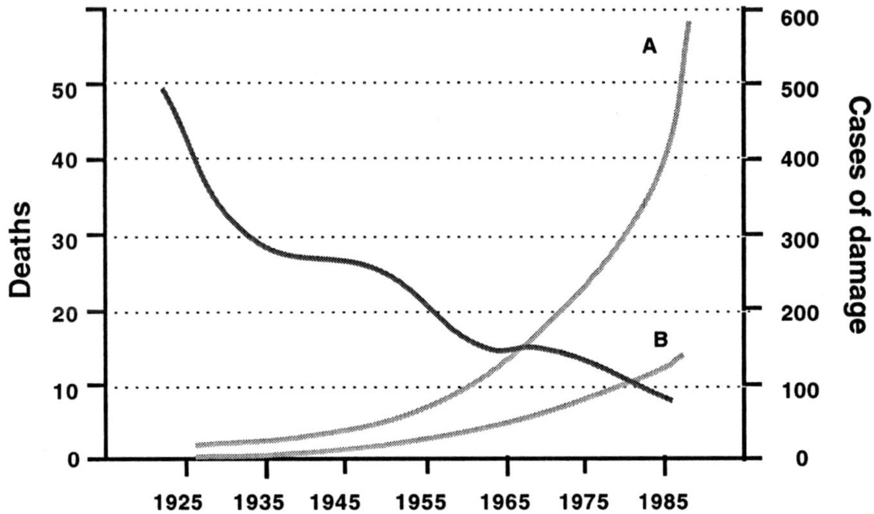

Figure 9.7 *The different trends in numbers of damaging incidents (light grey lines) caused by tornadoes and the number of deaths caused (dark line). Deaths in each decade (ending in the year marked) as number per million population in the 25 worst affected states of America. Number of incidents per decade causing more than $0.5–5 million damage (A) and greater than $5 million (B) (after Riebsame, Diaz, Moses and Price in Smith, 1992)*

Since people are more mobile, and have a stronger sense of self-preservation than historic or artistic objects, it is likely that the risks to collections should be predicted from the trends for damage to property rather than loss of life. However, the knowledge that the building of the Thames Barrier has reduced the annual death risk from 1 in 40 000 to less than 1 in a million can be taken as an indicator of reduced risk for collections in low lying areas of London.

Despite the reputation of England's weather it is usually quite benign. Very localized damage from extreme weather is not uncommon, there were 414 tornadoes in the UK between 1901 and 1975. However, every century or so there are 'great storms' which do considerable damage over widespread areas. The storm of November 1703 uprooted 10 000 trees and destroyed 14 000 houses, killing 8000 people. The storm of October 1987 destroyed 15 million trees but killed only 13.

Things falling out of the sky

If you fly into Heathrow Airport from Europe you are often afforded a beautiful aerial view of the V&A Museum. Conversely if you stand at the main entrance of the V&A you can see these huge passenger jets crawling slowly overhead as they cover the last few miles to the airport. What is the chance that a plane or part of one will land on the museum? About 65% of aircraft accidents actually occur at the airport (Laudan, 1994), so that reduces the risk a bit. People and museum objects have chosen to cluster under the Heathrow flight path. Since there is no early warning mechanism to reduce the risk to humans we can assume that the risks to the museum and the local population are of the same order. The annual risk of dying from anything falling on you is around 1 in 100 000. The annual risk of dying from an aircraft landing on you in the UK is around 1 in 50 million (five times better than in the US). Whatever logic you use to apply this countrywide average figure to a specific location it is unlikely you would come up with an annual probability greater than 10^{-5} of parts of a plane causing damage to some part of the collection.

The annual risk of death by meteorite is less than 10^{-9}.

Bad plumbing

The worst flood at the V&A in my memory was caused by a faulty temporary water main. Objects were stored in a basement which rapidly filled up with water. This flood was sufficiently interesting to get on national television. At a meeting of the Heads of Conservation of the National Collections a short while later, I learned that there had been smaller floods in three other London institutions within the same week which had not become public knowledge. Within the past 20 years I can recall at least five 'floods' at the V&A where objects were damaged or endangered. These were caused by burst pipes, badly fitted radiators or overtaxed rainwater pipes. Objects on walls suffered as badly as objects in cases.

It is apparent that small floods in museums are highly probable. The total annual risk caused by small incidents involving water is probably much greater than that from the grand flood that we like to imagine when preparing our disaster reaction scenarios.

The best preventive measures must be better routine maintenance and better supervision of labour. Regular patrols and swift reaction will limit the extent. Simple precautions like storing objects on pallets rather than directly on the floor will help.

Rain by itself is not automatically a hazard. If you know what rainfall to expect you can build guttering and drains to accommodate that volume of water. Disaster can strike if there is suddenly too much rain and the water starts to flow into the gallery or the store. In the UK it is quite common for one month's average rainfall to occur in one day. Once a decade three months' worth of rain can fall in 24 hours (Stirling, 1982). Will the drains cope?

Fire

Small fires in museums are like small floods, the statistic is not recorded. The annual risk of a fire of some sort in a museum may be around 2.4×10^{-5} per square metre (Michalski, 1994). In a museum the size of the V&A this should mean several small fires a year, which is a bit more than my anecdotal memory suggests is the case, but it is not more than an order of magnitude out. All the fires were dealt with quickly and no objects were affected. The distinction between a small fire and a big one may only be a matter of minutes.

The National Fire Protection Association in the US has published the most common causes of fires in museums and libraries (NFPA, 1991). Selected data is shown in Table 9.7. By far the largest impact was from fires caused in suspicious circumstances, 20 times as much damage as those caused by equipment or electrical installation.

Table 9.7 *Causes of fires in US libraries and museums 1980–88*

	Museum %	*Library %*
Electrical distribution	27.5	22.4
Incendiary or suspicious	25.0	46.7
Equipment	12.5	10.0
Smoking	10.0	7.1
Open flame	10.0	6.2
Cooking	7.5	2.9
Child playing	3.8	2.9
Natural causes	3.8	1.9

The preventive measures obviously relate to good security and maintenance. Extent can be controlled by rapid detection and rapid response. Sprinkler systems which used to have a bad press are now fashionable once more for protecting museums and libraries. Concern for the welfare of the planet has stopped the use of halon as a fire suppressant and alternatives are being sought (Roberts, 1993; Lafon, 1994).

Insects

The threat from animal and insect pests is similar to that from fire and flood in that the probability can be reduced by good maintenance

Table 9.8

Pests encountered	*Occurrence % respondents*	*Posing a serious threat % respondents*
Dermestid beetles	45	35
Moths	42	15
Anobiid beetles	40	8
Mites	25	8
Fungi	28	7
Psocids	28	6
Silverfish	25	
Rodents	10	
Tenebrionid beetles	5	
Cockroaches	5	

Table 9.9

	% respondents
Integration of new material	*34*
Ventilation system	*15*
Return of loaned specimens	*5*
Unknown	*36*
Other	*23*

procedures and the extent limited by regular inspection and quick response. Like fire and flood there will always continue to be frequent small incidents which if left unchecked could cause dramatic damage to whole collections. The potential for damage can be deduced from Table 9.8 which is taken from the results of a survey of natural history museums in Great Britain and Ireland (Linnie, 1987).

Some methods of reducing risk are suggested by the suspected cause of infestation (Table 9.9).

Something to think about

Is it fair to use humans as models for object behaviour when talking about the differences between rapid onset events and gradual attrition?

Some of the frequency curves in Figures 8.7 and 9.4 have a fairly flat portion. Why?

Why do natural disasters appear to be on the increase? Will these influences affect the total number of museum objects affected? Do these increases raise the risk for your collection?

References

ABAG Association of Bay Area Governments. http://www.abag.ca.gov

NCEDC http:quake.geo.berkley.edu/

Adams, Robert M. (1980) *The Lost Museum: Glimpses of Vanished Originals*. The Viking Press ISBN 0-670-44107-4.

Asmar, Camille (1995) Protecting Cultural Heritage in a Country at War. *ICOM News*, Vol. 48, p. 10.

Baer, Norbert S. and Slate Siena, Janet (1989) Disaster Planning Initiatives. Professional Notes. *International Journal of Museum Management and Curatorship*, **8**, pp. 105–110.

Barov, Z., Faber, C. and Sennett, R. (1994) The Development of an Earthquake-safe Mounting System for a Collection of Ancient Greek Vases. Preventive Conservation: Practice, Theory and Research. Preprints to the Ottawa Congress, 12–16 September. IIC, pp. 233–237.

Barrow, C.J. (1991) *Land Degradation. Development and Breakdown of Terrestrial Environments*. Cambridge University Press. ISBN 0-521-46615-6.

Benarie, M. and Druzik, J.R. (1992) Entropy and Risk Assessment of Cultural Heritage Conservation. *European Cultural Heritage Newsletter*, Vol. 6, No. 4, pp. 14–17. Quoting Richardson, L.F. (1960) *Statistics of Deadly Quarrels*. The Boxwood Press, Pittsburgh.

Calder, Nigel (1997) *The Manic Sun: Weather Theories Confounded*. Yelvertoft, Pilkington. ISBN 1-899044-11-6.

Clement, M. Etienne (1997) Risk Preparedness and the 1954 Hague Convention for the Protection of Cultural Property in the Event of Armed Conflict. International Symposium on Risk Preparedness for Cultural Properties. Kobe/ Tokyo, January.

Druzik, J.R., Stulik, D.C., Preusser, F. and Cass, G.R. (1991) The Presence and Transport of Ozone in the Museum Environment. Science, Technology and European Cultural Heritage. Proceedings of the European Symposium, Bologna, Italy, 13–16 June 1989, edited by N.S. Baer, C. Sabbioni, A.I. Sors. Butterworth-Heinemann for the Commission of the European Communities. ISBN 0-7506-0237-6, p. 807.

Fielden, Bernard M. (1987) *Between Two Earthquakes: Cultural Property in Seismic Zones*. Getty Conservation Institute. ICCROM. ISBN 0-89236-128-X.

Ganse, R.A. and Nelson, J.B. (1981) Catalog of Significant Earthquakes, 200BC–1979. Report SE-27, NOAA, Boulder, Colorado.

Haak, Wayne R. (1994) Base Isolation System for Large Scale Sculptural Works of Art. First World Conference on Structural Control. Los Angeles.

Hewitt, K. and Burton, I. (1971) The Hazardousness of a Place: a Regional Ecology of Damaging Events. Department of Geography. University of Toronto.

Informatica Museologica (1993) **24** (1–4) Muzejshi Dokumentacioni Centar, Zagreb.

International Federation of Red Cross and Red Crescent Societies (1997) *World Disasters Report*. Oxford University Press. ISBN 0–19–829290–2.

Jirásek, Pavel (1995) Institutions Form Network to Fight Art Theft. *ICOM News*, **48**, p. 8.

Laudan, Larry (1994) *The Book of Risks*. John Wiley and Sons. ISBN 0-471-31034-4.

Lafon, Jacques (1994) Protection des Oeuvres D'Art Contre L'Incendie Par Agent Extincteur Gazeux Inergen. Environnement et Conservation de l'Écrit, de l'Image et du Son. *Actes des Journées Internationales d'Études de l'ARSAG*. Paris. ISSN 0765–0248, pp. 232–242.

Levy, Matthys and Salvadori, Mario (1997) *Why the Earth Quakes*. W.W. Norton and Co., New York/London. ISBN 0-393-31527-4.

Lieberman, Gerald J. (1976) Fault-Tree Analysis as an Example of Risk Methodology, in *Energy and the Environment: A Risk Benefit Approach*. Pergamon Press. ISBN 0-08-020873-8. Quoting: Reactor Safety Study – An Assessment of Accident Risks in US Commercial Nuclear Power Plants. US Atomic Energy Commission, WASH-1400, August 1974.

Linnie, Martyn Joseph (1987) Pest Control: a Survey of Natural History Museums in Great Britain and Ireland. *International Journal of Museum Management and Curatorship*, **6**, pp. 277–290.

Koridze, A. (ed.) (1988) *Seismic Risk Assessment and Design of Building Structures*. Omega Scientific.

Koridze, A. (ed.) (1990) *Earthquake Damage Evaluation and Vulnerability Analysis of Building Structures*. Omega Scientific. ISBN 1-870199-07-3.

Morton, Oliver (1998) The Storm in the Machine. *New Scientist*, No. 2119, pp. 22–26.

NCEDC, North Carolina Earthquake Data Center, http://quake.geo.berkley.edu/

Phares, Joseph (1997) Man-made Disaster and Protection of Cultural Heritage in Lebanon. International Symposium on Risk Preparedness for Cultural Properties. Kobe/Tokyo, January.

Podany, Jerry (1995) The Protection of Cultural Heritage in Museum Collections from Earthquake Damage. The Symposium on the Conservation and Preservation of the Cultural Artefacts. Taipei.

Roberts, Barbara O. (1993) Fire Suppression and Life without Halon. *WAAC Newsletter* (ISSN 1052–066), Vol. 15, May, pp. 31–33.

Schneider, David (1997) The Rising Seas. *Scientific American*, Vol. 276, No. 3, March, pp. 96–100.

Smith, Keith (1992) Environmental Hazards – Assessing Risk and Avoiding Disaster. *Routledge*. ISBN 0-415-01217-1.

Stewart, Ian (1990) Risky Business. *New Scientist: Inside Science*, No. 33.

Stirling, Robin (1982) *The Weather of Britain*. Faber and Faber.

Tazieff, Haroun (1989) *Earthquake Prediction*. McGraw Hill Inc. ISBN 0-07-062992-7.

Thompson, S.A. (1982) Trends and Developments in Global Natural Disasters 1947–81. Working paper no. 45, Institute of Behavioural Science, University of Colorado, Boulder. Quoted in Smith.

Thornes, Robin (1995) Protecting Cultural Objects through International Documentation Standards. The Getty Art History Information Program. J. Paul Getty Trust.

Verdel, Thierry and El Shabrawi Atef (1994) The Seismic Risk on Ancient Masonry Structures Studied by the Use of the Distinct Element Method: Application to an Egyptian Monument. International Symposium on the Conservation of Monuments in the Mediterranean Basin, edited by V. Fassina, H. Ott and F. Zezza. Venice.

Weil, Stephen (1995) Stuff and Non-stuff. *Museums Journal*, July, p. 29.

10 Chemical reaction

The materials of which objects are made can be affected by substances in the environment. Prediction and control of damage is helped by an understanding of the mechanism by which these substances reach the objects and the factors that dictate the rate at which they combine with them.

Chemistry and reality

This is the second chapter about interactions between objects and their environment. The last chapter dealt with the effects of suddenly releasing large amounts of energy in the vicinity of museum collections. Although the types of damage were not described in detail, it can be imagined that they would involve severe physical change. This chapter is about more gradual changes of state brought about by interaction with specific substances in the environment. My traditional scientific education encouraged me to believe that there was a clear distinction between chemical and physical mechanisms of change. I hope that the inseparable nature of the two approaches to understanding rates of change will become apparent in the next two chapters.

This is not a book about physics or chemistry but about risk and conservation. The essential factors in risk are prediction and control. Prediction of the future relies on a thorough understanding of the past. The more we know about which changes in environment have resulted in different changes in state, the more probable it is that our predictions will be right. The more we understand the mechanisms of change, the more likely it is that we can control them.

The chemistry I learned at college consisted mostly of observations of the interactions of liquids with liquids. The reactions all took place in closed systems such as glass flasks. Each experiment had a definite beginning, where the reactants were thoroughly mixed together. There was a middle bit when something was going on, often involving the absorption or release of heat. Then, after a few hours at the most, there was an obvious end when the reaction was over and all of the reactants had been turned into products. Using pure reactants in known amounts there would be a high certainty that the experiment would yield the same products in the same time, no matter who did it or where it was done. Such an education is probably as much a hindrance as a help. The reaction of two chemicals in a flask is a grotesque simplification of the reaction of the chemicals in a historic object with the chemicals in its environment.

The vast majority of museum objects are solids, and in normal circumstances are surrounded on most sides by gas. This means that there cannot always be that intimate mixing of molecules generated by blending liquids in a reaction flask.

There are different degrees of 'solidity'. With a metal or a ceramic it is possible to imagine a clearly defined boundary between the object and the surrounding environment. A textile object is very much more intimately connected to its gaseous surroundings. Gases can pass through the holes in the web of the fabric and round each of the individual fibres that compose the yarn. The small gas molecules can even pass into the spaces between the much larger long molecules that make up the fibres. A single apparently simple classification such as 'stone' can cover a wide range of porosities.

Museum objects are rarely of one pure chemical substance, the presence of small amounts of impurity can have a dramatic effect on the rate or direction of reaction. Complex objects such as paintings may have several hundred chemical species present. The gaseous environment is not a single pure chemical but a dynamic cocktail of many hundreds of substances. Although the major constituents are very much the same wherever you are, the relative amounts of the minor components vary considerably from place to place, from year to year and even from hour to hour. Some chemical agents cause detectable damage at concentrations of only one molecule in every hundred million of air.

The reaction flask is a closed system where the amounts of reactants decrease until they are used up. The museum is an open dynamic system where the gaseous reactants are constantly replenished. The solid reactant, the object, is rarely used up chemically. The chemical reaction causes physical changes at the surface long before the bulk of the material is affected. New material may build up at the surface altering the way that the gases can get to the reactive material underneath. There may be a dramatic change in surface colour even though very little material has reacted. Chemical reactions may take place within cracks and between the grains of which the solid is composed. The boundaries between the physical components of the material are attacked, weakening its structural integrity. Physical disintegration will destroy the meaning of the object long before the chemical reaction is complete.

In the simple laboratory experiment the rate at which the reaction takes place is measured in terms of the rate of decrease in the amount of one of the reactants or the rate of increase in one of the products. With real objects our major concern is with decrease of utility. Utility is often determined by a complex mixture of properties. With this complexity added to the multiplicity of reaction components and reaction mechanisms, it is often difficult to talk about a specific 'reaction rate'. With whole objects it is probably easier to think in terms of the time taken to reach various stages of decreasing utility, eventually determining a 'time to failure'.

Observations of reactions between historic objects and their environments do not usually start until long after the reaction began. Observations may only start when the object is acquired or needed for exhibition. The timescales involved, which may be several human lifetimes, mean that there is great variability in the evaluation of the changes.

The college chemistry experiment is fairly value free. To the student, who is generally interested in the product or the process, it may have some positive value. On a historic object the same chemical reaction can produce patina or corrosion. Chemically identical products will have different effects on value for different observers.

Prediction and control

The changes that we want to control are very varied, ranging from change in colour to change in strength. The changes may only affect the surface or they may penetrate deep within the object. They may affect appearance but not life-span or they may affect life expectancy with very little visible change.

We can exercise little control over the current state of the object. We cannot significantly change the basic materials or construction. However, the more that is known about the state of the objects in a collection (materials and construction as well as condition), the more accurately we can predict how they will react in different environments. The more that is known about the states of individual objects, the more opportunity we have to make individual adjustments that will maximize the benefits of our actions for the whole collection and its users.

Since we cannot control the object we must control the environment. The four stages of risk assessment – release, exposure, consequence and risk estimation – were shown in Figure 2.1. We are interested in determining the sources of chemicals found to damage objects. We need to know the mechanisms by which they are transported to the vicinity of the object and in what quantities. We must find out what levels and combinations of chemicals cause detectable change and how quickly they do so. With this knowledge we can see if there are any affordable ways of control and predict how long the object will last in the presence or absence of these controls.

Most studies of durability are carried out where there is strong commercial, military or political influence. Most museum research is a refinement or an extrapolation of this much greater volume of work. The greatest numbers of publications are in areas where there is a large volume of material and a high demand for use. Paper, photographs, architectural stone and metals have received a great deal of interest.

Recent reviews or bibliographies on the effects of atmospheric pollution on specific materials can be found for stone (Schuster, Reddy and Sherwood, 1994; Smith and Warke, 1996; Price, 1996), metals (Graedel, 1994) and paper (Gurnagul and Zou, 1994; Fellers, Iversen, Lindström, Nilsson and Rigdahl, 1989). Artists' colourants are well covered in a series of papers by Grosjean (Williams, Grosjean and Grosjean, 1993). Effects on photographs have been studied at the Image Permanence Institute (Zinn, Reilly, Adelstein and Nishimura, 1994a, b). There are also general reviews dealing with the susceptibility of materials (Graedel and McGill, 1986) and mechanisms and effects (Camuffo, 1991; Brimblecombe, 1994).

Substances known to cause change in cultural property

Such a general description includes vast numbers of chemical compounds. In this chapter we are primarily interested in compounds that are transported through the air, which means that they must be volatile at ambient temperatures or found associated with particles that are small enough to be transported a reasonable distance through the air. Table 10.1 gives a brief list of some of the better known gases and volatile compounds. The concentrations are for the lower atmosphere averaged worldwide. The bulk of the lower atmosphere, 78% nitrogen and 1% argon, is believed to have no direct chemical effect on inanimate cultural property at ambient temperatures. The levels of all but oxygen and carbon dioxide will vary considerably depending on location.

Where does it all come from?

There are both natural and man-made sources of chemicals in the outside air. Where levels are very much higher in urban areas it is reasonable to assume that the sources are due to human activity. The amounts will vary according to what those activities are. Figure 10.1 shows some of the origins of nitrogen oxides and sulphur dioxide for one location in Sweden

Table 10.1 *Average atmospheric concentrations of gases and volatile compounds implicated in damage to cultural property*

Parts per hundred	
Oxygen	21
Water	0–3
Parts per million	
Carbon dioxide	350
Parts per billion	
Ammonia	1
Formaldehyde	1–0.1
Carbonyl sulphide	0.5
Nitrogen dioxide	0.3
Sulphur dioxide	0.1–0.01
Hydrogen sulphide	0.05
Hydrogen chloride	0.001
Acetic acid	0.001
Formic acid	0.001

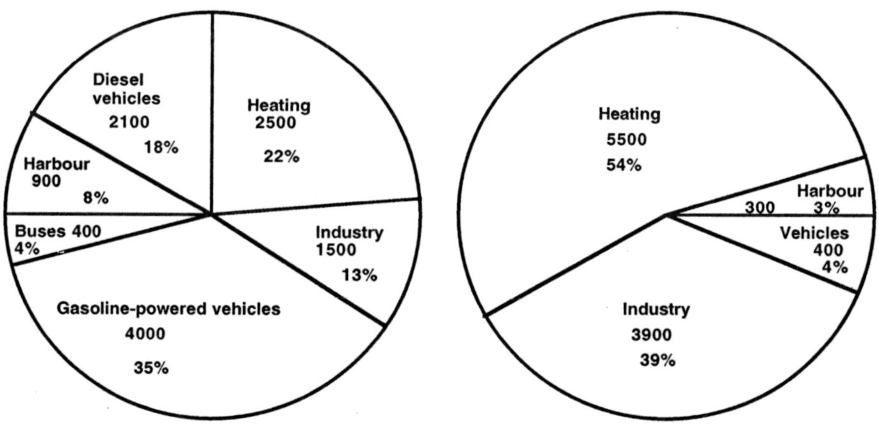

Figure 10.1 *Sources and quantities (tonnes) of sulphur dioxide and nitrogen oxides at Göteburg (Sweden) during 1984*

for one particular year (Rosvall and Aleby, 1988). Legislation on vehicle and industrial emissions will have some effect on total output and the balance between different compounds. The economy is also a strong influence. Improvements in UK air quality in the 1980s were largely due to the economic recession (Weale, 1992, p. 21). Countries striving for very high economic growth to catch up with the leaders in the developed world are likely to have high levels of pollution.

Vegetation such as trees, grasses and crops are natural sources of Volatile Organic Compounds (VOCs), principally small, unsaturated hydrocarbons such as isoprene and monoterpenes. Animals produce about 30% of the emissions of methane, the most abundant VOC. Anthropogenic sources of VOCs are landfill, oil and gas operations, road transport, chemical processes and use of solvents. The total emission of VOCs in Europe is of the same order as those for sulphur dioxide and nitrogen oxides at 23.8 million tonnes a year. The UK figures for 1989 were 1 777 000 tonnes man-made and 24 000 tonnes from natural sources (Hester and Harrison, 1995). The vast majority of these substances are not known to be harmful to cultural property. However, in warm conditions and bright sunlight the generally unreactive VOCs combine with nitrogen oxides from vehicle emissions to form more reactive compounds.

Maps of the distribution of pollutant gases in Europe are available (Kerrel, Briggs, Reeve and Wright, 1991; Lübkert and de Tilly, 1989). As a result of air quality regulations, levels of a number of pollutants are measured at a great many locations at regular intervals, so you should be able to find measurements for your own locality. Daily and seasonal fluctuations can be determined. Emissions from cars show daily peaks at traffic rush hours. Emissions from domestic heating show peaks in the colder months of the year. On a day-to-day basis the weather can have a dramatic effect in trapping the pollution in one area or in blowing it somewhere else.

Air indoors

Where levels of pollutants indoors are higher than outside the source must be local and internal. There are a number of potential sources (Baer and Banks, 1985). Nitrogen oxides are formed by burning gas used for cooking and heating. Formaldehyde is given off by thermal insulation foam and from the resins used to make plywood, particle boards and fibre boards. Formic and acetic acids are emitted by most timbers and from some timber products such as card made from wood pulp. Acetic acid can come from some adhesives and silicone sealants. Rubbers, paints and treated textiles are sources of sulphides.

The objects we are trying to protect may evolve products that are dangerous to other parts of the collection. Cellulose nitrate, used to make film stock and a variety of decorative objects, can degrade and give off nitrogen oxides. Cellulose nitrate has also been used extensively in materials used for conservation, so past preventive measures could be the cause of present damage. Cellulose acetate film negatives deteriorate to give acetic acid. Copies of coins and medals have been made using sulphur which is sufficiently volatile to affect nearby metals. Archaeological materials can retain soil that emits sulphides. Showcases may have adsorbed pollutants from the objects they contained. The cases will continue as sources after the offending objects have been removed (Green, 1993). The coatings and varnishes that are used to try to slow down emissions of VOCs from the materials used to make enclosures such as showcases may themselves give off VOCs (Tétrault and Stamatopoulou, 1997).

With luck museums are full of people. People emit a variety of gaseous substances some of which have the potential to do harm (Brimblecombe, 1992).

Mechanisms of transport

Water and oxygen are implicated in just about every known degradation reaction. Because they are necessary for life and comfort we do not think of them as pollutants. Because they are automatically around wherever there are people we don't consider their transport to the object in quite the same way as we do the chemicals that are generated by recent technology.

In perfectly still air, molecules of a pollutant gas from a localized source would diffuse outwards at a rate of a few centimetres a second. If the source was generating the pollutant continuously, a gradient of concentration would be established. Concentrations would be highest near the source, tailing off to nearly zero at some distance away. Air movements such as convection currents, drafts and winds disturb this gradient by carrying the bulk of the pollutant gas in a particular direction. Wind speeds near the ground are very low because of frictional drag. Where there are obstructions like the buildings in a city, wind speeds will be considerably reduced up to heights of several hundred metres, slowing down the movement of urban pollutants (Amoroso and Fassina, 1983).

A pollutant gas is removed from the atmosphere in a variety of ways. It may react with other gases in the atmosphere, be washed out by rain or be deposited on solid surfaces. Pollution deposited on buildings and sculpture causes obvious deterioration, but acid gases deposited onto the earth may also be affecting the cultural heritage. Sulphur dioxide deposition may be causing accelerated decay of archaeological metal in the ground (Scharff and Huesmann, 1997).

The level of pollution that is detected in the air at a particular site will depend on how fast it is being introduced compared to how fast it is being removed. Although this statement is a sufficient explanation it can be considered mathematically in more detail.

Imagine a volume of space, this could be a showcase, a gallery or just an imaginary 'box' of defined volume in the open air. The rate of change in concentration within this space is given by the rate of production within the space (or the rate of transport to the space) minus the rate of loss through various processes. The rate of loss of pollutant is dependent on its concentration, if there is more of a substance around the reaction goes faster. The process can be shown in an equation:

$$\frac{\mathrm{d}C}{\mathrm{d}t} = S - LC \tag{10.1}$$

In this case C represents the concentration of pollutant[1], S the rate of production from all Sources and L is a constant that determines the rate of Loss. The expression on the left-hand side is mathematical shorthand for 'the rate of change of C with time'. The possible interactions between different gases, the rates of deposition on different surfaces and the possible influence of light can be entered into a computer simulation which predicts concentrations that will be found in a gallery (Nazaroff and Cass, 1986).

A state of 'dynamic equilibrium' is reached if $S = LC$. This state is called 'dynamic' because new pollutant gas is constantly being introduced and then removed. It is called 'equilibrium' because the measured level of pollution remains constant, the rate of change is zero. The resultant concentration is then given by:

$$C = \frac{S}{L} \tag{10.2}$$

If S gets smaller or L gets bigger then C, the equilibrium concentration, will decrease. If the source of pollution is outside a physical enclosure, such as a museum building or a showcase, the rate of transport of the pollutant can be lowered by decreasing the exchange of air between the inside and the outside. For a building this exchange rate is very dependent on wind pressure and stack effects due to temperature differences. Some control is achieved by closing windows and doors. The showcase is controlled by having good seals on the doors. The rate of loss will depend on what surfaces are available, how adsorbent or reactive they are and how much area is exposed for adsorption to take place. Pollutants such as sulphur dioxide are readily adsorbed onto stonework,

[1] If you borrow equations from a variety of fields it is inevitable that common symbols are used to represent different things. Although C was used in earlier chapters to represent Cost it is also sensibly and universally used to represent Concentration in other contexts. At least L still stands for Loss even though the meaning is slightly changed.

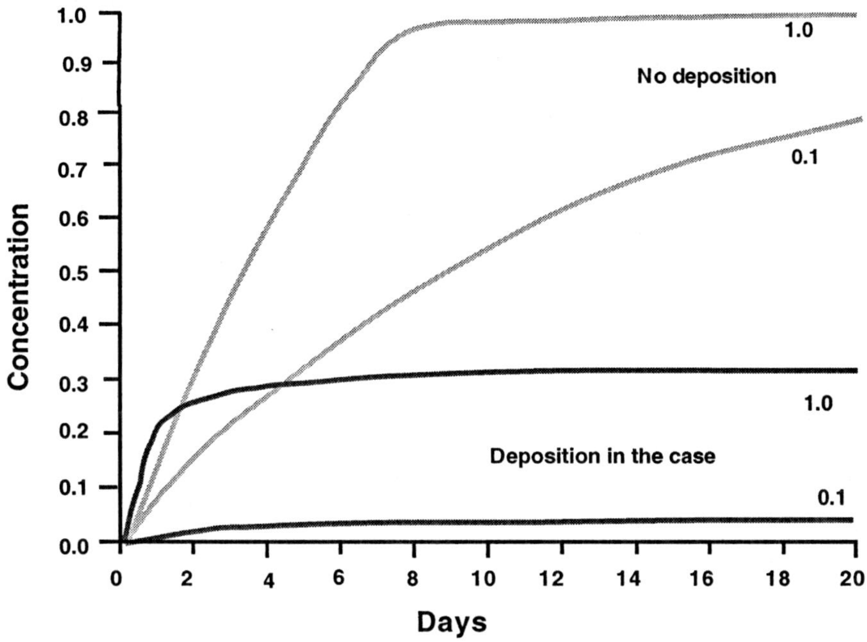

Figure 10.2 *Simulation of levels of pollutant inside a case at different rates of air exchange. The concentration is given as a fraction of the external level. If there is nothing to adsorb the pollutant inside the case the internal level will always eventually reach the external concentration*

furnishings and wall coverings (Braun and Wilson, 1970; Walsh, Black, Morgan and Cranshaw, 1977). Deposition or absorption does not necessarily imply chemical reaction, but chemical change is the usual outcome.

Imagine a case containing unpolluted air placed inside a polluted gallery. A computer model can be built using a simple spreadsheet[2] by assuming that, at the end of every hour, a certain proportion of the air at the internal concentration is replaced by air at the external concentration. If this stepwise calculation is plotted over a long enough period it can be seen as a continuous process. Figure 10.2 shows the graphical output of such a spreadsheet. If there is no mechanism for the pollutant to be absorbed inside the case then, at one air change a day, the level of pollution inside becomes the same as it is outside after a few days. At one-tenth of an air change each day the internal level takes more than 20

[2] I have used spreadsheets as the main tool for computer modelling in this book because of their availability and simplicity. They usually come in the bundle supplied with a home computer and require very little programming knowledge.

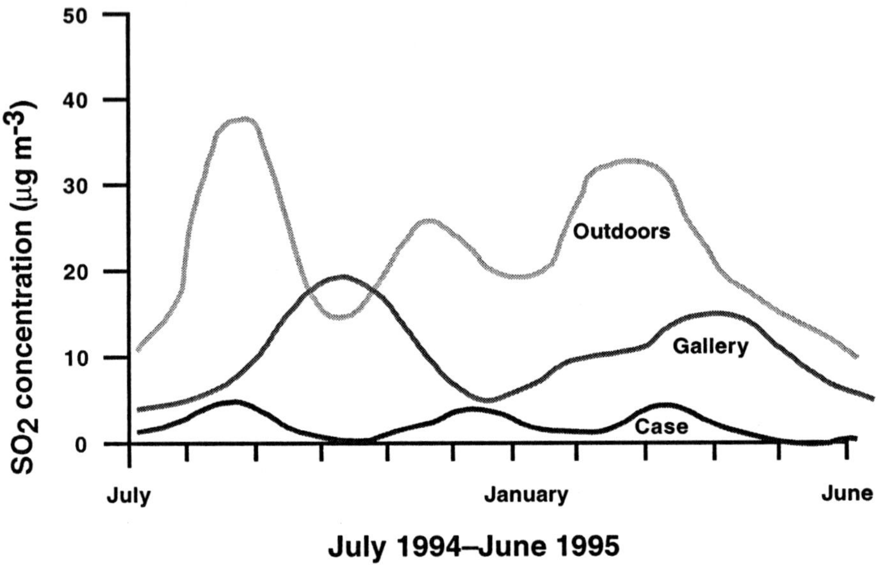

Figure 10.3 *Levels of sulphur dioxide measured at the Victoria and Albert Museum. Outdoor levels are generally higher than indoors. Levels inside a showcase are always lower*

days to reach the level outside. The spreadsheet can be altered to simulate the removal of pollutant by deposition at a rate proportional to the internal concentration. If the pollutant is absorbed onto the furnishings (and objects) in the case, equilibrium is set up much faster and the equilibrium concentration is much lower. If the rate of exchange of air is reduced by 90% then the equilibrium concentration is reduced to about one-tenth of the former value, as would be predicted by equation (10.2).

Observations in the real world match the mathematical predictions. Figure 10.3 shows levels of sulphur dioxide inside and outside the V&A Museum over one year (Blades, 1996). Levels of pollution are generally lower indoors and lower still inside a showcase.

If a source of pollution is placed inside an enclosure, the level will build up until an equilibrium is reached between the rate of production from the source, the rate of deposition on the available surfaces and exchange with the air outside the enclosure. Figure 10.4 shows the graphical output of a computer spreadsheet simulation.

The smaller the fraction of air changed each day, the more slowly the system reaches equilibrium. The equilibrium concentration for each rate of air change can be seen to be near to that predicted by equation (10.2) Jean Tétrault gives an alternative version of this equation:

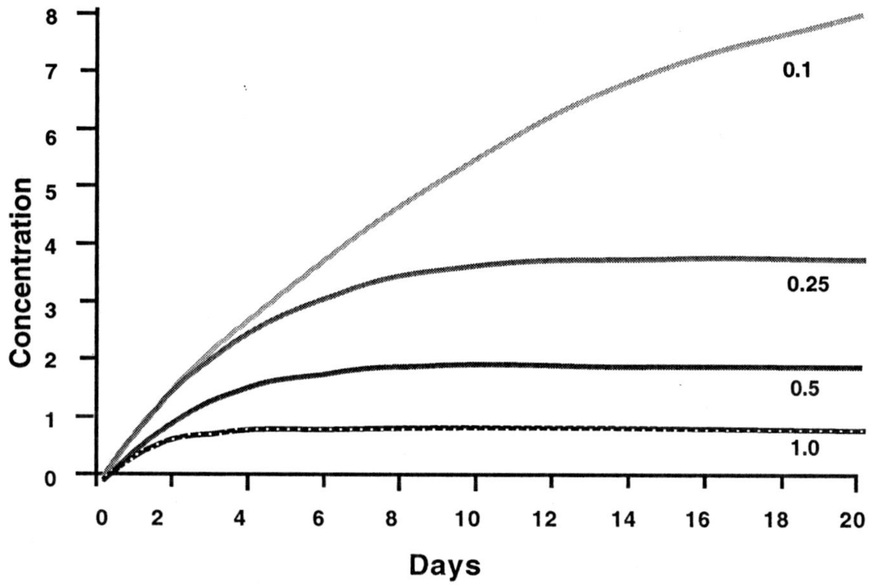

Figure 10.4 *Simulation of the effect of putting a source of pollution inside an enclosure with differing levels of air exchange*

$$C = \frac{EA}{VN} \tag{10.3}$$

Where E is the emission rate of the pollutant per square metre and A is the area of material emitting it, V is the volume of the chamber and N is the number of air changes in unit time (Tétrault, 1994). This equation ignores the possibility of anything absorbing the pollutant (including the objects!).

Using the model implied by equation (10.1) Brimblecombe uses figures for rates of generation and deposition of a number of substances from which equilibrium concentrations can be calculated for a small gallery (Brimblecombe, 1989). European legislation limits the levels of certain pollutants in houses and offices. This means that sources of indoor pollution are well studied and average levels recorded for several different environments (European Concerted Action, 1989; Crump, 1995).

Getting inside enclosures

Pollutants can enter (or leave) an enclosed space, such as a showcase or a storage box in several different ways (Passaglia, 1989; Michalski, 1994):

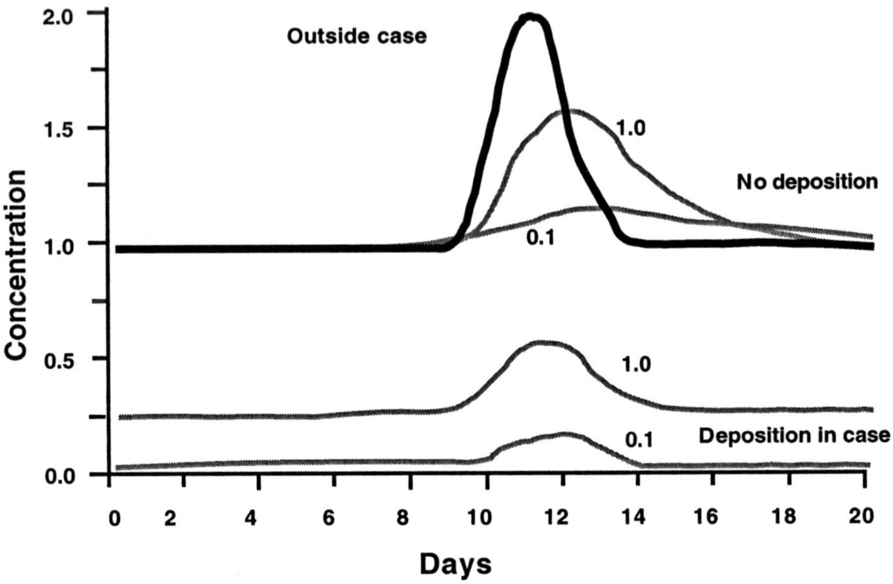

Figure 10.5 *Simulation showing that if the level of pollution outside an enclosure increases for a short while (dark line) the variation inside is very much smaller depending on the air change rate and the presence of an adsorbent*

- flow of the air/pollutant mixture through openings
- diffusion of pollutant molecules through still air in any openings
- permeation of molecules through solid walls

Solids such as dust can only enter by the first mechanism. The rate at which air flows in and out will depend on the size, number and position of openings such as cracks. It will also depend on differences in temperature, relative humidity and barometric pressure between the inside and the outside. Permeability is dependent on the material that the container is made from and on the pollutant in question. Acrylic sheet is very permeable to water but not to sulphur and nitrogen oxides.

A case with a one to two millimetre crack at the top and bottom (average fitting door) could have up to 30 air changes a day. With very well fitted doors the best to be hoped for practically is 0.03 air changes a day (0.003 is theoretically possible). The V&A standard specification is 0.1 air changes a day (Cassar and Martin, 1994). Cases which have cracks at only one level will leak much more slowly than those with cracks at top and bottom. Tall, thin cases will leak up to 10 times faster than cuboidal cases. For a case with cracks top and bottom, air flow is the dominant mechanism of exchange if the cracks are more than 0.3 mm wide. Diffusion through the case materials is usually several thousand times slower than diffusion or infiltration through openings.

For an enclosure to be an effective barrier against externally generated gaseous pollution it must have a low air exchange rate and also have internal surfaces that will adsorb the pollutant. Even if the object is the only surface on which deposition takes place it is still better off inside an enclosure, especially if there is a good seal. If the object is not a surface on which deposition takes place there isn't much point in spending money to protect it.

The enclosure will give protection against temporary increases in pollutant levels. Figure 10.5 shows a computer simulation of an incident in which the levels of pollution are doubled for a period of two or three days. Suppose that the object is the only surface on which the pollutant is deposited. If the rate of damage is proportional to the concentration of pollutant in the case, the leaky case has reduced the additional damage caused by the pollution surge by 90% and the more air-tight case has reduced it by 97%.

What affects rate of reaction?

We now have an idea of the extent to which we can predict or control the release of substances harmful to the objects in collections. We also have some ideas about how well we can control exposure of the objects to these hazards. There are several other properties of the object and of its environment that have an effect on the rate at which changes in state occur.

For the museum solid/gas reaction the amount of available reactive gas remains constant as it is replenished continuously. The rate of deterioration will be dictated by the availability of reactive sites on the surfaces of the object. In Chapter 8 the reaction rate was shown to decrease over time as the number of sites where reaction could take place slowly diminished (see Figure 8.5). This means that the increase in damage is rapid at an early stage but then begins to level out. The curve becomes horizontal at the point that all possible damage has been done (see Figure 10.6). The slope of the curve at any point indicates what the rate of reaction is, the steeper the faster. Whether this behaviour is actually observed will depend on a number of factors. For instance, if the property that is being measured relates to strength, the object may have fallen into pieces long before the maximum weakness is achieved. During the period of time that the object is intact the curve can be treated as if it were a straight line.

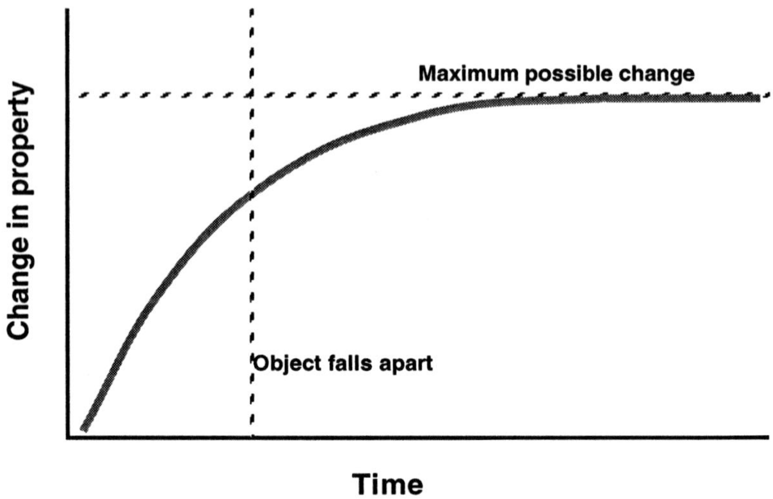

Figure 10.6 *Theoretical change with time in the property which defines damage. The maximum possible change may not be reached if other physical changes intervene*

If the property being measured as damage is a change of colour, the maximum damage may be reached, since the physical integrity of the object is not affected. With colour changes, what is being measured is a scientific interpretation of the human eye's reaction to chemical change at the object's surface. It is not a direct measure of the concentration of a particular chemical species. So the plot of colour change against time may not appear to follow the curve in Figure 10.6. Changes in colour caused by thermal ageing are often nearly linear with time.

Access to reactive sites will be denied if the products of reaction get in the way, this will lead to a convex curve, the rate diminishing with time. The amount of damage still increases although slowly. If something such as rainfall or regular cleaning removes the reaction products, constantly revealing a fresh reactive surface, the rate remains constant until the object is completely eroded.

Concentration of reactive gas

The assumption that the rate of a damaging reaction is directly proportional to the concentration of the pollutant turns out to be the case for the majority of solid/gas deterioration reactions. Reactions that show this relationship are called 'first order'. The rate of reaction, which is the rate of change of some chosen property x with time, is equal to some number k times the concentration C:

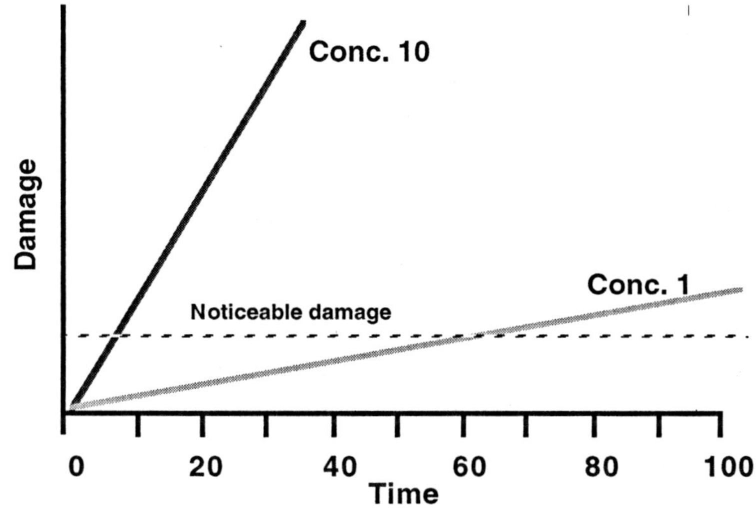

Figure 10.7 *For many materials the rate of reaction is linear with time and increases in proportion to the concentration of pollutant. The extent of damage is proportional to the rate, so a concentration 10 times higher leads to noticeable damage 10 times sooner*

$$\text{Rate} = \frac{dx}{dt} = kC \qquad (10.4)$$

The number k is called the rate constant which is specific to the reaction between two specified substances at a particular temperature. For the time being we will assume that the rate of reaction stays constant. If the concentration of a damaging pollutant is 10 times higher at one location than at another, then the rate of reaction will be 10 times faster and, as shown in Figure 10.7, the time before damage is noticed will be one-tenth of that for the lower concentration. The Extent of damage E will be given by:

$$E = kCt \qquad (10.5)$$

where t is the time of exposure. You should note the similarity of this to equation (8.1) and (8.12) in an earlier chapter.

Material

For any particular pollutant some materials will be more susceptible than others. This effect and the effect of concentration can be seen in Table 10.2 which shows the depth of corrosion on different metals after 10 years' exposure in different environments (Wranglen, 1985).

Table 10.2 *Depth of corrosion μm*

	Urban	*Rural*
Steel	500	100
Aluminium alloy	10	0.5
Copper	10	5

Figure 10.8 shows that different compositions of historic stained glass have different susceptibilities (Fitz, 1986).

The presence of small amounts of some substances can greatly affect susceptibility. Less than 0.2% of tin in a lead alloy can provide protection against the attack of VOCs (Heath and Martin, 1988). Figure 10.9 shows differential attack on lead inlay on a Japanese lacquer inro caused by differences in tin content.

Physical differences can also affect rate. The degree of crystallinity (regularity in the way the cellulose molecules fit together) in Japanese paper is much greater than in paper made from wood pulp. Japanese papers are less easily oxidized (Inaba and Sugisita, 1990).

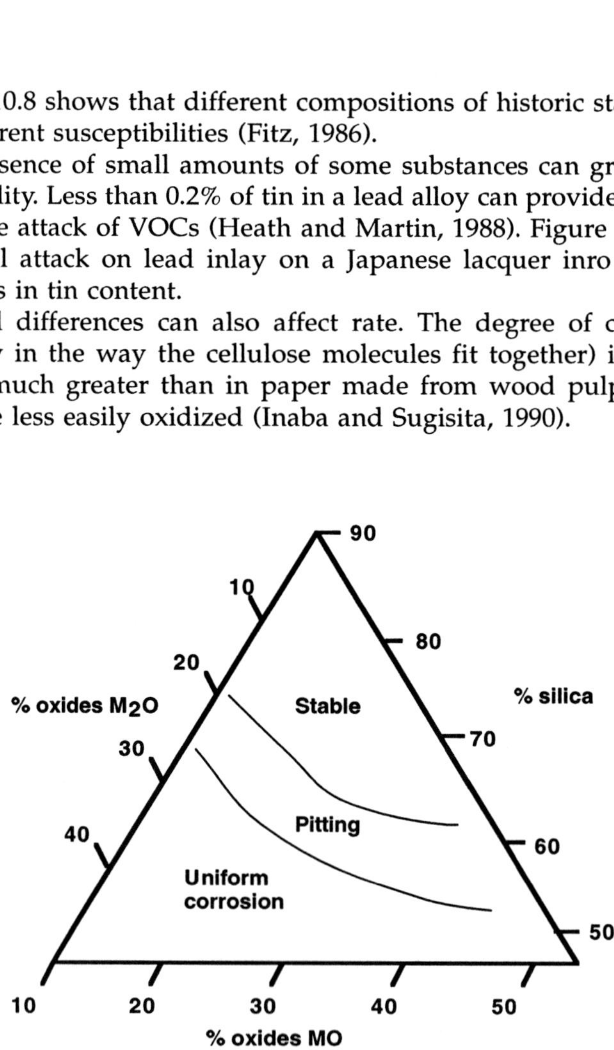

Figure 10.8 *Different compositions of a material with a single description 'mediaeval glass' have different susceptibilities. (The triangular graph allows the plotting of three composition variables) (after Fitz)*

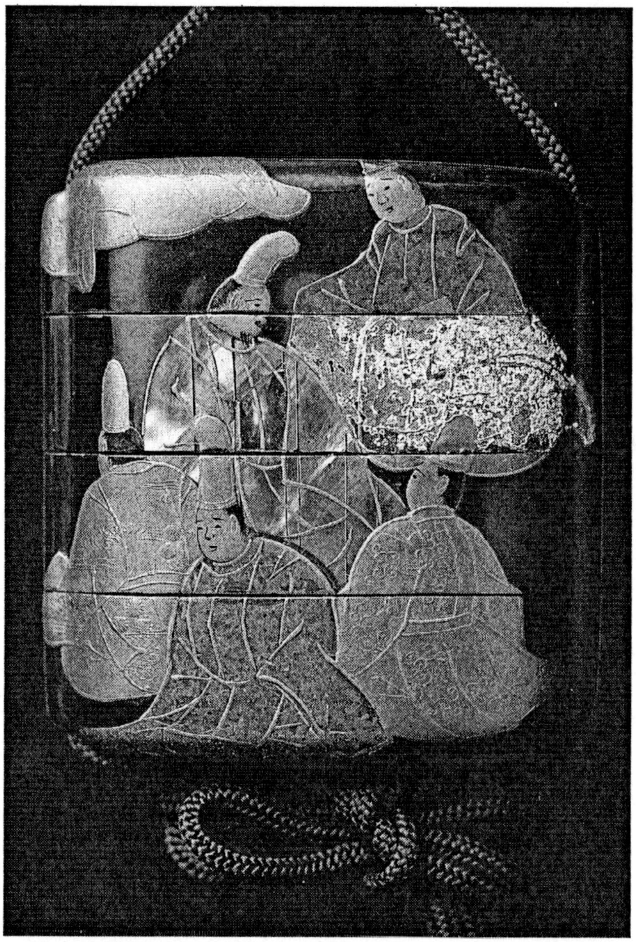

Figure 10.9 *Lead inlay on a Japanese inro is protected from attack by VOCs by small quantities of tin in the alloy used for part of the decoration*

Presence of moisture

Water is an aggressive chemical substance that causes the deterioration of a number of materials. If the temperature remains the same and the relative humidity doubles then the concentration of water in the atmosphere has doubled. As expected this causes an increase in the rate of the chemical reaction called hydrolysis in porous materials such as paper and textiles.

As the humidity increases, so the amount of water absorbed on the surface of non-porous substances increases. This layer of water is only a

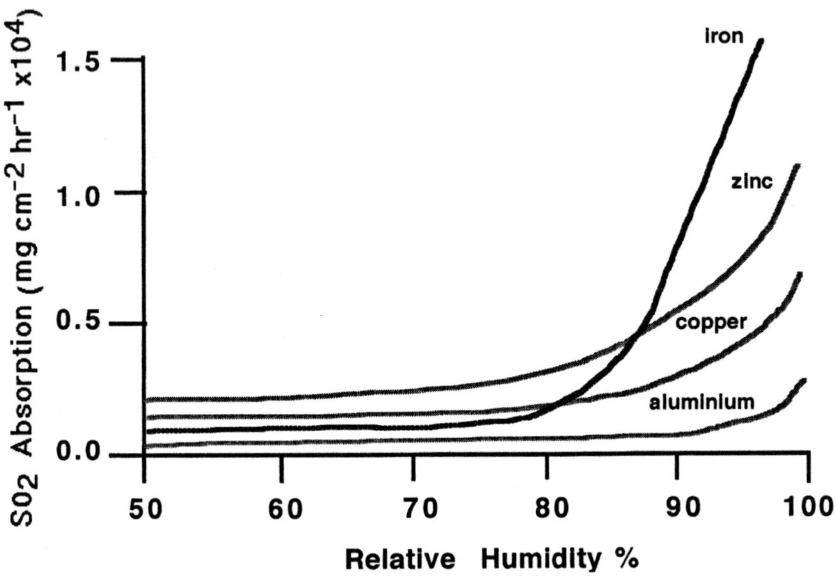

Figure 10.10 *The rate at which sulphur dioxide is adsorbed onto a clean metal surface is strongly dependent on humidity (after Sydberger and Vannerberg)*

few molecules thick. When it reaches a certain thickness it can dissolve pollutants and salts, at which point corrosion becomes very rapid. Figure 10.10 shows this effect where the rate of adsorption of sulphur dioxide onto the clean surface of different metals is rapidly accelerated at relative humidities greater than 80% (Sydberger and Vannerberg, 1972).

Porosity

The more porous an object is, the more surface area there is for reaction to take place. Pores can also retain moisture, allowing reactions to continue when the ambient humidity has decreased. Table 10.3 shows how the composition and porosity of several types of stone used in building interiors affect the rate at which they react with sulphur dioxide (Furlan and Girardet, 1991).

The compactness of a material will determine how strong the effect of humidity is on the rate of reaction with pollutants. Limestone is more open than marble. Reaction with sulphur dioxide is stimulated at lower humidities as shown in Figure 10.11 (Spiker, Comer, Hosker and Sherwood, 1992).

Table 10.3 *Effect of porosity and composition*

	Calcium carbonate %	*Porosity %*	*Relative deposition*
Sandstone			
Villarod	16	15	100
Bollingen	40	7	70
St Magarathen	8	7	28
Limestone			
Jaumont	95	23	117
Carrara	99	1	47

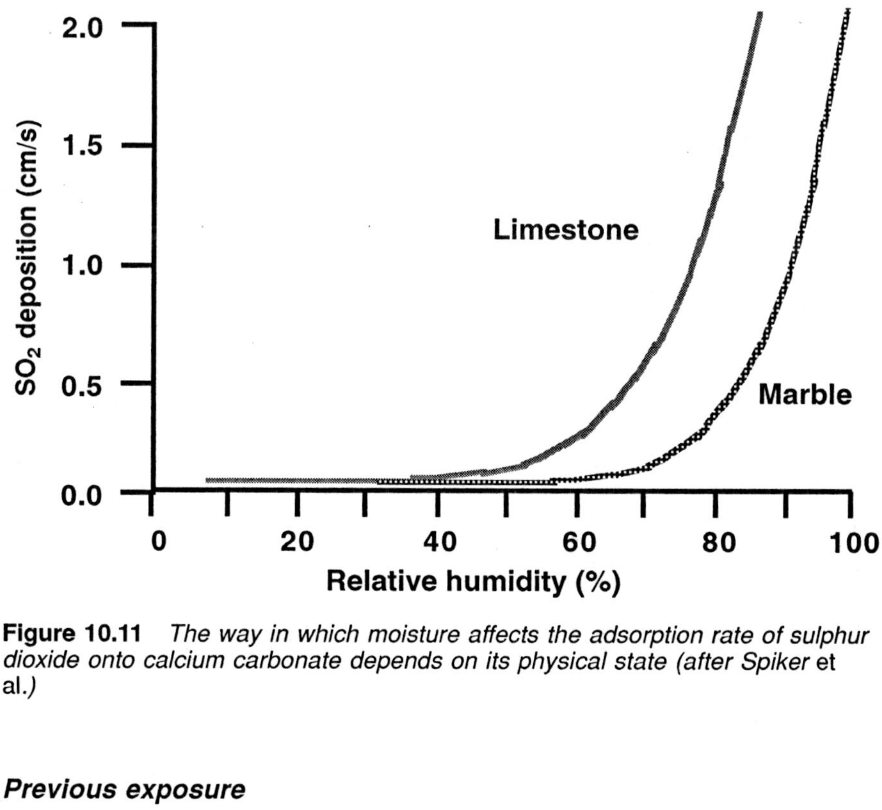

Figure 10.11 *The way in which moisture affects the adsorption rate of sulphur dioxide onto calcium carbonate depends on its physical state (after Spiker* et al.*)*

Previous exposure

Many of the scientific studies of reaction rate are done on freshly prepared, clean samples, whereas the objects we are concerned with may have been exposed to cycles of weathering and exposure which may have altered their susceptibilities.

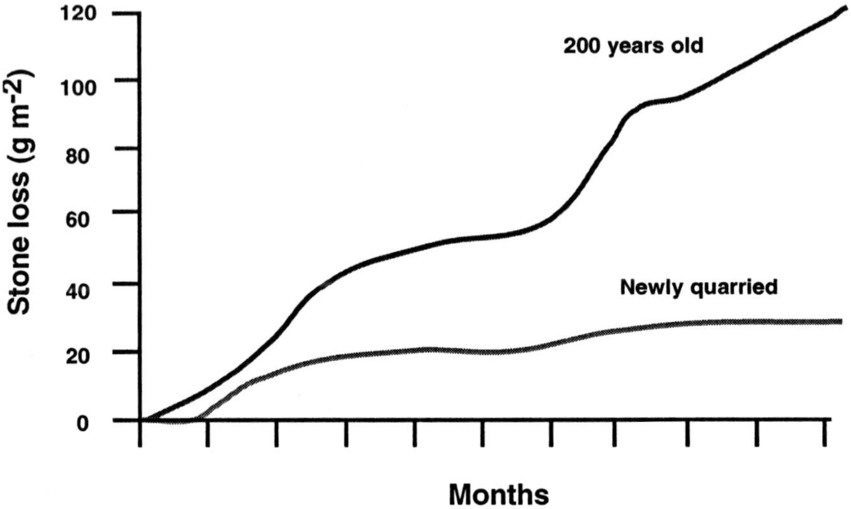

Figure 10.12 *Differences in rates of erosion of weathered stone and stone that has recently been quarried (after Cooper* et al.*)*

Figure 10.12 shows the difference in rate of stone loss between 200-year-old and freshly quarried Portland stone (Cooper, O'Brien and Jeffrey, 1992).

Previous exposure alters the relationship between reaction rate and moisture. Iron and zinc react more rapidly at lower humidities if they have been previously exposed to pollution (see Figure 10.13). The corrosion products on the surface can absorb the pollutant at lower humidities and store it until higher moisture levels occur (Sydberger and Vannerberg, 1972).

Catalysis

A catalyst is a substance which makes a reaction go faster without getting used up in the process. If a small amount of this substance is present then reactions which might normally only occur at high temperatures may take place in ambient conditions. Metals and metal compounds can act as catalysts. They are necessary for the conversion of sulphur dioxide into sulphuric acid. Metals can be found in small quantities associated with objects in the form of natural inclusions, debris from the process of manufacture, as pigments dyes or inks, or as dirt and dust.

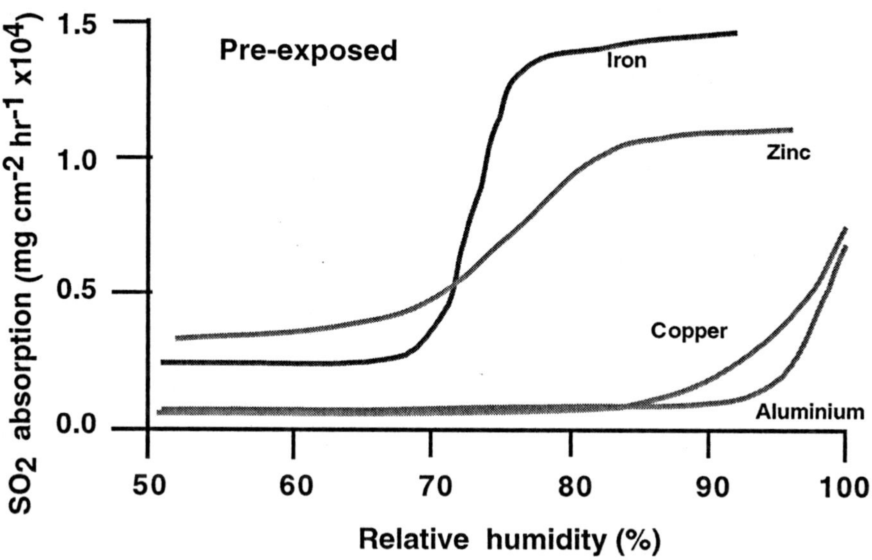

Figure 10.13 *Metals that have been previously exposed to pollution react faster at lower humidities than clean surfaces. Compare Figure 10.10 (after Sydberger and Vannerberg)*

If the catalyst is an essential or accidental part of the object then the control must be by limiting moisture and pollutant levels. If the catalyst is an unnecessary addition control must be by removal and prevention of dirt.

A number of important deterioration reactions are 'auto-catalytic' which means that one of the reaction products catalyses further reaction. The reaction becomes faster and faster. Acetic acid generated by the decay of cellulose acetate film accelerates further deterioration. In some cases the first reaction product is unstable and reacts further with substances in the atmosphere such as moisture or carbon dioxide. This second reaction releases the initial pollutant, allowing it to initiate further reaction.

The reaction of unstable archaeological copper corrosion (bronze disease) is of this type as is the reaction of lead objects with acetic acid from wood. If the catalyst cannot be removed then control must be by adjustment of humidity or temperature.

Synergy

Scientific investigations of reaction rates often test one pollutant at a time. However, the real world consists of mixtures of pollutants. The effect of a mixture can be much greater than the sum of the effects of the

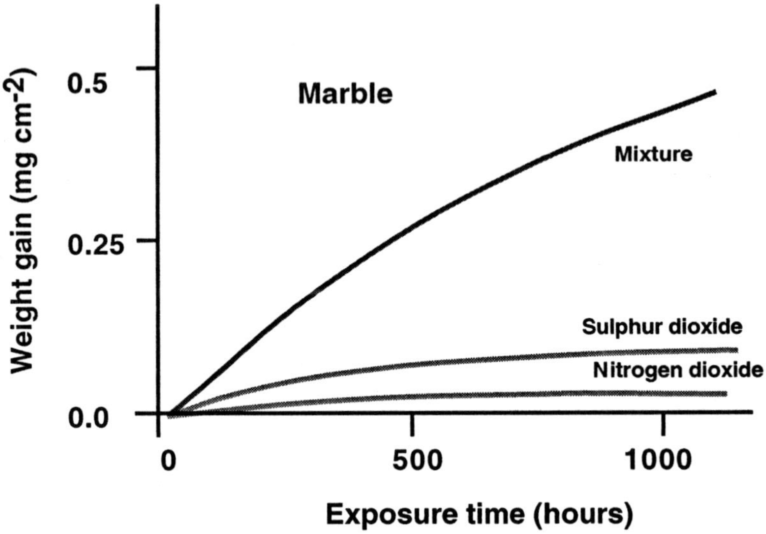

Figure 10.14 *The synergic effect. Damage caused by a mixture of nitrogen dioxide and sulphur dioxide is greater than the sum of the damage caused by each pollutant on its own (after Johansson* et al.*)*

component pollutants tested individually. Although levels of sulphur dioxide are decreasing in many cities around the world, levels of nitrogen oxides are increasing. There is a strong synergic (some people say synergistic or synergetic) effect between these two which affects the rate of attack on paper, leather and stone. The effect is shown in Figure 10.14 for marble (Johansson, Lindquist and Mangio, 1988).

In some cases the pure gases will not react at all. In most black-and-white photographs the image is composed of small particles of silver. Tests have shown that on its own the reactive gas ozone has no effect on the image and neither does hydrogen sulphide. Experience in the real world suggests otherwise. It was not until the two became accidentally mixed in one experiment that the strong synergic effect of these two pollutants was studied systematically (Zinn *et al.*, 1994a).

Temperature

In the laboratory a reaction can be speeded up by raising the temperature of the reaction flask. As a rule of thumb the rate of change doubles for every 10°C rise. So if we heat a solution in water from room temperature (20°C) to boiling (100°C) we will speed the reaction more than 250 times, which is the basis of much food preparation. In a museum, because we expect people to mingle with the objects, we don't usually find a range of

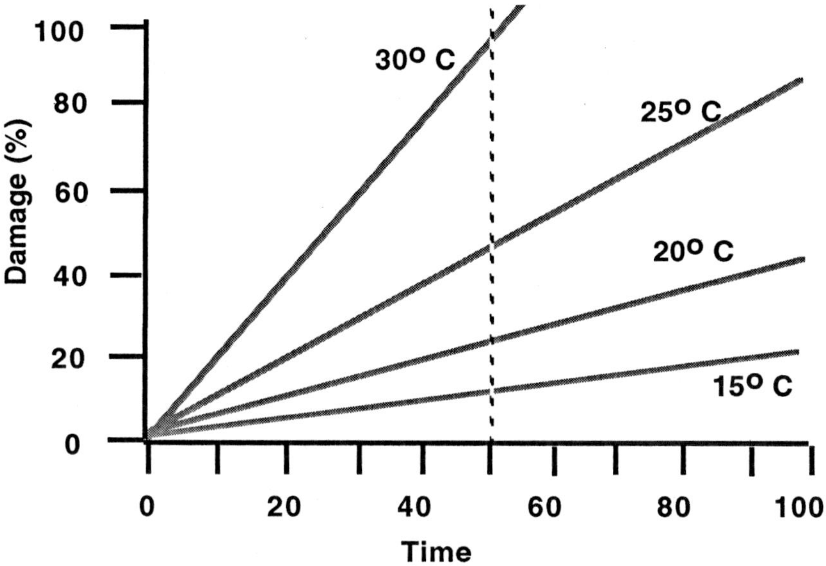

Figure 10.15 *Predicted rates of deterioration for at different temperatures. The materials are decaying eight times faster at 30°C than at 15°C*

temperatures greater than say 15–25°C. Some important reactions, such as the degradation of cellulose (paper, textiles), double in rate for every 5°C rise. So by more careful control of temperature we might be able to slow the rate of decay by two or three times even within the range of human comfort.

The progress of deterioration at four different temperatures is shown schematically in Figure 10.15. At the time indicated by the dotted line, an object would be completely destroyed if maintained at 30°C, but at 15°C only about 10% damage would be done. Another way of looking at this is to say that seven minutes at 30°C is equivalent to an hour at 15°C. A short time at an inappropriately high temperature can have a large effect on the predicted life span of an object.

It is because raising the temperature effectively compresses time that accelerated ageing tests are carried out at elevated temperatures. (This is discussed further in Chapter 15.)

It is possible to combine the effects of changes in temperature and humidity in a graph that can be used to predict relative life span of materials such as paper (Sebera, 1988). Figure 10.16 shows such a graph. Each of the curved lines is called an 'isoperm' as it connects points of equal permanence. The dotted lines cross at 50% relative humidity and 20°C. The curve that passes through this point represents a certain permanence which is given a value of 1.0. Any set of conditions on that

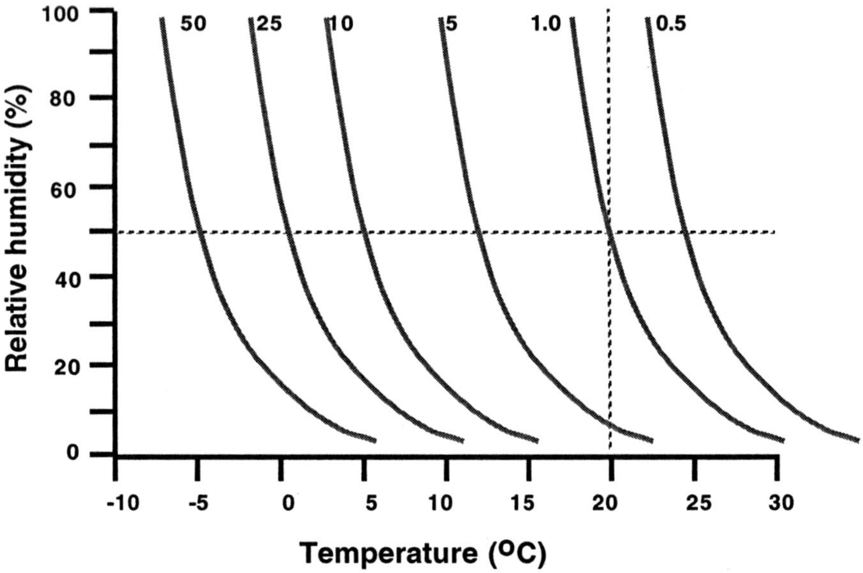

Figure 10.16 *Isoperms are lines joining points of equal permanence. These lines are calculated for the decay of paper. The number at the top of each curve represents the relative lifetime compared to the curve that passes through the standard conditions of 20°C and 50% relative humidity (after Sebera)*

line would have the same permanence. We can raise the temperature as long as we decrease the humidity and vice versa. If we move along the 50% RH line until we reach a new isoperm we can see that changing the temperature has a dramatic effect. Raising the temperature 5° halves the lifetime. Lowering it to –5°C makes the collection last 50 times longer. This is why it is worth doing the cost–benefit analysis to see whether cold storage is an achievable option.

Damage functions and prediction

If enough observations are made of the various factors that affect the rate of deterioration it is possible to combine the most important of these into a mathematical equation called a damage function. The amount of change in whichever property we have chosen to represent damage can be predicted if appropriate values for things like levels of humidity and pollution are put into the equation. Once again a computer spreadsheet is a convenient tool because you can take a quite complex relationship and by altering one variable at a time instantly see the long-term effect in terms of a number or a graph. The deterioration of outdoor calcareous

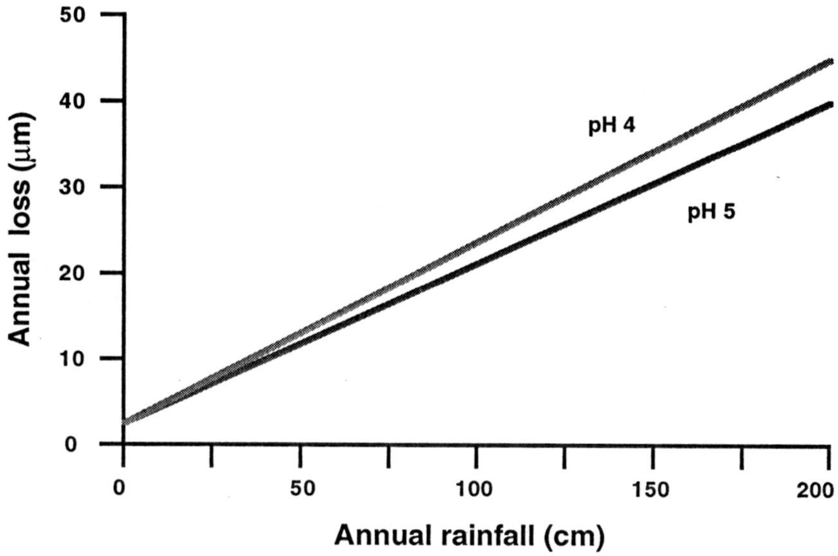

Figure 10.17 *Damage function for calcareous stones plotted as a graph of stone loss against rainfall. Levels of pollution typical of Northern European cities are included. The effect of a change in acidity of the rain can be seen (after Lipfert)*

stone has been studied for a long time and a damage function that combines the amount of rainfall, the acidity of the rain and the levels of sulphur dioxide and nitrogen oxides has been established (Lipfert, 1989). Figure 10.17 shows a graph plotting the output of this function in terms of loss of depth in the stone and annual rainfall. About 85% of this loss is due to the fact that calcium carbonate is soluble in water. Whether the rain is more or less acid has a relatively small effect. At an average rainfall of 100 cm a year we would expect the surface to recede at a rate of about 2 mm per century. Typical erosion at about this rate is shown in Figure 10.18.

The rate of loss of outdoor sculptures made of bronze (Mirabelli and Massa, 1991) has been fitted to a general damage function for metals which is of the form:

$$L = At^b \tag{10.6}$$

The Loss of metal L (in grams per square metre) is a function of t which is the time of wetness, that is, the time at which the object was above a threshold humidity, say 90%. A is a number that depends on the concentrations of sulphur dioxide and salt in the atmosphere. The number b depends on the particular patina and the acidity of the rain. If

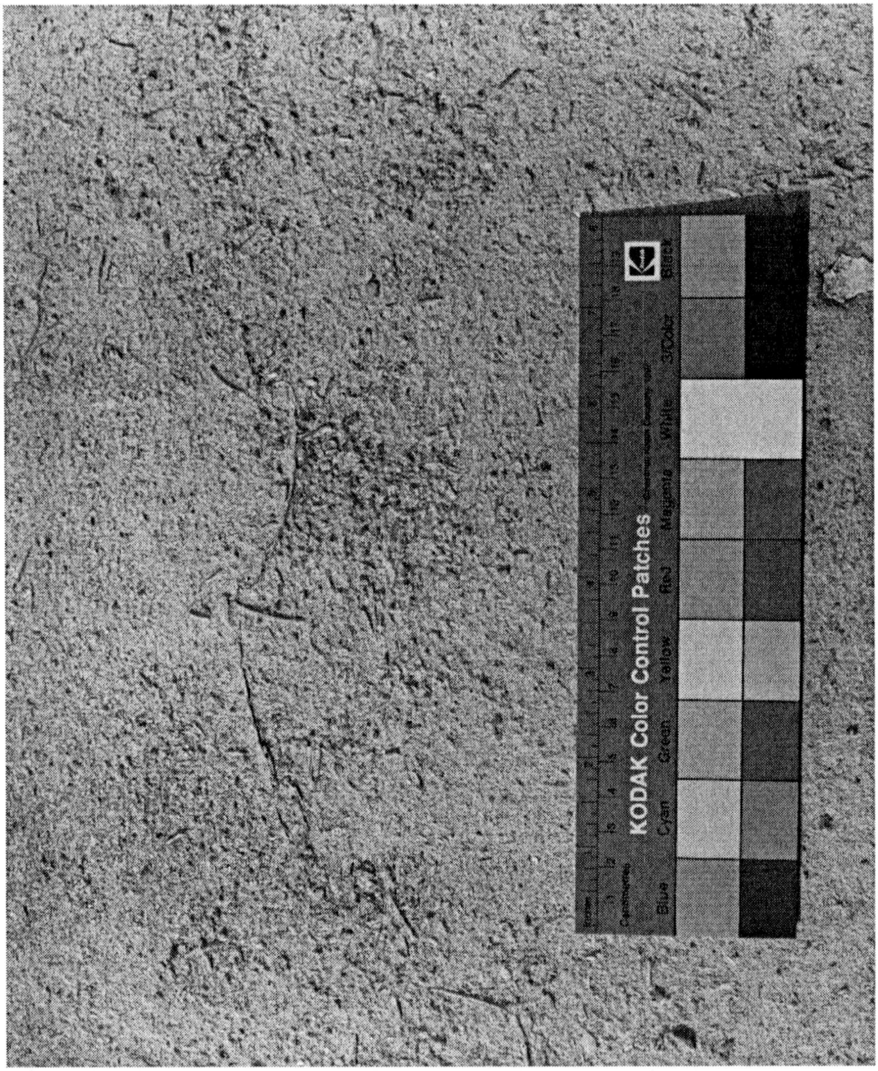

Figure 10.18 *The façade of the Victoria and Albert Museum has been exposed for 90 years, the inclusions are standing about 2 mm proud of the eroded surface*

the number *b* is less than 1.0, the reaction is one where the rate decreases with time. A corrosion velocity for bronze of only 0.2 μm per year (0.2 mm per 1000 years) has been calculated, which makes outdoor bronze a physically pretty stable material even if it does change colour dramatically (Figure 10.19).

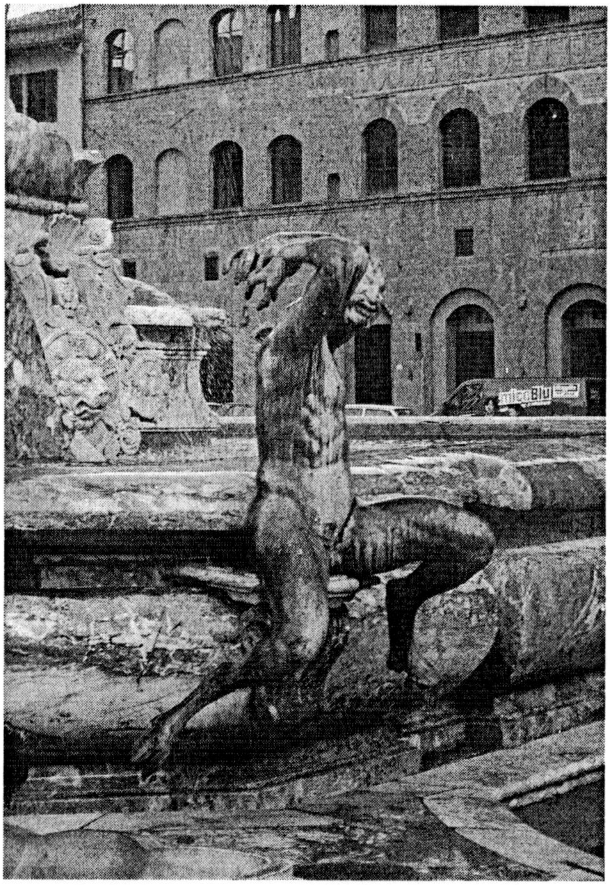

Figure 10.19 *Although very little material has been lost the effect of chemical change can be quite dramatic. Is it pleasing or disturbing?*

Thresholds

Methods of preventing pollutants getting to the objects, such as air filtration, showcases, cardboard boxes or protective lacquer coatings, all have costs in terms of money and interference with access. At certain levels of pollution you may want to take positive action because the rate of damage is large compared with the costs in cash and inconvenience. But is there a level below which you don't need to worry at all? There are theoretical limits dictated by the thermodynamics and kinetics of the reactions (Brimblecombe, 1994, p. 71). With human beings there are often levels of potentially damaging substances that can be tolerated without detectable long- or short-term effect. The human body has ways of

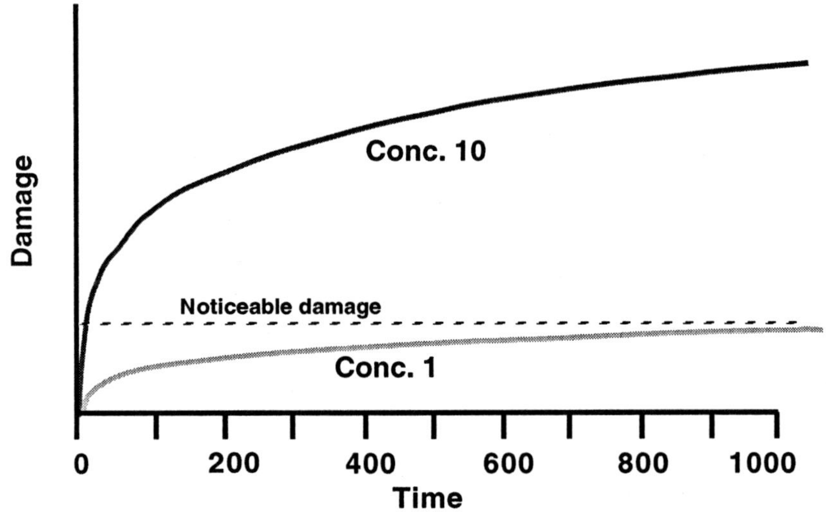

Figure 10.20 *If the rate of decay follows a 'parabolic' function (see equation (10.6)) it takes a very long time for damage to be noticed at low concentrations of pollutant. Compare with Figure 10.7*

disposing of poisons at low levels and also self-repair mechanisms. It is also true that humans are going to die of something at some time anyway. Very slow damage is not noticed because the experiment is interrupted by death.

Objects do not have self-repair mechanisms but there do appear to be concentrations of pollutants which do not seem harmful, whereas at levels only slightly higher noticeable damage is taking place. As we have seen, the level of humidity can act as a threshold. The corrosion of medieval stained glass does not occur at humidities below 20% even with high levels of pollution. At humidities of around 60% it does not proceed detectably at low levels of sulphur dioxide (Fitz, 1986, p. 234). Tétrault could not detect any reaction between acetic acid and lead at humidities below 75% where the acid concentration was less than $0.43\,\mathrm{mgm^{-3}}$ (Tétrault, Sirois and Stamatoplou, 1998).

The corrosion of metals follows the general form shown in equation (10.6). In the majority of cases the rate of reaction decreases with time as a layer of corrosion products builds up on the surface, interfering with further interaction (coefficient b less than unity). The early stages of the corrosion of lead by substances emitted from timber has been shown to follow this equation where the value of b is about 0.5 and t is the total time of exposure (Berndt, 1990). This behaviour is shown in Figure 10.20 for two concentrations of pollutant. It takes nearly a thousand times as long to reach a point where the damage is noticed as it does with a level of pollution only 10 times greater. So although there may be detectable levels of aggressive VOCs in the air, lead objects in galleries do not appear to corrode in the way that objects in wooden cases do. As a manager you might decide to think of this very slow rate of damage as below the threshold for immediate action.

Something to think about

Which do you think poses the greatest risk, chemicals generated outside the museum, inside the museum or inside the object?

How would you calculate loss of value for a bronze sculpture disfigured by a streaky patina or a newspaper weakened by exposure to atmospheric pollution?

If the average stone loss is predicted to be a mere 2 mm a century, why have some outdoor sculptures lost much more than this?

In Figure 10.3 levels of pollution inside the museum appear to be rising while they are falling outside. What could cause the graph to appear this way?

References

Amoroso, Giovanni G. and Fassina, Vasco (1983) *Stone Decay and Conservation: Atmospheric Pollution, Cleaning, Consolidation and Protection*. Elsevier.

Baer, Norbert S. and Banks, Paul N. (1985) Indoor Air Pollution: Effects on Cultural and Historic Materials. *International Journal of Museum Management and Curatorship*, **4**, pp. 9–20.

Barbara Lübkert and de Tilly, Soizick The OECD-MAP Emission Inventory for SO_2, NOx, and VOC in Western Europe. *Atmospheric Environment*, **23**, p. 3.

Berndt, Harald (1990) Measuring the Rate of Atmospheric Corrosion in Microclimates. *Journal of the American Institute for Conservation*, **29**, pp. 207–220.

Blades, Nigel (1996) Assessment and Monitoring the Environment of Cultural Property. Final Report. EU Contract EV5V-CT92–0144 'AMECP'.

Braun, P. and Wilson (1970) The Removal of Atmospheric Sulphur by Building Stones. *Atmospheric Environment*, **4**, p. 371.

Brimblecombe, Peter (1989) A Theoretical Approach to the Pollution of Air Volumes Within Museums. *The Conservator*, **13**, p. 15.

Brimblecombe, Peter (1992) *Biological Materials as Sources of Pollution in Museums. Life After Death*. UKIC. ISBN 1-871656-15-X.

Brimblecome, Peter (1994) The Balance of Environmental Factors Attacking Artifacts, in *Durability and Change: The Science, Responsibility, and Cost of Sustaining Cultural Heritage*, edited by W.E. Krumbein, P. Brimblecombe, D.E. Cosgrove and S Staniforth. John Wiley and Sons. ISBN 0-471-95221-4, pp. 67–80.

Camuffo, D. (1991) Environment and Microclimate. Science, Technology and European Cultural Heritage. Proceedings of the European Symposium, Bologna, Italy, 13–16 June 1989. Butterworth-Heinemann for the Commission of the European Communities, p. 37.

Cassar, May and Martin, Graham (1994) The Environmental Performance of Display Cases. Preventive Conservation: Practice, Theory and Research. Preprints to the Ottawa Congress, 12–16 September. IIC, pp. 171–174.

Cooper, Timothy P., O'Brien, Paul F. and Jeffrey, David W. (1992) Rates of Deterioration of Portland Limestone in an Urban Environment. *Studies in Conservation*, Vol. 37, No. 4, p. 228–238.

Crump, Derrick R. (1995) Volatile Organic Compounds in Indoor Air. Volatile Organic Compounds in the Atmosphere, in *Issues in Environmental Science and Technology*, 4, edited by R.E. Hester and R.M. Harrison. The Royal Society of Chemistry. ISBN 0-85404-215-6.

European Concerted Action (1989) Indoor Air Quality and Its Impact on Man. Environment and Quality of Life. COST project 613. Office for Publications of the European Communities, Luxembourg.

Fellers, Christer, Iversen, Tommy, Lindström, Tom, Nilsson, Thomas and Rigdahl, Mikael (1989) Ageing/Degradation of Paper: a Literature Survey. FoU-projektet for papperkonservering. Report No 1E. Stockholm. ISSN 0284–5636.

Fitz, Stephan (1986) Do Air Pollutants Damage Historic Stained Glass Windows? *Proceedings of the Electrochemical Society*, **86**, pp. 227–238.

Furlan, V. and Girardet, F. (1991) Attack of Atmosheric Pollution (Sulphur Compounds) on Interior Building Stones. Science, Technology and European Cultural Heritage. Proceedings of the European Symposium, Bologna, Italy, 13–16 June 1989. Butterworth-Heinemann for the Commission of the European Communities, p. 426.

Graedel, T.E. and McGill, R. (1986) Degradation of Materials in the Atmosphere. *Environmental, Science and Technology*, **20**, pp. 1093–1100.

Graedel, T.E. Mechanisms of Chemical Change in Metals Exposed to the Atmosphere, in *Durability and Change: The Science, Responsibility, and Cost of Sustaining Cultural Heritage*, edited by W.E. Krumbein, P. Brimblecombe, D.E. Cosgrove and S. Staniforth. John Wiley and Sons. ISBN 0-471-95221-4, pp. 95–106.

Green, L.R. (1993) The British Museum. Conservation Research Section Report No. CA1993/20.

Gurnagal, Norayr and Xuenjun Zou (1994) The Effect of Atmospheric Pollutants on Paper Permanence: A Literature Review. *Tappi Journal*, Vol. 77, pp. 199–204.

Heath, Diana and Martin, Graham (1988) The Corrosion of Lead and Lead/Tin Alloys Occurring on Japanese Lacquer Objects. The Conservation of Far Eastern Art. IIC. Kyoto Conference, edited by John S. Mills, Perry Smith and Kazuo Yamasaki, pp. 137–141.

Hester, R.E. and Harrison, R.M. (eds). Volatile Organic Compounds in the Atmosphere, in *Issues in Environmental Science and Technology,* 4, The Royal Society of Chemistry. ISBN 0-85404-215-6.

Inaba, Masamitsu and Sugisita, Ryuitiro (1990) Permanence of Washi (Japanese Paper) (Part II). Materials Issues in Art and Archaeology II. Symposium 17–21 April, San Francisco. Materials Research Society, pp. 799–804.

Johansson, L-G., Lindquist, O. and Mangio, R.E. (1988) Corrosion of Calcereous Stones in Humid Air Containing SO_2 and NO_2, in *Air Pollution and Conservation: Safeguarding Our Architectural Heritage. Durability of Building Materials*, 5, edited by Jan Rosvall and Stig Aleby, pp. 255–265.

Kerrel, E., Briggs, D.J., Reeve, D. and Wright, A. The CORINE Environmental Information System: Applications to the Protection of Europe's Cultural Heritage. Science, Technology and European Cultural Heritage. Proceedings of the European Symposium, Bologna, Italy, 13–16 June 1989. Butterworth-Heinemann for the Commission of the European Communities, p. 825.

Lipfert, F.W. (1989) Atmospheric Damage to Calcareous Stones: Comparison and Reconciliation of Recent Experimental Findings. *Atmospheric Environment*, **23**, pp. 195–201.

Michalski, Stefan (1994) Leakage Prediction for Buildings, Cases, Bags and Bottles. *Studies in Conservation*, **39**, pp. 169–186.

Mirabelli, M. and Massa, S. (1991) Ancient Metal Objects in Outdoor Exposure: Causes, Mechanisms and Measurements of Damage. Science, Technology and European Cultural Heritage. Proceedings of the European Symposium, Bologna, Italy, 13–16 June 1989. Butterworth-Heinemann for the Commission of the European Communities, p. 190.

Nazaroff, William W. and Cass, Glen R. (1986) Mathematical Modelling of Chemically Reactive Pollutants in Indoor Air. *Environmental Science and Technology,* **20**, pp. 924–934.

Passaglia, Elio (1989) The Characterisation of Microenvironments and the Degradation of Archival Records. *Restaurator,* **10**, pp. 123–150.

Price, C.A. (1996) *Stone Conservation: An Overview of Current Research*. The Getty Conservation Institute. The J. Paul Getty Trust. ISBN 0-89236-389-4.

Rosvall, Jan and Aleby, Stig (eds) (1988) Air Pollution and Conservation: Safeguarding Our Architectural Heritage. *Durability of Building Materials,* 5, p. 419.

Scharff, W. and Huesmann, L.A. (1977) Accelerated Decay of Metal Soil Finds Due to Soil Pollution. Metal 95. Proceedings of the International Conference on Metals Conservation edited by Ian D. Macleod, Stépane L. Pennec and Luc Robbiola. James and James. ISBN 1-873936-67-2, pp. 17–20.

Schuster, P.F., Reddy, M.M. and Sherwood, S.I. Effects of Acid Rain and Sulfur Dioxide on Marble Dissolution, in *Durability and Change: The Science, Responsibility, and Cost of Sustaining Cultural Heritage,* edited by W.E. Krumbein, P. Brimblecombe, D.E. Cosgrove and S. Staniforth. John Wiley and Sons. ISBN 0-471-95221-4, pp. 173–190.

Sebera, Donald K. (1988) A Graphical Representation of the Relationship of Environmental Conditions to the Permanence of Hygroscopic Materials and Composites. Proceedings of Conservation in Archives. International Symposium. Ottawa, Canada, 10–12, May pp. 51–74.

Smith, B.J. and Warke, P.A. (eds) (1995) *Processes of Urban Stone Decay. Proceedings of SWAPNET'95*. Belfast, Donhead. ISBN 1-873394-20-9

Spiker, E.C., Comer, V.J., Hosker, R.P. and Sherwood, S.I. (1992) Dry Deposition of SO_2 on Limestone and Marble: Role of Humidity. 7th International Congress on Deterioration and Conservation of Stone, edited by J. Delgado Rodrigues, F. Henriques and F. Telmo Jermias. Lisbon, Portugal, pp. 387–406.

Sydberger, T. and Vannerberg, N.G. (1972) The Influence of Relative Humidity and Corrosion Products on the Adsorption of Sulphur Dioxide on Metal Surfaces. *Corrosion Science*, **12**, p. 775.

Tétrault, Jean (1994) Display Materials: the Good the Bad and the Ugly. Exhibition and Conservation. Scottish Society for Conservation and Restoration. Edinburgh.

Tétrault, Jean and Stamatopolou, Eugénie (1997) Determination of Concentrations of Acetic Acid Emitted from Wood Coatings in Enclosures. *Studies in Conservation*, Vol. 42, pp. 141–156.

Tétrault, Jean, Sirois, Jane and Stamatopolou, Eugénie (1998) Studies of Lead Corrosion in Acetic Acid Environments. *Studies in Conservation*, Vol. 43, pp. 17–32.

Walsh, M., Black, A., Morgan, A. and Cranshaw, G.H. (1977) Sorption of SO_2 by Typical Indoor Surfaces Including Wool Carpets, Wallpaper and Paint. *Atmospheric Environment*, **11**, p. 1107.

Weale, Albert (1992) *The New Politics of Pollution*. Manchester University Press. ISBN 0-7190-3067-6, p. 21.

Williams, Edwin L., Grosjean, Eric and Grosjean, Daniel (1993) Exposure of Artists' Colorants to Sulfur Dioxide. *J. American Institute of Conservation*, **32**, pp. 291–310.

Wranglen, Gösta (1985) *An Introduction to Corrosion and Protection of Metals*. Chapman and Hall. ISBN 0-412-26050-6.

Zinn, Edward, Reilly, James M., Adelstein, Peter Z. and Nishimura, Douglas W. (1994a) Air pollution Effects on Library Microforms. Preventive Conservation: Practice, Theory and Research. Preprints to the Ottawa Congress, 12–16 September. IIC, pp. 195–201.

Zinn, Edward, Reilly, James M., Adelstein, Peter Z. and Nishimura Douglas W. (1994b) Preservation of Colour Photographs: the Danger of Atmospheric Oxidants in the Storage Environment. Environnement et Conservation de l'Écrit, de l'Image et du Son. *Actes des Journées Internationales d'Études de l'ARSAG*. Paris. ISSN 0765–0248, pp. 25–31.

11 Physical effect

Hazards in the environment cause physical changes in objects. Deposition of dirt causes changes in appearance that are easy to measure but more difficult to evaluate as damage. Changes in temperature can cause significant changes in state, and there is an interesting relationship between temperature and time. Under normal museum conditions temperature changes do not on their own constitute a risk for most object types. Interaction with moisture in the environment can cause dramatic changes in certain classes of object depending on their composition and construction. The degree to which these changes are cumulative or permanent is discussed.

Chemical/physical

This is the third and final chapter about the risks to objects just sitting still. It is about the probability and extent of physical changes of state that result from interaction with the environment. The last chapter dealt with accumulated damage caused by reaction with substances in the environment. The greater the dose of that substance the greater the damaging change. If we could remove the hazardous agent the reaction would stop, but the change would normally be permanent. In certain circumstances the visible effects of the change could be reversed by the intervention of a conservator.

Irreversible chemical changes are similar to extreme physical changes such as fracture and disintegration. They are steps down the path by which the structure and order imposed at the point of creation of the object are destroyed. They are signs of the general law that the randomness of the universe is increasing. Such changes are only reversible with effort.

Dirt and dust

The subject of dirt forms a perfect bridge between chemical and physical phenomena. Very small particles behave much like individual molecules in the way that they move around through the atmosphere. Larger particles are subject to physical forces such as gravity. The effect that dirt has on objects is mostly physical, due principally to the addition of material rather than to changes in chemical composition. However, the presence of dirt or dust may accelerate some chemical changes. Some types of soiling are very difficult to reverse.

Just as with gaseous pollution there are internal and external sources of airborne dirt and so there are different dirt populations inside and outside a museum building. The composition of airborne particles varies with location and season. The constitution of dirt inside museums and the rates and mechanisms of deposition are well reviewed (Thomson, 1986; Brimblecombe, 1990; Phenix and Burnstock, 1990; Nazaroff *et al.*, 1992, 1993).

If there is no filtration system the level of fine particles indoors will be about 90% of that outdoors. A good filtration system can reduce this to below 20%. Without filtration, the amount of coarse particles in the air will be about 50% of the outdoor level. Filtration can reduce this to about 10%. Figure 11.1 shows the sizes of various types of particles. Most of the coarse particles (greater than 1 μm, one-millionth of a metre, in diameter) are formed by mechanical abrasion at ground level or are ejected directly into the air as ash or seaspray. Most of the very fine particles are actually formed in the air following various combustion processes (automobiles and industry) or by reactions between pollutants. These small particles

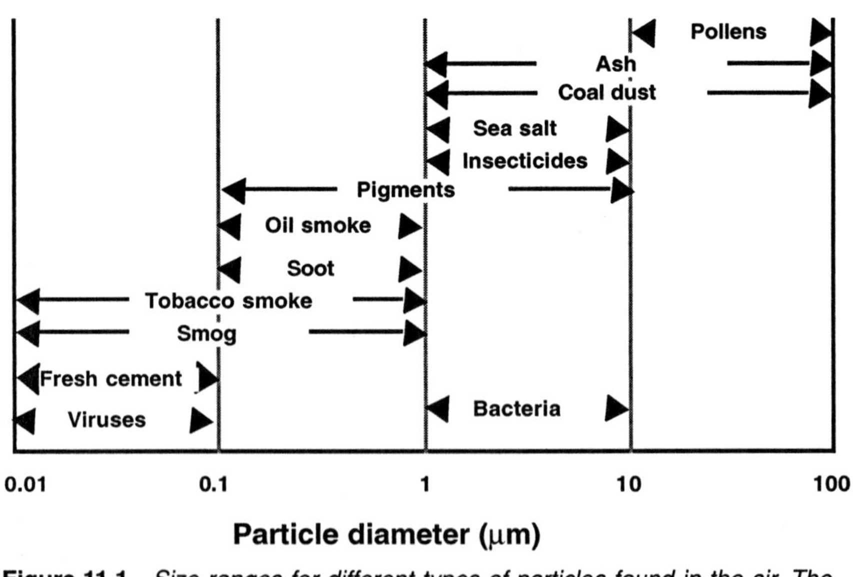

Figure 11.1 *Size ranges for different types of particles found in the air. The dividing line between fine and coarse particles is around 1 μm*

Table 11.1 *Composition of particles by mass (%)*

Type	*Airborne*	*Vertical surface*	*Horizontal surface*
Soot and organics	24.0	13.5	10.5
Sodium compounds (sea salt)	0.9	1.7	2.2
Sulphates	40.9	4.7	13.5
Lead compounds	2.1	1.7	2.3
Metals	11.2	32.2	27.1
Soil	11.7	35.4	36.7
Miscellaneous	10.8	9.3	7.7

often accumulate to form larger ones in the range 0.1–2 μm. This size range includes most of the black and tarry particles responsible for visible soiling and also carries the greatest amount of adsorbed gaseous pollutants. This is probably the most hazardous type of dirt.

In still air, particles over 15 μm settle out quite quickly, nearly all on to upward facing horizontal surfaces. Below this size the particles stay in the air until they hit something and stick to it, whether horizontal or vertical. An example of substances of which the particles are composed is shown in Table 11.1 (Nazaroff *et al.*, 1992, p. 143). This breaks the compositions into seven broad categories, each containing many subcategories. The figures shown are for a building without mechanical ventilation.

The analytical method used to determine these compositions would tend to underestimate the mass of small organic particles. Despite this it seems that in the air the organics and sulphates (from sulphur dioxide pollution) predominate but the particles that are more readily deposited on surfaces are the metals and particles from soil (from the Earth's crust, materials containing silicon and aluminium).

The models developed for levels of gaseous pollutants in the last chapter can be applied to particulate pollution. The amount of particulate matter suspended in the air in a gallery will be dependent on the rate at which dirty air enters the space and the rate at which the particles are deposited indoors. Less than half a per cent of the 0.1 μm particles that enter a building are actually deposited on surfaces. However, even if the process is slow, the amount of dirt in the air is what dictates the amount that will end up on things like objects. For elemental carbon, the blackest of particulate pollutants, this could be as much as 0.5 $\mu g\ m^{-2}\ d^{-1}$ (millionths of a gram per square metre per day) on walls and ceilings and 50 $\mu g\ m^{-2}\ d^{-1}$ on floors. At this rate white surfaces become noticeably soiled within a few months. So there is value in trying to reduce levels.

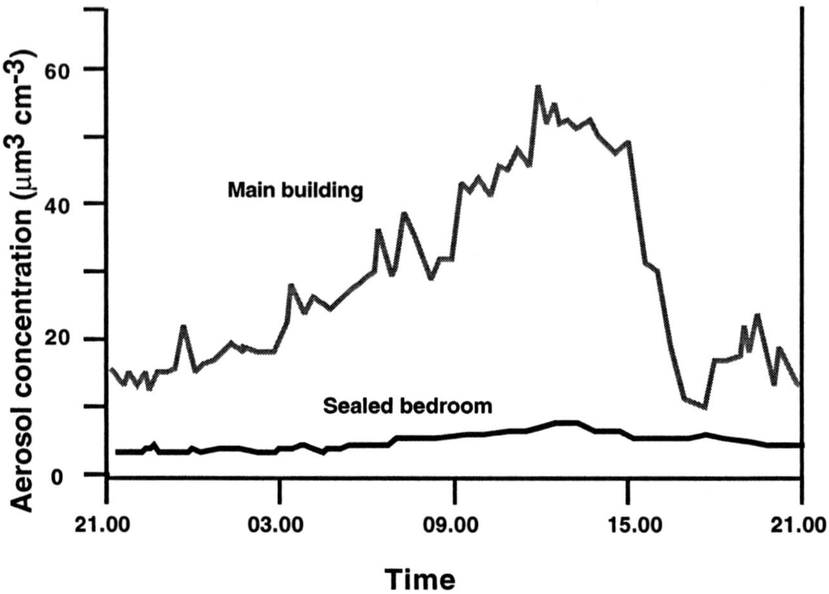

Figure 11.2 *The effect of sealing a room. Levels of particulate pollution in the main building are consistently higher (after Nazaroff* et al.*)*

Mechanically controlling air flow, recycling and filtering the air, can extend the time to visible soiling from months to decades. There are obviously high capital and running costs associated with this. Adaptation of an existing building has additional costs in terms of appearance and is likely to be less effective.

Reducing air exchange by simpler, cheaper means will help. Nazaroff and coworkers describe the effect of sealing off a bedroom and its delicate contents in Sepulveda House in El Pueblo de Los Angeles State Historic Park in downtown LA (Nazaroff *et al.*, 1993, p. 118). The visiting public were allowed into a glass enclosure just inside the door, but otherwise the room was isolated from the rest of the museum. This is a technique that has been used in several historic houses in Britain, such as Knole House in Kent. Figure 11.2 shows that the amount of particles in the range c.0.1–2 µm is greatly reduced and that daytime peaks in the main building are not noticed in the sealed room. The distribution of particles inside the room is different from that outside (see Figure 11.3). The proportion of particles greater than about 0.2 µm is very much lower.

The rate at which dirt is deposited on surfaces does not depend solely on the airborne concentration of particles. It also depends on the rate of transport to the actual surface. The particles must pass from the bulk of

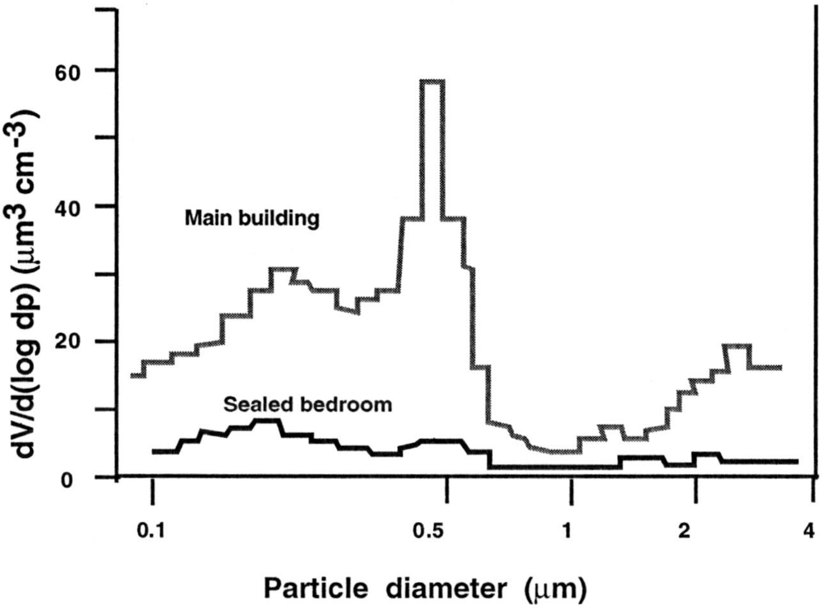

Figure 11.3 *Sealing the room alters the distribution of particulates in the air. There are far fewer large particles (after Nazarof* et al.*)*

the air across the thin boundary layer immediately against the surface. If the air flow over a surface is slow and not turbulent, deposition rates will be low. Air flow near doors, windows and ventilation grilles is likely to be faster and more turbulent than the average air movement in the rest of the gallery, leading to preferential deposition of dirt. Temperature differences can lead to convection currents that disrupt the boundary layer, leading to accelerated soiling.

In still air, particles will diffuse slowly outward from a source in the same way as pollutant gas molecules. The heavier particles are affected by gravity and tend to fall downwards onto up-facing surfaces. The smaller particles are kept airborne in random motion by collisions with the gas molecules that make up the atmosphere. If there is any reason for the gas molecules on one side of the particle to be consistently more energetic than those on the other, the particle will move in a particular direction. Temperature differences in the air will drive particles in one direction, from hot to cold. This is known as thermophoresis and is why colder patches on walls get badly soiled. If the walls are sufficiently cool for moisture to condense on them, the particles will also be driven in this direction by water molecules, the majority of which will be diffusing toward the wall.

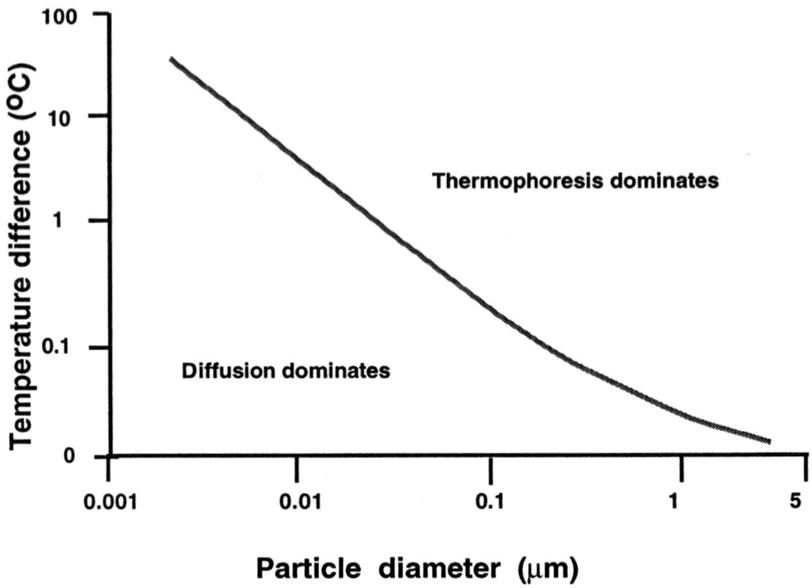

Figure 11.4 *Soiling of surfaces can be driven by differences in temperature. The larger the difference the larger the particle size affected*

Where there is a small temperature difference, thermophoresis is the dominant mechanism for the smaller particles. As the temperature difference increases so larger and larger particles are driven by this mechanism (see Figure 11.4). The thermal difference between air and surfaces will vary throughout the day depending on plant operation, display lighting and solar gain. There may be different convection currents and thermophoretic gradients at different times of day leading to cycles of soiling.

Simple controls consist of placing objects away from turbulent air and eliminating temperature gradients through the use of thermal insulation or isolation from exterior walls.

Indoor sources of dirt

Levels of certain types of dirt, such as organic materials, are higher inside than out, suggesting internal sources. The most obvious source is people. Tobacco smoking is a source of small tarry particles and for this and other reasons is usually not tolerated in museums. People lose flakes of skin (c.5 g a week). Their clothes continually shed fibres. As they walk about they grind fibres from carpets and particles of wax and wood from hard floors. Most of these particles are larger than 10 μm diameter and settle out on up-facing surfaces close to the source. However, the movement of people through galleries increases turbulence which may increase soiling of vertical surfaces.

Construction and renovation are sources of particulates. It has been suggested that new concrete can continue to emit dangerous levels of ultrafine alkaline particles for as much as two years unless the surface is suitably sealed (Toishi and Kenjo, 1975). Filters will need to be changed more frequently if there are high levels of construction dust.

Paradoxically, one of the causes of interior dirt is the desire to be clean. The waxing of floors has been postulated as a source of organic particles. The increasing use of cleaning materials in handy spray bottles must contribute. A feather duster obviously does nothing but move dirt from one surface to another, adding a few more particles of its own as it disintegrates. The vacuum cleaner gives small particles a second chance. Dirt that had already come to rest is sucked up into the machine. Large particles are broken into smaller pieces and small ones pass through the filter on their way to a new home.

Dirt and damage

From a knowledge of internal and external sources, and an understanding of air flows and temperature gradients in a building, it is possible to predict future levels of dirt deposition on objects in a gallery (see Table 11.2). It is considerably more difficult to say what the damage associated with that deposition is. It is therefore more difficult to judge appropriate levels of investment in preventive or curative methods.

Table 11.2 *Predicted rates of deposition on indoor surfaces ($\mu g\ m^{-2}\ d^{-1}$) (data from Nazaroff* et al., *1993)*

		Carbon	*Soil dust*	*Total*
1. Mechanical control				
a. laminar air flow	ceilings	0.003	0.00	0.003
	walls	0.05	0.01	0.3
	floors	52	560	1540
b. homogeneous turbulence	ceilings	0.54	0.1	3.6
	walls	0.64	0.23	6.2
	floors	53	560	1540
2. Natural ventilation	ceilings	0.4	0.32	1.4
	walls	0.69	0.7	2.8
	floors	280	8500	24 000

In my experience, museum visitors do not comment on the levels of soiling of objects on display. It is not surprising if historic things look old. If there is enough dust on a polished surface to write 'dust me', visitors see this as a sign that the museum does not care for its collections generally, not as an obstacle to interpreting the particular object beneath the dust. Deposition on upward facing projections will accentuate the surface profile, this might be disturbing or helpful. The scientific basis of visual effects of soiling on paintings is discussed by Eastaugh who concludes that shifts in colour are likely to be more important than changes in gloss (Eastaugh, 1990). However, recent evaluation of dust in museums has relied on reduction in gloss of glass slides exposed in galleries (Ford, 1997). This is likely to be a reasonable means of quantifying the effect of deposition on reflective surfaces on metals, ceramics and polished furniture, and has the benefit that it is independent of the colour of the dirt.

It is relatively easy to carry out scientific experiments that result in statements such as 'for black particles on white surfaces, soiling is perceptible when 0.2% of a smooth surface is effectively covered'. It is more difficult to say whether this degree of soiling has the slighest effect on the use of the object or whether it is actually or potentially causing permanent change.

It is possible to conceive of a number of mechanisms by which dirt could cause permanent damage to objects, but there is very little systematic research or anecdotal evidence to suggest that it is a serious hazard. Theoretically, particulates are likely to be acidic, contain metallic catalysts and attract moisture, all of which should accelerate chemical deterioration. Perhaps it is just so obvious that no one has bothered to study this systematically. Perhaps objects get cleaned sufficiently often for other reasons. The dirt doesn't stay long enough to cause noticeable damage.

There are definitely secondary effects of dust. If objects look neglected they are more likely to be treated carelessly, resulting in physical damage. If dust containing organic material is allowed to accumulate it will attract and harbour biological agents such as fungi and insects.

The most important factor in assessing dirt as a risk is that all methods of removing it are extremely hazardous to the objects. This is summed up in a statement from a report on the effects of air pollutants on modern textile fabrics and dyes:

> 'Unless fabrics are exposed to the abrasive action of wind-blown particles or are soiled with highly abrasive particles and repeatedly flexed, they are not directly deteriorated by soiling, a familiar (but aesthetically objectionable) process in which airborne particles settle on objects. The major impact of soiling results from the need for more frequent dry cleaning and laundering, which not only

> represent added expenses but, more importantly, hasten the day when fabrics are no longer serviceable.' (Upham and Sabin, 1975)

For fragile objects, such as historic textiles, damage by cleaning is certain, but the extent of damage at each cleaning operation has yet to be fully quantified. The more fragile the object, the more time consuming the careful cleaning will have to be. High future costs of cleaning must be weighed against current costs of preventive measures and continuing maintenance.

Effects of temperature and humidity

The extreme physical changes that can result from explosions or earthquakes could be explained by saying that:

> 'The rate of change in the environment affects the rate of change of the object.'

The chemical alterations discussed in the last chapter could be described by the statement:

> 'The state of the environment affects the rate of change of the object.'

In the rest of this chapter we will be discussing physical changes that are best described by:

> 'The state of the environment affects the state of the object.'

A simple example of this is the traditional liquid-in-glass thermometer. If the temperature of the environment rises, the length of liquid in the tube increases. If the temperature drops, the length of liquid decreases. This change in state is directly related to a change in the environment but is not permanent and needs no effort to reverse it. In 50 years of hypochondria and child-rearing I have never known a clinical thermometer that wore out through the repeated oscillation of the mercury. It was always extreme physical change caused by biting or dropping that resulted in irreversible damage.

Some physical changes appear to be totally reversible through a large number of cycles. To assess the risk we need to determine whether there are factors such as the size of the change, or the total number of cycles, that will tip the balance from reversible change to permanent damage. We need to know whether there are chains of events or combinations of small alterations that can result in catastrophe.

Temperature

The reason that we are able to measure temperature at all is that certain physical characteristics of materials change in a reliable and reversible way as they absorb or release heat. We have to be careful how we use the word 'reversible'. There are some transformations, such as melting and solidifying, that take place on raising and lowering temperature. These do not perceptibly change the chemical composition of a material and may not permanently alter many of its measurable properties such as density, colour, conductivity or solubility. But the shape changes!

Leaving aside certain scientific specimens that are kept below freezing point, very few objects are likely to be damaged by melting at temperatures that would normally be found in galleries or stores. Waxes are among the lowest melting materials of which artifacts are likely to be made. The majority of fats and waxes have melting points above 35°C. To allow a margin of safety 25°C should be taken as a maximum for objects made of these materials.

The melting and freezing of water in the outdoor environment can have a deleterious effect on materials that absorb water, such as stone. The change in volume on going from liquid to solid is enough to cause cracking and spalling. In these circumstances it is the number of passages through this transition temperature that is more important than the length of stay at any extreme either side of this point (Warke, 1996).

The change from solid to liquid is called a phase change. Solid-to-solid phase changes are also possible. Since these entail changes of volume and structure they might be potentially damaging. The best known of these changes in the solid phase is 'tin pest' where the metal tin theoretically changes crystal structure and disintegrates if the temperature falls below 13°C. This applies only to the pure metal tin and not to its commonly found alloy pewter. Moreover it is difficult to get even pure tin to perform the trick (Peal, 1971).

The majority of materials of organic origin are polymeric, that is they are composed of very long molecules bunched together. This fundamental feature of the structure of materials such as textiles, paper and wood has a profound effect on how they behave with changes in the environment. Depending on the temperature they can behave like glass or like rubber.

Independent of the environment, polymeric materials 'age', that is, their physical properties change slowly with time. This is not due to chemical degradation but to the fact that the long molecules are slowly easing themselves into more comfortable positions more closely packed together. During the process of creation or manufacture the material has been left 'frozen' in an unstable state. The process of ageing is the material slowly trying to reach its most stable configuration. This process has been reviewed in the context of conservation (Fellers, Iversen, Lindström, Nilsson and Rigdahl, 1989).

As the polymer molecules pack closer together the material becomes smaller in volume, stronger yet more brittle. As this happens it should also become less affected by moisture and by pollutants. The rate at which materials age physically depends on the temperature and on the specific nature of the polymer. For each material there is a particular temperature above which it is easy for the long molecules to slide past one another. This is called the glass transition temperature and given the symbol[1] T_g. Below this temperature the material acts like a brittle glass: above T_g it is more flexible. The nearer the ambient temperature is to the glass transition temperature, the more quickly the material will age. Physical ageing has been observed in wool, in cotton and in other cellulose fibres found in paper (Atalla, 1981).

The changes in properties of materials around the glass transition and the consequences for preservation have been reviewed (Schilling, 1989; Michalski, 1991). Materials above their glass transition temperature tend to be tacky and to imbibe dirt, this is a particular problem for acrylic paints whose T_g is around room temperature. If materials that we expect to behave flexibly become more rigid because the temperature has fallen below T_g there may be risk in moving or using the object. The change in stiffness for an idealized acrylic paint is shown in Figure 11.5. The material becomes a thousand times stiffer as the temperature drops. Since the glass transition is dependent on the presence of additives, contaminants and moisture (most of which bring it down) it is not possible to give a definitive list of materials and their T_g.

Objects expand and contract as the temperature changes. Environments with people in are unlikely to suffer temperature changes greater than 10°C. The increase in any one dimension for a 10° temperature rise is less than 0.02%. The forces that could be generated by this small dimensional change are a fraction of that needed to break or permanently distort everyday materials. This is obvious from the fact that objects such as automobiles and windows do not regularly crack or buckle when the outdoor temperature drops rapidly by more than 10° as night falls.

Ceramics and glass expand about a tenth of the amount that metals do for a particular temperature rise. If metals and ceramics are found in close combination, as in enamels, it is possible that temperature changes could set up damaging stresses due to differential expansion.

[1] It is also given the symbol t_g but I shall reserve lower case *t* to refer to time.

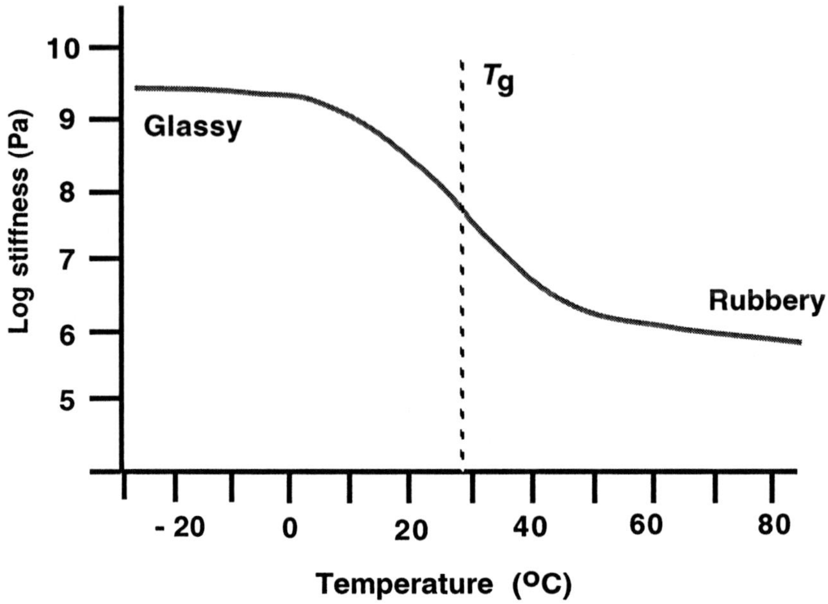

Figure 11.5 *Many polymeric materials rapidly change physical properties, such as stiffness, if they are heated above a temperature called the glass transition point*

For a 10° change the induced stress is still well within the ability of the more brittle material to accommodate it. Again this is obvious from the fact that the preparation and decoration of enamel involve much greater temperature ranges. Enamel-coated metals are used for ovenware. If the enamel layer is thin, poorly attached, scratched or deteriorated, a change of more than 5° might possibly do harm. Figure 11.6 shows loss of enamel that was apparently caused by an overnight fall in temperature that could not have been greater than 20°C. There is a synergic effect between humidity, pollution and temperature change in the mechanisms of enamel degradation (Pilz and Troll, 1997).

The rate at which the temperature changes could be important. The difference in thermal expansion will be exaggerated if only one component of a complex structure gets hot before the rest of the object has a chance to reach the same temperature. Objects in direct sunlight or close to spotlights can heat up rapidly. Depending on the material and the circumstances the temperature rise could be as much as 40°C. There are very rare reports of ceramics, glass and enamels cracking on display where radiated heat has added that little extra stress to those that were probably already there.

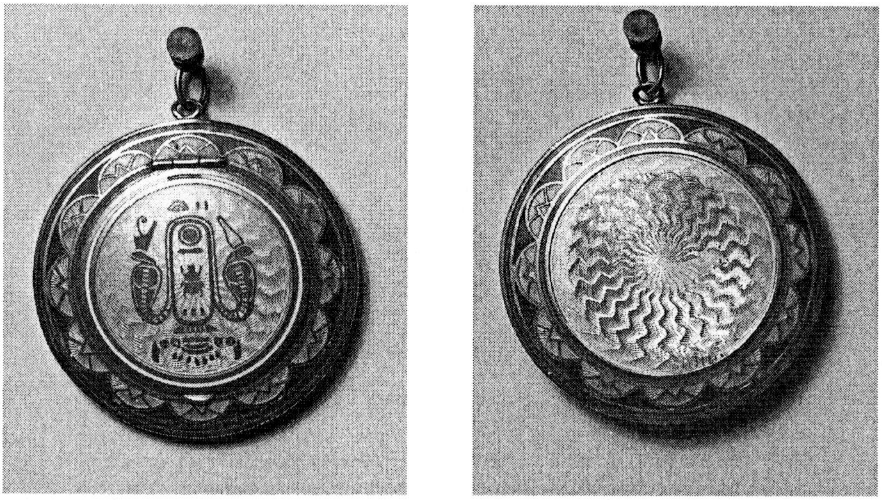

Figure 11.6 *Front and back view of a nineteenth-century enamel pendant. Disintegration of the front panel was due to a drop in temperature*

Temperature and time

There is an interesting relationship between temperature, time and physical change that is worth some effort to explain.

If sufficient force is applied to a material it will distort. The way that materials behave under mechanical stress is usually shown using a stress–strain curve. If a sample of material is held at both ends and pulled it can behave in several different ways. Four typical types of behaviour are shown in Figure 11.7. The terms glass, elastic, plastic and rubbery are used in this context as technical terms to describe differing responses to stress. These terms can be applied to a range of different materials. There may be types of material called by these names that do not respond as their names suggest. A very clear description of the mechanical properties of materials of the sort found in museum objects has been written by Lorna Gibson (Gibson, 1988).

Glass-like materials are stiff and need a lot of stress (force applied per cross-sectional area) to generate any strain (fractional increase in length). Only a small amount of strain can be tolerated before fracture occurs. For stresses lower than those that cause the sample to break, the behaviour is reversible. If the stress is removed the strain disappears (see Figure 11.8(a)). This is called elastic behaviour. Rubber-like materials stretch very easily under small stresses and can take very large strains before they break. This behaviour is also reversible (see Figure 11.8(d)). The same

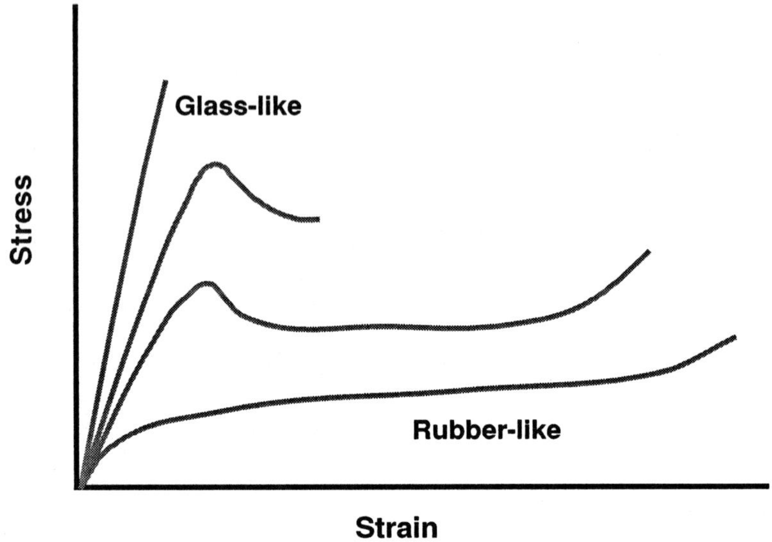

Figure 11.7 *Four different stress/strain behaviours of a polymeric material at different temperatures*

polymeric material can display both behaviours depending on the temperature. At intermediate temperatures the material will show intermediate behaviour, responding elastically to begin with but then starting to deform more rapidly before breaking. The deformation may not be reversible if the material is stretched beyond the yield point, the point where elastic behaviour turns to plastic behaviour. The material will have a permanent strain, shown by the distance between the up and down portions of curves b and c in Figure 11.8.

The rate at which the stress is applied is very important. If it is applied very rapidly the material will behave like glass and may fracture. If the stress is applied very, very slowly the material can tolerate this stress by behaving like a highly stretchable material. There is a relationship between time and temperature. A deformation for a short period of time at one temperature is equivalent to a longer period at a lower temperature (Nicholson, 1991). So rather than temperature shown along the horizontal axis in Figure 11.5 we could have time as shown in Figure 11.9.

If stress is maintained over long periods the material can begin to creep, that is, slowly deform to relieve the stress. The higher the temperature the faster this will occur. Museum objects are kept under stress for long periods. The force is usually provided by gravity. Some, like tapestries, are displayed in tensile stress as they hang from a support at the top. Many others like sculpture and furniture are in compressive stress as the

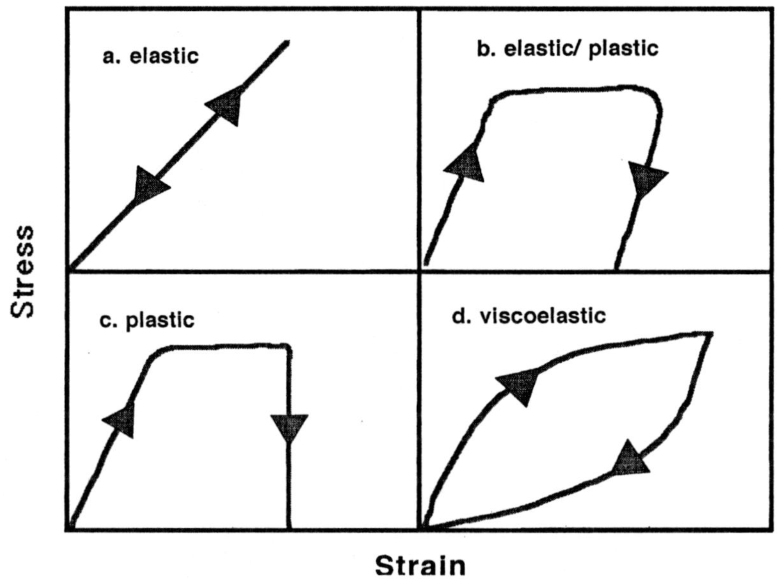

Figure 11.8 *The degree of reversibility of four different/stress strain behaviours. The plastic response in b and c results in permanent deformation. The arrowed lines do not return to the same point*

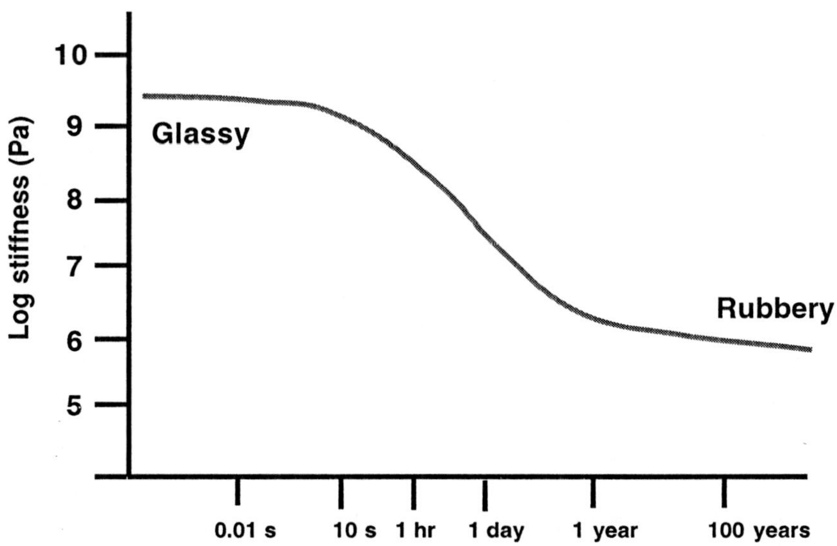

Figure 11.9 *The speed at which strain develops determines the apparent stiffness of the material. Rapid response may be damaging*

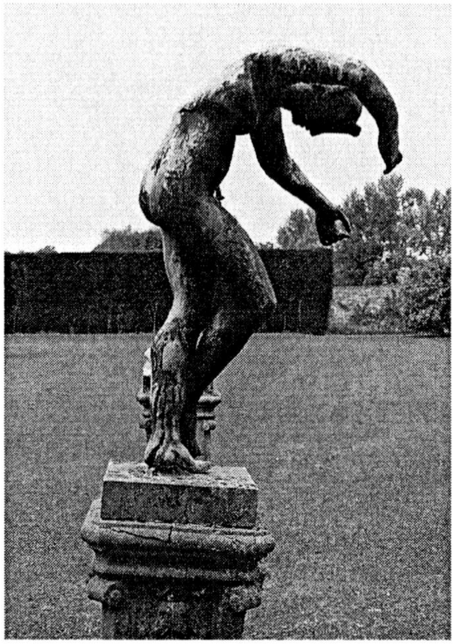

Figure 11.10 *As the internal iron support rusted away this sculpture slowly deformed under the stress of its own weight*

force of their weight is resisted by the floor. Since creep relieves stress it may not always be a bad thing. It will only constitute damage if there is noticeable irreversible change in shape. This is only likely to be a problem for polymeric materials in museums if there is a mount or hanging system with a small cross-section which causes high local stress.

In metals at ambient temperatures creep only becomes a problem if the melting point of the metal is less than about 500°C. The necessary stresses are only likely to occur if the density of the metal is high and size of the object is big. Unless it has adequate internal support, lead sculpture can deform over periods of a century or so (see Figure 11.10).

Humidity and strength

Humidity in the air around us is frequently measured as 'relative humidity', RH. This is certainly the way curators and conservators talk about humidity, although engineers and scientists may have other ways of expressing it. At least once a year someone new to museum work says 'Why on earth do we use RH rather than . . .?' But we seem to be stuck with it. RH is an indication of how much more water the air could contain

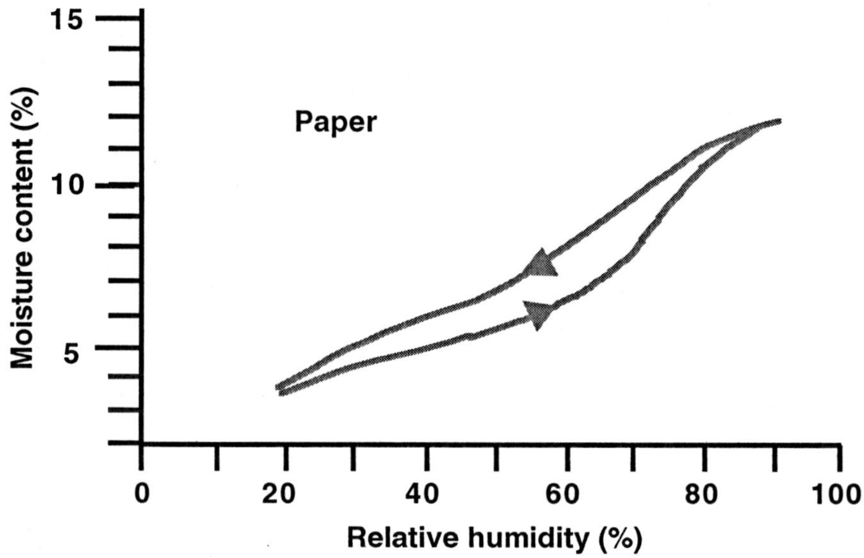

Figure 11.11 *Moisture content changes for Kraft paper in response to rising and falling relative humidity*

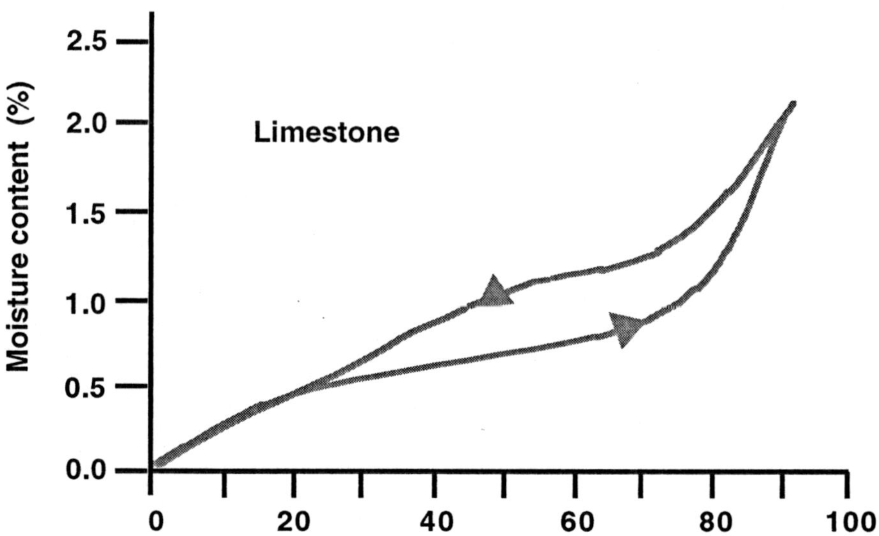

Figure 11.12 *Moisture content changes for limestone in response to rising and falling relative humidity. Note the much lower water content for the inorganic material*

at that temperature. 0% RH means the air contains no moisture and could hold a lot more. 100% RH means the air cannot hold any more moisture. Air at 50% RH contains different amounts of water depending on the temperature, 5 grams per cubic metre at 10°C and 10 grams at 20°C. As long as the temperature remains constant, a change in RH is a change in the concentration of water in the air.

A dynamic equilibrium is formed between water molecules in the air and water molecules adsorbed onto or into an object. As the RH rises so the amount of water in the object will rise. As the RH falls so the amount of moisture in the object falls. Although the relationship is easy to state, it is not so simple if we look closely. Figures 11.11 and 11.12 show the effect on the moisture content of two different materials of increasing and then decreasing RH. Although the amount of water absorbed is very different there are similarities between the curves for paper and limestone. There are portions of the curve that are steep and portions that are relatively flat. Each material has more water in it at 50% if the RH was previously higher, than it does at 50% RH if the humidity was previously lower. This effect is known as hysteresis. This means that even if we know the RH quite accurately we can't be so sure about the moisture content unless we know the object's recent history.

For objects made of materials like paper or leather that are degraded by hydrolysis (reaction with water) it is the moisture content that will dictate the rate of reaction. Following the curve in Figure 11.11 it can be seen that there will be a smaller increase in reaction rate going from 30 to 60% than going from 60 to 90%.

Physical properties of absorbent materials, such as textiles and paper, change with changes in moisture content. The effects of different humidities on the tensile behaviour of three different textile fibres is shown in Figure 11.13 (Ballard, 1995). All three become more flexible at higher humidities. Cotton becomes weaker, as well as less flexible, at low humidities. The changes in three mechanical properties for paper as the humidity deviates from 50% RH are shown in Figure 11.14. Tensile strength is a maximum at 30–40% RH but decreases rapidly as humidity increases. For a collection that is not physically handled, but subject only to the stresses of being restrained by mounting methods, tensile strength may be a useful measure. In this case a relative humidity of below 50% would be appropriate.

Other measures of strength, such as fold endurance and tear strength, show increases with rise in humidity. If the values derived from these mechanical tests actually bear a relationship to the way in which materials are abused by handling, a higher humidity would be appropriate in active libraries and archives. It was surely a librarian's vision, of an infinite number of malicious readers systematically folding

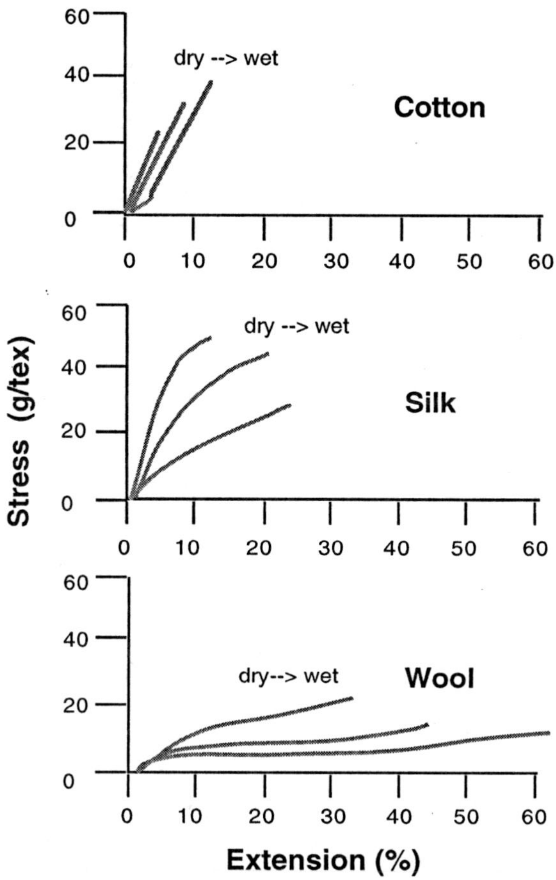

Figure 11.13 *Textile fibres become more flexible as humidity increases (after Ballard)*

the corners of pages to mark which ones they were about to tear out, that led to the specification of 60% RH as the set point in the British standard for archives BS5454.

However, the benefits of safer handling at higher humidities must be weighed against the increased rate of chemical damage. Mechanical damage is easily noticed and so may receive more attention than slow chemical degradation. Mechanical damage can, however, be reversed by simple interventive treatment, whereas reversal of chemical damage needs more invasive methods.

Polymeric materials become softer and more flexible as they absorb moisture. To that extent the change can be equated to those that occur

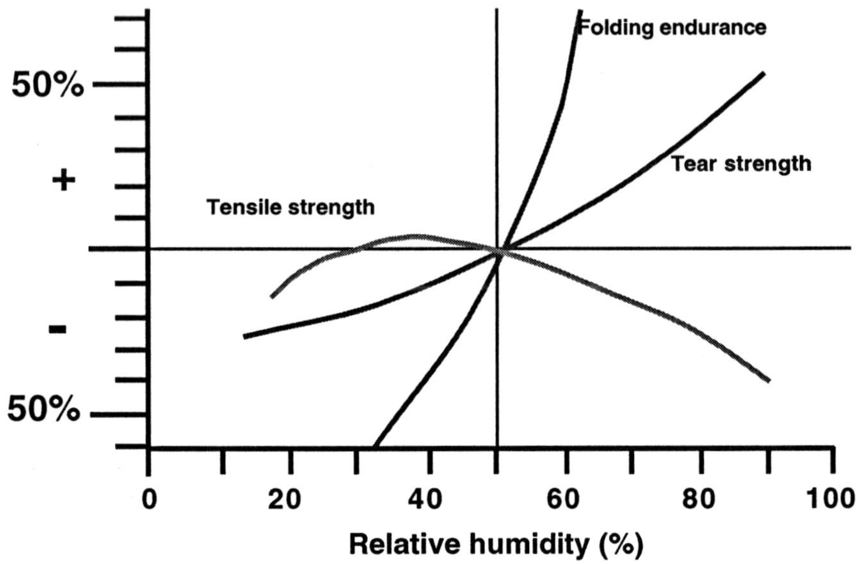

Figure 11.14 *Variations in mechanical properties of paper with changing RH, shown as percentage change compared to standard conditions of 20°C and 50% RH (after Smook)*

with rising temperature. High RH could lead to a change from glassy to rubbery behaviour. This could be a problem if you are relying on stiffness to hold an object together, or on flexibility to allow the object to accept stress. At 20°C and 50% RH hide glue is in the leathery stage between glass-like and rubbery behaviour. At very low humidities, 5%, it is glassy and very stiff. At high humidities, 80%, it is very many times more flexible.

Humidity and mould

High moisture content will encourage attack by insects and moulds. The rate at which mould grows will depend on how nutritious the object is and on what other nutrients are around in the form of 'protective' coatings or dirt. Figure 11.15 shows the lowest humidity that will support mould growth on a highly nutritious surface and how this decreases with increasing temperature. It also shows how long it takes for mould to develop if well fed. Risk management comes from constant monitoring of the state of the collection as well as from control of temperature and humidity. If you only look once a year you might miss something.

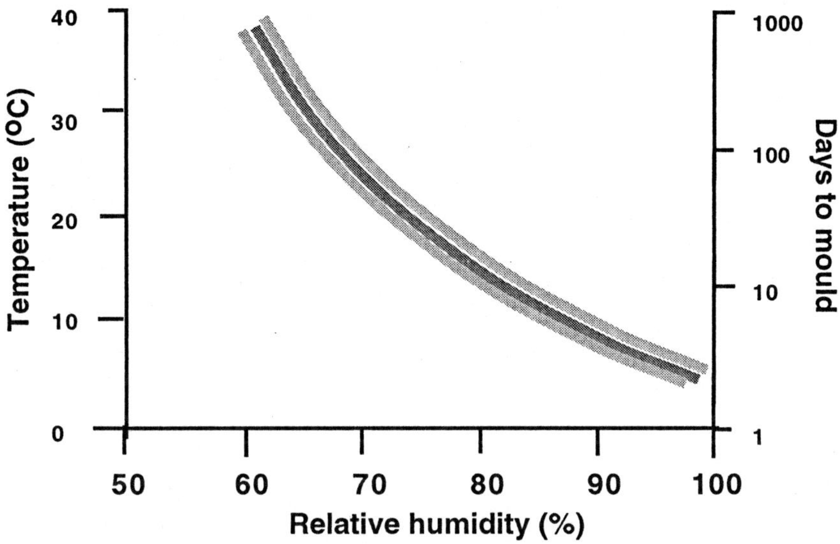

Figure 11.15 *Likelihood of mould growth on a nutritious substrate as a function of temperature and humidity. The right-hand axis gives an indication of the time before growth becomes apparent (after Michalski)*

The appearance of mould is not necessarily equivalent to damage. On many surfaces the mould can be brushed off without visible or structural change. However, some moulds cause staining that is very disturbing and difficult to remove. Yet again a small degree of foxing is more aesthetically allowable today than it was 20 years ago. Although my experience is limited, I have not seen serious structural deterioration caused by mould except where there was a supply of liquid water in the form of constant condensation or permeation through a wall. Transport of water by capillary action is much faster than diffusion of vapour. Remember that the moisture content increases rapidly at high RH and that because of hysteresis, an object once wet tends to stay damper. Immersion in water can lead to higher moisture contents than that reached at equilibrium with 100% RH. Loss of water is usually much slower than absorption.

Humidity change

Probably the most familiar effect of varying humidity is that it causes changes in dimension, especially in timber. If the dimensional change is constrained in any way, damage such as cracking can result. If the object has a layer structure of materials with different moisture responses then damage is possible through differential movement. Paintings, especially those on wooden panel, have long been known to be damaged by fluctuations. It has become part of the conservator's catechism that humidity fluctuation is a bad thing. The physical effects of humidity on materials in the museum environment are well reviewed (Thomson, 1986; Berger and Russell, 1990; Michalski, 1993; Erhardt and Mecklenburg, 1994, 1997).

For some reason the damaging effects of humidity fluctuation have become exaggerated. The susceptibility of the minority of sensitive objects has been generalized to cover the majority of materials and constructions. One way to wean yourself away from worry is to observe the changes that take place to the books, clothes and furniture in your own home or office. I have kept a cheap portable RH monitor at home and at work for the last few years to see what sorts of changing environment my heaps of stuff were subjected to. Through variations of plus or minus 25% RH I have observed no changes attributable to humidity fluctuation in a wide range of objects. Obviously this period is too short to detect slow chemical change or slow cumulative physical damage. But then again some of my stuff is at least 150 years old. I recommend this practical educational experience. Not because I think museums should treat their valuable and vulnerable objects as carelessly as I treat my own possessions, but just because it's a good way of keeping a sense of proportion. Many conservators seem unable to make the bridge between everyday observations and museum predictions.

It is easy to reason that no fluctuation at all is the ideal situation, but it is 'ideal' in the sense of unachievable. If people are to be allowed in the same space as objects then no amount of money and technology will provide a totally stable environment. The range of fluctuation will depend on the type of building, the form of humidity control used, its state of maintenance, and the style and amount of access granted to gallery users.

A cost-conscious manager will ask whether a further investment in plant or casing will actually bring increased benefits, or whether freedom of access could be restricted in order to give better protection to the objects. These questions could be asked in a more technical way that relates to the materials and construction of the object. How large a fluctuation is damaging? Are fluctuations in a dry climate more damaging than those in a humid one? The answers to the first question are given in Table 11.3 (Michalski 1994).

Flexible organic materials are not affected unless they are restrained somehow, in which case the risk is the same as for wood. Or they may be covered by brittle image layers, in which case the risk is the same as for paintings. Construction and conservation treatment history are as

Table 11.3 *Risk of fracture in stiff or brittle organic materials due to RH fluctuation*

Fluctuation	*Material*	*Risk of fracture growth*
±5%	P, A, W	None
±10%	P	Tiny
	A, W	None–tiny
±20%	P	Small
	A, W	Tiny–small
±40%	P	Severe
	A, W	Small–severe

P = oil and tempera paintings and polychrome; A = acrylic paintings; W = wood

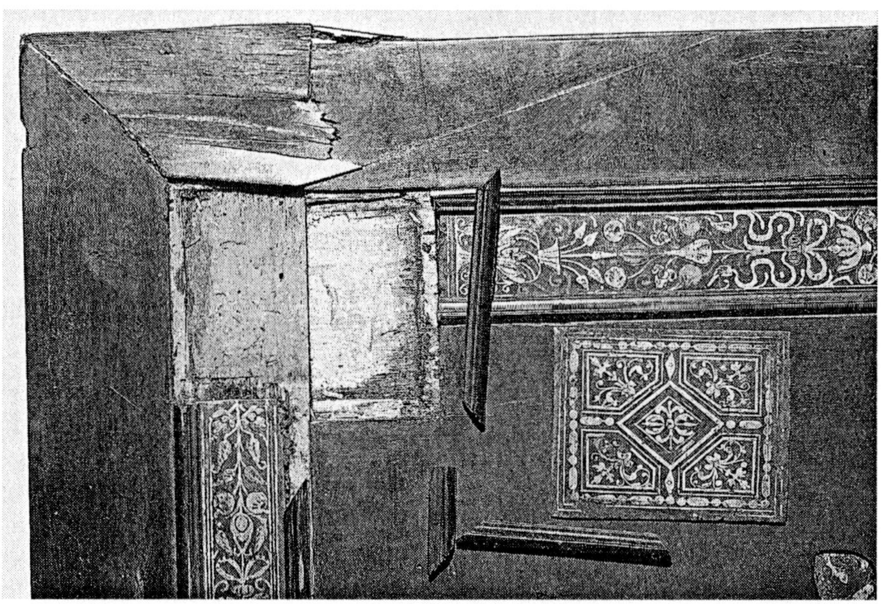

Figure 11.16 *Damage caused by shrinkage at low RH. The grain of the veneer is at right angles to one of the supporting members*

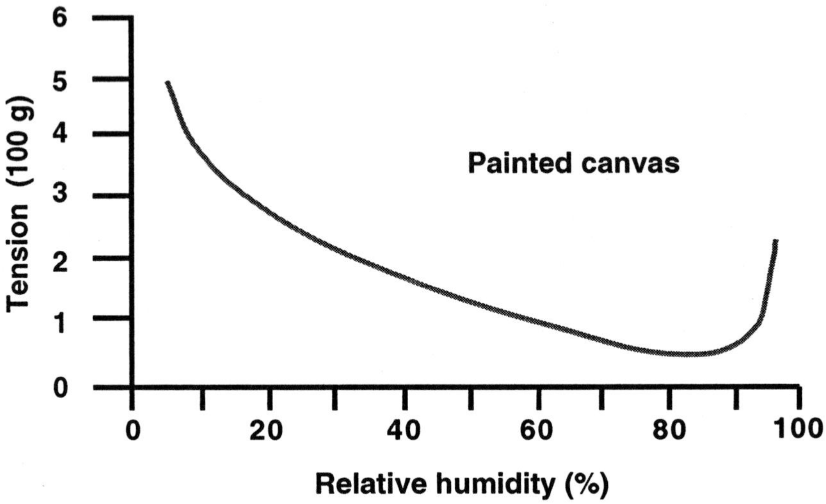

Figure 11.17 *Change in uniaxial stress in painted canvas with change in RH (after Hedley)*

important in calculating the risk as the materials in question. Different structures involve different chances of restraint and induced stress. Certain construction techniques accentuate the effects of small dimensional changes (see Figure 11.16).

The shape of the curves in Figures 11.11 and 11.12 is called sigmoidal after a fairly tenuous resemblance to the letter S. The letter U is also fairly well represented in graphs showing changes of property with changes in ambient moisture. Figure 11.17 shows how the tension in a sample of painted canvas alters as the humidity is increased (Hedley, 1993). The layered structure does not show uniform behaviour. As humidity increases the canvas relaxes, but at very high humidities the tension suddenly rises steeply. The steepest parts of the curve, the parts where stresses are greatest and change most rapidly, are at either end of the humidity scale. It might be inferred that there was much less risk of damage in the mid-range, 40–80% RH, than at the wet and dry extremes.

Another roughly U-shaped curve is shown in Figure 11.18. This gives an indication of how the gelatin layer on a photographic negative might behave with changes in humidity (McCormick-Goodhart, 1995). The rate at which the gelatin expands with each small humidity change is dependent on the ambient humidity. The rate of change is much higher at the extremes and shows a minimum in the mid-range at about 50% RH. So, if the assumption is that the smaller the amount of dimensional change the more stable the object, the area of least risk is somewhere around 40–60%.

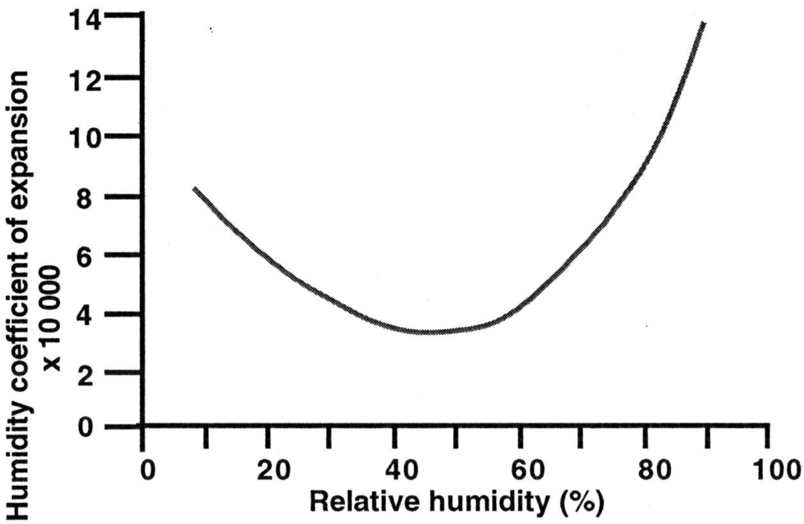

Figure 11.18 *Change in moisture coefficient of expansion for gelatin with change of RH (after McCormick-Goodhart)*

Indeed the U-shaped curve could be used as the model for risk from environmental humidity as suggested by Figure 11.19. Somewhere around the mid-range the risk is at a minimum. The further you move away from that minimum in either direction the greater the risk, rising quickly to very high risks at very high or very low humidities. Small to medium fluctuations around the minimum do not greatly increase risk. Very large excursions away from the mid-point dramatically increase risk. Towards the extremes even a small environmental fluctuation can have a dramatic effect on risk.

This pattern of behaviour has been demonstrated for paintings by research published over the past few years by Mecklenburg and coworkers at the Smithsonian Institute in Washington (e.g. Mecklenburg and Tumosa, 1991). They have carried out great numbers of actual measurements on the individual elements of the layered structure of paintings and used these values in computer models that predict changes of strain with changes in temperature and humidity. Their conclusions are that, in the mid-range of humidity, oil paintings on canvas and on panel can be subjected to greater fluctuations than are usually specified for these object types. There have been criticisms of the limitations of the computer simulation and there are dangers in extrapolating from one type of object to another. However, the sigmoidal shapes of the curves generated by the model are hardly surprising and the conclusions drawn closely match my own observations.

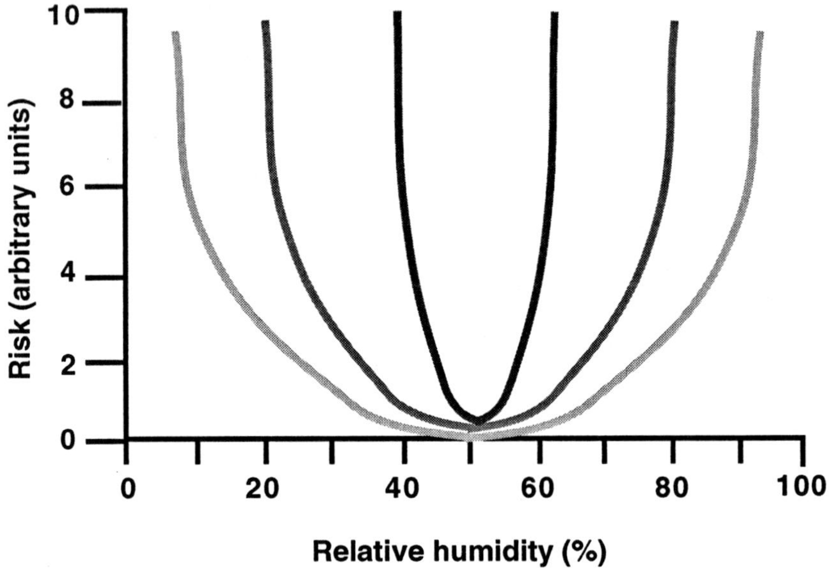

Figure 11.19 *Generalized curves showing that risk (probability and extent of damage) increases with distance from a set mid-point*

Fluctuation, fatigue and failure

The mid-range of behaviours illustrated in Figures 11.7 and 11.8 is shown in a generalized way in Figure 11.20. Up to a certain stress the material behaves elastically. When the stress is released the material will return to its original dimension, just like a spring. If the material is stretched beyond a certain point it begins to deform plastically. When the stress is released the material no longer returns to exactly its original size but has been permanently deformed. The degree of stretching at which this transition from elastic to plastic behaviour takes place is called the yield strain. Much larger stresses will lead to a deformation so great that the material is torn apart – the breaking strain.

Repeated cycles of stress that take the material beyond its yield strain will lead to a cumulative deformation. Theoretically, repeated cycles of stress that lead to cycles of deformation smaller than the yield strain can be carried out indefinitely. However, in reality, there will be slight changes at the molecular level for each cycle that may develop into permanent deformation and possibly to failure after a very large number of cycles. There is a point for some materials (about 25% of the yield strain) below which the stress/strain behaviour seems to be infinitely reversible and no fatigue behaviour is observed. Fluctuations of ±10% RH

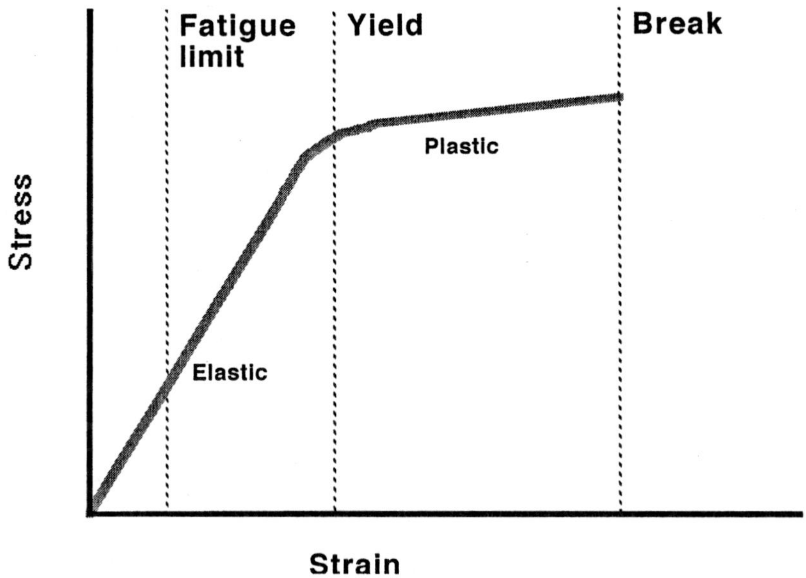

Figure 11.20 *Idealized stress–strain diagram showing area below fatigue limit where repeated fluctuations can be tolerated*

would have to go through millions of cycles for brittle materials such as gesso or paint to fail. At fluctuations of ±20% RH it would take a milion cycles to damage a tough (non-brittle) material such as wood (Michalski, 1992). I have met conservators who were sceptical about this, believing that even the tiniest of changes must accumulate. Chemical bonding relies on flexible 'springs' between the atoms. Since we know that matter persists for extremely long periods we can assume that these molecular springs are not subject to fatigue. So there has to be some level of fluctuation of stress that can be accommodated indefinitely. The process of fatigue is clearly described by Ramesh Talreja (Talreja, 1987).

Marion Mecklenburg's work shows that for a painted wooden panel, which has become accustomed to a humidity of 50%, the strain in the paint film does not exceed the yield strain within the range c.35–60% RH (Figure 11.21) (Richard, Mecklenburg and Tumosa, 1997). He uses the most conservative values for physical properties in his model and specifies yield strain rather than break strain for the upper limit of deformation. If the model is correct it seems that ±10% RH could be considered a very safe range rather than the more conventional ±5% or the technically possible but fairly idealistic ±3%.

Figure 11.22 shows the behaviour of a panel equilibrated to a higher humidity, 70%. The sigmoidal curve is slightly shifted, but more importantly, the equilibrium humidity occurs at a point where the strain

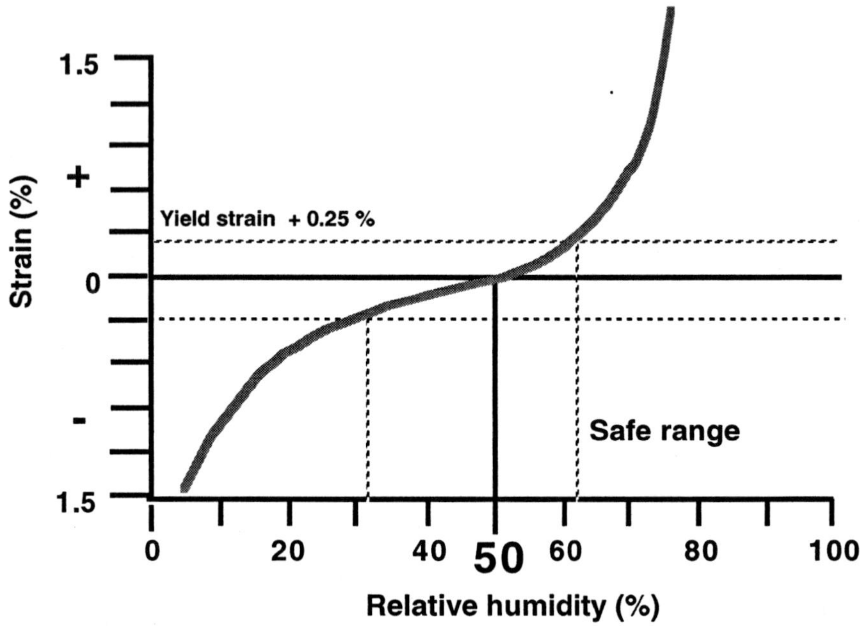

Figure 11.21 *Change in strain for paint on panel in the tangential direction with change in RH. The panel has been acclimatized to 50% humidity (after Mecklenburg* et al.)

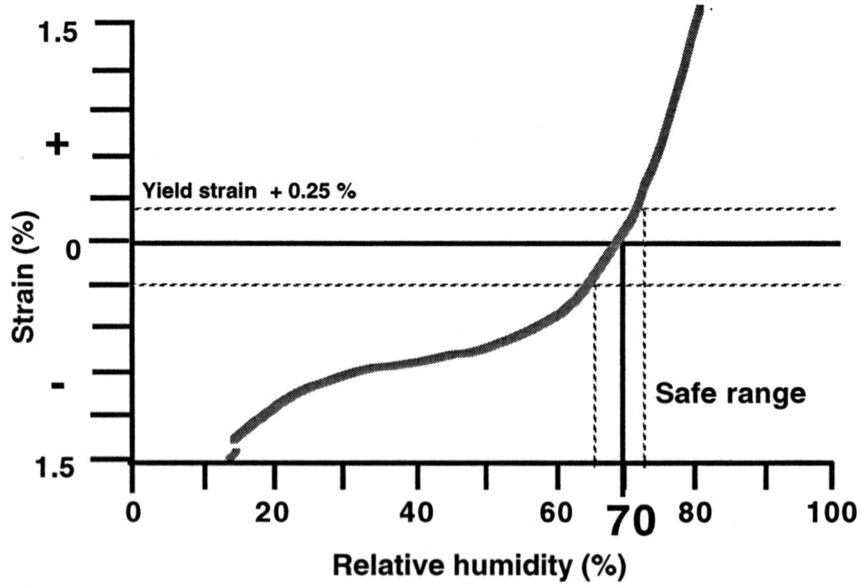

Figure 11.22 *As for Figure 11.21 except that the panel has been acclimatized to 70% RH. At this steeper portion of the curve the safe range is much smaller*

curve is very steep. A very small fluctuation from the set-point can lead to strains greater than the yield strain leading to cracking or tenting of the paint film.

The 'safe range' at 70% does not overlap that at 50%. This means that to introduce 'ideal' conditions, such as 50 ± 5%, to an environment where the objects have become used to much higher humidities will almost certainly cause damage. This damage has been observed a number of times where objects have been brought from cold, damp environments such as churches or country houses to warm, dry museums for temporary exhibitions. Moving objects from dry conditions (30% or less) to the ideal mid-range could be equally damaging. Damage to the timber in furniture is usually caused by one long-term change rather than an accumulation of small changes.

Speed of change

The simulations just described assumed that an object can become 'acclimatized' to a particular humidity. This suggests that somehow material at 30% RH could become acclimatized to 50% or 70%. How can a potentially damaging change take place without damage?

The rate at which an object will absorb or desorb moisture will depend on several things. For any particular material the most important factors are the mass, the surface area and the presence of an impermeable surface layer. A large, wooden object with a coating of varnish or wax will not notice changes in humidity for several days. A thin, uncoated panel, which has a large surface area for its weight, will react more quickly (Stevens, 1960). If the stresses induced by a dimensional change are applied slowly then there is a good chance that the materials will behave in a viscoelastic fashion and accommodate the strain without damage. If they occur rapidly then the chances of sympathetic behaviour are reduced.

If an object must be moved from one environment to another there is a good chance that wrapping it in a reasonably impermeable covering, such as polythene sheet, for a few months will slow down the response to a changing environment long enough for the object to cope with the induced stress.

Rapid oscillations in atmospheric moisture will not be noticed by many objects. Very slow changes may well be accommodated, which is why many objects survive yearly seasonal changes. Changes in environment that are large enough to cause permanent changes in moisture content, but still too fast for safe viscoelastic response, are most damaging. These are the sort of change that may occur if air-conditioning plant breaks down or if its replacement takes weeks rather than days.

Minerals, salts and patina

Just as there are phase changes in materials at certain temperatures, sudden physical change can occur in some materials at particular humidities. Some compounds contain water in their crystal structure and change in volume as they move from one hydrated form to another at a specific RH. Above a certain humidity some compounds attract moisture in sufficient quantity that they form liquid solutions rather than solid crystals. This is called deliquescence. When the humidity drops, the crystals reform. If this change takes place at a vulnerable surface considerable physical damage can take place. This can occur in walls, sculpture, ceramics and natural history specimens. It is advisable to keep such material in an environment with a humidity well away from the transition point. Most people opt for keeping it in the dry phase since migration and chemical action are prevented. Small fluctuations in humidity may be very damaging if they occur around the critical humidity. Although the RH levels at which these transitions take place are well known for individual chemical species it is more difficult to predict how mixtures will react. Salts with individually high deliquescence points may form mixtures that transform from liquid to solid at much lower levels (Price and Brimblecombe, 1994).

Chemical degradation of some compounds is very much accelerated above specific humidities. This may be due to deliquescent behaviour which forms a liquid medium in which reaction is more feasible. A number of physico-chemical deterioration reactions classified by medical analogies – bronze disease, pyrite disease and sick glass – fall into this category. It may be expensive, time consuming or even damaging to keep specimens with these problems absolutely dry. It is wise to gain some knowledge of the mechanisms of reaction and the relevant chemical substances involved and do the minimum necessary to stay away from the threshold humidity.

Critical humidities for a wide range of minerals have been published (Waller, 1992). The critical humidity for bronze disease has been reassessed to be as high as 46% (Scott, 1990).

Age

When we discussed chemical change in the last chapter there were times when the reaction might be faster for weathered samples. Age alone does not appear to cause dramatic changes in response to humidity. The physical and mechanical properties of archaeological wood have been reviewed. The differences in equilibrium moisture content and moisture response between new and very old wood are not consistent in direction and are always very small (Schniewind, 1990). A more recent study has confirmed this. Although slight chemical differences could be detected between twentieth-century and seventeenth-century pine there were no substantial changes in physical response (Erhardt, Mecklenburg and Tumosa, 1996).

Something to think about

Some permanent changes, such as small amounts of plastic deformation, reduce the possibility of future stresses. Can this be called damage?

Why is it believed that constant air movement will prevent mould growth, even at high humidities?

Wood/adhesive combinations for industrial use are designed to withstand a hundred million cycles of stress without failure. Why does it only take a few cycles to wiggle a mortice and tenon joint loose?

References

Atalla, Rajai H. (1981) *The Crystallinity of Cellulose Fibers. Preservation of Paper and Textiles. Part II.* American Chemical Society, pp. 169–177.

Ballard, Mary (1995) Mechanical Properties: Preview and Review. *Textile Conservation Newsletter.* Ottawa, Canada, No. 28, pp. 14–27.

Berger, Gustav A. and Russell, William H. Deterioration of Surfaces Exposed to Environmental Changes. *Journal of the American Institute of Conservation*, **29**, pp. 45–76.

Brimblecombe, Peter (1990) Particulate Material in Air of Art Galleries, in *Dirt and Pictures Separated*, edited by Stephen Hackney, Joyce Townsend, Nick Eastaugh. UKIC. ISBN 1-871656-08-7, pp. 7–11.

Eastaugh, Nicholas (1990) The Visual Effects of Dirt on Paintings, in *Dirt and Pictures Separated*, edited by Stephen Hackney, Joyce Townsend, Nick Eastaugh. UKIC. ISBN 1-871656-08-7, pp. 19–24.

Erhardt, David, Mecklenburg, Marion F., Tumosa, Charles S. and McCormick-Goodhart, Mark (1997) The Interface between Science and Conservation. British Museum Occasional Paper No. 116. ISBN 0-86159-116-X, pp. 153–164.

Erhardt, David, Mecklenburg and Marion F. (1994) Relative Humidity Re-examined. Preventive Conservation: Practice, Theory and Research. Preprints to the Ottawa Congress, 12–16 September. IIC, pp. 32–38.

Erhardt, David, Mecklenburg, Marion F. and Tumosa, Charles S. (1996) New versus Old Wood: Differences and Similarities in Physical, Mechanical and Chemical Properties. ICOM Committee for Conservation. 11th Triennial Meeting. Edinburgh, pp. 903–910.

Ford, David (1997) Slides and Frisbees – Determining Dust Deposition Rates. *V&A Conservation Journal*, No. 22, January. ISSN 0967–2273, pp. 19–20.

Gibson, Lorna L. (1988) *Cellular Solids: Structure and Properties*. Pergamon Press, Oxford. ISBN 0-08-035910-8.

Hedley, Gerry (1993) *Measured Opinions*. UKIC, London. ISBN 1-871656-21-4.

McCormick-Goodhart, Mark H. (1995) Moisture Content Isolines and the Glass Transition of Photographic Gelatin: their Significance to Cold Storage and Accelerated Aging. Research Techniques in Photographic Conservation. Proceedings of the Conference in Copenhagen, edited by Mogens S. Koch, Tim Padfield, Jesper Stub Johnsen and Ulla Bøgvad Kejser. Royal Danish Academy of Fine Arts, pp. 65–70.

Mecklenburg, Marion F. and Tumosa, Charles S. (1991) Mechanical Behaviour of Paintings Subjected to Changes in Temperature and Relative Humidity, in *Art in Transit*, edited by Marion T. Mecklenburg. National Gallery of Art, Washington. ISBN 0-89468-163-X, pp. 173–216.

Michalski, Stefan (1991) Paintings – Their Response to Temperature Relative Humidity, Shock and Vibration, in *Art in Transit*, edited by Marion T. Mecklenburg. National Gallery of Art, Washington. ISBN 0-89468-163-X, pp. 223–249.

Michalski, Stefan (1992) Temperature and Relative Humidity: The Definition of Correct/Incorrect Values. A Systematic Approach to the Conservation (Care) of Museum Collections. Canadian Conservation Institute.

Michalski, Stefan (1993) Relative Humidity: A Discussion of Correct/Incorrect Values. ICOM Committee for Conservation, 10th Triennial Meeting, Washington, pp. 624–629.

Michalski, Stefan (1994) Relative Humidity and Temperature Guidelines: What's Happening? *CCI Newsletter*, No. 14, September. ISSN 1180–3223, pp. 6–8.

Nazaroff, William W., Ligocki, Mary P., Salmon, Lynn G., Cass, Glen R., Fall, Theresa, Jones, Michael C., Liu, Harvey I.H. and Ma, Timothy (1992) Protection of Works of Art from Soiling Due to Airborne Particulates. GCI Scientific Program Report. The J. Paul Getty Trust.

Nazaroff, William W., Ligocki, Mary P., Salmon, Lynn G., Cass, Glen R., Fall, Theresa, Jones Michael C., Liu, Harvey I.H. and Ma, Timothy (1993) Airborne Particles in Museums. The Getty Conservation Institute. The J. Paul Getty Trust. ISBN 0-89236-187-5.

Nicholson, J.W. (1991) *The Chemistry of Polymers*. Royal Society of Chemistry. ISBN 0-85168-413-9.

Peal, Christopher A. (1971) *British Pewter and Britannia Metal*. John Gifford, London, p. 28.

Phenix, Alan and Burnstock, Aviva (1990) The Deposition of Dirt: A Review of the Literature with SEM Studies of Dirt on Selected Pictures, in *Dirt and Pictures Separated*, edited by Stephen Hackney, Joyce Townsend, Nick Eastaugh. UKIC. ISBN 1-871656-08-7, pp. 11–18.

Pilz, Monika and Troll, Carola (1997) Simulation of Gold Enamel Degradation. The Interface Between Science and Conservation. British Museum Occasional Paper No. 116. ISBN 0-86159-116-X, pp. 193–202.

Price, Clifford and Brimblecombe, Peter (1994) Preventive Conservation: Practice, Theory and Research. Preprints to the Ottawa Congress, 12–16 September. IIC, pp. 90–93.

Richards, M., Mecklenburg, M.F. and Tumosa, C.S. (1998) Technical Considerations for the Transport of Panel Paintings. The Structural Conservation of Panel Paintings. Proceedings of a symposium at the J. Paul Getty Museum, April 1995 (ed. Kathleen Dardes and Andrea Rothe). J. Paul Getty Trust. ISBN 0-89236-384-3.

Schilling, Michael R. (1989) The Glass Transition of Materials Used in Conservation. *Studies in Conservation*, **34**, pp. 110–116.

Schniewind, Arno P. (1990) Physical and Mechanical Properties of Archaeological Wood. Archaeological Wood: Properties, Chemistry, and Preservation. *Advances in Chemistry Series*, 225, edited by Roger M. Rowell and R. James Barbour. American Chemical Society, pp. 86–106.

Scott, David A. (1990) Bronze Disease: A Review of Some Chemical Problems and the Role of Relative Humidity. *Journal of the American Institute for Conservation*, **29**, pp. 193–206.

Smook, Gary A. (1992) *Handbook for Pulp and Paper Technologists*. Vancouver, Angus Wilde Publications.

Stevens, W.C. (1960) Rates of Change in the Dimensions and Moisture Contents of Wooden Panels Resulting from Changes in the Ambient Air Conditions. *Studies in Conservation*, pp. 21–25.

Talreja, Ramesh (1987) *Fatigue of Composite Materials*. Technomic Publishing Co. Ltd, Lancaster. ISBN 87762-516-6.

Thomson, Garry (1986) *The Museum Environment*. Butterworth-Heinemann. ISBN 0-7506-2041-2.

Toishi, K. and Kenjo, T. (1975) Some Aspects of the Conservation of Works of Art in Buildings of New Concrete. *Studies in Conservation*, **20**, pp. 118–122.

Upham, James B. and Sabin, Victor J. (1975) Effects of Air Pollutants on Textile Fibers and Dyes. Prepared by North Carolina University for the National Environment Research Council. Distributed National Technical Information Service. US Department of Commerce. PB-241 507.

Waller, Robert (1992) Temperature- and Humidity-sensitive Mineralogical and Petrological Specimens, in *The Care and Conservation of Geological Material*, edited by F. Howie. Butterworth-Heinemann, pp. 25–50.

Warke, P.A. (1996) Inheritance Effects in Building Stone Decay, in *Processes of Urban Stone Decay*, edited by B.J. Smith and P.A. Warke (1995). Proceedings of SWAPNET'95. Belfast. Donhead. ISBN 1-873394-20-9, pp. 32–43.

12 Light entertainment

Damage by light is easy to control. Studies of perception and enjoyment give some idea of sensible levels at which to light objects, but can't be used to set absolute standards. Knowing how fast an object changes, acknowledging thresholds of acceptable damage and defining total service life can lead to logical, flexible systems to reduce risk. Costs and benefits are best assessed when information is available about the state of each individual object.

Light and use

This is the first of three chapters dealing with changes to objects resulting from use. Damaging agents such as tornadoes, pollution or dramatic changes in temperature and humidity are incidental to the use of an object. They will occur whether or not anyone is studying the object, consulting the record or enjoying the view. For most people, most of the information from an object is received in the form of light reflected from its surface. This is true whether the purpose of an object is purely aesthetic or purely archival.

The amount of light falling on the object is fairly easy and cheap to control. For an object indoors there is no reason why light should fall on its surface except when there is an expectation that someone will look at it. If an object is made with materials that change on exposure to light the amount of change should be related to the amount of use. Use automatically means damage. We are faced with the concept that some damage must be acceptable. There is only a certain amount of damage that an object can take before it ceases to have a value derived from use. This means we must choose criteria that we will use to ration the exposure.

The amount of change that occurs is dependent on the nature of the object and the control of the light falling on it. The lighting control factors are the intensity, the duration and the wavelength distribution of the light. The amount of benefit derived from use depends on the intensity of light reflected from the surface and the information this brings the viewer about the state of the object. We cannot control the nature of the object but we can minimize damage and optimize benefit by control of the light.

The damaging effects of light and possibilities for control are well reviewed (Feller, 1964; Thomson, 1986; Michalski, 1987, 1990, 1997).

Susceptible objects

The categories of object that are considered light sensitive should be very familiar: textiles, works of art on paper, photographs, paintings. However, we must be careful about the classification. Some classes are more sensitive than others and within each class there may be a dramatic range. The description 'photograph' covers a broad sweep of sensitivities. Exposure at the recommended level of 50 lux would cause a noticeable change in an early salt print within a few weeks, in a colour photograph in months, but no change at all over several centuries in a well-processed modern silver-gelatin photo (Ware, 1994).

There are different routes by which types of object have entered the class of light-sensitive objects. No one disputes that dyed textiles fade because an awful lot of textile objects in museums look miserably faded. This fading used to be a familiar household experience. It is less familiar now because of improvements to the product and the way we constantly change possessions and decorations for the sake of conspicuous consumption. Objects prized for aesthetic rather than archival merit, especially paintings, are classified as light sensitive because they have durable class value and every aspect of them has been closely and expensively studied. Some members of the group are sensitive but the overall rate of change is small compared to the fading of textiles. Furniture is infrequently classed as light sensitive, although the colours of timber and surface coatings can change more dramatically than the pigments of an oil painting. Seen as rubbish that will eternally damage the world's ecology, objects made of plastic are not considered sensitive. Since they do not have durable value, who cares anyway? However, there are now a great number of plastics objects gaining respectability in museums, and many of these are very susceptible to damage by light and ultraviolet radiation.

Some groups gain the reputation of being sensitive because its easiest to teach things that way. It seems too complicated to keep qualifying a general statement. The warning about the sensitivity of some works of art on paper has slowly been made to encompass all objects made of paper. It is the thin image layer of a water-colour painting that is most likely to

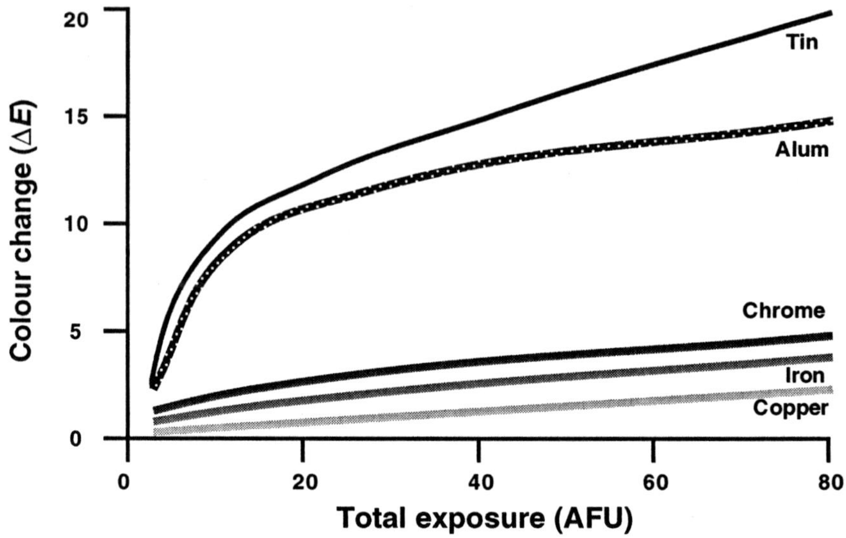

Figure 12.1 *The rate of change is dependent on small differences in the state of the object. The mordant which holds the dye to a fabric is a key factor. Note that at high rates of damage there appear to be two rates, the initial and the final. At low rates, the increase in damage is linear with total exposure (80 AFU is approximately 10 megalux hours) (after Crews)*

be damaged, not the support. High-quality white rag paper is extremely durable.

Small differences in the composition of objects can lead to significant differences to the way objects respond to light. Figure 12.1 shows the change in colour of natural dyes depending on the mordant used. The tin mordanted dyes changed four times as much and five times faster than those with copper as mordant (Crews, 1982). Indigo on cotton fades quickly, indigo on wool barely at all. These differences in composition may be discovered by chemical analysis or the information may already be available in the catalogue entry for the object.

The more we know about the state of individual objects the more we will be able to make recommendations about rationing exposure on an individual basis. We don't want to cause damage unnecessarily but we don't need to discriminate against objects that are tough enough to take it. The change in the amount of damage and the change in the benefits derived must be weighed against the cost of inspecting and classifying each object and against the risk of making an incorrect analysis. It has recently been proposed that a fading 'spot' test could be undertaken using an intense light directed at a very small area of material through fibre optics (Michalski, 1997, p. 102).

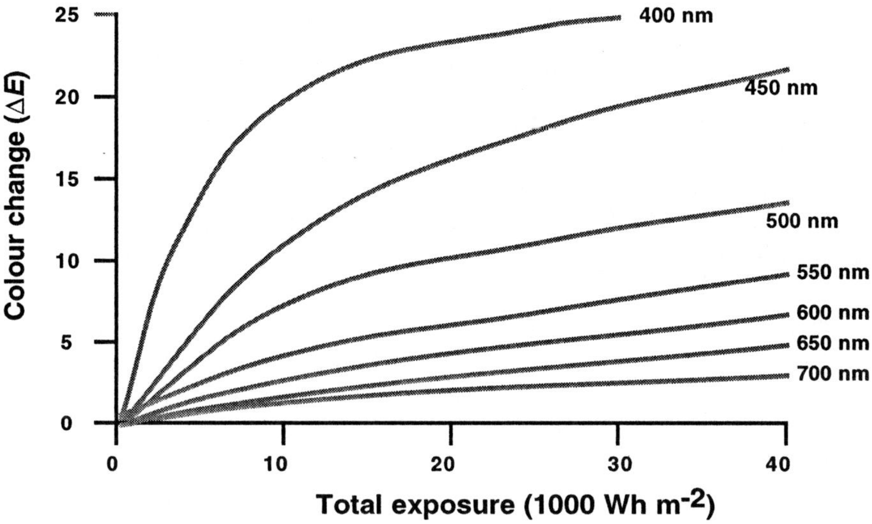

Figure 12.2 *Rate of colour change at different wavelengths of visible light. At low levels of damage the relationship appears to be linear (after Saunders and Kirby)*

Wavelength

The fact that we see different colours results from the ability of eye and brain to discriminate between different wavelengths of radiation. The range of wavelengths that can be perceived by the human eye runs from about 400 to 700 nm (nm = nanometre = 10^{-9} metre). Radiation from different sources contains different distributions of these wavelengths and also some that are not directly perceived, such as the short-wave ultraviolet (UV) and the longer infrared.

The amount of change caused by the different wavelengths of visible light is shown in Figure 12.2 (Saunders and Kirby, 1994). In this case the damage is the fading of a natural dye. The change caused by the shorter wavelengths is very much faster than by the longer wavelengths. As the maximum possible damage is approached the rate of reaction decreases. At lower levels of damage the rate appears to show a linear relationship between total exposure and damage. The total exposure indicated would be equivalent to display at 50 lux, eight hours a day for about 60 years.

A generalized view of the relationship between the wavelength of light and the relative amount of damage caused by the same dose of radiation at different wavelengths is shown in Figure 12.3. Historic artifacts are generally not exposed to wavelengths below around 300 nm because

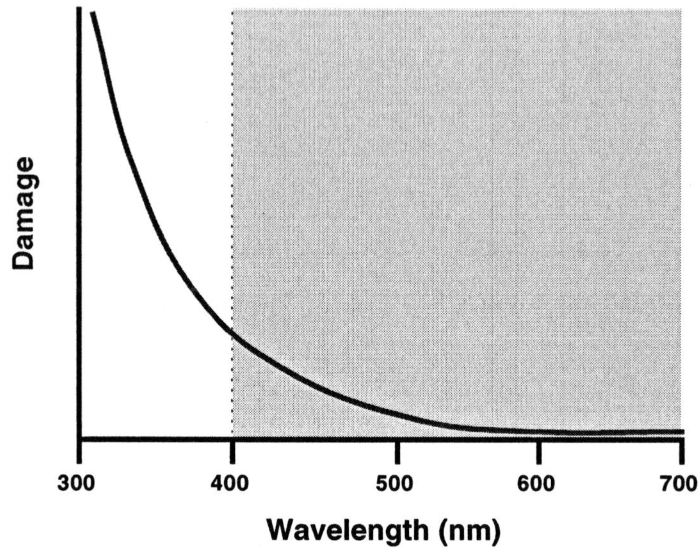

Figure 12.3 *Rate of damage versus wavelength. The shaded area covers the wavelengths necessary to see the object. Most of the damage for most types of objects takes place in the UV region between 300 and 400 nm*

these are absorbed by the atmosphere and by window glass. This graph is intended to indicate many types of damage, fading of dyes, the yellowing of wool, loss of strength of wood-pulp paper, embrittlement of polymers and decrease in solubility of resins. Red light (600–700 nm) can do some damage to a number of material types, blue light (400–500 nm) does much more damage and to more materials. Ultraviolet radiation (wavelengths below 400 nm) affects many types of materials especially polymers and can cause damage at rates more than 10 times greater than blue light.

The damage caused by light and UV is usually explained in terms of photo-*chemistry*, the interaction of radiation with the molecules near the surface of the object. The chemical changes are nearly always measured as changes in *physical* properties rather than changes in the amounts of chemical species. The changes caused by UV radiation often show up as physical damage; chalking, crazing, cracking.

It can be seen that the total amount of damage caused by the ultraviolet radiation (which is not needed to see the object) is at least five times that caused by the visible light (without which the object cannot be seen). It is for this reason that conventional conservation wisdom is to filter out the UV to reduce the rate of damage. It should be remembered that the remaining visible light is still damaging and so UV filters can never

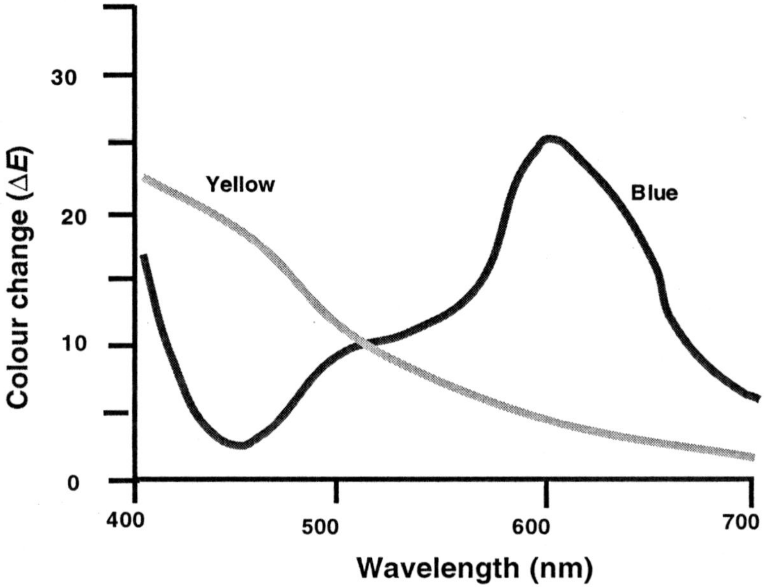

Figure 12.4 *Red and yellow materials often follow the damage/wavelength relationship shown in Figure 12.3. Blue and green materials reflect the blue light and are more damaged by the longer (redder) wavelengths (after Saunders and Kirby)*

provide complete protection. Removing the UV portion of the radiation has little effect on fugitive materials but will increase the lifetime of more stable substances up to 10 times.

Some materials such as natural dyes (and the colours in cheap felt-tip pens) are very sensitive to visible light and UV filters have been shown to have little or no effect on rate of fading (Crews, 1989). For these materials most of the damage is done by blue light and, as long as the appearance of the object is not distorted too much, the use of yellow filters that absorb blue light can reduce fading. The light from tungsten spotlights contains much less blue than daylight and is less damaging than UV filtered daylight.

The colour of materials is determined by the wavelengths of light that are absorbed and those that are reflected. Yellow objects absorb blue light, blue objects reflect it.

It would be expected that blue objects would be less damaged by light with a lot of blue in it than red or yellow objects would be. The rates of damage at different wavelengths for a blue wool standard and a yellow natural dye are shown in Figure 12.4. This confirms that the blue material is less damaged by blue light.

Dose

The total dose of light that falls on an object is the product of the intensity of the light, I, and the duration of the exposure t. The deterioration is a function of the total dose.

The Extent of change is given by the equation:

$$E = k\,I\,t \tag{12.1}$$

This is a similar relationship to those shown in equations (8.12) and (10.5).

The constant k is the amount of that type of deterioration produced for that material by a standard dose of light, e.g. 1 megalux hour. If it were possible to agree on the relationship between physical change and perceived damage you could have a constant that related loss in value to total exposure. In this case the risk would be given by:

$$R = k\,I\,t \tag{12.2}$$

Figure 12.5 shows the linear relationship between intensity of light and deterioration. At very high intensities it is possible that the linear relationship breaks down, but for reactions such as fading of dyes at

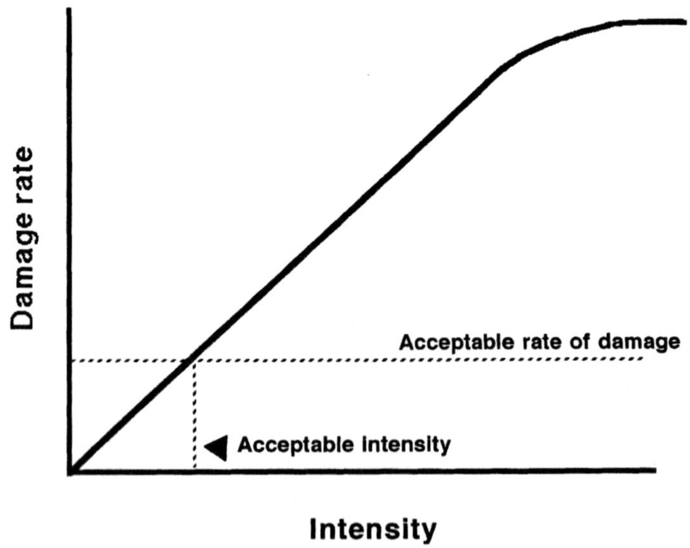

Figure 12.5 *The relationship between rate of damage and intensity of light is linear except at very high intensities. If a particular intensity is acceptable then so is that rate of damage*

normal display lighting levels a straight line dependency can be assumed. Certain maximum light levels such as 50 lux or 200 lux are often specified. It doesn't matter how low the light level is, you are always causing damage. So you can never get it right. If 50 lux represents an acceptable intensity of light it implies that a certain rate of deterioration is acceptable. If a certain rate of deterioration is acceptable then it follows that more stable objects can be displayed at higher light intensities.

In Britain, for ease of application of the law, it is assumed that all drivers with a certain number of milligrams of alcohol in 100 ml of blood are perfectly safe on the road but those with just one milligram more are irresponsible killing machines. No account is taken of differences in body weight, metabolic rate, driving skills or drinking experience. Whatever your views on drinking and driving (historically there has not always been total social abhorrence) you must see that this is an arbitrary division to make decision-making easy. Some teetotal drivers are far less competent than some drinkers. The spirit of the law suggests that the more you drink the more likely you are to cause an accident. The letter of the law makes an arbitrary division into good and bad. In museums we should be wary of introducing rigid laws for the sake of convenience. The traditional specifications are only indicators. They lead to a reasonable

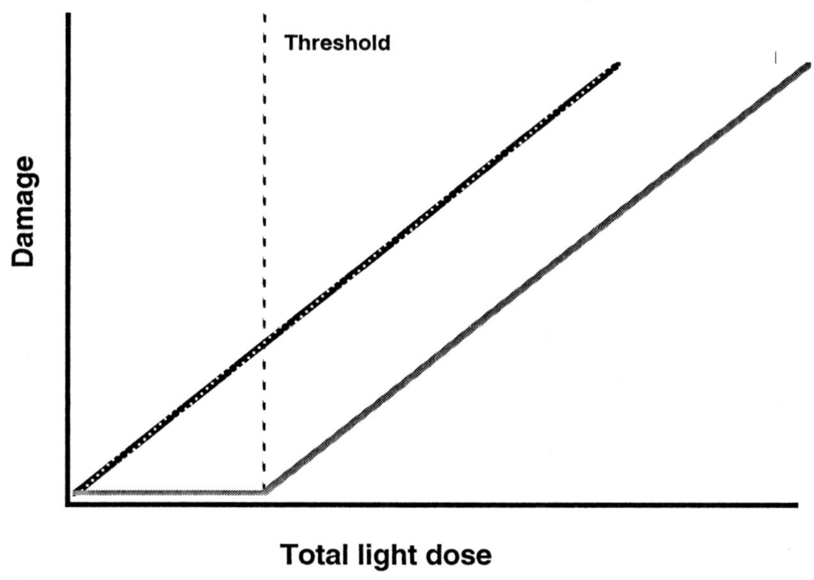

Figure 12.6 *The law of reciprocity suggests that the total amount of damage increases with the total dose of light. One exception to this is when there is an induction period during which no change is apparent but the fact of change is getting closer*

balance between being able to enjoy the object and minimizing, rather than encouraging, decay. 51 lux is not a sin.

If you multiply the units of both axes in Figure 12.5 by units of time you get a graph of light dose against damage sustained. Figure 12.6 shows this linear relationship (judging by Figure 12.2 it can only be considered linear at low levels of damage). To allow flexibility in application of light intensities it has become popular to consider controlling the total light dose rather than the light intensity. You specify a certain maximum dose per year for a particular type of object. You can shine a brighter light for a shorter period and do no more damage than if you had shone a dimmer light for a longer time. This allows flexibility in display but is still based on arbitrary assumptions about an acceptable rate of decay. It assumes that there is consensus about how long an object should be allowed to live. It does not entirely avoid the possibility of rigid interpretation and mechanical enforcement by the conservation police.

For some objects (e.g. plastics materials) an initial dose of light appears to cause no damage. Once a certain exposure has been reached, further doses cause damage that can be seen. So while there can only ever be an arbitrary threshold intensity there may be an actual threshold dose (Feller, 1977). This delayed decay could fool you into thinking that an object is not light sensitive. Except in impossibly controlled circumstances, you cannot know how close you are to the threshold.

Other factors

Other factors beside susceptibility, wavelength and dose affect the rate of degradation. Very few photo-chemical reactions are purely the interaction between light and the molecules that make up the material. The light induces reactions between different chemical species. For many types of photo-deterioration it is the reaction between the substrate and oxygen in the atmosphere that is important. This is called photo-oxidation. The light reacts with the chemical species creating molecules that are in higher energy states. These 'excited' molecules then react together in the same way as in the reactions described in Chapter 10.

It follows that the sorts of thing that will accelerate 'dark' chemistry will also affect photo-chemistry (Suppan, 1994). Removal of oxygen will stop many reactions but this is not a realistic proposition for the majority of objects. Moisture affects reaction rate, high RH leading to much faster reactions (though rates at very low humidities can also be faster than in the mid-range of RH). A rise in temperature will speed up the reaction. The presence of metals or metal compounds can catalyse the decay.

The light itself is not a catalyst in the strictest sense because it does not remain unchanged at the end of the reaction. However, it can be thought of as having the same effect as a catalyst, enabling or speeding up reactions. Fading of dyes by pollutant gases, which can take place in the dark, is accelerated in the presence of light.

The reactions that are initiated by light may continue long after the stimulus is gone. Regardless of whether they darkened or faded during exposure, samples of paper darkened over time in dark storage (Lee, Bogaard and Feller, 1989). Papers with high lignin content and low pH darkened most.

Flashguns and photocopiers

Because the light from photographic flashes seems so intense there is a recurrent worry that it is unnecessarily hastening the demise of objects on display in museums.

The exposure from a typical hand-held flash unit is about 600 lux seconds (Saunders, 1995). For an object normally displayed at 50 lux, eight hours a day, one flash adds about a millionth to its annual dose. Because it is beneficial for the photograph the flashgun usually has a filter that removes most of the UV content. To double the rate of decay would need one flash every 12 seconds, which would be extremely annoying to anyone who wanted to study the object or had come to the museum for peace and contemplation. It is to avoid disturbance, and to protect copyright in the images of objects, that flash photography is discouraged in museums.

If the environment in which the sensitive objects are housed is used for other purposes, such as weddings or political meetings, then the frequency of flashes may be high but not disturbing. If the frequency of such events is kept low (once a week) there is no problem.

Professional photographers should be encouraged to use flash. The use of powerful halogen or discharge lamps leads to prolonged exposure while setting up the shot and between 'takes'. The National Gallery (London) rules for professional photographers permit the use of flash to a limit of 1250 lux seconds per exposure and stipulate that an ultraviolet filter must be used. The same guidance (Thomson, 1986, p. 47) suggests that for television recording 2500 lux is a maximum but that the time of illumination is so short that there is no need for a UV filter even on metal halide lamps. If the object is normally shown at 50 lux with UV filtering it would take two or three days' continuous filming at 2500 lux to double its annual dose. If the object is currently not being protected from light on display, then of course the additional lighting for photography or TV recording makes very little difference. Heat build-up, inattentive people and falling equipment pose greater risks and these can be avoided by keeping the light sources at a distance and by supplying concerned supervision.

Another source of intense light is the photocopier. If you think that only flat paper gets photocopied you have never worked in a museum. The object is held very close to a source that emits radiation with a high proportion of UV. Copying a document 26 times is equivalent to one hour's lighting by tungsten light at 50 lux (Neevel, 1995). Photocopiers designed for low volume work take longer for each copy and should be avoided. The biggest danger is mechanical damage from trying to squash the object flat to get a good image.

Neevel worries that the high intensity irradiation of flash photography and photocopying will lead to different or substantially faster reactions than lower levels of light. Saunders' work and that of David Howell suggest that these high intensities for short periods can be exactly equated to low levels for a longer period (*New Scientist*, 1995). The level of UV from some photocopiers is enough to generate ozone. The object being copied will not be around long enough to worry, but if objects are kept in the immediate vicinity of the copier they will be subjected to much longer exposure.

Enjoyment and understanding

Making images of an object does not seem to involve great risk. But for access by scholars and visitors the only way long-term damage can be reduced is by cutting down the time of access and the intensity of light in which the object can be viewed.

Cutting down the time of illumination is a question of management. It can be managed but does 'the management' dare to do it? It has become unfashionable to hide objects behind curtains. Even in this age of interactivity and discovery visitors still feel embarrassed about drawing back the curtain. Galleries that are dark except when a button is pushed to illuminate the object are uninviting and are seldom visited. The Japanese method of ceremonially unveiling objects for a limited period at intervals of a year or a decade raise objects to a level of reverence that is not fashionable in Europe. Keeping objects in store and only exposing them for short periods works very well unless the object is so famous that it must always be on display, e.g. the Leonardo cartoon at the National Gallery. In an age where the visitor's whims must be satisfied without stint, the limiting of exposure time during normal opening hours would seem to be unfashionably obstructive.

So we must minimize levels of illumination. Yet one of the most common complaints in museums (after the state of the toilets) is the low lighting levels in galleries containing textiles or paper. Does the visitor have the right to complain? If we are not illuminating the objects sufficiently to be enjoyed we are causing damage without the compensation of generating benefit.

The factors affecting visual acuity and colour discrimination have been reviewed (Boyce, 1987). Because of a concern about damage, the light levels in museums are measured on their way to the object not on their way to the visitor's eye. Paradoxically light levels in museums are measured on a scale that reflects the eye's sensitivity to colour and not the susceptibility of the object to damage (Padfield, 1994). The intensity of light coming from the object to the viewer (luminance) depends on how light absorbent the object is and how far away. The ability to interpret the information in this reflected light will be dependent on the eyesight of the visitor and their ability to discriminate small changes in contrast and colour at specific luminances.

My interpretation of the work reviewed is that:

- at 50 lux
- young people
- whose eyes have become adapted to that level of light
- looking at objects that reflect more than 10% of the incident light
- can discriminate small differences in colour
- and differences in contrast between sharply defined areas if the difference in luminance between the areas is greater than 30%
- as long as the background is not brighter than the object

This means that for the average visitor who is ticking off a list of 'important things to see', at the rate of one every 30 seconds, most objects could be shown at around 50 lux. Anyone who wants to appreciate dark objects with subtleties of texture and contrast will need more than this. Especially if the viewer is more than 50 years old. Large objects which must be viewed at a distance, but which still have detail that must be distinguished for full appreciation, may need more than 50 lux.

We can probably see most detail at 150 lux, but we would see even more at higher illuminances, which is why Garry Thomson is happy to allow restorers to work at 2000 lux (Thomson, 1986, p. 47). The Canadian Conservation Institute has devised a rule of thumb which takes 50 lux as the basic minimum and then allows this to be multiplied by up to three times for each of a variety of factors such as darkness of object, lack of contrast in the object, difficulty of task and age of viewer. Thus viewing a dark coloured object on normal display might need $50 \times 3 = 150$ lux. An aged conservator working on a dark low-contrast piece might need $50 \times 3 \times 3 \times 3 = 1350$ lux in order to carry out demanding repair work (Michalski, 1997, p. 100).

Another important point is that some objects just look better if more brightly lit. The work of David Loe, which quantified subjective responses

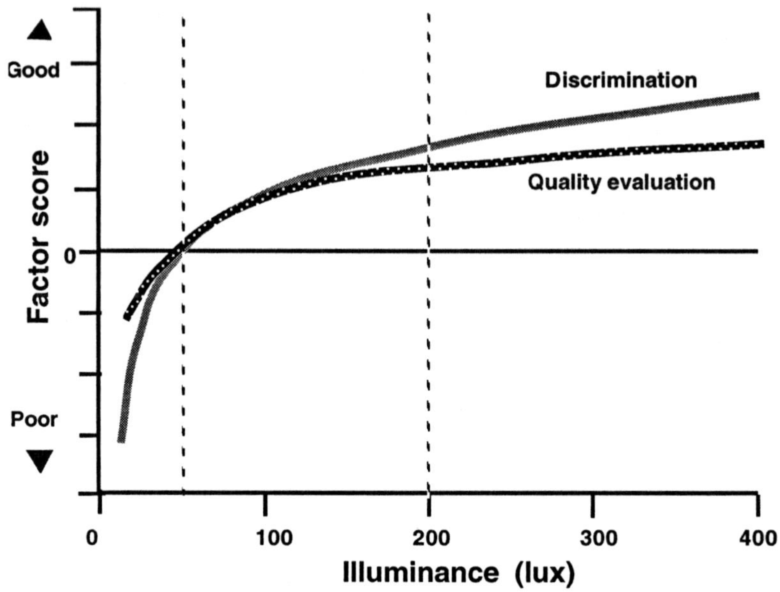

Figure 12.7 *Two subjective aspects of the appreciation of paintings are plotted against the illuminance of display. Below 50 lux the responses are poor. Above 200 lux higher levels of illuminance do not improve enjoyment significantly (after Loe)*

to various lighting arrangements for a small group of paintings, was influential in making Thomson raise his recommended maximum level from 150 to 200 ± 50 lux (Loe, Rowlands and Watson, 1982).

Some of Loe's results are summarized in Figure 12.7. Two major factors were determined by assessing the responses of 24 people to 18 different lighting arrangements. The 'discrimination' factor relates to the ability to appreciate small differences in colour and detail. The 'quality evaluation' factor is a measure of the degree of pleasure the painting instils. Below 50 lux the responses are poor. Above 200 lux the improvement gained by doubling the illuminance is very small. Somewhere between 50 and 150 lux the curve changes from steeply rising to levelling out. Lamps with warmer colour did less well. Variety in the distribution of the light was also important.

Although variety is essential to eliminate the blandness of some conservation lighting, the contrasts cannot be too great or the eye will find it difficult to keep adapting. On grounds of increased understanding and enjoyment there doesn't seem to be good reason to illuminate any object at levels greater than about 200–250 lux. On grounds of immediate understanding and enjoyment, some textiles may need higher levels of illumination than some oil paintings.

Acceptable damage and service life

If we recommend that a light-sensitive object is illuminated at no more than 50 lux we are not saying 'this object will now be safe'. We are saying 'please damage this object at a rate that I consider acceptable'. If we stipulate a certain total annual dose we are saying the same thing, but without being too fussy about the light level. Either way, after a certain period of time, an irreversible change will have taken place that has been defined as acceptable. Since we are discussing a continuous causal relationship, where extent of change determines the risk, this is a measure of acceptable risk.

Assume for simplicity a straight line relationship between value and total exposure. An object at a fixed moment in time has a value that can be defined as 100%, whatever its condition. Figure 12.8 shows the value slowly decreasing with increasing exposure at three different rates. When any of the lines hits the horizontal axis the value becomes zero, the damage is 100%. This is an indisputable definition of the limit of acceptable damage. There is only one point that represents 100% of value. The value is only 100% when exposure is zero. If we want to say that any value below 100% constitutes unacceptable damage then we can *never* expose or use the object in any way. In that case I would maintain that the object might as well not exist.

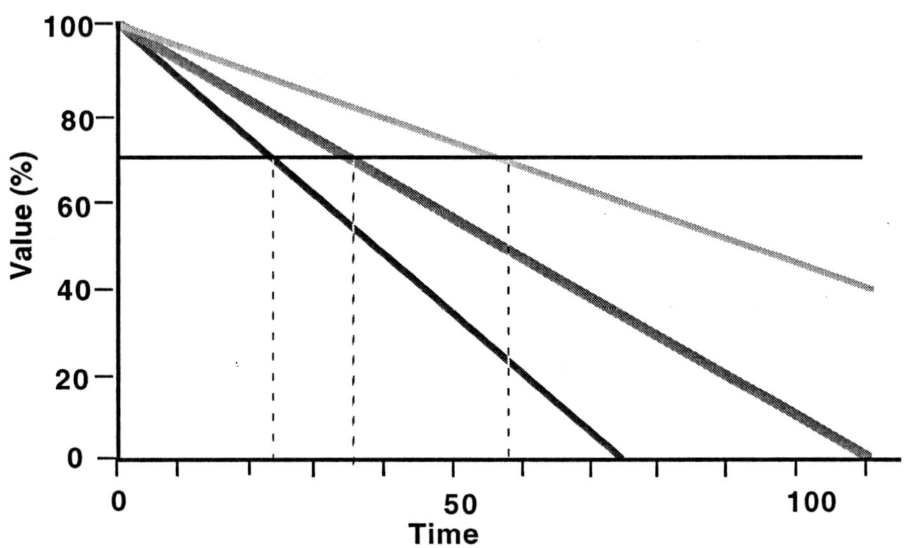

Figure 12.8 *Three different rates of damage. The points at which the lines reach the horizontal axis mark the end of the object's existence. The points at which they cross the arbitrary 30% damage (70% value) line mark the stage at which they cease to have value in a museum context*

So if the object is to be used we have to be prepared to choose an arbitrary number for the acceptable limit to damage somewhere between 0 and 100%. The number doesn't have to be totally *random*, it could be arrived at by discussion among a group of experts, art historians, for instance, who agree that at a certain level the object will no longer demonstrate those qualities for which it was acquired. Suppose this number is 70% of the original value. The vertical dotted lines show the times at which the object reaches this state for the three rates of exposure. These are the exposure times taken to reach the limit of acceptable damage – they define the service life of the object under different conditions.

If we as guardians of this valuable and vulnerable artifact want to control its *current* use, then we have to declare in advance how long we think it should be allowed to function *in the future*. I am not being cynical when I say that people will inevitably choose a minimum service life that is long enough to ensure that they are completely retired if not dead by the time the limit is reached. This would tend to make the minimum value ever proposed for minimum service life somewhere in the order of 40 years. (Museum directors and trustees last much shorter times than this – so beware.) If regular exposure at minimum light levels would lead to unacceptable damage in less than 40 years, additional control of total exposure must be instituted to ensure that the object lasts for at least this proposed service life. Service life will always be equal to or longer than exposure time at the minimum useful lighting level.

Forty years is likely to be the minimum ever proposed and most people would find the logic for choosing such a short period somewhat distressing not to say illogical. Can we decide on a maximum value for the minimum service life? Not on any logical grounds. By careful control of exposure times we could make even the most sensitive artifact last a thousand years, if light damage were the only risk. We do have to make a decision, however. People want to see the object *now*. At what rate should it be rationed? I would argue that it is meaningless to consider a planning horizon further than 200 years in the future. It's fairly difficult to predict the state of museums even 20 years into the future. Two hundred years is double the time that the majority of museums have been in existence. Suppose an object is going to receive unacceptable damage from regular exposure at minimum light levels in 50 years. Something must be done to prolong its life by control of exposure time. It is difficult to argue that current exposure, at a time when there is a guaranteed demand, *must* be rationed so that the object lasts considerably longer than 200 years.

This figure is my own and completely arbitrary. It is based on my pessimistic view of the future of museums in society and my perception of level of risk if the objects are left unexposed. Many light-sensitive objects also decay by thermal mechanisms in the dark. It makes no sense to deny access now if the object is not being preserved for later use. An accurate study of reaction rates in the dark might be a more scientific way of arriving at service life.

Thresholds of perceptible change

The way that the change in state is linked to the change in value is through the concept of the just noticeable difference (JND) (Ware 1994) or the just noticeable fade (JNF) (e.g. Michalski, 1997). These are two related measures of the smallest perceptible difference in state which is discernible by the observer under specified conditions of measurement. They form a bridge between the scientific 'any measurable change is damage' and a more realistic 'any change that a human might observe is damage' (but see Chapter 7). One JND is defined as a measured density difference of 0.01, the JNF is defined in reference to the colour difference between the steps in a grey scale and is an order of magnitude bigger. In the real world this threshold is dependent on the observer, on the colour and size of the test sample, and on the spectrum and intensity of lighting. However, it leads to a potentially transferable mechanism for defining the threshold exposure lifetime (TEL), which Mike Ware defines as the duration to exposure at 50 lux which results in one JND in a significant area of the object.

The susceptibilities of objects to fading by light are conventionally grouped into eight categories numbered ISO 1–8 (referring to the lightfastness of International Standard blue wool samples). ISO 1 is very fugitive and ISO 8 extremely stable. Table 12.1 gives a few representative

Table 12.1

Material	*ISO*
Colour photo print	1–2
Natural yellow and green dyes	1–2
Gamboge (pigment)	2
Indigo on cotton	3
Natural timber colours	3
Feathers	3–6
Dark fur or hair	4–6
Vermilion, alizarin (pigments)	4–6
Indigo on wool	7
Ultramarine, graphite, earth colours	8
Silver gelatin photograph	8

Table 12.2 *Annual exposure in days or weeks to achieve a just noticeable fade in 200 years of service (assuming no UV radiation)*

ISO	*50 lux*	*100 lux*	*200 lux*
1	5 days	3 days	1 day
2	2 weeks	1 week	4 days
3	6 weeks	3 weeks	1 week
4	19 weeks	9 weeks	4 weeks
5	1 year	30 weeks	15 weeks
6	(4 years)	1 year	47 weeks
7	(11 years)	(5 years)	1 year
8	(33 years)	(16 years)	(8 years)

values for a range of materials. Table 12.2 shows how long in any one year an object could be exhibited at various light levels to arrive at one JNF in a period of 200 years. It should be noted that one JNF is not the same as my definition of the limit of acceptable damage the service life of the object. The acceptable limit has to be the point at which you say 'there's no reason to keep this any more!' Total fade is about 30 JNF. In many circumstances 10 JNF might render an object useless. Multiply the figures in Table 12.2 by 10 if you are determined to fully use up the object within 200 years. Current museum practice probably gives one JNF in 20–50 years of display giving planning horizons til 'death' of 200–500 years.

The times shown in Table 12.2 should be multiplied by 50 if you believe that a total service life of 40 years is adequate or multiplied by 2 if you are more cautious and think that a millennium hence is a better planning horizon. Look at the effects of that decision on objects rated ISO 1.

There will be some objects where one JNF is not critical and others where the reason for an object's existence is that it is a continuing true record of colour. For instance, a textile sample from a manufacturer's pattern book will have most of its value removed if it changes colour perceptibly.

People who feel constricted by limiting the exposure time will argue that the damage has already been done. For dyes and pigments that fade rapidly initially, the final rate of fading makes them appear one or two ISO numbers more stable. Because the object has changed it doesn't mean that the maximum amount of damage has been done.

Costs and benefits

The limits to an acceptable rate of damage can be addressed by looking at the costs and benefits associated with that rate. The lower limit is set by

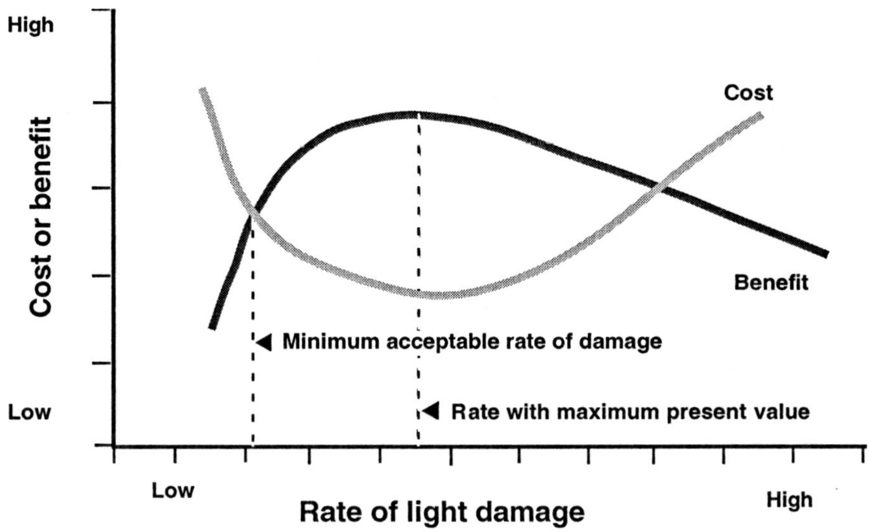

Figure 12.9 *Attempts to keep rates of light damage low increase costs and decrease benefits. The effects of high rates of light damage are to increase costs and decrease benefits. Where does the optimum net benefit lie?*

the cost of control and the fact that if you reduce exposure to damage you will reduce the benefit that is derived from exposure. For example, to minimize light damage we change displays of sensitive material. There is a manpower cost in constantly changing the display and also an additional risk of mechanical wear and tear. The benefit is severely reduced if levels of light are so low that aspects such as colour cannot be perceived or if objects are visible for so short a time that only a lucky few get to see them.

What about the upper limit to rate of damage? There are cost constraints on increasing the intensity or duration of exposure to damaging factors. For sensitive objects the cost is obvious damage. For robust objects it may actually cost too much to cause noticeable damage through increasing the intensity of lighting. Very high illumination levels cause distress to people as well as objects. With some types of increased exposure there will be diminishing returns in benefit. For instance, of the millions of people who went to the Tutankhamun exhibitions, which epitomized the new wave of heavily marketed displays, very few actually had time to appreciate the exhibits. Certainly any serious scholar would find it difficult to derive benefit from a blockbuster exhibition (Powers, 1978). So increasing exposure time may actually decrease some measure of benefit.

This general picture is indicated in Figure 12.9. At high rates of damage, benefits begin to decrease and costs rise. At low rates of damage, costs start to rise and benefits drop dramatically. Any rate of damage for which benefits exceed costs will be acceptable. If you are averse to risk, which by definition conservators and possibly curators are, you will be tempted to operate at the low end where costs begin to overtake benefits. You should be aware that at this point you are not maximizing net benefit. If the monetized costs and benefits have been discounted at an appropriate rate, the rate of damage that gives the greatest net benefit is the rate of damage with the highest present value.

Something to think about

For very light-sensitive objects, is it more important to spend money on UV control or simply dim the lights?

How would you argue with the fire and security officer who says that patrol lights must be left on all night in the galleries? After all this could be a matter of life and death, not just a bit of fading in an old object.

When would a change of one JND not constitute damage?

How did you feel when I proposed a service lifetime of only 200 years? How do you feel now after studying Table 12.2?

References

Boyce, P.R. (1987) *Visual Acuity, Colour Discrimination and Light Level.* Lighting. A Conference on Lighting in Museums, Galleries and Historic Houses held in Bristol. Museums Association, London, pp. 50–57.

Crews, Patricia Cox (1982) The Influence of Mordant on the Lightfastness of Yellow Natural Dyes. *Journal of the American Institute for Chemistry,* **21**, pp. 43–58.

Crews, Patricia Cox (1989) A Comparison of Selected UV Filtering Materials for the Reduction of Fading. *Journal of the American Institute for Conservation,* **28**, pp. 117–125.

Feller, Robert L. (1964) Control of the Deteriorating Effects of Light upon Museum Objects. *Museum,* **17**, pp. 71–98.

Feller, Robert L. (1977) Stages in the Deterioration of Organic Materials, in *Preservation of Paper and Textiles of Historic and Artistic Value,* edited by John C. Williams. American Chemical Society, Vol. 164, pp. 314–335.

Lee, S.B., Bogaard, J. and Feller, R.L. (1989) Darkening of Paper Following Exposure to Visible and Near-Ultraviolet Radiation. *Journal of the American Institute for Conservation,* **28**, pp. 1–18.

Loe, David L., Rowlands, E. and Watson, N.F. (1982) Preferred Lighting Conditions for the Display of Oil and Watercolour Paintings. *Lighting Research and Technology*, **14**, p. 173.

Michalski, Stefan (1987) *Damage to Visible Radiation (Light) and Ultraviolet Radiation (UV)*. Lighting. A Conference on Lighting in Museums, Galleries and Historic Houses Held in Bristol. Museums Association, London, pp. 3–16.

Michalski, Stefan (1990) Towards Specific Lighting Guidelines. 9th Triennial Meeting of the ICOM Committee for Conservation, Dresden, pp. 583–588.

Michalski, Stefan (1997) The Lighting Decision. Fabric of an Exhibition: An Interdisciplinary Approach – Preprints. Canadian Conservation Institute. ISBN 0-660-60261-X, pp. 97–104.

Neevel, J.G. (1995) UV-Belastung durch Elektronenblitz und Kopiergeräte. *Restauro*, March–April, pp. 98–102.

New Scientist (1995) Fabulous Fabrics Come out of the Shade. Article by Marcus Chown describing David Howell's work. *New Scientist* No. 1977, 13 May, p. 10.

Padfield, T. (1994) The Role of Standards and Guidelines: Are They a Substitute for Understanding a Problem or a Protection against the Consequences of Ignorance?, in *Durability and Change: The Science, Responsibility, and Cost of Sustaining Cultural Heritage*, edited by W.E. Krumbien, P. Brimblecombe, D.E. Cosgrove and S. Staniforth. John Wiley and Sons. ISBN-0-471-95221-4, pp. 191–199.

Powers, Sandra (1978) Why Exhibit? The Risks versus the Benefits. *American Archivist*, **41**, p. 297.

Saunders, David and Kirby, Jo (1994) Wavelength-dependent Fading of Artist's Pigments. Preventive Conservation: Practice, Theory and Research. Preprints to the Ottawa Congress, 12–16 September. IIC, pp. 190–194.

Saunders, David (1995) Photographic Flash: Threat or Nuisance. *National Gallery Technical Bulletin*, 16. National Gallery Publications, pp. 66–73.

Suppan, Paul (1994) *Chemistry and Light*. The Royal Society of Chemistry, Cambridge. ISBN 0-85186-814-2, p. 91.

Ware, Mike (1994) *Mechanisms of Image Deterioration in Early Photographs*. Trustees of the Science Museum, London. ISBN 0-901805-78-5, pp. 41–42.

13 The things people do

The effects of people on objects and their environments are many and varied. Most of the hazards can be controlled so that damage is minimized. Because most risks are easy to contain, much of the damage occurs through random failure of control procedures. This means it is often difficult to make useful predictions. The physical effects of numbers of bodies in one space can be calculated, as can the reduced lifetime of objects taken out of storage for study.

Use and risk

This is the second chapter about use. Many of the ways in which objects are used have a direct effect on their state or their environment. The users are people and people have an effect, whether they intend it or not. The current trend is to encourage greater numbers of people to use museums and historic sites. A common indicator for the success of a museum is number of visitors through the door. The distinction between display and storage is changing, as reserve collections are made increasingly accessible to avoid criticisms of hoarding treasures in the basement. Even for archival and scientific collections increased use is the indicator that is demanded for continued funding. As payment by tax is replaced by payment at point of access, greater use is the only way to survive. Growth is sustainable up to a point when the individual benefit starts to decline. This happens if access to the objects is spoiled by overcrowding, or if access is denied because the objects are being destroyed.

What are the risks of having people around? People have an effect on the environment just by being there. Once they start to study or enjoy their surroundings they increase the risk. They demand comforts and excitements in addition to access to the collections. Some of this added value may also add to risk. Occasionally, individual people choose to cause severe damage. The only way to eliminate the risk of theft or vandalism completely is to deny access. A certain level of risk must be accepted if there are to be any benefits.

People and space

Before they even consider looking at displays or consulting archives, humans have a basic set of demands. There must be air with sufficient oxygen and not too much carbon dioxide. Sighted visitors demand light in order to find their way about. People complain if temperatures are lower than 15°C or higher than 25°C. They will feel uncomfortable if the humidity falls below 30% or rises above 80%. They will feel unwelcome if there are unpleasant smells.

These basic demands are not incompatible with the preservation of a great many objects. Many objects were created by humans for use in the human environment, and so have a reasonable stability in that milieu. If levels of humidity are restricted for conservation reasons, it will not upset the visitors as long as the set point is around the mid-range. Since there is no 'ideal' temperature for objects, human comfort is the determining factor.

Having entered this comfortable environment the humans then set about disturbing the equilibrium. They consume oxygen, and emit carbon dioxide. They emit a variety of VOCs and sulpur-containing compounds. They scatter tiny fragments of their bodies and clothing. Most importantly they generate heat and produce water vapour.

If a number of people enter an unventilated and insulated space the temperature rises. This reduces the relative humidity but the moisture produced by the people is not sufficient to raise the RH back to or above the previous level. Garry Thomson asserts that the RH will always go down, and supports this view with a record of an event where this happened. A group of 16 people in a small space raised the temperature by about 2°C and lowered the humidity by about 2% (Thomson, 1986). My own experience is that RH may go up or down but never by very much. The heat output of a human being (70–120 watts) depends on ambient temperature, amount of clothing and degree of alcoholic intoxication. The water output (1–2 litres a day) depends on the ambient temperature and humidity and the degree of activity. There is a wide range of possibilities. The important fact is that for a space normally at about 20°C and 50% RH the ingress of a large number of people does not constitute a risk in terms of varying RH or temperature.

A very rough rule of thumb for the temperature rise is to divide 10 by the number of square metres floor space available to each person (based on a 3 m ceiling height). The result of this calculation gives the maximum temperature rise at the end of an hour. So, if a space becomes sufficiently crowded that there is only 2 m^2 of floor space for each person, the temperature could rise by 5°C.

The biggest worry is the fate of the additional water. Although the relative humidity may not have altered much, the absolute humidity, the actual mass of water in the air, has increased. If ventilation and insulation are poor this moisture will condense on to cold surfaces such as outer walls.

A traditional worry is the influx of a large group of children in wet raincoats suddenly raising the humidity to dangerous levels. Yes, you can sometimes see the effect on the graph. But it is a small and transient peak and only a risk to extremely sensitive objects such as thermohygrographs.

If the space in which objects are kept is normally much colder or much more moist than the conventional 15–25°C and 30–70% RH range, the risk from people is much greater. The heating of cold spaces for human comfort can cause dramatic changes in moisture content of objects and walls (e.g. Olstad, 1994). Changes in moisture content of walls can lead to cycles of efflorescence and deliquesence which may disrupt surface decorations.

Tombs and caves underground are often at relative humidities in the range 90–100% (e.g. Bettini, 1991). The air is in equilibrium with the wall. Letting people in to this space destroys the equilibrium. It encourages exchange of air between the damp cave and the much drier atmosphere outside. This combined with the heating effect of their bodies causes the RH to drop while they are there. This leads to cycles of evaporation and condensation at the wall which may damage surface decoration.

The people demand light and leave traces of organic matter. At high RH these two combine to encourage algal growth.

In limestone caves there is an equilibrium between the carbon dioxide in the air and the amount of limestone that is dissolved in moisture in the walls. If the level of carbon dioxide increases, more limestone will dissolve. If the levels drop, lime will be precipitated from solution possibly obscuring a wall painting. Introducing fresh air will lower the carbon dioxide levels and restricting ventilation will cause them to rise.

The only control is through regulating the flow of visitors (e.g. Maekawa, 1994). Where preservation of the object is dependent on payment for entry this may not be an easy option.

To summarize. If objects are kept in an environment where twentieth-century humans are comfortable then increasing the number of people does not increase risk of environmental damage. If the objects are kept in conditions very different from the comfort zone then introducing people is likely to increase risk. The greater the number of people the greater the risk. People have to pass from the outside into the space and then back out again. Every time this happens there is the possibility of exchange between the inside environment and that outside.

Added value

Museums encourage people to come by offering changing displays and exciting events. They encourage them to stay by offering food and drink. Funding for museums is encouraged by letting the rich and influential gain closer access to collections and museum spaces while wining and dining.

The demands for excitement and change in museum presentations add to the risks. The hazards associated with temporary exhibitions are dealt with in the next chapter. The hazards associated with entertaining sponsors and visitors with food and wine are subject to management. The presence of flowers and plants may well encourage insect pests, the possibility of food debris certainly will. Careful control of food preparation areas and scrupulous cleaning will reduce the risks. Candlelit dinners for corporate sponsors will increase fire risk and add to particulates in the air. Ventilation and supervision will reduce the possibility of damage.

The main dangers come from the possibility of local overcrowding close to vulnerable objects.

Wear and tear

It is obvious that where people come into contact with historic objects they cause wear and tear. The greater the number of people, the greater the rate of attrition. The obvious point of contact between people and cultural material is their feet treading on historic floor surfaces. They may also be obliged or tempted to touch door fixtures (see Figure 13.1). However, there are other ways that contact takes place. Tired people will lean against walls or furniture. People absorbed in looking at one object will back into another. Those on the edge of a crowd may have no option but to brush against walls or objects. All of these inadvertent contacts can be controlled but at a cost to the appearance and ambience of the space.

When all the acceptable physical and psychological barriers have been installed the only thing left is to control visitor numbers. There are good descriptions of the types of damage and of possible methods of control (Fawcett, 1984; Yates and Davison, 1996). Unfortunately there is very little work relating rates of damage to visitor numbers. The National Trust, which manages historic properties that may attract up to a million visitors a year, has started some studies (Lloyd and Mullany, 1994). Suspended timber floors and fine staircases are particularly suceptible to high-amplitude vibrations associated with high visitor numbers.

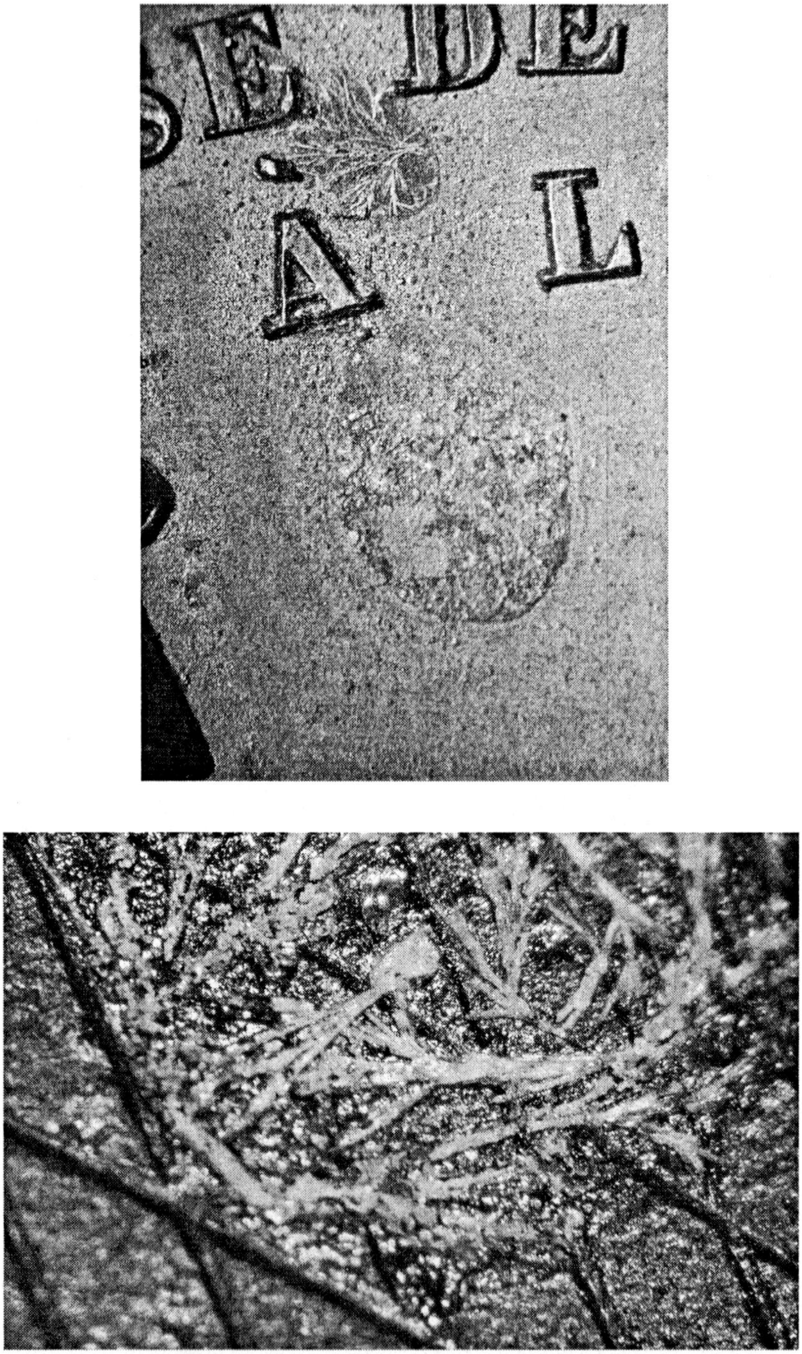

Figure 13.1 *Corrosion on a bronze medal associated with a fingerprint*

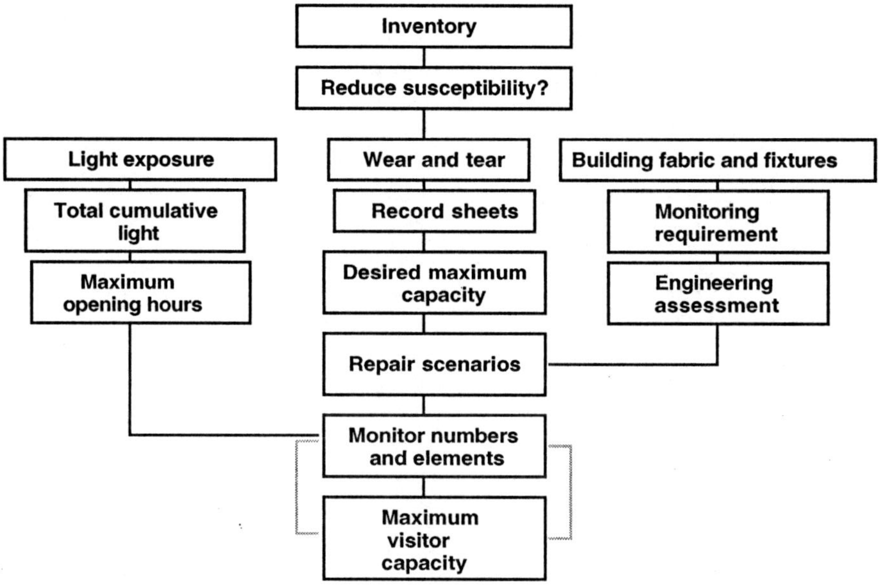

Figure 13.2 *Elements of a Visitor Impact Assessment (after Thomas* et al.*)*

The effects of visitors on the building and its contents can be estimated using the Visitor Impact Assessment (VIA) and a Vulnerability Index (Thomas, Seeley and O'Sullivan, 1997). The structure of the VIA is shown in Figure 13.2. It is recomended that this is carried out before any new visitor facilities or attractions are planned.

The rates of damage due to use should be calculable from records of use and surveys of damage. These can be the result of simple observation. For instance, there is an unprotected wooden staircase in my house. I know the date that I removed the carpet and I can calculate within one power of 10 how many times the stairs have been trodden on. Approximately 200 000 trips have worn away 1 mm of pine. In many cases the owners of property at risk will be able to keep better records of use, and more accurate measures of wear. Automated records in libraries and archives are most likely to be productive but I have not come across any published results.

Wear and tear can be modelled theoretically or physically. The easier it is to do a test, the more readily it will become accepted as a method of predicting behaviour. As pointed out in Chapter 7 a straightforward test may not necessarily represent the greater complexity of the real world. Folding endurance for paper has become accepted as a measure of mechanical permanence. 'Folding' sounds more gentle than 'creasing' and can be related mentally to the slow turning of pages in a library. That is until you see the test itself, where the paper is repeatedly bent under tension over a hard edge through around 300°. These conditions are not reproduced at any stage of careful use. Because these distortions induce plastic deformation they lead to cumulative damage, indeed the test depends on that accumulation. Care should be taken in interpreting the figures. A paper with high fold endurance will definitely endure high use. Within a service expectancy of a couple of centuries so might paper that failed the test.

Vandals and thieves

A survey of around 100 US museums revealed that during the previous five years 30% had suffered a theft and 23% some vandalism (Young, 1992). Most of the vandalism was minor and the work of pranksters. The one serious incident was politically motivated. The rate of thefts was highest in history museums and the objects were usually taken from open display in period rooms or from libraries and archives.

One of the first jobs I did as a trainee metals conservator was to make a small replacement part for a large decorative centrepiece that was on open display in a period room. It had been stolen by a trophy hunter. Knobs, finials, decorative mounts . . . anything that protrudes and is easy to pocket will go. Such damage can be avoided by separating the visitor from the object and by remote electronic or local human supervision. The loss of the original piece involved a greater loss in value than when my replacement was stolen some years later. However, in both cases there was the cost of making the replica. The continuing cost of replacement must be weighed against the loss of access and the cost of protection.

Objects on open display are also subject to touching and to artistic improvement.

The chemical risks of soiling are mentioned later in this chapter and the discussion in Chapter 10 is relevant. Artistic improvement frequently consists of the addition of moustaches or the accentuation of nipples on sculpture. Usually the effect is not permanent but there is a cost in the removal by trained conservators. Rarely, something sharper than a pencil is used, leaving a lasting mark. A sharp object such as a pencil has been used to poke out the eyes of unglazed portraits. This marks the borderline between adolescent idleness and malevolent or psychotic behaviour.

Occasionally a visitor decides to do a great deal of damage. Some years ago at the V&A, a paint tin was thrown into a case containing Venetian glassware, and on another occasion a visitor attacked a showcase with a fire extinguisher. Fortunately the showcase in the last incident was of robust high quality and the object inside was not damaged. These incidents are the only two that I can remember over a period of 20 years, call it one in every 10 million visits. The common features are that the culprits had had a bad day and that there was a heavy implement to hand. In these and most other incidents of vandalism, the action was over very quickly. No amount of supervision could guarantee to stop it in time. Prevention by separation and physical protection is the only way.

The presence of people in a space may increase the risks to security but in general it tends to limit theft and vandalism. The English Heritage risk categories for listed buildings involves a correlation of physical condition and occupancy. An occupied building is at lower risk (Keith, 1991).

Outside of wartime, the use of firearms to damage cultural objects is rare, the shooting of the Leonardo cartoon at the National Gallery, London, being the most famous example. Most vandals do not seek to destroy a particular object but one that happens to be convenient. To that extent the effect can be considered random. The cost of bullet proof glass is prohibitively high for inclusion in routine physical protection.

Where mechanical means have been used to attack an object, most of the damage is done in an instant. Chemical attacks take time and so swift action can minimize the effect. It is necessary to make a speedy identification of the chemical and to have the cure ready at hand. Attack by acid or solvent is likely to remove more information-laden material than slashing by a knife. So loss of value and expense of repair are likely to be greater.

In peace time, and in economically stable countries, the incidence of theft and vandalism is mostly dependent on local factors such as the nature of the collection, the methods of display and the levels of security in any particular institution. There is reluctance to publish figures or share information. The notices of thefts published in museum and art periodicals would have to be taken as a low minimum. Any assessment of risk as a part of collections care would probably be best based on pooled local knowledge rather than appeal to global statistics. The annual risk per object is probably in the order of one in a hundred thousand. The loss in value will depend on whether, and in what state, the missing item is recovered.

Working objects

There is no doubt that people get enjoyment out of seeing clocks, cars and steam engines actually working. There is little doubt that making museum objects work creates wear and tear, and increases the possibility of catastrophic damage. The risks, costs and benefits can be calculated in the same way that we did for light damage except that there is usually the possibility of repair. The arguments about loss of value from wear and tear are covered in Chapter 7 and the loss of information as original material is lost and replaced will be discussed in Chapter 15. Peter Mann has discussed some of the curatorial problems of working exhibits (Mann, 1989). He notes that significant cumulative degradation is common but catastrophic destruction is rare. Cumulative degradation through modification may occur, even without wear, in order to improve the reliability or repeatability of a demonstration.

The serious student

The majority of museum visitors do not have an opportunity to do more than look at objects from behind a rope barrier or through the glass of a showcase. The serious student is sometimes granted the privilege of much closer contact. After misappropriation, the major risks associated with this come from:

- removing the object from its current environment
- handling the object

The problems of handling can be separated into those associated with touching and those that come from changing the pattern of physical stresses in the object by turning it around or flexing it.

The hazards of touching are the transfer of reactive chemicals and the transfer of soils. Whether touching causes deterioration will depend on the chemicals that are transferred and the materials of the object. Whether the change that takes place is serious damage will depend very much on the object and how it is valued.

The chemicals that are likely to be transferred are fats, fatty acids, water and salt. Diet can have an effect on the content of breath and sweat. Over-indulgence in garlic increases the concentrations of sulphur compounds that can react with materials in art objects (Arnold, 1983; *New Scientist*, 1986).

The materials that are particularly susceptible to touching are polished metal, especially iron and silver, and photographic negatives and prints. The slighest change in any polished surface is likely to be visually disturbing. If discovered quickly the damage may not be permanent. The cost is the time and risk of cleaning. However, if the chemicals are left on the surface for a long time, especially at higher humidities, further reactions may take place. Figure 13.3 shows corrosion on the surface of a medal which was associated with a fingerprint. It was not possible to clean this off without leaving some staining on the metal. Given the way that medals are valued for their perfect surface, this blemish caused a considerable loss of value. Some people are significantly more corrosive than others. In the steel industry tests have been developed to screen out 'rusters' (Nishimura, 1997).

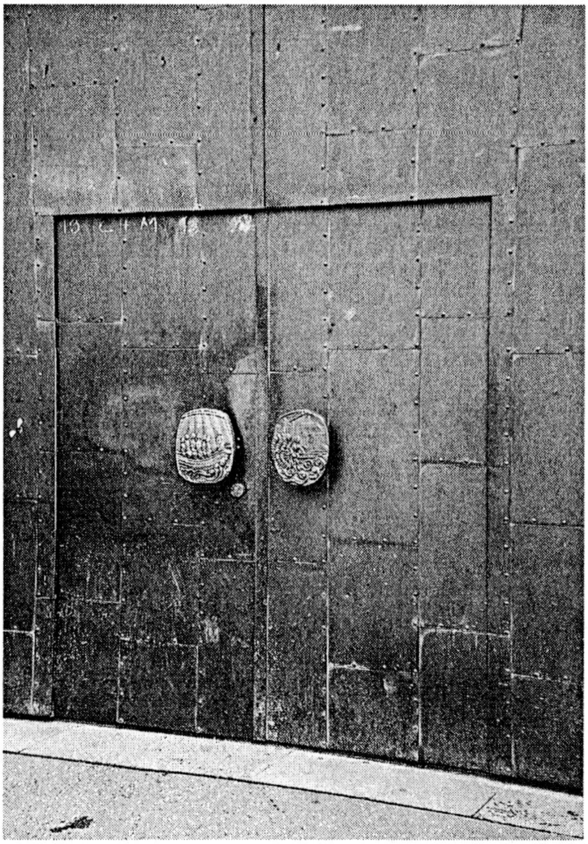

Figure 13.3 *Loss of patina on a bronze door through repeated handling*

If left, fingerprints can etch the surface of gelatin on photographs and cause sulphiding of the image silver (Hendriks, 1994). The probability of severe damage is relatively small but it can be completely avoided by simple techniques such as wearing gloves and handling more discretely.

The degradation of paper and textiles is theoretically accelerated by the presence of acids. Repeated handling would be expected to increase acidity and therefore increase deterioration. As bank notes circulate they become more acidic and the water repelling qualities of the resin sizing is destroyed by lactic acid in sweat (Fellers *et al.*, 1989). I am not aware of any study of the effects of acidity from handling involving historic objects. The risks from acids generated in poor wood-pulp papers and from the strong acids due to atmospheric pollution are likely to be much greater.

Physical damage due to mishandling or dropping can be controlled by common sense, supervision and training. The greatest danger is the researcher wanting to deal with too much material at once. No single type of accident should happen frequently, as lessons should be learned and steps taken to avoid repetition. Once an accident has occurred it should be investigated to see if procedures to prevent it were ignored or need to be modified.

Kitty Nicholson describes some unusual incidents at the National Archives, Washington, where historic documents fell into the paper feed tray of a photocopier (Nicholson, 1989). In a couple of instances the toner was fused into a dense black layer obscuring the original text. The public are allowed to photocopy original material once it has been reviewed by staff. Self-service photocopying is prohibited for several types of material including oversized documents. The three documents damaged in this way were all oversized but staff review failed to detect them because they were stored folded and presented in large batches of documents. The accidents occurred because the particular geometry of the photocopier meant that overhanging parts of large documents were perilously close to the paper intake. The incidence of such accidents was small, three in two years from among nearly half a million photocopies. This low incidence would not suggest changing the policy of allowing self-service photocopying. A simple temporary physical modification to the machine made any further incidents unlikely. The machine was eventually replaced with one whose geometry made this type of accident impossible.

It is also possible to predict whether changes in student behaviour will lead to increasing low-level damage. Post-it notes are now a part of everyday life and can be very useful as bookmarks when carrying out research (there are 10 sticking out of the edges of the pile of books and photocopies on my desk at the moment). They are forbidden in a number of libraries. The cry goes up 'but the adhesive is very weak and totally reversible!'. Even after only a few weeks the note can become permanently attached, especially to coated papers. Library policies should be in place before the student population becomes addicted.

Removal from cold-storage

Because the rates of degradation at room temperature are so high some photographic materials are stored at low temperatures. Controlled removal to a study area at room temperature is not risky as there is no damage from thermal shock. If the RH in storage and study environments is similar, the material can come in and out of cold-storage as frequently as necessary without fear of cumulative damage (McCormick-Goodhart and Mecklenburg, 1993).

Table 13.1 *Effect on permanence of removing photographs from cold storage (RH 40%)*

Storage temperature (°C)	*Time out of storage (days)*				
	0	*1*	*2*	*5*	*10*
24	1.0	1.0	1.0	1.0	1.0
15	3.3	3.3	3.2	3.2	3.1
7	10	10	10	9	8
2	19	18	17	15	13
–3	37	34	31	25	19
–10	100	79	65	42	27
–18	305	166	114	59	33
–26	1000	268	154	68	35

There is a cost every time the objects are retrieved and resealed before placing back in the cold-store. Maintaining the store at low temperatures is expensive. If the objects are going to be consulted frequently there may be no purpose in going for the most expensive option. Table 13.1 shows the relative permanence of chromogenic colour dyes in colour photographs at different storage temperatures.

Because the relationship between temperature and reaction rate is exponential, as much damage is done in one day at room temperature as in a month at around freezing point. The phenomenal benefits of very low temperatures, a thousandfold increase in lifetime at –26°C, are considerably reduced if the object is out of storage for 10 days each year (bottom right number in the table). The difference between –18 and –26 becomes negligible at 10 days out of storage, but there is a twofold increase in lifetime if the object is only out for one day. The running costs of a store held at –3 are at least double those for a store at +2. The longer the object remains out of storage, the less necessary it seems to accept this additional cost.

Opening the door

A similar argument can be used about the expense of showcases. The advantages of a well-sealed showcase are the greater stability of relative humidity and the decreased deposition of pollution. A well-sealed showcase can be very expensive. If the case is going to be opened frequently so that objects can be removed for study there may be no advantage in paying for the good construction and a tight seal.

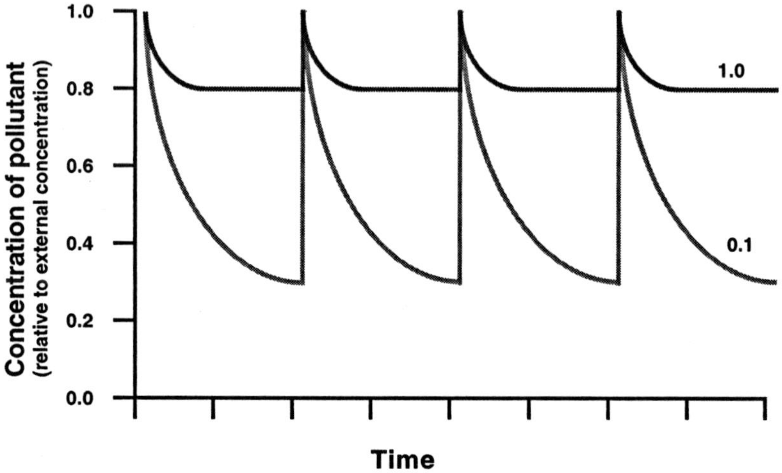

Figure 13.4 *Computer simulation showing the concentration of an externally generated pollutant inside showcases with differing exchange rates. The cases are opened at regular intervals to remove objects for study. It is assumed that when the doors are open the atmosphere in the case becomes the same as that outside*

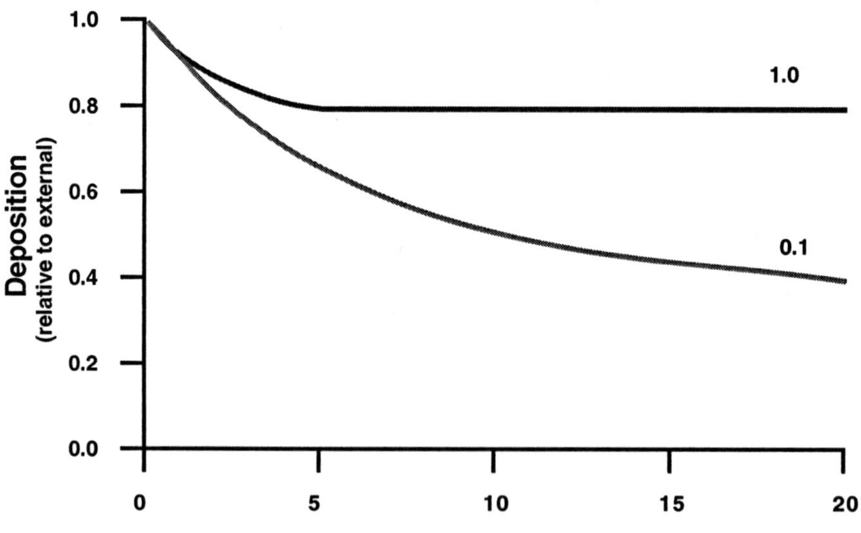

Figure 13.5 *Plot of frequency of opening against the relative benefit of being inside a case. The vertical axis is the ratio of pollutant deposition inside and outside the case. A low air exchange rate always gives better protection*

Table 13.2 *Permanence of objects affected by pollution in different locations*

Location	*Days out of storage*			
	0	*100*	*200*	*300*
Room	1.0	1.0	1.0	1.0
Leaky case	1.3	1.2	1.1	1.0
Airtight case	2.5	1.8	1.4	1.1

Figure 13.4 shows a computer simulation of the concentration of an externally produced pollutant gas in two showcases that are opened at regular intervals. One showcase has an air exchange rate of 1 change per day, the other 0.1 per day. The slope of the curves will depend on the nature of the pollutant and on the absorbent surfaces, so this can only be an example. The actual amount of deposition is related to the area under each curve. No matter how often the case is opened the low exchange rate case wins out. Figure 13.5 shows the rates of deposition in each case, relative to the rate that would occur if the objects were not cased, plotted against the frequency of opening. The case with a tenth of the air exchange ends up being twice as good at protection. It would depend on the relative costs of the showcases, the rate of damage and cost of repair and the value of the objects whether this constituted the best buy.

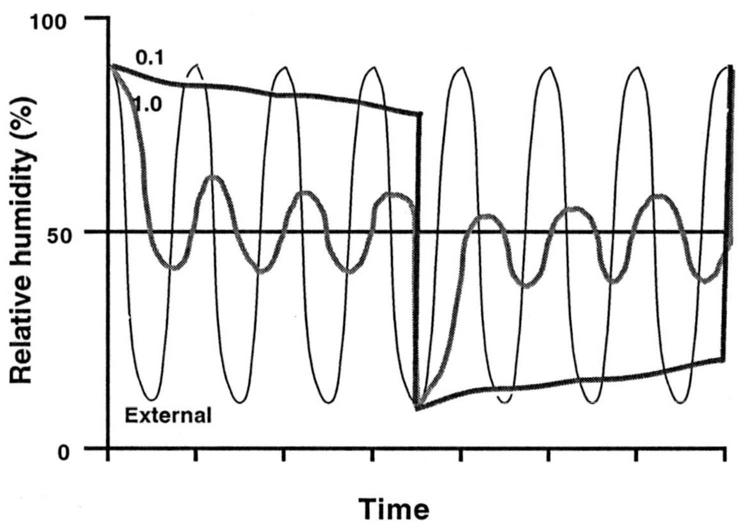

Figure 13.6 *Opening a case with a low air exchange rate could lead to a larger RH change than for a more leaky case*

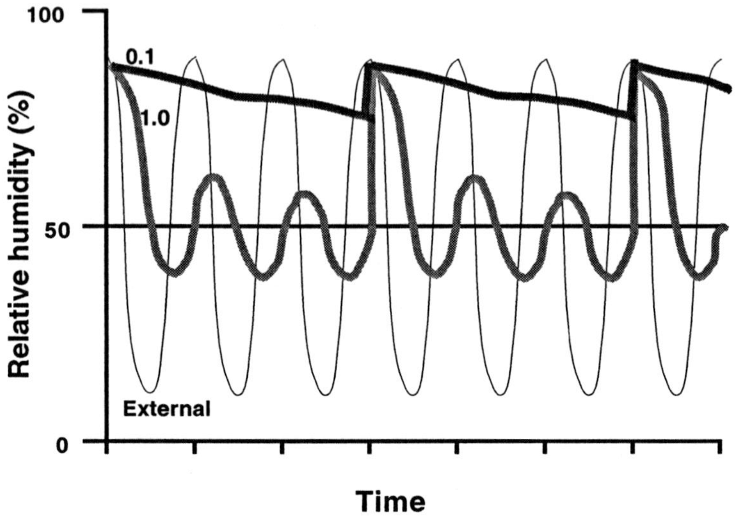

Figure 13.7 *Because a case with a low exchange rate holds its environment better, opening it at periods of high RH will mean that the average RH in the case remains higher than the average outside*

If the objects are removed from the case for study in an area that has the same pollution levels as the gallery then the rate of deterioration will increase. This increase is not as dramatic as for removal from cold storage. Table 13.2 shows the decrease in permanence associated with keeping an object out of its protective case.

The situation with relative humidity is a little more complex. Remember, some damage is caused by continuing high levels of humidity and some may be caused by changes or fluctuations. An airtight showcase will tend to maintain the environment that was in it at the time the door was closed. This could be a good thing or a bad thing. If any case remains unopened it will slowly reach the average humidity of the external air.

Take as examples two computer simulations which, although they show extreme situations, demonstrate the relevant points. Figure 13.6 is a plot of humidity against time. The thin line shows the RH in a gallery fluctuating wildly on a regular basis. The other two curves show the RH inside two cases in that gallery, one is leaky, the other airtight. Everytime the cases are opened they rapidly assume the RH of the gallery at that time. The cases are opened at the point of highest humidity on one occasion and then, some time later, at the lowest point. The largest changes take place in the airtight case; the most frequent changes in the leaky case. In both cases the average RH is the same as that in the gallery.

Figure 13.7 shows what would happen if the cases were always opened at the point of highest humidity. The largest and most frequent changes take place in the leaky case. The RH is continuously maintained at a high level in the airtight case.

If the general level of fluctuation shown for the leaky case is thought not to be damaging then there is no need to go for the airtight case. Increasing the frequency of opening the leaky case does little to increase risk. If there are good reasons to keep objects in an extremely stable environment then the airtight case is justified, but increasing the incidence of opening increases the risk. The value of higher capital cost has to be justified by continuing good management. The case should not be opened if external conditions are radically different from those inside the case.

The examples just given take no account of the effect of buffering materials in the case or of the buffering effect of the objects themselves. Buffering would decrease risk in both cases. Much more buffering material is needed in the leaky case.

If you intend to study objects frequently or for long periods in unfavourable environments there is no great advantage in providing expensive storage facilities for the times in between. If you have gone to the bother of providing a protective environment the object is best served by leaving it there undisturbed.

Something to think about

What are the risks of holding a private view where wine and food are served in a gallery where the objects are in showcases? What chains of events would be necessary for damage to occur?

What are the risks of allowing visually impaired visitors to handle objects? What are the costs and benefits?

What are the political and social implications of restricting access to sites that are at risk from use?

What are the risks, costs and benefits of keeping historic clocks in working order?

References

Arnold, Andreas (1983) Der Braungefleckte Polierwiess-Engel. *Maltechnick-Restauro*, p. 157.

Bettini, G. (1991) Preservation Problems: Visitors and Deterioration on the Painted Etruscan Tomb. Science, Technology and European Cultural Heritage. Proceedings of the European Symposium, Bologna, Italy, 13–16 June 1989. Butterworth-Heinemann for the Commission of the European Communities, p. 761.

Fawcett, Jane (1984) Greater Churces: Damage by Visitors. *Transactions of the Association for Studies of the Conservation of Historic Buildings*, **9**, p. 6.

Fellers, Christer, Iversen, Tommy, Lindström, Tom, Nilsson, Thomas, and Rigdahl, Mikael (1989) Ageing/Degradation of Paper: a Literature Survey. FoU-projektet for papperkonservering. Report No1E. Stockholm. ISSN 0284–5636.

Hendriks, Klaus B. (1994) *Fundamentals of Photograph Conservation: A Study Guide*. Lugus, p. 422.

Keith, Crispin (1991) *Using Listed Buildings*. English Heritage. ISBN 1-85074-297-9, p. 29.

Maekawa, Shin (1994) Preventive Strategies for Reducing the Impact of Visitors on the Microenvironment of Caves at the Magao Grottoes. Preventive Conservation: Practice, Theory and Research. Preprints to the Ottawa Congress, 12–16 September. IIC, pp. 76–79.

Mann, Peter Robert (1989) Working Exhibits and the Destruction of Evidence in the Science Museum. *International Journal of Museum Management and Curatorship*, Vol. 8, p. 369.

McCormick-Goodhart, Mark H. and Mecklenburg, Marion F. (1993) Cold Storage Environments for Photographic Materials. IS&T 46th Annual Conference, pp. 277–280.

New Scientist (1986) No. 109, p. 24.

Nicholson, Kitty (1989) Photocopier Hazards and a Conservation Case Study. *The 1989 Book and Paper Group Annual*. AIC, pp. 39–57.

Nishimura, Doug (1997) Note entitled 'white gloves', in Conservation On Line. Cons Dist. 22 April.

Olstad, Tone M. (1994) Mediaeval Wooden Churches in a Cold Climate – Parish Churches or Museums. Preventive Conservation: Practice, Theory and Research. Preprints to the Ottawa Congress, 12–16 September. IIC, pp. 99–103.

Thomas, Paul, Seeley, Nigel and O'Sullivan, Patrick, (1997) The Processes of Visitor Impact Assessment. *Journal of Architectural Conservation*, No. 1, pp. 67–84.

Thomson, Garry (1986) *The Museum Environment*. Butterworth-Heinemann. ISBN 0-7506-2041-2, p. 230.

Yates, Tim and Davison, Sandra (1966) *Tile Pavement and Floorwear. A Future for the Past*. A joint conference of English Heritage and the Cathedral Architects Association, March 1944, edited by Jeanne Marie Teutonico. James and James. ISBN 1-873936-45-1, pp. 99–107.

Young, Janie Chester (1992) The State of the Art and the Artifact: A Regional Survey of Museum Collections. *Technology and Conservation*, pp. 11–17.

14 Travelling shows

The contributions to benefits, costs and risk of travelling exhibitions are listed. The concept of risk perception is introduced. An attempt is made to determine a threshold of acceptable risk.

Exhibitions and risk

It has become common practice for exhibitions composed of large numbers of objects to travel from one venue to another around the world. The general area of lending and borrowing works of art, and the particular subject of touring exhibitions, causes heated debate.

This debate is of interest because it involves all the possible conflicts that result from a museum trying to balance its internal needs with external pressures. There are conflicts between preservation and access, conflicts between the pressures of economy and the maintenance of professional standards, and conflicts between risk to the objects and benefits to the funders and to the public.

Museums expect to lend. The National Heritage Act allows the Trustees of the V&A to lend any object, whether or not the object is for public exhibition and whether or not the loan is to remain in the United Kingdom. Julian Spalding, former Director of Glasgow Museums, in his 'touring exhibitions manifesto' goes one step further, demanding that there be no obstacles to lending because touring exhibitions *are* museums. 'They are the means by which museums will lose their chains' (Spalding, 1995).

On preservation and access Spalding notes that 'huge investment has been made in the science of conservation in recent years and we must expect as a result great improvements in both safety and accessibility'. He makes the point that I stressed in Chapter 6, that without access there is no benefit and so no value. We will return to the conflicts between economy and standards a little later but first we need to spend some time looking at the benefits and the risks.

Benefits

The risks of a venture such as a touring exhibition are among the factors to be considered when making decisions about which objects should travel where and when. In Chapters 3 and 5 we learned that the Expected Value of a decision is composed of the net benefits and the risks. The highest Expected Value will indicate the best option if the probabilities of loss are very low. We should be aiming to maximize benefit and reduce costs so long as this does not significantly increase risk.

Rather than considering a range of options we are often just considering doing one thing rather than doing nothing. We must keep in mind that there are benefits, costs and risks associated with the routine of the status quo. We have to look out for *differences* between the current situation and that which is proposed. Even if there are difficulties in quantifying the absolute values of the proposed and the existing states, it may be possible to define the differences.

Table 14.1 indicates a list of possible benefits from touring an exhibition rather than leaving the objects in store or on 'permanent' exhibition at the home institution.

There may be income but only rarely will this cover total costs. There may be a fee paid to the lender, or the promise of additional funds for research and conservation treatment. Visitors seem more willing to pay an entrance charge for a temporary exhibition than for a permanent display.

The exhibition can be used to promote the name of the museum and encourage new visitors to the static exhibits at the home site. The 'brand' of a museum is increasingly important, the quality of the exhibition reinforces the quality of the brand. Marketing the exhibition markets the name. Manufactures and retailers will pay to be associated with that name. The exhibition is also a point of sale for museum publications and other merchandise.

Table 14.1 *Benefits of a touring exhibition*

- Money
- Marketing
- Merchandising
- Enjoyment
- Outreach
- Scholarship
- Conservation
- Understanding

Almost certainly more people will get to see the objects at an exhibition than would have if the objects had stayed at home for the same period. The relevance of the objects is usually better explained and they are usually more excitingly displayed. So there is a net increase in global enjoyment. The people who *do* attend might never, for social or financial reasons, have come to a permanent display at the home institution. They may come to something more local, less daunting and more immediately relevant.

The historical research for the exhibition and the opportunity to view objects not normally seen in juxtaposition can be of lasting benefit to scholars. It is true that the benefit of the scholarship during preparation could well have been produced by work on the permanent display, but an exhibition deadline seems to improve productivity if not quality. The benefit of scholarship deriving from display will disappear if the exhibition is too populist or too popular. If, in calculating benefit, scholars are given a greater weighting than 'ordinary' visitors, more benefit might derive from leaving the objects where the cognescenti expect to find them (Powers, 1978).

Objects that might not have attracted attention may now receive necessary conservation treatment. Conservators worry that exhibitions and loans distort conservation priorities and that objects are treated for no other reason than to withstand the rigours of travel. On the first point, the time directed to loans and exhibitions is only 'distorting' if these activities are seen as a burdensome addition to the 'proper' duties of museum staff. On the second point, the treatment necessary to make an object fit for travel may not be unethical if you believe that the object's purpose is to be seen and enjoyed by a large number of people. It may be unethical if you firmly believe in minimum intervention at all costs. This point will be discussed further in the next chapter.

Costs

Some of the costs listed in Table 14.2 are aimed at maximizing benefit and some at minimizing risk.

All the costs, except possibly the last one, Damage, are directly measurable as money. This is money spent on staff time, materials or services bought. All of these costs, except the last one, can be predicted with great accuracy before the objects travel.

Each object *must* be examined to see that it is in a fit state to travel and to be exhibited. This may be a cost for a borrower as well as a lender if the borrower is acting responsibly. If either party deems that the object is not fit to travel it will need some treatment or preparation.

Table 14.2 *Costs of travelling exhibitions*

- Examination
- Preparation
- Scholarship
- Administration
- Transport
- Packing
- Courier
- Monitoring
- Insurance
- Damage

It must be packed in a way that relates to its size, weight, complexity and fragility. This must account for its sensitivity to changes in temperature and humidity. Good packing is expensive and it also adds to the volume of the shipment which increases the costs of transport. Trying to save on packing is a false economy.

When exhibition organizers try to cut costs they often try to eliminate the courier. Undoubtedly there are times when the object's best interests would be served if someone *did* eliminate the courier. But when someone who understands the physical nature of the object and its relationship to the environment is selected as courier, then both the object and the exhibition can benefit.

It is wise to monitor the environment to which the object is going and relate this to the environment to which it has become accustomed. This incurs a cost in logging equipment and in time to analyse the data. The loggers serve as a signal that the lender is overseeing the borrower's ability to fulfil promises made during the initial negotiations.

Insurance can contribute greatly to the expense, in extreme cases as much as a third of the total cost of an exhibition (Hiscox, 1991).

The costs are inter-related as shown in Figure 14.1. The insurance premium may be lower if packing and supervision costs are higher. If the packing is good, less supervision may be needed but transport costs may be higher (Cannon-Brookes, 1986).

If we consider the benefits of an exhibition and compare them with the costs, we are doing a cost–benefit analysis. In museums it is rare for this to be a very formal exercise. Usually the director or a senior curator makes a quick subconscious assessment. The benefits, which are difficult to quantify but easy to justify, can readily be made to outweigh the costs, most of which may be charged to the borrower anyway. The decision is often made easier if there is any promise of income, whether or not this relates to

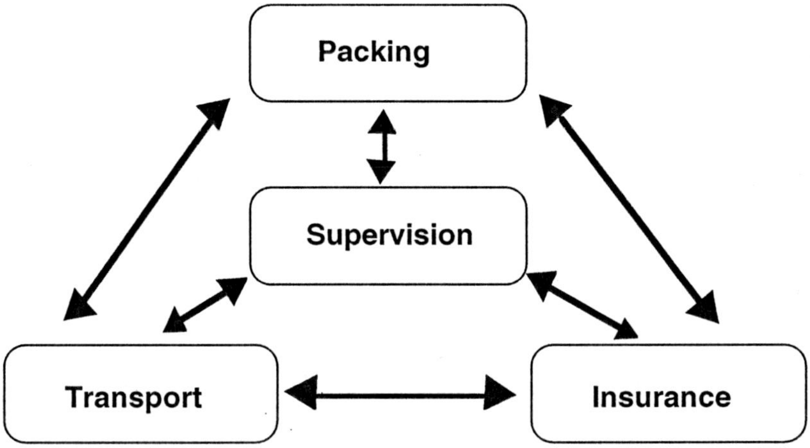

Figure 14.1 *The manner in which the costs of art in transit are inter-related*

total costs. It is very unlikely that anyone actually carries out a systematic assessment of the risks for each loan. Insurance premiums are likely to be based on a developing relationship of trust between insurers, museums and shippers rather than a rigorous study of every aspect of a proposed trip. Deliberate and inevitable damage, such as fading, will not be insured against, but must be part of the museum's assessment of risk.

Risk

The risks can be divided into those where the object is just sitting still and those while it is on the move. The risks of sitting quietly apply at the home institution as well as at the new venue. These hazards, summarized in Table 14.3, should be very familiar if you have read the preceding chapters.

Which of these is likely to be different at another location? It has to be assumed that the people organizing the venues for the travelling exhibition have a basic degree of professionalism and that the location passes basic criteria for physical security. Obviously if the objects are lent to inexperienced borrowers with no understanding of fundamental conservation and security, then the risk will be substantially higher. We need to look at the additional risks where experience has shown that even seasoned professionals have not got their act together.

Light will constitute an additional risk if the object is not on permanent display at home. This should be the case if the object is particularly light sensitive.

Table 14.3 *Hazards of just sitting quietly at home or abroad*

- Dust
- Light
- Air pollution
- Case pollution
- Humidity variation
- Temperature variation
- Humidity extreme
- Temperature extreme
- Earthquake
- Fire
- Theft

New, temporary showcases are often erected at each venue. Screens and walls will be repainted. There is a very much higher risk of case pollution and damage caused by VOCs. It is not easy to build a cheap, temporary case that will maintain a constant humidity which is substantially different from that in the gallery. Faster than normal humidity changes are possible unless an object travels with its own microclimate.

Figure 14.2 shows an example of the provision of a microclimate case for a panel painting that is not too visually intrusive.

The difference of risks of earthquake damage depend on location. Moving from a seismically active area to a location that has no seismic history will reduce the probability. However, expertise in seismic risk mitigation ought to be higher where the probability is higher, so the resultant damage may not be great. With appropriate display strategies, exhibition in a seismically sound structure should not involve excessive risk. This is obviously the view of those who continue to live and to collect important items of historic and cultural value in locations that are known to suffer earthquakes on a regular basis.

Inasmuch as insurance premiums represent actual risk, they can be used to assess differences between locations and activities. A representative estimate of the different contributions to insurance premiums is shown in Table 14.4. These are for imaginary situations but are not unrealistic (Hiscox, 1991, p. 80).

Although it is not made explicit in the text from which this data is taken, the word 'museum' is taken to indicate a location where a permanent collection is housed and exhibited, and 'gallery' to refer to a space primarily dedicated to changing displays. The numbers refer to a valuable 'Old Master' painting lent for a period of 30 days.

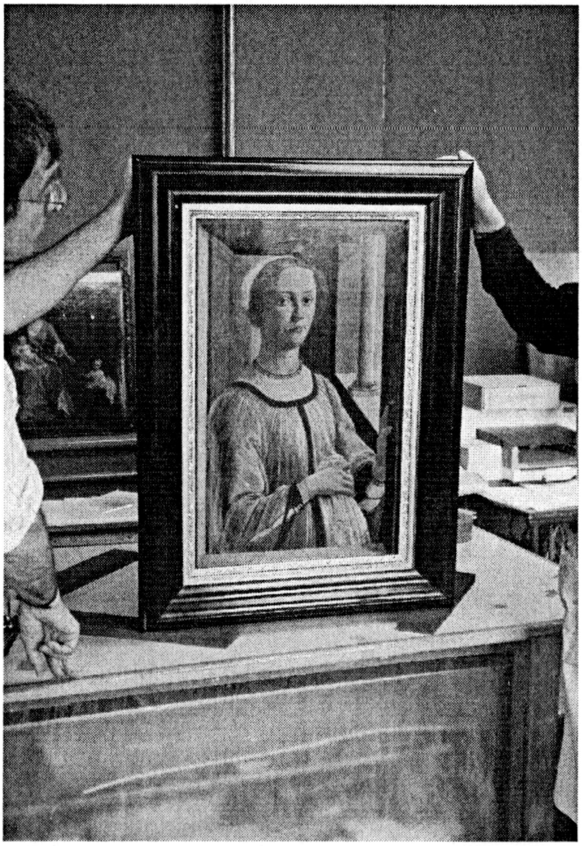

Figure 14.2 *Wooden panel inside a sealed microclimate case which is hidden by the picture frame*

Table 14.4 *Premiums expressed per thousand (0.1%)*

Hazard	*Display*		*Transit*	
	Museum	*Gallery*	*Museum*	*Commercial*
Catastrophic (e.g. fire, plane crash)	0.03	0.075	0.05	0.075
Vandalism	0.02	0.005	0.00	0.00
Theft	0.04	0.10	0.25	0.525
Accidental damage (water damage, breakage)	0.01	0.02	0.10	0.60
Total	0.10	0.20	0.40	1.2

Table 14.5 *Hazardous times and events for objects on the move*

- Moving
- Packing
- Plane crash
- Road crash
- Vibration
- Temperature extreme
- Humidity extreme
- Pressure drop
- Case drop
- Unpacking
- Object drop
- Installation
- Theft

The figures for transit relate to a transatlantic journey of up to 30 days. The difference between 'museum' and 'commercial' is an indication of the rigorous control exercised by museums over shipping techniques and the use of experienced art shippers.

The hazards to objects 'on the move' are summarized in Table 14.5. Which of these are additional risks for touring exhibitions?

Judging by the totals at the bottom of Table 14.4, being on the move is around four times riskier for an object than sitting quietly in a museum. It may be true that one transatlantic crossing is four times more risky than one month of actually sitting still, but objects do not sit quietly in museums for ever. Photography, conservation, study, temporary and 'permanent' redisplays, rotations of light-sensitive materials, new storage facilities and, once in a while, new museum buildings; all mean that objects *within* museums do not sit still for long. For moves between museum buildings, 'plane crash' is probably not a hazard. For moves within a single building, 'road crash' and accidents from 'packing' and 'unpacking' are not likely. The remainder, among which are the gravest risks, apply at home as well as abroad. Staying at home may reduce the frequency of some hazardous events but does not eliminate them.

Let's examine the hazardous phases of going from one 'safe' location to another.

Moving

The safe moving of objects is worth a book on its own. If the movers are trained, well equipped, used to working as a team, well briefed, well directed, familiar with the object, familiar with the current installation method and familiar with the location, the risks are low. The use of different teams at different locations on a tour will inevitably increase risk.

The scientific rules of safe handling are quite simple:

(a) An object that stands on the ground is used to being compressed by its own weight. Lifting it by the top will cause load-bearing parts to go from compression to tension. Points of weakness, such as cracks and abrupt changes of shape, tend to fail when put in tension.
(b) Objects are usually designed or mounted to withstand stresses in the vertical plane, whether in compression or tension. Moving horizontally inevitably induces horizontal stresses which the object was not designed to take. The greater the horizontal acceleration, the greater these unfamiliar and unforeseen stresses will be.
(c) The energy of a moving object increases with the square of the velocity. If you double the speed you quadruple the energy available for damage when the object is suddenly stopped in its tracks.
(d) The energy of a moving object is also dependent on its mass. It will always be more difficult to control a massive object such as a piece of stone sculpture.
(e) Objects held below their centre of gravity are unstable (see Chapter 9).

Not all objects provide hand-holds which allow elimination of unusual stresses or complete stability. To move at all there must be some acceleration and some velocity. It is impossible to remove all risk.

Packing

The process of packing involves handling, with its attendant problems of touching and altering stresses. It may entail mechanical activities such as screwing new fixings to frames, with risk of vibration and possibilities of tools slipping or falling. Packing material has to come into contact with the object's surface, so there is a risk of abrasion, generation of dust and transfer of colour. The object will be enclosed with the packing materials so they must be chemically inert (Erhardt, 1991). For a long tour the objects may remain in their cases for considerable lengths of time without ventilation.

The first packing may take place in a well-equipped and well-lit space. It may be carried out by experienced staff who are familiar with the packing methods because they devised them, and may be familiar with the individual objects. Subsequent repackings at the end of each showing may be carried out by people who are less familiar with objects and materials, who are working in less than ideal conditions.

Plane crash

I have not come across published details of numbers of museum objects lost in plane crashes. This is probably because there are so few as to be negligible. There are legendary losses of band leaders and pop musicians but not of famous art objects.

To reach some figure for probability you could look at data for human fatalities.

The most dangerous parts of a plane trip are take-off and landing. For each of these flight events, there is a risk of around one point three fatalities in every one million, a probability of a death of one in 750 000 for a return flight (Taylor, 1988). Air crashes tend to kill more than one person at a time. People are less well packed and die of things other than physical shock, so the probability of a well-packed consignment of objects being destroyed can be assumed to be of the order of one in a million per flight.

It is possibly as low as one in 10 million for some journeys. Some airlines have much worse records than others. (Fatalities per 10 million departures between 1977 and 1989, Aeroflot 25, JAL 15, British Airways 0.) Some air space is more dangerous. (Fatalities per million flights between 1973 and 1984, Turkey 1717, Netherlands 384, UK 57, US 37, Australia 1.) (Further details in Laudan, 1994.)

Road crash

For air travel the risks are more or less independent of length of the trip. This is not true of road travel where the risks are more evenly distributed throughout the journey. The consequences of a crash are more variable. Length and type of journey are important. A crash in a built-up area is more likely, but the probability of damage is greater for a motorway accident. For a large truck, assuming a sober, mature and experienced driver, travelling below the appropriate speed limit, and taking the expected rest periods, the probability of a damaging accident must be less than one in a million for each 100 miles.

Vibration

Vibration is a phenomenon that can cause damage in a static display as well as one on the move. Vibrations from visitor traffic, air-conditioning, road traffic and underground trains can make objects move about on shelves or cause the objects or their mounts to resonate (Koestler, 1997). Vibrations during travel depend on the mode of transport and the nature of the object. The vibrations caused by different types of vehicle have been well studied (ASTM, 1987) and excellently reviewed (Marcon, 1991).

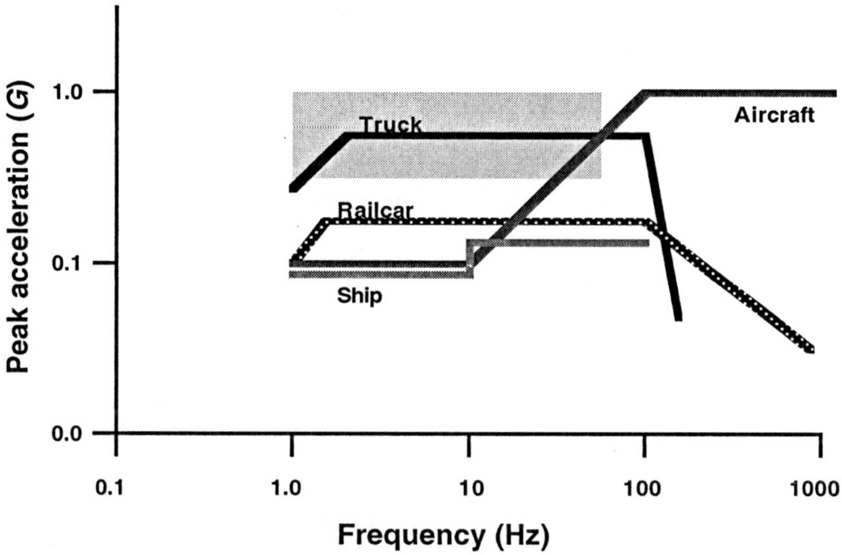

Figure 14.3 *Vibration spectra for different transport types. The vertical axis is a measure of severity. The shaded area marks the range of frequency and acceleration that humans find 'intolerable'*

Figure 14.3 shows the different ranges of vibration that are continuously produced by different transport types. The horizontal axis shows the frequency of the vibration in cycles per second. The vertical axis shows the peak acceleration which can be taken as a measure of severity. The shaded area marks the range of frequency and acceleration that humans find 'intolerable'. The data for the truck relates to journeys over rough terrain, an air-ride vehicle on a good road would show a much lower maximum.

Vibrations of the frequency and severity shown are not likely to be damaging (Mecklenburg and Tumosa, 1991). There may be damage if some part of the object is flexible and resonates at one of the frequencies to which it is subjected. For objects in good condition the damage will be from abrasion or impact of the part set in motion. For unsound objects it is possible that resonant vibrations could encourage crack propagation and separation of poorly joined layers. Some objects can be treated to minimize the risk of vibration; the primary vibration mode of a canvas painting can be prevented by provision of a backboard or by a false lining (Green, 1991). Some, but not all, frequencies can be prevented from reaching the object by choice of suitable foam cushioning.

In addition to the continuous drone of engine and road vibration there are transient peaks of high acceleration caused by a truck going over a rail

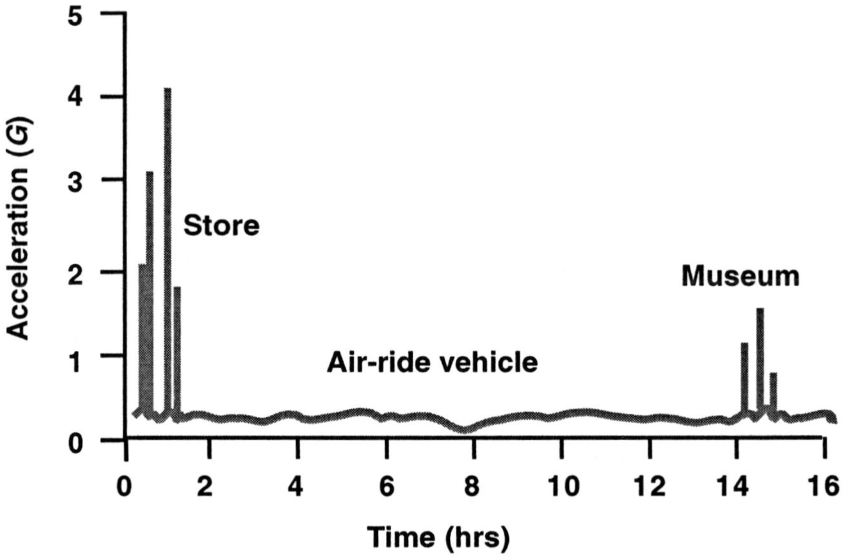

Figure 14.4 *Graph of peak accelerations suffered by a large packing case on its way from a store to a gallery. The central flat region is the road journey in an air-ride vehicle*

crossing or an aircraft hitting turbulent air. For normal air, sea and road trips these shocks are unlikely to exceed 1.1 *G*. This is just sufficient to cause an object to bounce, so everything should be firmly secured to prevent movement. In a bad sea, peak accelerations in a ship could reach 1.5 *G*. On a very bad road a pot-hole could cause a shock of 5 *G*. Shocks of around 40 *G* have been measured during coupling operations on railways.

Most objects are packed on the assumption that they can stand accelerations of 40–60 *G* without damage. For instance, a 30 *G* impact along the edge of a painting induces maximum stresses that are only 3% of that needed to cause cracks in a paint layer (Mecklenburg and Tumosa, 1991).

If an air-ride road vehicle is used it is unlikely that rigid structures such as frames or cases will suffer shocks exceeding 0.5 *G*, although flexible parts of objects may move at up to 1 *G* (Saunders, 1991a). The shocks associated with manual handling are usually greater than this. Figure 14.4 shows readings from an accelerometer attached to a packing case containing a painting in a warehouse in Osaka, Japan. The case was loaded onto a trolley and taken in a lift to the ground floor where it was loaded into an air-ride vehicle. After a 10-hour journey it was unloaded and man-handled up nine flights of stairs. In the lorry (the central section of the graph) there is no measurable shock or vibration. While the paintings were entirely in the hands of the object handlers there was some slight shock. But while the object was being moved in what might be considered the most careful way, in a purpose built store, using trolleys and lifts, it suffered accelerative forces of up to 4 *G*. And although these are quite small for a robust object such as an oil painting, the important point is that they are considerably greater than anything suffered during 10 hours on the road. They equate to what is probably happening routinely in a busy museum.

Temperature and humidity extremes

As we know from earlier chapters, for many objects we only need to worry about very large and lengthy divergence from the middle range of humidity and temperature. These are only likely to happen if something goes wrong with the travel schedule, such as a consignment missing a flight or a truck breaking down. These delays would have to be accompanied by external extremes of environment; a truck breaks down in subzero temperatures, a packing case is left in direct tropical sunlight on an airstrip.

It used to be a worry that the temperature in the cargo hold of a plane would drop very low. This is now not a normal occurrence on scheduled flights in large aircraft where temperature-sensitive cargoes such as live chicks are commonly carried. Even if there are prolonged environmental extremes the risk of damage is small for many classes of material if the packing is of high quality. The probability of these events occurring is anyway very small if the journey is well planned.

The ability of a packing case to maintain a temperature which is different from that of the external environment is usually measured in terms of its thermal half-life. Suppose a packed case was originally at 20°C but is then placed in an environment at 0°C. If the internal temperature reaches 10°C in 4 hours then the thermal half-life is 4 hours, the time taken for the internal temperature to change by half the original difference in internal and external temperatures.

If you look at Figure 14.5 you will see that after a further 4 hours the temperature will have reached 5°C, and 2.5°C after a further 4. After 24 hours the inside temperature will be indistinguishable from that outside. More insulation will slow the cooling process but can never stop it.

The hygrometric half-life of a packing case is usually very much longer than the thermal half-life. A well-packed object could stand many days in an external humidity extreme before the internal RH reached that on the outside. Some danger arises from changes in the RH of the packed air and

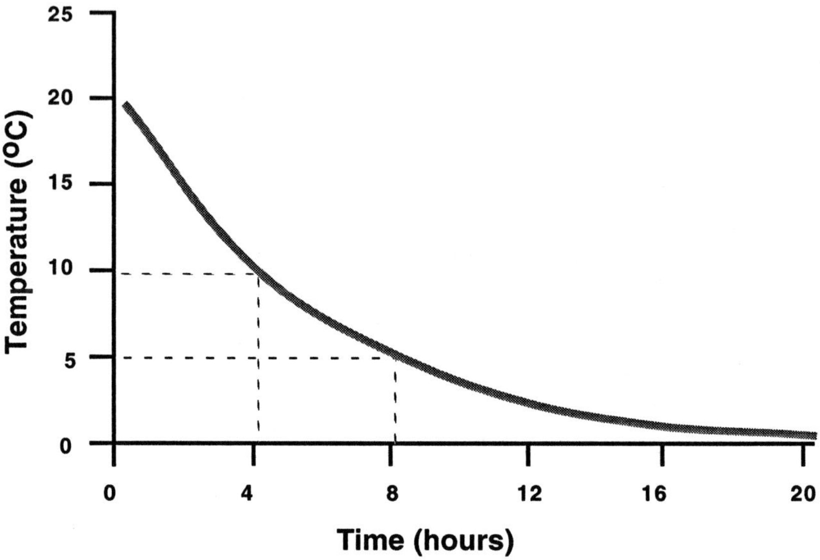

Figure 14.5 *Rate of change of temperature inside a case which was packed at 20°C but is now in an environment at 0°C. The case has a thermal half-life of 4 hours*

moisture content of the packed object if the temperature within the enclosed space drops too much.

If the objects and packing materials are unabsorbent, the RH in the space will increase as the temperature decreases. If the objects were packed at 20°C and 50% RH then condensation will start once the internal temperature falls below 10°C. The outer layer, that is the packing, will get coldest first. This is where the condensation will occur. If the objects are wrapped in polythene, condensation may occur on the inside of the plastic sheet. The amount of free water will be very small, only a few drops, but could conceivably cause damage to some decorative surfaces if it dripped on to them. Because of the low temperature, corrosion and mould are unlikely in the short term.

A hygroscopic material such as wood will absorb moisture as the temperature decreases. To maintain the same moisture content in the wood, the RH of the environment must decrease. In a packing case the water absorbed by the object is being removed from a small unventilated space, so the RH automatically falls. (Transient increases in RH are sometimes observed if the temperature drop is very rapid, Figure 14.6.) For a wrapped object with a small airspace around it, the amount of water being transferred between environment and object is very small. The temperature drop has to be dramatic, at least 20°C, and there has to be

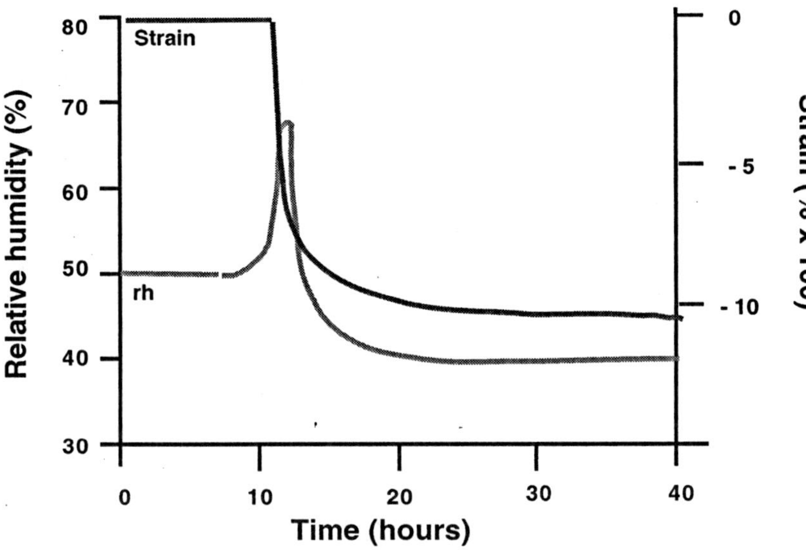

Figure 14.6 *An uninsulated case containing hygroscopic material is kept at 22°C for 10 hours. The temperature is then dropped to –18°C. After an initial rise the RH settles at a new lower level. The strain measured in a sample of wood inside the case does not appear to be affected by the temporary rise in humidity*

access to atmospheric moisture, for the equilibrium moisture content to change in a way that could cause damaging dimensional changes. The increase in strain in a sample of wood shown in Figure 14.6 is mostly due to thermal changes. It has been calculated that a 40°C drop would be enough to cause an increase in stress sufficient to lengthen cracks in a wood panel whose dimensional response was constrained in some way (Richard, 1993).

Pressure drop

The atmospheric pressure inside an aircraft decreases when the plane is in flight. Measurements taken in a cargo hold show that the pressure drops to about 80% of the normal atmospheric pressure experienced at sea-level. This lower pressure level could be achieved on land by climbing to a height of around 1600 metres. La Paz, the capital of Bolivia, is more than twice this height and there are navigable passes in Europe and Asia at 2–3000 metres above sea-level.

There is possible danger from a pressure drop if air at the original pressure remains trapped in a space that does not have sufficiently strong or rigid walls:

- Bubbles in glazes or enamels might explode.
- Sealed microclimate cases might distort or explode.
- Cushioning foams with closed cell structure might expand or become rigid.

The evidence so far seems to suggest that the first two do not happen, and if the third phenomenon occurs there are no harmful effects.

There is the possibility of full decompression in an aircraft, but such accidents are rare. Even if the pressure did drop by 100% there is little evidence that damage would occur to objects. As part of a technical study I have placed metals, ceramics, enamels, pearls and gemstones in the vacuum chamber of a scanning electron microscope without any sign of damage. Lower pressure equates to lower RH and so hygroscopic materials would begin to dehydrate. They might eventually warp or crack if pressure were not restored within a few hours.

Colleagues at the V&A measured pressure inside and outside a microclimate case constructed of Perspex, during a flight from Tokyo to London with stopover in Anchorage, Alaska. The pressure dropped inside and outside the case each time the aircraft was in the air. The pressure inside and outside quickly equalized, suggesting that the inevitable distortion of the butt-jointed plastic sheets allowed sufficient passage of air to prevent explosion. The RH inside the case was barely affected while outside the packing case in the cargo hold it dropped below 25%.

If the pressure inside had not equalized there would be a force of about 2000 kg on each square metre of Perspex. While it is equalizing, there is bound to be some distortion. The faces of the microclimate box will become convex while the plane is ascending and concave while it is descending. The greatest pressure difference between the inside and outside is likely to be about 3 kPa (3% of sea-level atmospheric). This is enough to cause a 2 cm deflection of the centre of an acrylic sheet 76 × 60 cm (Richard, 1994). During recompression there is the possibility that the front plate might bend sufficiently to touch and damage the surface of the object.

Case drop

There are many factors that can lead to a packing case being dropped, most will be due to poor planning, poor case design or handling crews working too fast and too long. A probability would have to be determined by monitoring a particular institution or by equating institutions, which judged by other factors, appear to be equally professional.

The impact of dropping a case can be more accurately predicted. Table 14.6 is the well-known assessment of likely drop height for different types

Table 14.6

Weight (kg)	*Handling method*	*Drop height (cm)*
10–20	1 person carrying	90
20–45	1 person carrying	75
45–115	2 people carrying	60
>115	Handling equipment	45

of package. A small parcel is likely to be carried at around waist height and placed on a table. A large, heavy package may be held half way up the side so the distance between the ground and the bottom of the crate (the maximum drop height) is not that great.

The possibility of a single crate falling from the tail-lift of a truck is much greater than the longer drop from the scissor lift moving the palletized consignment into the aircraft cargo hold.

Another aspect of air travel that may be forgotten is that the packing cases will not remain vertical. The angle of take-off is about 17° and the angle of banking can be between 10° and 25°. The effect on take-off will be accentuated by acceleration. Tilting while turning may be somewhat compensated by the effects of centrifugal force. However, the packing should reflect that there will be a horizontal component to the forces exerted.

Unpacking

The action of unpacking is potentially risky because the environment inside the case may be radically different from that in the space in which the case is opened. As you must know by now the difference would have to be large for there to be damage. One possible scenario is that the case has been in a very cold environment with which the contents have become equilibrated. This might not be obvious to someone at the receiving institution, as the outer surface of the case may have warmed up again. But it will take another 16 hours before the objects inside the insulated case reach the gallery temperature. If the case is opened immediately on arrival there is the possibility of condensation onto the surface of the object. In this instance there is plenty of water available to condense from the large volume of conditioned gallery air.

The period of unpacking is also hazardous because, unless the packing is well designed, the object may have to be held at an awkward point, possibly while it still has a plastic or tissue wrapping.

Object drop

The final stage of offering an object up to its fixing on a wall or transferring from a trolley into a showcase is possibly the most risky of the whole journey. No matter how good the control has been up until that point it will almost certainly be slightly worse at the critical stage. Once again planning, testing and experience are the only things that can minimize risk.

Installation

To an outsider the last few days or hours before the opening of a temporary exhibition look chaotic. This is the period when everyone's schedules have slipped but everyone has to meet the same deadline. Large numbers of people are carrying out a variety of tasks that ought to be sequential but seem to be going on simultaneously. People are milling around in a very small space. Objects are somewhere between their packing cases and their final display location. An accident seems inevitable. If you are one of the people involved, it may all seem more organized and more purposeful. Even so everyone is aware of stories of accidents that have happened at this very active stage. Planning, organization and a cool head will prevent most problems but opening an exhibition at a new venue is always an exciting time and it is asking a lot that everyone should remain cool.

Table 14.7

Factors increasing risk perception		*Factors decreasing risk perception*	
Factors	*Example*	*Factors*	*Example*
Involuntary hazard	Radioactive fallout	Voluntary	Mountaineering
Immediate impact	Forest fire	Delayed	Drought
Direct impact	Earthquake	Indirect	Drought
Dreaded hazard	Cancer	Common	Road accident
Many fatalities per event	Air crash	Few per event	Car crash
Deaths grouped in space/time	Avalanche	Random in space/time	Drought
Identifiable victims	Miners	Statistical victims	Smokers
Process ill understood	Nuclear accident	Well understood	Snowstorm
Uncontrollable hazard	Tropical cyclone	Controllable	Ice on highway
Unfamiliar hazard	Tsunami	Familiar	River flood
No belief in authority	Private industrialist	Belief in authority	University scientist
Much media attention	Nuclear plant	Little attention	Chemical plant

Theft

From the data in Table 14.4 it appears that theft in transit is around five times more likely than in a display space. Different forms of transit carry different risks. The longer a packing case remains unsupervised the greater the risk that the contents can be removed and the longer it will be before this removal is noticed. Complex journeys, with changes of vehicle, changes of supervision and interim stays in warehouses, pose the greatest threat.

The perception of risk

We first met the concept of risk perception in Chapter 2. Different people have different ideas about how safe or how risky any particular activity or event may be. This is particularly true of the subject of travelling exhibitions. The same event may be exciting and virtually risk free to one person and hard work and a great worry to someone else. People have different perceptions of risk depending on their education, their past experience and their current involvement. Sensible decision-making in museums demands an accurate knowledge of the risks, but this accuracy is not always possible. Some people would rather not seek too hard for the information they need to make a choice. So the arguments that surround decisions are often highly coloured by personal perceptions of the risk.

Some factors will tend to make most people overestimate the risk and others will tend to make the majority underestimate. Table 14.7 shows one way in which these factors have been categorized for natural and anthropogenic hazards to human life (Burton, Fowle and McCulloch, 1982).

If we look at these factors and translate them into the museum and exhibition context we see the same ways of thinking. There is a tendency to overestimate the risks of overwhelming disasters and underestimate the risks of slow attrition. There is concern about the mechanical damage caused by the environment and less about chemical deterioration. There is worry about very small risks that cannot be controlled such as plane crashes, yet there is indifference to larger manageable risks such as bad handling.

The factors of motivation, involvement and authority are relevant to the management of travelling exhibitions. People for whom the event is voluntary, who plan to get something out of it, will tend to underestimate the risks. People who get nothing but hard work out of the event, such as conservators preparing the objects, will tend to overestimate them. This will lead to argument which could have been avoided if involvement and motivation were improved. People who are familiar with all the stages of exhibition preparation, especially the frenzied final hours, will not have as great a fear of unwanted outcomes as someone who does not have that experience or who has only observed the apparent chaos as an outsider, a courier bringing in a single object.

Acceptable risk/acceptable damage

Suppose you were contemplating sending a specific group of objects to a known series of venues by known modes of transport, with agreed total display times in controlled environments. It would be possible to list all the marginal risks, the additional risks caused by the exhibition that the objects would not be exposed to if left in the museum.

For each of the items on the list it would be possible to put a figure, or range of figures, for risk using appropriate formulae from Chapter 8. For some of the categories there would be considerable uncertainty, but for many it would be possible to arrive at figures within one order of magnitude. Not all of the hazards listed in Table 14.5 are mutually exclusive, e.g. installation is a time when all sorts of hazards are present including 'object drop'. So you would have to be careful to avoid double counting. If any of the factors showed a surprisingly high level of risk you would want to address this to find ways of removing the factor or reducing the effect.

It would be possible to add all these separate figures to form one 'total marginal risk'. For a known set of costs and benefits you would be able to decide whether this risk was acceptable or not. This calculated level of risk could be used as a benchmark for other enterprises.

At one end of the possible scale of risks is total certainty of complete loss ($P = 1$, $V = 1$, $R = P \times V = 1$). This would always be defined as unacceptable. At the other end of the scale there are very small values of R, of the order of 10^{-8}, where the risks are comparable to those of being kidnapped by aliens. We daily accept much greater risks than these. Somewhere between the two ends of the scale there must be an area where it is difficult to decide whether the risk is tolerable or not. This is the threshold of acceptable risk.

The upper limit to such a threshold would be of the order of 10^{-4}, that is, a chance of 1 in 10 000 of absolute loss. It has been noted by the health and safety executive that an individual annual risk of death of 10^{-3} is the most that is ordinarily accepted under modern conditions for UK workers. The Royal Society Study Group on Risk argued that:

> 'few people would commit their own resources to reduce an annual risk of death as low as 1 in 100 000'.

These and other discussions about acceptable levels of risk are well reviewed by the Environmental Risk Assessment Unit at the University of East Anglia (Goats and Ball, 1994).

A risk of around 10^{-5} should certainly be acceptable for an enterprise that expects to obtain both immediate and long-term benefits. That is the equivalent of total certainty of the loss of one hundred thousandth of the value of the exhibited collection. For a collection worth £1 million this is the absolute certainty of £10 worth of damage. Which is less than an hour's work for a conservator touching in a scratch, or a small paint loss.

If we accept a risk we must admit that this is the same as accepting damage. We will accept this damage if the net benefits are worth pursuing. In Chapter 3 we noted that there was a critical value P_c for the probability of total loss that made the expected value of a decision greater than zero. To be on the safe side we thought that the actual probability P of total loss should be a thousand times smaller. Using this criterion, for a risk of 10^{-5} to be acceptable, the net benefit must be at least 1% of the value of the collection.

Something to think about

If the damage due to travelling is measured as conservator-hours of repair how much damage is accepted by your institution at the moment?

What are other appropriate ways of estimating damage?

Is it reasonable to claim that a conservator will always perceive risks as greater than they actually are? What events are likely to cause a conservator to underestimate risk?

References

ASTM (1987) *Performance Testing of Shipping Containers*. ASTM Committee D-10. 2nd ed. 03–410287–11.

Burton, I., Fowle, C.D. and McCulloch, R.S. (1982) Living with Risk: Environmental Risk Management in Canada. Monograph 3. Institute of Environmental Studies, University of Toronto.

Cannon-Brookes, Peter (1986) The Evolution and Implementation of a Transportation Strategy for Works of Art. *The International Journal of Museum Management and Curatorship*, **5**, pp. 163–169.

Erhardt, David (1991) Art in Transit. Material Considerations, in *Art in Transit*, edited by Marion T. Mecklenburg. National Gallery of Art, Washington. ISBN 0-89468-163-X, pp. 25–36.

Goats, G.C. and Ball, D.J. (1994) The Management of Risks Posed by Food Chemical Contaminants: Scope for Rationalisation? Research Report No. 24. UEA. ISBN 1-873933-75-4.

Green, Timothy (1991) Vibration Control: Paintings on Canvas Supports, in *Art in Transit*, edited by Marion T. Mecklenburg. National Gallery of Art, Washington. ISBN 0-89468-163-X, pp. 59–68.

Hiscox, Robert (1991) Insuring Works of Art in Transit, in *Art in Transit*, edited by Marion T. Mecklenburg. National Gallery of Art, Washington. ISBN 0-89468-163-X, pp. 79–84.

Koestler, Robert (1996) Note in Cons DistList. Conservation On Line. Inst. 10:34 3 October.

Laudan, Larry (1994) *The Book of Risks*. John Wiley and Sons. ISBN 0-471-31034-4.

Marcon, Paul J. (1991) Shock, Vibration, and the Shipping Environment, in *Art in Transit*, edited by Marion T. Mecklenburg. National Gallery of Art, Washington. ISBN 0-89468-163-X, pp. 121–132.

Mecklenburg, Marion F. and Tumosa, Charles S. (1991) An Introduction into the Mechanical Behaviour of Paintings under Rapid Loading Conditions, in *Art in Transit*, edited by Marion T. Mecklenburg. National Gallery of Art, Washington. ISBN 0-89468-163-X, pp. 137–171.

Powers, Sandra (1978) Why Exhibit? The Risks Versus the Benefits. *The American Archivist*, **41**, No. 3, pp. 297–307.

Richard, Mervin (1991) Control of Temperature and Relative Humidity in Packing Cases, in *Art in Transit*, edited by Marion T. Mecklenburg. National Gallery of Art, Washington. ISBN 0-89468-163-X, pp. 279–297.

Richard, Mervin (1994) The Transport of Paintings in Microclimate Display Cases. Preventive Conservation: Practice, Theory and Research. Preprints to the Ottawa Congress, 12–16 September. IIC, pp. 185–189.

Spalding, Julian (1995) The Touring Exhibitions Manifesto. Touring Exhibitions, in *The Touring Exhibitions Group's Manual of Good Practice*, edited by Mike Sixsmith. Butterworth-Heinemann, Oxford. ISBN 0-7506-2518-X, pp. xiii–xv.

Taylor, Laurie (1988) *Air Travel – How Safe is it?* BSP Professional Books, Oxford.

15 Ethics and intervention

The risks of interventive treatment depend on the predicted changes of value. State and value are both multivariate and the relationship between them is necessarily complex. However, the maximum possible changes in some types of value are not always as great as would be expected from the attendant fuss. Actions that reduce current or potential value are described as unethical. A mathematical approach to conservation ethics is compared with a more conventional view.

Treatment and risk

In the model described in Chapter 4 treatment of the collections is seen as one of the ways in which resources can be used to affect the benefits that the museum provides. A different view of the model is shown in Figure 15.1. It is a necessary consequence of treatment that the state of an object is altered. This alteration of state may have an effect on the value of the object. The act of interventive conservation or restoration often reveals new information. The addition of new information to the documentation associated with the object will also have an effect on the value. Changes in value will affect demands for use. Increased use should bring increased benefits.

When the activity of treatment was broken down into its component parts in our discussion about decision-making (Tables 3.1 and 3.2) it was found to be a very complex operation. It was felt that there was some correlation between the complexity of an operation and risk. That accidents are inevitable in complex operations with highly inter-related component parts is one of the basic tenets of Natural Accident Theory (Perrow, 1994).

When we considered costs and benefits we looked at decisions which could have a good outcome in terms of increasing or maintaining the value of an object. As part of that model we also considered unfavourable outcomes and their probabilities, that is, the risk of something going wrong. Undesirable outcomes were defined in terms of decrease in value or utility.

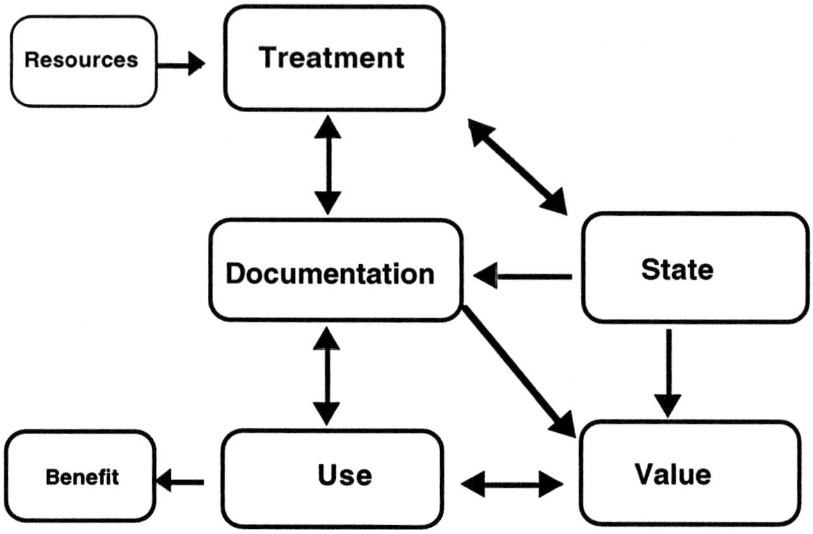

Figure 15.1 *The connections in the network that link treatment to the benefits that the collection provides*

Treatments that are acceptable to the professional peers of the conservator and to the guardians of the treated objects are called ethical. It has been said that all codes of ethics can be summarized as 'Do no deliberate harm!' (Drucker, 1977). In the context of this book, an alternative ethical one-liner is:

- Do nothing to reduce value

Perceptions

The arguments about treatment can become quite heated. In some instances the rights and wrongs of treatment become the subject of international public debate. Once again some of the differences of opinion are about different perceptions of the risk. Look again at Table 14.7, then think about the cleaning of the Sistine Chapel ceiling. For interested onlookers and academic art historians the cleaning of major international monuments can be seen as involuntary, since they neither commission nor control the work. Cleaning brings an immediate impact with identifiable victims and much media attention. Whether or not there was damage in previous treatments, the perception will be that future proposals carry a high risk.

A conservator who is used to treating individual objects sequentially will assume that the risks of a mass treatment such as de-acidification must be high. This is because of the large numbers involved, because the process is not familiar and not well understood, because at the level of individual objects the process appears uncontrollable.

A conservator working without publicity, using familiar and controllable techniques, will probably underestimate the possibility of damage. This is called confidence.

Effects of treatment on value

A desirable outcome for treatment of an object is that its value (however defined) is maintained or increased. A treatment is damaging or unethical if the value decreases. Treatment that has no effect is a waste of time and money (which by other standards is also unethical).

The various effects of treatment can be classified by changes in the physical state of the object and by whether such change was intentional or not (Table 15.1). Here the word '*un*intentional' will be used to indicate that the result was not the primary motive of the treatment. The conservator may have fully understood that it was a necessary consequence of the chosen course of action. This is not the same thing as the intended treatment going wrong through lack of experience or control.

Table 15.1

• Material is permanently added	
intentional:	protective coating, consolidant, lining, restored part
unintentional:	residual enzymes in paper and paint films, biocide residues in paper and textiles
• Material is permanently removed	
intentional:	old repairs, insect damaged wood, discoloured varnish, corrosion, dirt
unintentional:	sizing washed from paper, original metal polished away
• Material is permanently rearranged	
intentional:	bent metal reshaped, paper and textiles 'relaxed'
unintentional:	metallographic structure changed by heating, thermoluminescence state changed by X-radiography, shaping and creases in dress lost by relaxation
• The physical state of the object is temporarily altered	
intentional:	heating or freezing to kill insects, humidification treatments
unintentional:	permanent change from accelerated ageing due to extreme environment

In determining risk we must assess whether the intended treatment, if successful, would actually increase or maintain value. We need to know what the probability of an adverse outcome is and how this will affect value. We need to know the probabilities of unintentional consequences and determine their effect on value.

If we look at the contributions to value that we discussed in Chapter 6 we can examine them to see which of these are seriously affected by any of these aspects of treatment. As shown in Table 6.2 major contributors to value are age, rarity, material, complexity, quality, history, identity, information, context, potential and condition.

Age, identity and rarity

Some of the contributions to value are extrinsic properties independent of the object's state. Treatment cannot affect age, rarity, material, history, or identity, if these are already known. The appearance of age may be affected temporarily by addition of material, or permanently by removal. Evidence of age, history and identity may be permanently lost by removal or rearrangement of material. This evidence has the potential to change value, but if there is already other convincing evidence it may not be that important if the information intrinsic to the object is lost. If a walking stick belonging to Charles Dickens appears with him in a photograph and is documented as a gift to the museum from his family, it may not be such a disaster if cleaning has removed traces of his sweat from the handle.

Complexity

Complexity and the appearance of quality could be improved by treatment, usually by the removal of material obscuring details on the surface of the object. Similarly there is a possibility that treatment will decrease complexity by hiding or removing detail.

Information

The information an object can supply about itself, and about its connection with other objects, ranges from what is obviously visible to what must be determined by extremely sensitive (and expensive) technical instrumentation. For an object such as a painting the vast majority of the information is visible, the rarity of the object makes it unlikely that there will be hidden information that will connect with, or affect the value of, many other objects. The opposite may be true of a collection of natural history specimens where there is a great deal of information that is not immediately visible and interpretation of the hidden information may well lead to establishing connections within this group, and with other groups. This will increase the value of the collection as a resource.

This hidden information is what may be unintentionally lost by treatment. In some cases we know something of the nature of the information and what may damage it. For instance, thermoluminescence information, used to date ceramics and bronzes, is affected by heat and by radiation. With this knowledge it is possible to avoid damaging treatments. Yet, before this was known, many bronzes may have been repaired using heat or investigated using X-rays.

It is only in recent years that that the wealth of information that can be derived from samples of DNA has been recognized. Until techniques of analysis are developed we do not always know what the potential information is or what treatments would eradicate or distort it. This is often used as a reason for avoiding treatment.

Context

An object may be part of a larger ensemble, such as a gilt bronze fitting on a piece of furniture, or a piece of furniture placed in a room setting. A treatment such as cleaning, which might enhance value in an isolated object, might decrease its value in context. Extremely bright ormolu decoration may look garish against the muted tones of faded veneers. The restored cabinet may stick out like a sore thumb in the context of darkened woodwork and nearly monochrome tapestries. The effect of cleaning one part is to decrease the value of the whole.

Potential

In the discussion about contributions to value the 'potential' was seen as important. The future use of the object contributes to its present value. Interventive treatments such as insect eradication, consolidation or lining are devised to make the object last longer. The primary effect on value is potential. The current exchange value or aesthetic, symbolic or documentary value may not have changed but the net present value based on the continued provision of these other values has. Non-interventive preventive treatments such as humidity control or inert atmospheres are also intended to increase potential. If a museum object is enabled to live longer, its age obviously increases and so its age value may well do the same. As other less well cared for examples disappear the rarity value of the preserved object will increase. The effect of treatment on potential is dealt with in more detail later in this chapter.

Condition

Since it is usually defined in terms of need for treatment, 'condition' will change favourably if material is added or subtracted deliberately, unfavourably if material is lost or rearranged unintentionally.

Maximum possible loss

The risk of a treatment for one object is the sum of all the risks to each of the different types of value:

$$R = \sum_{i=1}^{n} w_i P_i L_i \qquad (15.1)$$

In this equation we are considering n different types of value and pessimistically assuming that all of them will decrease. In one person's view the different contributions to value, or probabilities of failure, will have different weighting and this is reflected in the factor w. Each value of w could be a fraction such that

$$\sum_{i=1}^{n} w_i = 1. \qquad (15.2)$$

We need to decide whose point of view is relevant. Is it one conservator or one curator, or the Board of Trustees, or representatives of one profession, or the public or one select section of the public?

If we try to look for any change in the benefits to society as a whole, the cleaning of one painting or even a national gallery-full of paintings will have an infinitesimal effect. If we choose measures of willingness to pay (WTP) we may not have much more success. The previous dirtiness of the ceiling of the Sistine Chapel did not deter people from queuing and paying. The cleaning has generated so much publicity that an increase in WTP must be predicted. By that measure the value has gone up, yet the claim of the critics is that damage has been done.

Just as we found when considering deterioration, a change of state does not automatically lead to a significant change in value. The maximum possible proportionate loss in any particular type of value is probably small. The exception being a treatment so drastic that it destroys the whole object or the part of it that carries the majority of information, such as the emulsion layer of a photograph. When we get upset about unethical treatment we are usually talking about something that affects very few people and which makes very little lasting emotional or financial impact on even those few. As long as we remember that, we can get as irate as we please.

Most complaints of damage following treatment are about deviation from a current convention for typical appearance – old things should look old, medals shouldn't be polished bright, Chinese funerary bronzes should be covered in corrosion. I have carried out some research into the effect of treatment on monetary value of a variety of object types sold at auction houses in London[1]. The loss in value due to poor or unconventional treatment is rarely more than 50% and usually much less. This matches well with the view that, for objects in reasonable condition, treatment is unlikely to increase value by more than 100% and usually by much less. It is true that if you restore a total wreck, such as an upholstered armchair with no upholstery, it might be possible to increase the value by 400%. The majority of 'ethical' museum conservation treatments are not this radical. Treatment may contribute to a more extreme increase in value if it discloses information about identity or rarity.

It is often cited that a mended object is worth less than a complete one, as if it were the restoration rather than the previous damage that had lowered the value. It is merely proof that treatment can raise value, that is, restore value to a devalued object.

Given the history of public fuss, the largest maximum proportionate losses are likely to be in the cultural and emotional categories of value. The two types that make the news are the aesthetic and the spiritual.

In countries that were colonized with extreme prejudice to the previous residents there is now growing sympathy for the religious beliefs of the remaining descendants of the dispossessed. The way in which the artifacts of native cultures are cared for in museums is changing with the recognition that a select group within the potential museum public believe that these objects have spiritual value (Clavir, 1994; Drumheller and Kaminitz, 1994). Incorrect care or treatment can have a dramatic effect on the magical power or spiritual status of sacred objects. This is one category where a very small change in state could result in 100% loss of one type of value.

Those who argue about loss of aesthetic value resulting from cleaning, over-cleaning or removal of later restorations (this sort of discussion is nearly always restricted to European easel paintings) would probably admit that a great deal of the beauty intended by the artist or maker still remained. Changes to the subtleties of modelling or the balance of colour are unlikely to remove 100% of the beauty of the composition. Would you settle for 20% max?

The weighting that you would give to the valuations of either of these two groups, the first peoples or the art critics and historians, depends on the political and economic power they wield in the community, which is not necessarily related to how loud they can shout.

[1] A substantial part of the legwork was carried out by my colleague Dorothy Rogers.

Potential value and utility

If we are going to include considerations of the future, another way of defining ethical treatment in one line is:

- Do nothing to reduce net present value[2]

Changes in potential value are changes in the future in the benefits that result from use. We need to consider the degree to which the treatment could increase or decrease the benefit. We need to look at how long the treatments make the object last. We also need to know how much they cost and how frequently they must be repeated. These questions need answers if we are to attempt the estimations of Expected Value we discussed in Chapter 5.

Before we can use NPV or RPV to assess the importance of treatment, we need to make two important decisions. First, we must decide how far in the future we need to look. In Chapter 12 it was proposed that there was not much point in extending our forward horizon beyond 200 years. We also need to decide on an appropriate discount rate.

The effect of different discount rates on NPV is shown in Figure 15.2. Assume that an object or collection produces an annual net benefit of one (arbitrary) unit. If we look at the next 200 years, and there is no discounting, the NPV is 200. If we only considered the next 100 years the NPV would be 100. As the discount rate increases so the NPV decreases, becoming around 20 at a rate of 5%. The value of looking very far into the future also becomes significantly less the higher the discount rate. At 10% it makes no difference if you look 50, 100 or 200 years ahead.

There is considerable debate about an appropriate discount rate in the areas of health and ecology (Reviewed in Arrow, 1976; Soby and Ball, 1992; Hanley and Spash, 1993) and one can imagine the same would be true for museum conservation. The main argument is that discount rates that are linked to financial investment rates will always produce a short-term view. This will always favour exploitation rather than conservation. The use of discounting also suggests greater freedom to make financial choices than is actually allowed to institutions that are dependent on central funds.

If we ignore discounting and assume that all objects will last for ever, then the NPV of every object becomes infinite. The Expected Value of all options becomes the same and it is not possible to make a choice. If we set a planning horizon of say 200 years then different objects and actions may have different potentials, and choices become possible. However, without discount, events occurring in 150 years' time are deemed to have the

[2] NPV strictly relates to a *proposal* to do something. In this instance the proposal is to continue to use and maintain the object.

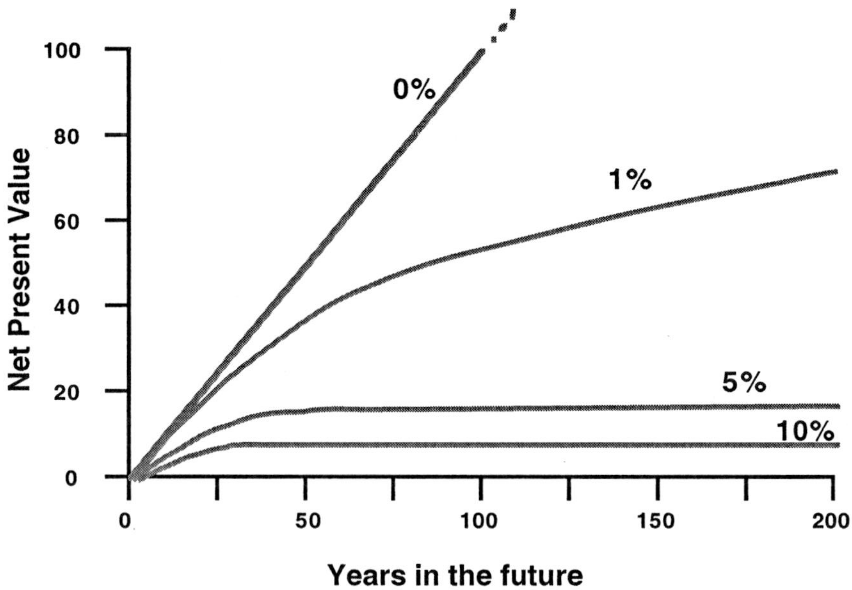

Figure 15.2 *The effect of different discount rates on Net Present Value. The larger the rate, the less important future events become*

same present value as nearer events that we can predict more accurately. Far distant changes in the use of objects become as important as our current decisions about access and display. It seems wise to set an arbitrary discount rate which matches the planning horizon, so that events close to that horizon do not have exaggerated importance now. A rate of just below 1% fits that description. It also conveniently gives an NPV of the order of 100, based on an annual benefit of one unit.

The present value of future benefits over a 200-year period at a discount rate of 0.8% is shown in Figure 15.3.

If we allow a capital/revenue approach to museum collections then there will be a relationship between the value of an object and the annual benefit it produces. If we were modelling our decision-making in a totally commercial environment we would feel obliged to use a rate of return on capital similar to that we used as our discount rate. If we study recurrent costs as a measure of present value of collections in major UK museums, then we do indeed find a rate of return of the order of 1%. However, the societal benefits of museum collections tend to spread by a chain reaction to areas that have no direct connection with the museum. Whereas a commercial organization could not lay claim to these secondary benefits, an institution with a wider social role may do so, and is justified in postulating a higher rate of return.

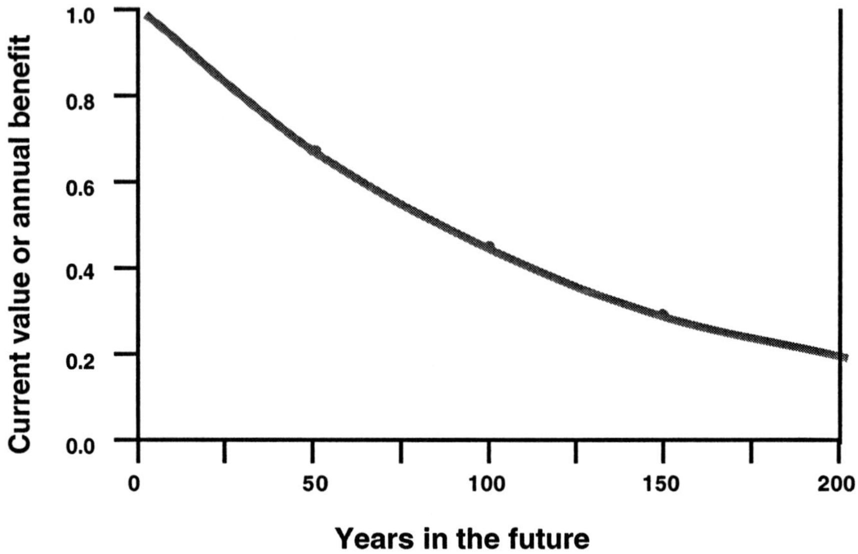

Figure 15.3 *The effect of applying a discount. The present value of future events is reduced. At a discount rate of 1% the present effect of events two centuries in the future is reduced to around 20% of events in the next few years*

This is a very long and complicated way of saying something simple yet important. Following treatment, immediate changes in some types of value may appear small (0–20%), yet changes that affect future utility can have a much greater effect on present value (100–200%). Actions that decrease future utility decrease present value, and should be considered unethical.

Maximum potential value and maintenance

There may be a maximum possible rate of benefit B_{max} for any one object because there are a finite number of people who can simultaneously derive pleasure, knowledge or inspiration from it, and a finite number of hours in the day. This provides a ceiling to the present value which we could call NPV_{ideal}. This ideal maximum can only be reached when costs of maintenance have been minimized and if there is no deterioration from constant use:

$$NPV_{ideal} = \sum_{t=1}^{200} B_{max} \tag{15.1}$$

The object may be deteriorating anyway and the amount of use may be further shortening its useful life. There may therefore be a maximum possible present value for an object which derives from a varying rate of net benefit which is always below B_{max}. We could call this maximum potential value, which is the maximum realizable present value, NPV_{max}. Elsewhere I have described a similar concept, the Total Potential Benefit, which is a function of the maximum realizable rate of benefit and the lifetime of the object, but has no arbitrary cut-off point in the future (Ashley-Smith, 1995a,b). It suggests that you can manage the use of the object in such a way that provides maximum benefit for a short time, or a lesser benefit for a longer time, and still achieve the same total benefit. This is a little bit like Jack London's declaration 'The proper function of man is to live, not exist. I shall not waste my days in trying to prolong them. I shall use my time.' It is also to some extent the same as the notion of 'maximum dose' used to control damage caused by light. However, the components of maximum dose, which are intensity and duration, are independent and controllable. There are many hidden components in total potential benefit or NPV_{max} and they are inter-related. Moreover, they can be altered by passive or interventive treatment.

However, it is quite easy to devise computer models that calculate NPV from varying rates of benefit, rates of deterioration and discount, and the costs, frequencies and effects of treatment. I recommend that you have a go yourself because an interactive computer program can demonstrate so many more possible interactions and outcomes than can be described in a static linear text.

The use of the concept of NPV_{max} is shown in graphical form in Figure 15.4 (the effects of discounting have been ignored). Four different situations are represented. The uppermost line, marked 1, indicates a continuing annual benefit of one unit every year for the next 200. The total benefit is $1.0 \times 200 = 200$, the same as the NPV. This is equal to the area of the graph under the line. If $B_{max} = 1$ then $NPV_{ideal} = 200$. This may not be achievable and the line marked 2 represents the more likely situation that there is deterioration at this rate of use. This decreases the net benefit. The area under this line is smaller, NPV = 120.

Line 3 indicates a deliberate attempt to control access at a lower level, $B = 0.8B_{max}$, where the rate of deterioration is lower. In this case the NPV is 130, higher than case 2. This is the hoped for outcome of good collections management. The correct balance between access and preservation should result in NPV_{max} getting as near to NPV_{ideal} as possible. Line 4 shows a situation where deterioration is totally under control but the rate of benefit is low. NPV is down to 20.

Such a low NPV is not acceptable (ethical) if it is being maintained by denying access where there is a demand. The equilibrium between costs, benefits and deterioration was approached from another direction in

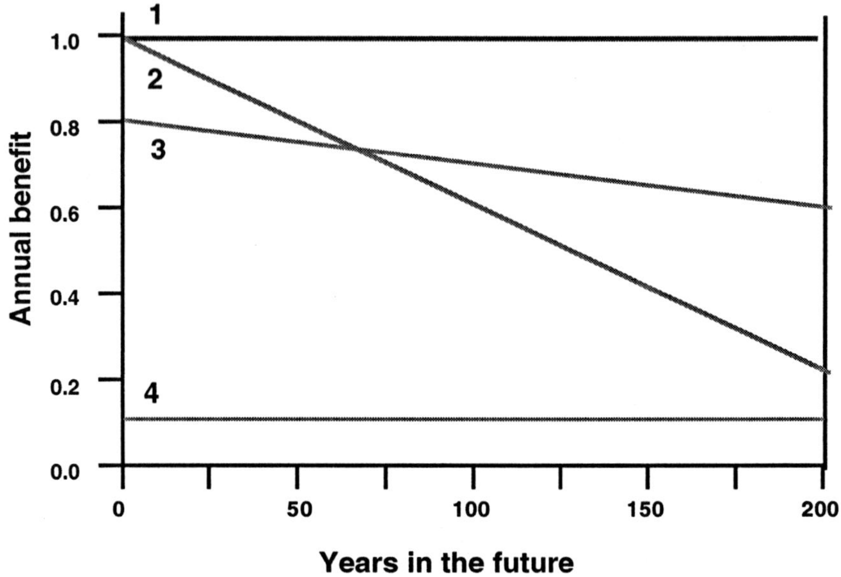

Figure 15.4 *Representations of changes in annual benefit with time. The total potential benefit is given by the area under each line. The area under line 3 is greater than that under line 2 even though this starts at a higher rate of benefit*

Figure 12.9 when we were discussing the untreatable damage caused by light. For a large range of object types much damage can be treated and can be used to increase NPV_{max}.

Suppose the reason for the limited access is the custodian's assessment of the poor but stable condition of the object. A traditional conservation view might be to leave a stable object alone. Yet treatment could increase use, thus increasing NPV. Alternatively the low rate of access might be a public reaction to the poor but stable condition of the object, no visitor being interested in such a dismal and dirty little thing. Treatment such as cleaning would increase NPV. This effect is shown in Figure 15.5. The sooner the treatment is carried out, the larger the NPV. The rate of deterioration would have to increase seriously following treatment for these interventions to reduce NPV, that is to be deemed unethical.

A regular series of small interventions may result in a greater NPV than a delay followed by one dramatic intervention as shown in Figure 15.6. Roberto Nardi has proposed that regular maintenance following major conservation treatment of monuments will decrease the need for future expensive intervention (La Rocca and Nardi, 1994). However, such a conclusion is very dependent on the proposed levels of intervention and the actual costs. It also depends on the exact role of the maintenance staff.

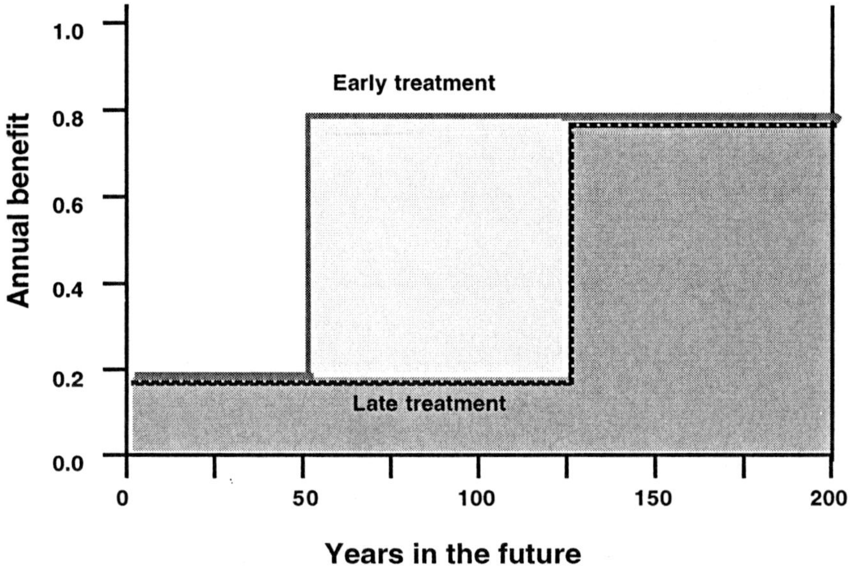

Figure 15.5 *The square shaded area marks the additional Net Present Value derived from early treatment that improves the rate of benefit derived from the object*

They must be trained to look out for and understand signs of accelerating decay. Regular maintenance by untrained workers may merely continually remove evidence of underlying deterioration.

Jan Rosvall has suggested that maintenance is what helps property sustain value during the critical phase implied by Rubbish Theory. It allows an object to be available at the point that its value picks up again (Figure 15.7) (van Gigch, Rosvall and Lagerqvist, 1993).

It can be seen from Figures 15.6 and 15.7 that the effect of maintenance is actually to slow the rate of damage rather than maintain a particular state. As the state of the object deteriorates different types of intervention will be necessary. In some cases the intervention, or its reversal, may be so disturbing that there is a limit to the number of times it can be applied. I have been told that no painting can take more than five relinings. It is important that the proposed time interval between inspections or interventions relates to the state of the object and predicted rate of deterioration.

In another reference to Rubbish Theory, Robert Barclay has proposed that there are four phases to the life of a historic musical instrument where the degree of maintenance and intervention is related to the value given to the object. He defines: the Utensil phase, the Rubbish phase; the Restoration phase; and the Conservation phase (Barclay, 1995).

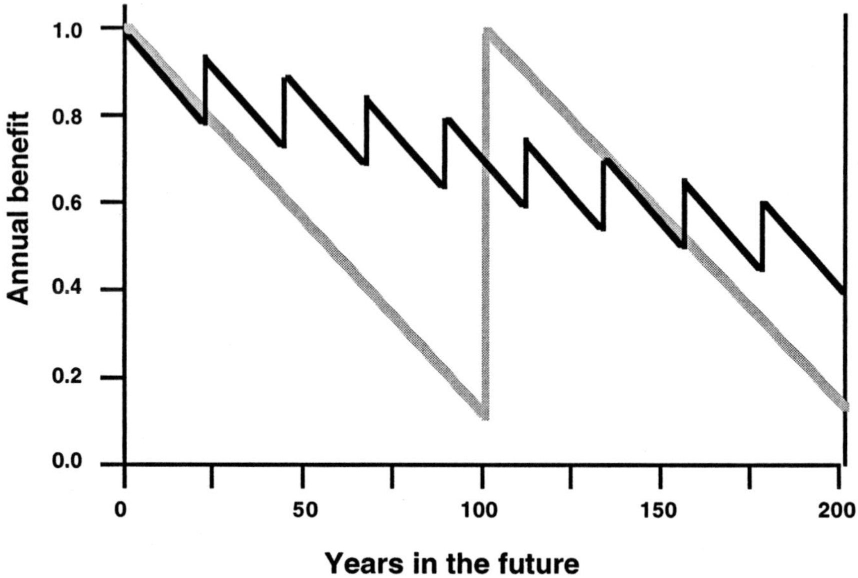

Figure 15.6 *Regular treatment may give better value than infrequent but radical interventions. In this case the area beneath the dark sawtooth maintenance line is greater than the area under the lighter line depicting treatment after considerable decay*

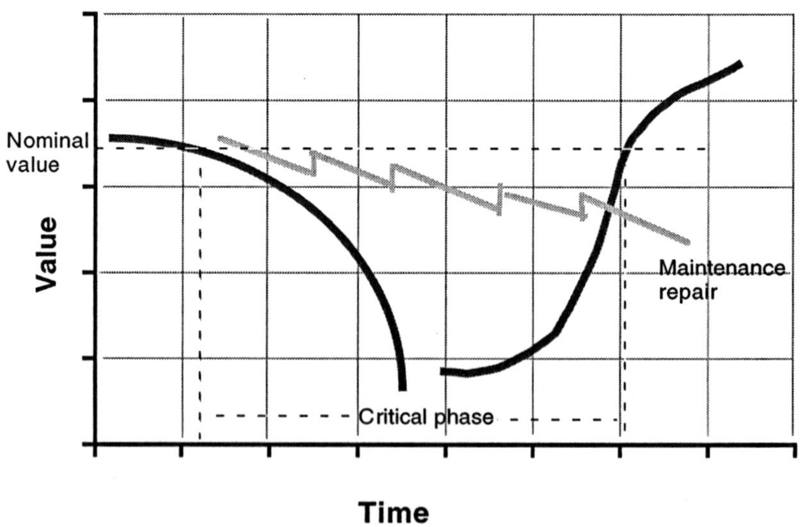

Figure 15.7 *Maintenance slows the loss of value during the critical Rubbish Phase (after Rosvall)*

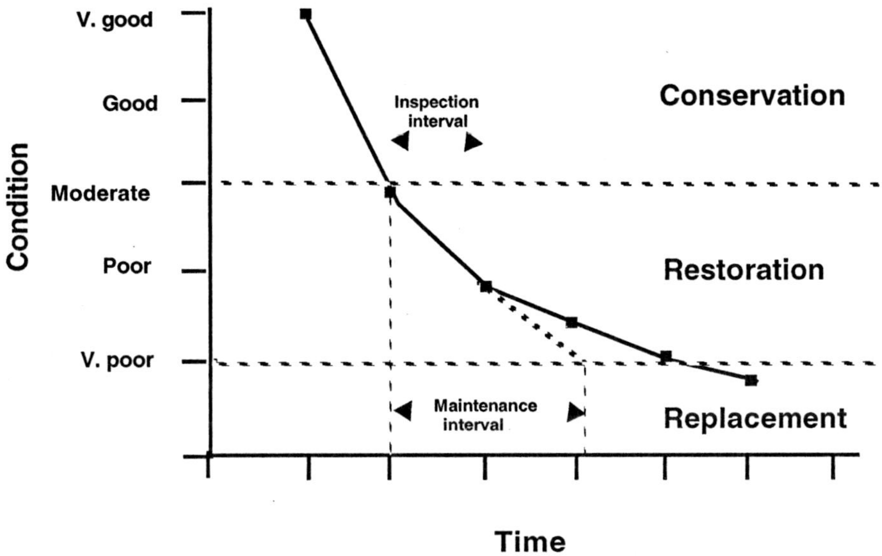

Figure 15.8 *Three approaches to treatment depending on the state of the object. The time for the next treatment is extrapolated from the most recent estimation of decay rate derived from inspection at regular intervals (after Thomas* et al.*)*

The change of intervention type and the determination of a 'maintenance interval' is shown in Figure 15.8 (Thomas, Seeley and O'Sullivan, 1997). This model was derived for building components of historic houses that are subject to wear from visitors, but is transferable with a little thought to other types of object. As the item slowly deteriorates, the appropriate type of intervention changes. It becomes increasingly necessary to use techniques such as replacement that significantly affect the historic integrity of the whole. The present rate of deterioration can be judged from differences in state on two consecutive inspections. The point at which treatment will become necessary can be found by extrapolating the present damage rate and seeing where it would cross into a different condition/treatment type. This will set the maintenance interval.

There may be financial reasons to attempt to make the time interval between interventions as long as possible, that is, to specify that treatments should last for a long period. The reasoning may be couched in terms of minimum intervention, politically correct professional behaviour. This hints at the idea that all interventions, however well intentioned, are in fact damaging. However, the wisdom of this policy will depend on the nature and cost of the intervention and the skill of the operator. There may be some benefits in developing a symbiosis between conservator and collection. Continuing intervention may be the only way that necessary skills are maintained.

A time to break down, a time to build up

It is fashionable to assume that intervention should be postponed until the last possible moment. Yet it is a curious interpretation of preventive conservation that suggests that appropriate action should be taken only when signs of deterioration are obvious. There are many instances when intervention is far less risky than leaving something untouched.

Donald Sebera has published some simple yet elegant modelling relating to the treatment of paper archives which promotes the idea that early action is sometimes advisable (Sebera, 1990). The model can be extended to a range of treatments for a variety of object types. In this section I will develop some of these ideas.

In Figure 15.9 the dark line represents an object decaying from a state of 100% to 0% over a period of 50 years (or some other unit of time). After 20 years a treatment is carried out that returns the state to 100% (Sebera refers to this as a strengthening treatment, an example of which would be the sizing of paper). After treatment the decay rate is still the same, but the object lasts for 20 years beyond the original prediction.

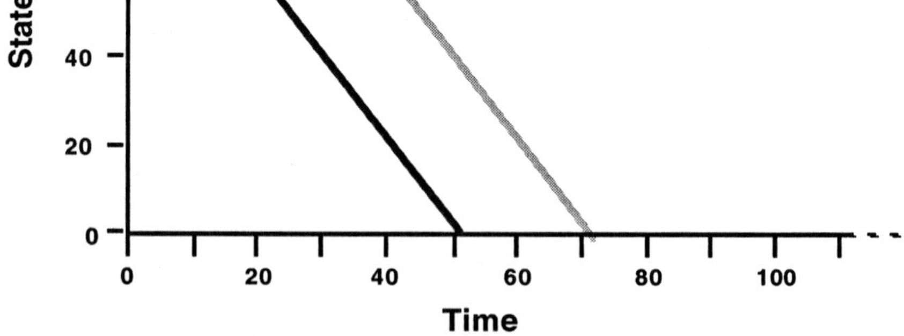

Figure 15.9 *Effect of a treatment that strengthens an object but does not affect the rate of decay (after Sebera)*

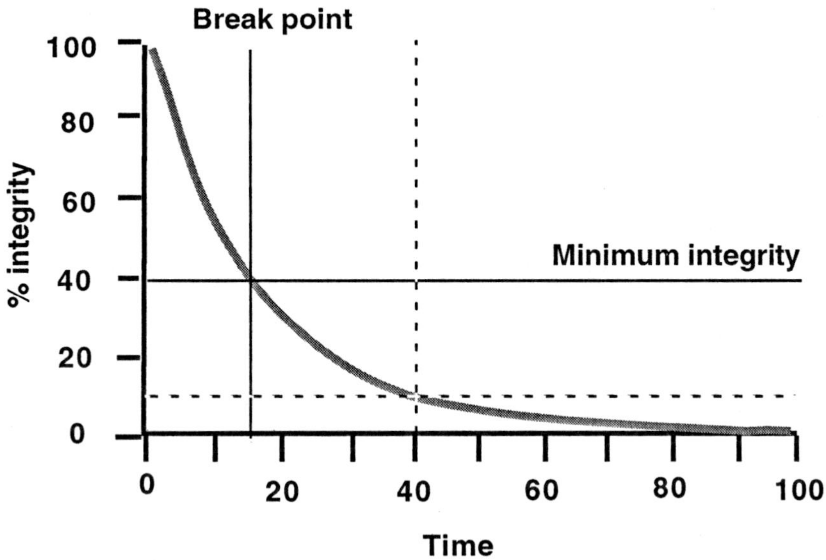

Figure 15.10 *Representation of loss of strength due to deterioration. The time for which the pieces hold together is increased by adding a support even though the rate of decay remains unaltered*

If the treatment always returns the state to 100% then the best extension of life is achieved when the object has nearly decayed to nothing. Such a treatment would be very radical, that is, 'risky'. If the strengthening treatment has the same absolute effect, in this case about 40 percentage points, then it doesn't matter at what time the treatment takes place (test this for yourself on the graph). However, it is a reasonable supposition that the effect of a treatment is dependent on the state of the object at the time of treatment. Suppose the effect is directly proportional to the state, then treatment becomes less and less effective the longer we leave it. The greatest extension of life comes from the earliest treatment.

Another form of strengthening treatment is lining for support. Figure 15.10 shows a graphical representation of the decay of a hanging textile. The decay is approximately first order, as the loss of supporting threads in the woven network is random. The object is slowly losing structural integrity and will fall apart at some point long before every possible reaction site has been attacked. This is shown as the break point, the moment in time when the object reaches its minimum integrity.

Attaching a support does not affect the rate of decay it just holds the pieces together for longer. It does this by reducing the minimum integrity

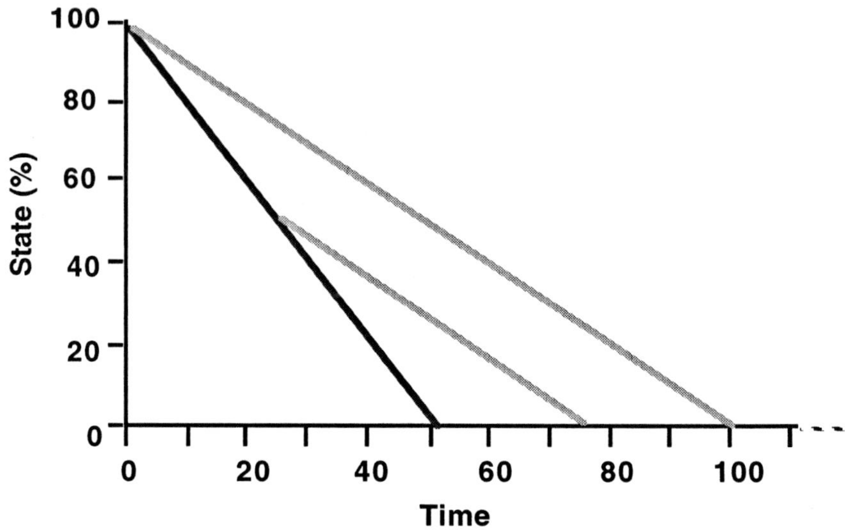

Figure 15.11 *Graphical representation of treatment that affects the rate of decay. Early treatment has a greater effect on prolonging the object's life expectancy (after Sebera)*

as shown by the dotted lines on the graph. There is no *dis*advantage in adding a support at any time. If you wait until the object is about to fall apart you will need more skill and more 'confidence'.

If the treatment does actually slow down the rate of deterioration, then there is always an advantage in applying it as early as possible. Sebera gives as an example the deacidification of archive material. The linear decay of an object is represented in schematic form in Figure 15.11. After a while the damage becomes visible. At some later time it becomes untreatable or the object becomes unusable, a state referred to as 'terminal'. If the rate of decay is slowed down before the damage is visible (shown by the shallower slope of the line) the object will last longer than if treatment is delayed until it is observed to be necessary. As Figure 15.12 shows the combination of strengthening and rate-slowing effects has the greatest effect on longevity.

Passive methods involving control of the environment will prolong the useful life of objects. Such measures should of course be applied as soon as possible (affordable). However, there are a number of circumstances where chemical intervention is necessary to reduce rates of decay, in which case treatment should be sooner than later. This might involve addition of an alkaline reserve in paper or the removal of acidic soils from textiles by washing.

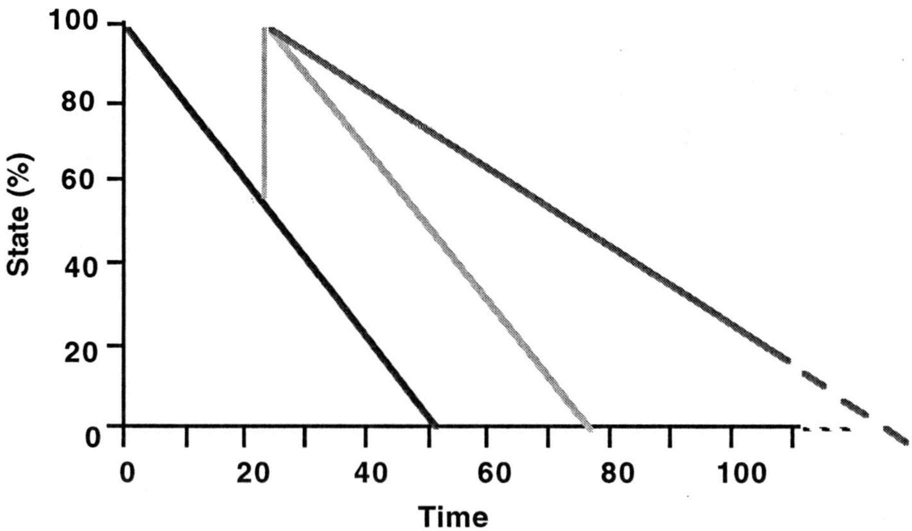

Figure 15.12 *The joint effect of a strengthening treatment and one that decreases the rate of decay. The best result (after Sebera)*

Prediction and evaluation

From the preceding discussions it has emerged that an important consideration in proposing a treatment is that it should make the object last longer and that this effect should be long lasting. But how can we predict that this will be the case?

The most obvious way is to follow the progress of objects that have undergone similar treatments in the past. There are several disadvantages to this method which may account for it being a rare occurrence:

- The historic records of condition and treatment do not exist.
- Access to treated objects may be difficult.
- Such a survey may not be seen as a good use of conservators' time.
- Newly devised treatments have not been in use long enough.

Even if it is possible to see and assess a number of objects there may be objections to any conclusions drawn because:

- The number of objects studied may be small and not representative.
- There may be variation in the application of a material or technique.
- Post-treatment histories are unknown or very varied.
- Even within one object type there may be a large variation of material and construction.

A good example of a successful survey and evaluation was carried out by staff at the Canadian Conservation Institute (Stone, 1996). One important conclusion from this exercise was that even where historic records of condition and treatment exist they are rarely compiled in a way that is useful to a future researcher.

The more frequent approach is the use of laboratory simulations. The correct approach to laboratory testing and an analysis of the conservation profession's success in achieving statistically valid results have been reviewed (Reedy and Reedy, 1988, 1992). The alternative to the study of the natural ageing of objects and conservation treatments is accelerated ageing. This involves preparing a sample or token that in some measure represents the materials and techniques used, and then placing this in a space where one or more of the properties of the normal environment are exaggerated. This should increase the rate of degradation thus, in effect, compressing time.

There are limits to how far time can be compressed while the conclusions drawn remain meaningful. There are limits to how far it is sensible or possible for the experimental conditions to diverge from those normally found in storage or display. For instance, it is not possible to vastly increase the amount of available atmospheric moisture, the norm is around 50% RH and the limit is 100%. High humidity can lower T_g which could mean that the physical state of the test piece did not resemble that found in normal circumstances. There is no point in accelerating cycles of humidity if the sample does not have time to respond to these changes. Since desorption is usually much slower than absorption, rapid cycling may merely result in maintaining a high moisture content. This could lead to the false conclusion that fluctuating conditions caused damage when in fact it was merely accelerated hydrolysis.

Even though it is possible to increase the concentrations of some pollutants quite considerably, the physical and chemical form in which they are adsorbed may be different at high concentrations. This could lead to different reaction pathways and products.

For many materials the law of reciprocity holds for reactions induced by light. For these materials it is possible to simulate a long exposure at a low light level in an experiment that uses very much higher intensities but for a shorter time. However, some dyes used in photography have high reciprocity failures.

Raising the temperature has the most noticeable effect on increasing rate of change. If you are measuring the effect of a wax-based preservative there is no value in raising the temperature above its melting point. It may be misleading to carry out tests above the glass transition temperature of the material. If there is more than one degradation reaction high temperatures may favour one that is not a major problem at room temperature.

Despite these worries, accelerated ageing is a common approach to predicting the efficacy of treatment. The theory and practice have been reviewed in a number of places including one of the books in the useful series published by the Getty Conservation Institute (Feller, 1994), in a number of papers in the Proceedings of the Conference on Research Techniques in Photographic Conservation held in Copenhagen (e.g. Reilly, 1996; Edge, 1996) and in a short but comprehensive article by E. Ströfer-Hua, whose publications always provide an appropriate mixture of science, philosophy and realism (Ströfer-Hua, 1990).

The validation of predictions based on accelerated ageing can only be achieved by comparison with natural ageing. Examples where there is good correlation are studies of permanence in the fields of paper and photographs (Wilson and Parks, 1980; Anderson and Ellison, 1992). However, a notable failure in photography was the prediction that triacetate film base was very much more stable than cellulose nitrate.

But there are problems with studies of even short periods of natural ageing. The validity of observations depends on the completeness and accuracy of the initial measurements. The first measurements of the series must by necessity have been gathered by what is now deemed to be outmoded technology. Bertrand Lavéndrine relates a study of colour film where, after 10 years of ageing, there was no longer any computer hardware available to read the original data. Once this hurdle had been overcome by much manual labour the correlation was quite good (Lavéndrine, 1996).

Other methods of prediction assume that techniques tested on small standard samples will have the same effect when transferred to larger and more variable objects. Where the real thing is very large, like a house or cathedral, there may be noticeable divergence between what is seen in the laboratory and what is eventually observed in the real world (Snethlage and Sattler, 1990; Smith, 1996). Some difficulties of using small blocks for testing stone decay are:

- Edge effects are accentuated – influencing internal temperature, humidity and salt distribution during environmental cycling.
- They are not subject to the confining pressures that building stones are subjected to.
- Unless set into a larger surface they alter air flow which influences deposition rates.
- Because of differing volume/surface area ratio, they have different thermal response.
- In most tests many surfaces are exposed, but in the real world only one face is exposed to the environment.

- Many actual decay features have dimensions greater than those of test blocks. For instance, solution rates are influenced by the length of stone surface over which run-off flows.

In some cases the immediate efficacy of treatment may not be apparent. A paper sheet that has been deacidified may appear much the same as one that has not. Two sheets that have been through the same process may not have been altered to the same degree. The prediction that both sheets would have the same improved life span may not be true. When a large number of objects go through an automated process sequentially, or are treated by a single batch process, it is necessary to know how uniform the results are. Since this is not visible to the unaided eye, mechanized analytical techniques are necessary. For instance, the distribution of magnesium and zinc in paper deacidified by a number of mass treatments was studied by Energy Dispersive X-ray Fluorescence and Atomic Absorption Spectrometry (Daniel *et al.*, 1994). A great deal of heterogeneity was found in both the solvent-based and gaseous treatments. It was concluded that the lowest concentrations of alkaline reserve were sufficient to give a protective role. Only a real time study will show whether this is true.

In some cases the immediate effect of a treatment is obvious. Physical transfer of a photographic image from a decaying base onto a more stable one may not always be successful. If the process is carried out on a large number of objects, then the success score to date becomes the figure you use to predict the risk of the next attempt (Thurgood, 1994).

To summarize, many of the current methods of predicting the outcome of treatment have a degree of uncertainty. If the purpose of treatment is to effect an immediate visible change then the major factors in predicting success will be knowledge of past performance of the materials and techniques and the experience and skill of the conservator. These are things that involve and can be encompassed by human feelings and understanding. The predictions will be right most of the time. If the purpose of the treatment is to make a significant increase in the life expectancy of the object, the prediction will be based on scientific examination, laboratory simulation and mathematical modelling. These predictions will not have the same success rate.

Mathematics and ethics

This book is about damage and risk. In it I have adopted a quasi-mathematical semi-quantitative approach. The preceding discussion contained judgements about the ethics of treatment based on numerical prediction of outcome. This is probably not merely obscure to many practical conservators, but totally alien. What about considerations of preservation of original material or reversibility, the real stuff of ethical debate? What about the battle between conservation and restoration?

Restoration is condemned as highly interventive. Some think it unethical to reweave a missing area of tapestry or replace a missing nose on a piece of sculpture. Yet in terms of the physical and potential chemical interaction with historic material these actions are far less interventive than say consolidating worm-eaten wood or supporting brittle silk by sticking *or* stitching. We would therefore make a prediction that reweaving or a nose job might increase NPV slightly but carry no risk of decreasing it.

Interventions for the sake of appearance can often bring benefits to stability. Replacing missing veneer will prevent further veneer from lifting under the influence of changes of humidity or the tug of the duster. The irreversible process of washing a discoloured piece of paper may improve stability by raising pH and improving flexibility. The chances of these processes decreasing NPV appear slight.

If you washed the paper with the sole purpose of raising the pH, it might have the added advantage of removing unsightly discoloration. But, in general, it is less usual for intervention, whose intention is to improve stability, to have side effects that improve the appearance. Indeed when it comes to non-interventive conservation such as encapsulation, boxing, placing in showcases and turning the lights down, the effect is always to detract from the appearance of the object, and reduce the amount of information it can provide at that moment. A mathematical approach is necessary to determine whether the total potential benefit of the object is actually reduced by such preventive measures.

The systematic analytic approach to the change in various types of value calls into question the almost religious obsession for preserving every minute scrap of original material. The chances are extremely small that one tiny fragment of the bulk material contains unique information. The amount of time involved in reintegrating tiny splinters of wood or ceramic may be out of all proportion to the change in value or utility of the mended piece. It almost certainly involves unnecessary addition of foreign material. The relatively low value of original material is accepted in some disciplines of conservation where non-visible material is removed to make a stronger mend, e.g. drilled out to accept a dowel.

The limitations of the concept of reversibility have been admirably reviewed by Barbara Applebaum (Applebaum, 1987). Obviously, many ethical conservation treatments are not completely reversible. A widely distributed homogeneous material, such as dirt or a consolidant, cannot be completely removed or so accurately reversed that the same particles or molecules return exactly to their previous position. However, if it is possible to reconsolidate or resoil an object, the changes in value on going in one direction are likely to be of the same magnitude as those on doing the reverse. Using a maths-based approach we can achieve perfect reversibility.

Since the aim is to make objects last for a very long time (Applebaum suggests 'forever') it is highly likely that attempts will be made to treat again in the future. A treatment that prevents future retreatment is bound to have a profound effect on the potential of the object to be useful. Early impregnations of stone with wax have had this effect, as did some of the first consolidations with silanes. Since changes to potential value are generally more important than alterations in other value types retreatability becomes the most important definition of reversibility.

Something to think about

Do you believe that failures of treatment (accidents) are inevitable?

Is putting an object in a showcase or deliberately interfering with its oxygen and moisture content through environmental control non-interventive?

In what circumstances will the application of a discount rate actually alter the ranking of different proposals?

If treatment increases value isn't this the same thing as increasing risk (the product of probability and value)?

What physical interventions are likely to reduce rate of decay?

What effect does non-interventive restoration through the making of reproductions, models or computer simulations have on total potential benefit?

References

Anderson, Stanton and Ellison, Robert (1992) Natural Aging of Photographs. *JAIC*, **31**, pp. 213–223.

Applebaum, Barbara (1987) Criteria for Treatment: Reversibility. *JAIC*, **26**, pp. 65–87.

Ashley-Smith, J. (1995a) Response and Responsibility. Text of a talk given at UKIC Conference, November 7 1995. Available on request from the author.

Ashley-Smith, J. (1995) Definitions of Damage. Text of a talk given at the AAH conference. London, April 1995. On the World Wide Web at http://www.palimpsest.stanford.edu.

Arrow, Kenneth J. (1976) The Rate of Discount for Long-Term Public Investment, in *Energy and the Environment: A Risk Benefit Approach*. Pergamon Press. ISBN 0-08-020873-8, pp. 113–140.

Barclay, Robert L. (1995) Treatment Phase Analysis in Restoration and Conservation. Actes du 4e Colloque International de l'ARAAFU. Paris.

Clavir, Miriam (1994) Preserving Conceptual Integrity: Ethics and Theory in Preventive Conservation. Preventive Conservation: Practice, Theory and Research. Preprints to the Ottawa Congress, 12–16 September. IIC, pp. 53–57.

Daniel, F., Flieder, F., Juchauld, F. and Yver, C. (1994) Study of the Homogeneity of Mass Deacidification Treatments using Atomic Absorption Spectrometry. Preventive Conservation: Practice, Theory and Research. Preprints to the Ottawa Congress, 12–16 September. IIC, pp. 217–222.

Drucker, Peter (1977) *Management*. Pan Business Management. ISBN 0-330-256386.

Drumheller, Ann and Kaminitz, Marian (1994) Traditional Care and Conservation, the Merging of Two Disciplines at the National Museum of the American Indian. Preventive Conservation: Practice, Theory and Research. Preprints to the Ottawa Congress, 12–16 September. IIC, pp. 58–60.

Edge, Michelle (1996) Lifetime Prediction: Fact or Fantasy? Research Techniques in Photographic Conservation. Proceedings of the Copenhagen Conference, 14–19 May 1995. ISBN 87-89730-18-6, pp. 97–100.

Feller, Robert L. (1994) *Accelerated Aging: Photochemical and Thermal Aspects*. J. Paul Getty Trust. ISBN 0-89236-125-5.

Hanley, N. and Spash, C.L. (1993) *Cost–Benefit Analysis and the Environment*. Edward Elgar Publishing.

Lavédrine, Bertrand (1996) Prediction of Dark Stability of Colour Chromogenic Films Using Arrhenius Law and Comparison after Ten Years of Natural Ageing. Research Techniques in Photographic Conservation. Proceedings of the Copenhagen Conference 14–19 May 1995. ISBN 87-89730-18-6, pp. 71–76.

Nardi, Roberto and La Rocca, Eugenio (1994) Preventive Conservation and Restoration: a Matter of Costs. Preventive Conservation: Practice, Theory and Research. Preprints to the Ottawa Congress, 12–16 September. IIC, pp. 24–31.

Perrow, Charles (1994) The Limits of Safety: The Enhancement of a Theory of Accidents. *Journal of Contingencies and Crisis Management*, Vol. 2, pp. 212–220. ISSN 0966–0879.

Reedy, Terry J. and Reedy, Chandra L. (1992) *Principles of Experimental Design for Art Conservation Research*. J. Paul Getty Trust.

Reedy, Terry J. and Reedy, Chandra L. (1998) *Statistical Analysis in Art Conservation Research*. J. Paul Getty Trust. ISBN 0-89236-097-6.

Reilly, James M. (1996) Accelerated Aging Tests. Research Techniques in Photographic Conservation. Proceedings of the Copenhagen Conference, 14–19 May 1995. ISBN 87-89730-18-6, pp. 77–84.

Sebera, Donald (1990) The Effects of Strengthening and Deacidification on Paper Permanence – part 1. AIC. *The Book and Paper Group Annual 1990*, p. 66.

Smith, B.J. (1996) Scale Problems in the Interpretation of Urban Stone Decay, in *Processes of Urban Stone Decay*. Donhead. ISBN 1-873394-20-9.

Snethlage, Rolf and Wendler, E. (1990) The Application of Laboratory Processes and Studies to Real Structures. Analytical Methodologies for the Investigation of Damaged Stones. Pavia, 14–21 September.

Soby, B.A. and Ball, D.J. (1992) Consumer Safety and the Valuation of Life and Injury; Research Report No 9. Environmental Risk Assessment Unit, School of Environmental Sciences, UEA, Norwich NR4 7TJ.

Stone, Thomas G. (1996) Artifacts Revisited: The Evaluation of Old Treatments. ICOM-CC. 11th Triennial Meeting, Edinburgh, 1–6 September. ISBN 1-873396-50-8, pp. 643–649.

Ströfer-Hua, E. (1990) Experimental Measurement: Interpreting Extrapolation and Prediction by Accelerated Aging. *Restaurator*, **11**, pp. 254–266.

Thomas, Paul, Seeley, Nigel and O'Sullivan, Patrick (1997) The Processes of Visitor Impact Assessment. *Journal of Architectural Conservation*, No. 1, pp. 67–84.

Thurgood, Brian (1995) National Archives, Canada. Personal Communication.

van Gigch, John P., Rosvall, Jan and Lagerqvist, Bosse (1993) Setting a Strategic Framework for Conservation Standards. ASTMS Symposium on Standards for Preservation and Rehabilitation. Fort Worth, Texas, 10–11 October.

Wilson, William K. and Parks, E.J. (1980) Comparison of Accelerated Aging of Book Papers in 1937 with 36 Years Natural Aging. *Restaurator*, **4**, pp. 1–55.

16 Purpose and presentation

This purpose of this chapter is to show that the information gained in the past chapters can be used in systematic ways to enable consistent decisions and the formulation of strategies. Examples of some strategic collections management initiatives that have been proposed or implemented in the last decade are reviewed. These include the elements of prediction, impact, use, value, costs and benefits that indicate a relationship with risk analysis, even though the vocabulary employed does not always suggest this. The relationship between simplified ranking systems and more quantitative assessments is explored. Quantitative assessments of past decisions provide benchmarks for future decision-making.

Using risk information

Information about the likelihood of unwanted events and their impact on the collections should be a part of decision-making in museums. But is it? Is the quantitative or semi-quantitative approach, which relies on estimates of what many people consider unquantifiable, likely to succeed? Is risk one of those things that people write books about but never use?

Decision-making in museums can be divided into two broad categories.

- Strategic – where the nature and mission of the institution is understood but guidance is needed about which activities should be allotted priority in terms of sequence or resources.
- Tactical – (a) where courses of action have been proposed and one option must be selected
  (b) where courses of action have been decided and damage limitation is called for.

There are a number of instances where some or all of the elements of risk analysis have been included in all of these types of decision-making. But not always consciously.

Strategy – the Delta Plan

Probably the largest collections management strategic initiative has been the Delta project in the Netherlands. The General Audit Office, advising the Dutch Parliament on the efficient use of taxpayer's money, advised that a general evaluation of the state of national collections was necessary, as there were deemed to be significant backlogs of objects in need of care or conservation treatment. Following this there should be a rescue plan and a revised cultural heritage policy. The Delta Plan for the Conservation of the Cultural Heritage was launched in 1990. Details can be obtained from the responsible ministry (Ministry of Welfare, Health and Cultural Affairs, 1992). Curators and conservators have described their involvement, and their need to modify and develop the methodology in their respective disciplines (Krikken, 1997; Kantzenbach, 1996; van Veek, 1995).

The most interesting aspect of the initial surveys was the classification of collections and individual objects by value. The allocation of funds would not depend solely on perceived conservation need but on an assessment of the importance of each collection. The use of a widely accepted valuation system was essential to the success of the Plan. There were four basic categories labelled A to D.

A. Objects (collections or individual items) of extremely high value, being irreplaceable or having a high reference value. Indispensable to the museum's mission and the Netherlands' cultural heritage as a whole.

B. Objects of value, worthy of preservation because they are regularly shown or requested for temporary exhibitions; objects belonging to an ensemble of cultural or historic value. Objects of great documentary value.

C. Objects of indeterminate value in some way relevant to the collection. On study such objects might be reclassified as A or B.

D. Material not worthy to be kept in the collection.

Different institutions and disciplines worked out different criteria for placing objects in one of the four value categories The method adopted at the National Museum of Natural History, Leiden, is given in Table 16.1 This involved the use of 13 named criteria.

Category A requires fulfilment of criterion 1 plus at least one out of 2–4
Category B requires fulfilment of criterion 1 plus at least one out of 5–12
Category C requires fulfilment of criterion 1 only
Category D requires fulfilment of criterion 13 only

Table 16.1

Number	*Name*	*Criterion*
1	Minimum	Fits the objectives and scope of the institution
2	Rarity	Irreplaceable, extremely rare or extinct *in situ*
3	Symbol	Within the discipline is of global symbolic or cultural significance
4	Nomenclatural reference	A nomenclatural type or has global reference value
5	Distributional	Documents spatiotemporal occurrence of a species, rock type or another phenomenon of nature
6	Presentation	Has demonstrable presentation value: informative, educative, attractive, spectacular, aesthetic
7	Verification	Carrier of published scientific information (including illustrations) that needs to remain verifiable
8	Research	Potential carrier of new scientific information
9	Historical	Documents the history of the relevant discipline
10	Ensemble	Derives value from association with other A or B objects
11	Anticipation	Awaits further analysis as to its presumed value
12	Transit	Given in custody, not the institution's property but satisfying relevant criteria from 1–11
13	Disposal	Nothing to do with the objectives and scope of the institution

As you can imagine this did not initially put much material into category C, a situation which had to be resolved in discussion with the audit office inspectors. The tendency to put natural history specimens in category B comes from the great unpredictability of the future information value, as discussed in the last chapter.

A set of five 'Categories of Specimens' using similar criteria has been defined at the Canadian Museum of Nature (Price and Fitzgerald, 1995). The middle three categories, between priceless and worthless, are actually given approximate monetary values: >$10 000; $1000–10 000; <$1000.

A complementary part of the Delta Plan was an assessment of the condition of the object. Because the aim of the survey was to estimate the need for resources, the condition was assessed in terms of need for treatment. A four-stage classification was used, category 4 needing urgent

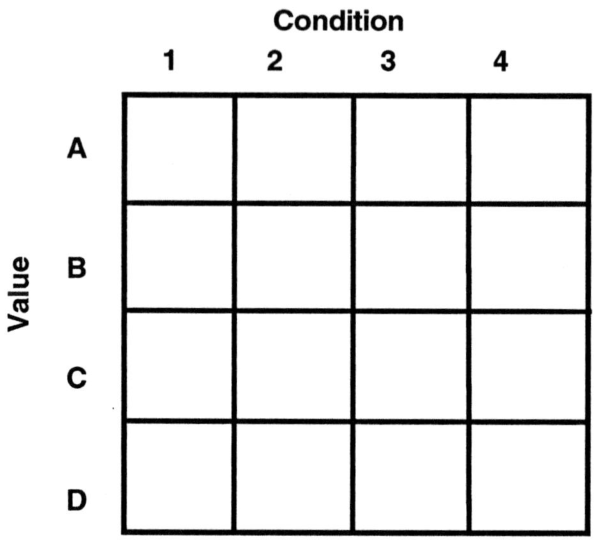

Figure 16.1 *Matrix giving 16 possible risk or priority scores with coordinates based on classifications of value and condition into four categories each*

treatment (see Chapter 7). With a four-point definition of value and a four-point definition of condition, one can construct a matrix with 16 possible categories (Figure 16.1). If the need for treatment is construed as an evaluation of the current extent of damage, and as a prediction of the future probability or extent of damage, then each of the squares in the matrix categorizes a different magnitude of risk. A4 must constitute the highest risk since something of very high value stands a good chance of losing much of that value very soon. D1 must be the lowest risk since there is no probability of the loss of even a small amount of value.

In Figure 16.2 I have put numbers (in brackets) against the letters A–D and below the condition ratings 1–4. In each square of the matrix I have put the sum of the two numbers whose row and column intersect at that point. The numbers chosen are in line with the proposal by Stefan Michalski that there are only eight orders of magnitude for the value of objects (excluding zero) and six orders of magnitude for annual rate of risk or deterioration (excluding zero) (Michalski, 1994). Remember that when multiplying numbers expressed as powers of 10 the answer is obtained by adding the orders of magnitude. Risk is related to the product of the value and the probability or rate of deterioration. By definition, category D objects have no value, so there can be no risk associated with them. This is why there are only zeros below the double line.

Value	Condition: 1 (0)	2 (2)	3 (4)	4 (6)
A (8)	8	10	12	14
B (5)	5	7	9	11
C (2)	2	4	6	8
D (0)	0	(0)	(0)	(0)

Figure 16.2 *Applying quantities to the matrix. The number in each cell is the sum of the two figures in brackets at the end of the relevant row and column. Class D objects have no value to the institution and are automatically assigned zero risk*

If the policy were to give priority to the individual objects or whole collections with the highest risk, squares A3–A4 would have highest priority and C1–C2 the lowest. There is overlap between all three classes. However, there could be a broad division into, say, four groups (risk numbers 2–4, 5–7, 8–11, 12–14) that would demand different strategies. That would lead to five strategies if you include the task of disposing of class D objects which were ranked as zero. You could try to see how changing the ranges of value and condition alters the number and distribution of distinct classes of risk.

The funding body may not respond to very high risk in the same way that the owning institution might. The central funding agency might question why highly valuable objects had been allowed to deteriorate to such an extent, and suggest confiscation and reallocation of the collections rather than increased funds to cope with the problem.

In the Netherlands, different types of institution have developed differing responses to the initial survey depending on the nature of the collections, the numbers in each category and the previous history of conservation. The National Museum of Ethnology has proposed a five-level approach shown as a pyramidal model (Figure 16.3). The lower the level, the greater the proportion of the collection to which it may apply. The

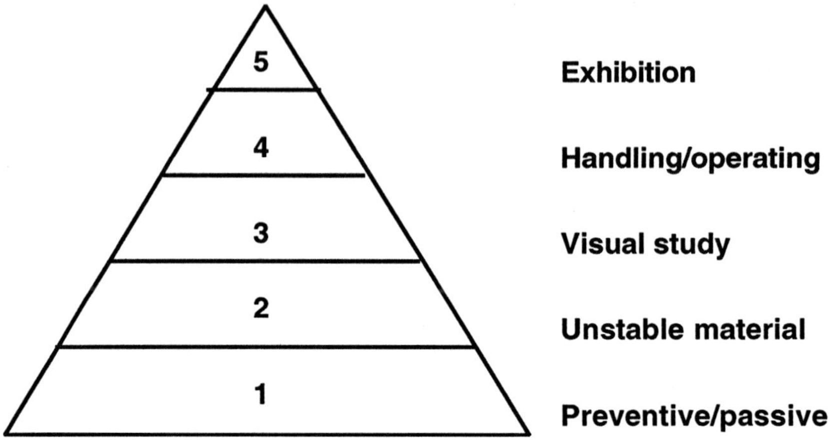

Figure 16.3 *Pyramidal model for five levels of action. The higher up the pyramid, the less important it is to reach the next stage and the fewer the number of objects that will be affected (after Kantzenbach)*

lowest levels have the highest priority. Working at level 1, providing appropriate environmental conditions for all classes of object, and level 2, dealing with materials that are still unstable in these circumstances, is equivalent to moving all objects from condition category 4 to category 3 and from 3 to 2. Levels 3 and 4 involve interventions which enable useful study by looking at complete, assembled and cleaner objects or by making the objects function. Level 5 applies to the smallest number of objects and involves intervention, including restoration and mounting, for the purposes of exhibition. These levels correspond to moving from condition category 2 to 1. It is implicit in the descriptions of value classes A and B that there will be more candidates for levels 3–5 in these groups.

At first sight this strategy is mostly driven by conservation condition, rather than any assessment of risk that involves value. It is, however, driven by attempts to increase present value by passive control and preventive intervention (levels 1 and 2) and increase of utility through structural and aesthetic intervention (levels 3–5). The relative increases in value due to these different phases would be for local determination, as would the costs of executing the changes. In 1996 the Ethnology Museum was only at the stage of conducting pilot studies to proceed to level 2.

Strategy – the Canadian contribution

Probably the best known and widely published preservation strategies based on risk are those that have come from Canada. The Canadian

Conservation Institute (CCI) has developed wallcharts and interactive computer programs that are designed to lead museum managers to identify areas of risk and which suggest ways of minimizing them (Michalski, 1992, 1994; Marcon, 1997). The Canadian Museum of Nature has developed systematic methods of risk assessment for collections and has held training workshops in Canada and the UK (Waller, 1994; Canadian Museum of Nature, 1995). Much of the content of this book relies on the foundation of this work.

The Canadian Museum of Nature approach is to look at each distinct collection in turn. For each of 23 distinguishable agents (Table 2.6) the maximum possible proportional change in utility of that collection is estimated. The degree to which it will actually happen is estimated in terms of probabilities or extent, and the fraction of the collection susceptible to that agent. The period under consideration is set at 100 years. It is assumed that current conditions persist throughout that period. No considerations of absolute value are used. The extent of change is not approached in quite the same way as proposed in Chapter 8. In this book, extent is treated as if related to idealized chemical kinetics, using functions of intensity and exposure time. Although the result is identical, Waller treats extent in a more pragmatic way, using it to modify the worst possible case.

The assessments are entered into an array which allows the magnitude of risk for each agent to be given a ranking. The results of the assessment can also be presented in a graphical form that enables differences in susceptibilities of the collections to be recognized quickly. Figure 16.4 shows a simplified and idealized presentation of the risk to two fictitious collections using the Museum of Nature format. Looking at these profiles you could try to work out what object types they represent.

If you are presented with this information about your collections, what should you do? Which of these risks is acceptable and which should be addressed immediately? Waller makes no comment about acceptability but indicates that risk mitigation methods should be proposed and subjected to cost–benefit analysis. In Chapter 14 I proposed that a risk of 10^{-5} for an event such as an exhibition was easily acceptable. If the annual net benefit from the static collection is of the order of 1% (which I have stated is the usual minimum), an annual risk of 10^{-5} is justified. This is equivalent to a risk of 10^{-3} for one century, or 0.001 as shown in Figure 16.4. Risks per century below 10^{-3} are not worth worrying about, risks per century below 10^{-2} may have to be accepted unless they are very cheap and easy to eliminate. Risks per century above 10^{-2} are unacceptable and must be addressed. In Figure 16.4 strategies to reduce risk from fire and pests are needed for collection 1.

Risk management strategies will involve eliminating the source of hazard, creating a barrier or monitoring and controlling the effect

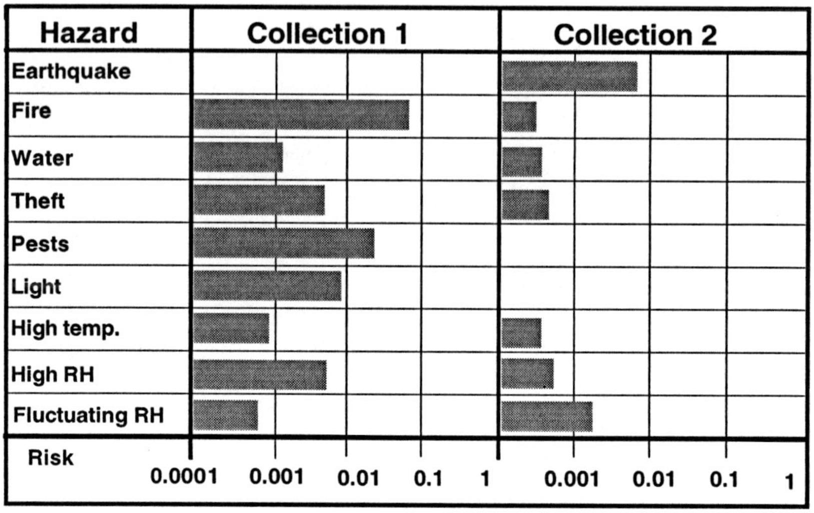

Figure 16.4 *Method of displaying risk information. The bars represent the magnitude of risk per century due to each agent for a particular collection (after Waller)*

(Ashley-Smith, 1986). Five stages of control avoid, block, detect, respond and recover – borrowed from fire prevention theory form an integral part of the CCI methodology and are now widely taught. They are in priority order:

1. *Avoid* sources and attractants of the agent – but if unable to do this...
2. *Block* the agent – but if you cannot be certain of a total block you will need to...
3. *Detect* the agent or its effects – enabling you, in a swift and timely manner, to...
4. *Respond* to the agent – if the response is not swift or timely, you will be forced to...
5. *Recover* from the effects of the agent on the objects.

The methods proposed to reduce risk may include changes to the building; changes to hardware such as shelving, air-handling plant, locks and alarm systems; or changes to procedures.

The conservation and preservation strategies described above have only been started within the last five to 10 years, have not been completed and are still being developed. One common feature mentioned in all of the reports from the Netherlands and from Canada is that with the strategic reappraisal of whole collections comes a great improvement in communication and motivation across all the disciplines within the institution. 'The heuristic value of applying an intuitively acceptable set of valuation criteria ... whatever its drawbacks, has proved to be considerable to managing staff, curators and technicians alike.' 'Introducing the model to the staff ... had a positive effect. It very quickly created a common language that made communication between different departments much easier and more successful.' 'The exercise of performing the risk assessment ... produces many benefits ... A sense of the value of their own ideas and knowledge is instilled in staff. Collection care staff tend to accept changes because they were intimately involved in defining problems and proposing and evaluating possible solutions.'

The Delta Plan and the Museum of Nature assessment involve time and staff in large quantities. There may be more rough and ready approaches to determining areas of risk that require priority action. Stefan Michalski has suggested a simplified system in which three properties – object value, object susceptibility and presence of each agent – are each given a score of 1 to 5 (very low–very high) for each of the nine fundamental agents recognized in the CCI methodology (1 Direct physical forces, 2 Thieves, vandals, displace, 3 Fire, 4 Water, 5 Pests, 6 Containments, 7 Light, UV, 8 Incorrect temperature, 9 Incorrect relative humidity). The scores for each agent are added to arrive at a rough ranking of risk. Almost in the same breath, Michalski warns against using simplified methods which merge fundamental notions from different bodies of knowledge. Thus 'susceptibility' (defined mathematically in Chapter 8) mixes cultural and technical judgements without it being clear which dominates the final outcome.

I have proposed an even cruder simplification. As a result of reading the literature, having a personal gestalt picture of the state of your collection, and knowing the types of damage most frequently treated by conservator colleagues, ask yourself:

1. Which object types are deteriorating at a rate detectable within a working lifetime?
2. Of these, which objects lose the highest percentage of their information value as they deteriorate?
3. Of these, which have highest absolute value?
4. For which of these are there well-known methods of control?

If your institution already has a roof, locks on the doors and fire alarms, this method will probably correctly lead you to your greatest preservation priority. Nineteenth-century paper and early photographic negatives come high on my list.

Preservation procedures

An elegant procedure for assessing the preservation priority of archive material has been devised by the Society of American Archivists (SAA) in collaboration with the Research Libraries Group and the Commission on Preservation and Access (Tennison, Van der Reyden, Tsai and Parrish, 1996; Tennison, Van der Reyden, Tsai, 1996). It contains many of the elements that are found in the strategic appraisals mentioned above, but it has been designed as a procedure for *implementing* a strategy or policy, rather than as a guide for devising one. In stepwise fashion it requests answers to questions about value, housing provision, use, exposure and condition. It uses 3 × 3 matrices to compare three-category ratings for two properties at a time (compare this with the single 4 × 4 matrix in Figure 16.2). Interim scores are obtained from these matrices which are used to direct specific courses of action such as disposing of the collection, or reformatting material for use by researchers. These scores are fed into further matrices, the last of which provides a priority score.

The procedure is divided into three major stages called Value Assessment, Risk Assessment and Preservation Priority.

Three types of value are identified:

- Evidential: administrative, fiscal, legal or institutional significance.
- Informational: research value for historical, educational or genealogical reasons.
- Intrinsic: artifactual, monetary, symbolic or sentimental.

These can be seen as individual examples or combinations of the value types explored in Chapter 6.

A Value score is obtained from plots of evidential value against informational value (Figure 16.5). Different matrices are used depending on the importance of the records to the institution. If they are important because of value to researchers, matrix 3 is used; if to meet operational needs matrix 2 is used; if both, then matrix 1 is applicable. Study the different distribution of scores within the three matrices. Matrix 1 is symmetrical about the top left–bottom right diagonal, whereas the other two impose different biases on the scoring. If the intrinsic value of the records is also high, there is discretion to move the value score one higher.

The Risk Assessment consists of several stages. A Holdings Maintenance Need score is obtained from considerations such as housing needs, difficult formats and damaging attachments. A Use score is obtained by plotting evidence of past use against prediction of future use. This Use score is plotted against the Holdings Maintenance Need score to

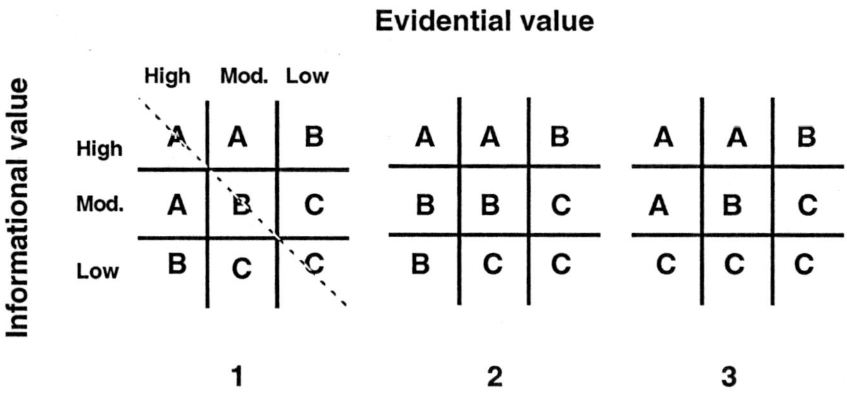

Figure 16.5 *Three matrices used to determine a value score for a particular collection of archive material. Only matrix 1 is symmetrical about the diagonal, the others impart a bias to the score depending on the importance of the collection to different types of user (after Society of American Archivists)*

obtain an Exposure score. A Condition score is obtained by plotting existing deterioration against the presence of unstable materials (Figure 16.6(a)). Note the bias.

Finally Condition is plotted against Exposure in a symmetrical matrix to obtain what is called a Risk score. The Risk Assessment stage does not contain any judgement of value. The combination of value and the predicted extent of deterioration occurs in the final step, Preservation Selection. In the vocabulary adopted in this book, the Preservation Matrix shown in Figure 16.6(b) forms the *true* risk assessment. Although there are nine possible distinct risk scores, they are grouped to form only three levels of priority (1–3, 4–6, 7–8, shown separated by the dotted lines). The distribution of these groups is not symmetrical, as the scores have not been entered on the grid in order. It shows a deliberate institutional policy bias. All low value material is seen as a low priority, regardless of exposure or condition. High value material at moderate risk and moderate value material at high risk are deemed equally important. It is interesting to note that the same geometry is obtained if you choose only three groups from the risk numbers in the 16 cell matrix shown in Figure 16.2 (0, 2–8, 9–14).

The more ranks you choose for each property such as value, use or condition, the greater the possible evaluations of risk and the greater the potential number of strategies or actions to choose from. However, it is unlikely that anyone would want to deal with more than five or six

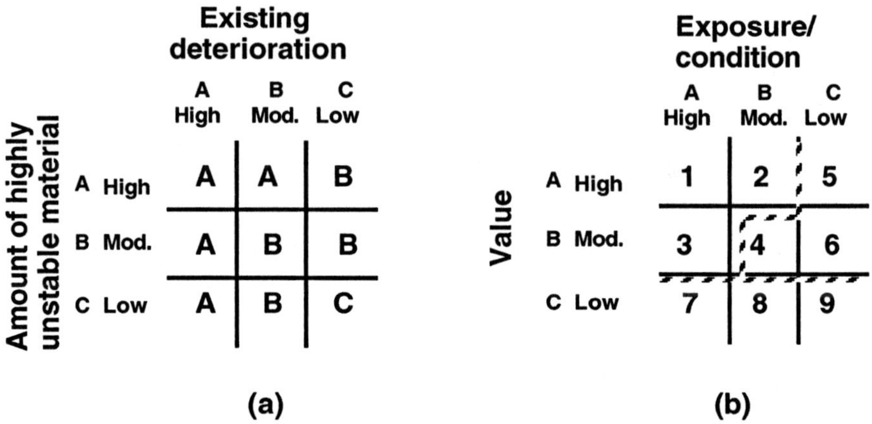

Figure 16.6 *(a) Matrix to determine a condition score showing a bias towards existing damage. (b) Matrix to determine a final priority score. This shows a bias against low value material whatever the predicted state of the material and predictions of use (after Society of American Archivists)*

priorities. The Delta Plan used four rankings, the SAA system chose three. It would be possible to limit yourself to two – high/low, or good/bad – and still arrive at a choice of three priorities or possible directions. Procedures using four and six cell matrices have been developed and incorporated into interactive computer programs for library preservation assessments (Research Libraries Group Inc., 1993).

Risk assessment for disaster preparedness

Attempts have been made to assess the vulnerability of institutions to disaster. One method, developed at CCI, forces evaluations of Event History, Event Probability and Event Criticality, into a series of 0–5 rankings (Stewart and Tremain, 1994).

The criteria for deciding which ranks are appropriate are worth noting. The ranking of the Loss Event History combines both frequency and impact (Table 16.2); however, it is not used in the final ranking of risk. It is more an exercise to help understand the different concepts and to guide people to make subjective assessments of future probabilities. It also acts as a check, because there would have to be a good reason why the proven and the predicted risk were substantially different.

The Loss Event Probability criteria are shown in Table 16.3. If the prediction period is 25 years then the once-a-century storm has a

Table 16.2 *Loss event history*

Rank	*Criterion*
0	No loss events of this type have occurred before
1	One or two minor occurrences. Minimal damage; few people affected, with no injuries: minor problems easily handled; little monetary loss: few resources affected
2	Less than four minor occurrences. Minor damage; several persons affected, perhaps with minor injuries; some difficult problems; minor monetary loss; few resources affected
3	More than three occurrences. Some major damage, but restricted in areas or facilities involved; many people involved, with some major injuries or many minor injuries; several difficult problems; major monetary loss; resources affected
4	More than three occurrences. Extensive or major damage; large numbers of people affected, with personal suffering, many injuries, and personal property damage; many difficult problems; heavy monetary loss; many resources affected
5	More than three occurrences. Very heavy or extensive damage; large number of people affected, including many deaths and injuries; many complex problems; unbearable monetary loss; heavy loss of museum resources

Table 16.3 *Loss event probability*

Rank	*Criterion*	*Probability (%)*
0	Virtually impossible in the future under currently existing circumstances	0
1	Could happen but data insufficient to determine probability	1–19
2	Improbable in the future	20–49
3	Moderately probable in the future	50–79
4	Highly probable	80–99
5	Virtually certain to occur in the future under circumstances currently existing	100

Table 16.4 *Loss event criticality*

Rank	*Criterion*
5	Fatal. The loss would be disastrous, resulting in the long-term or permanent closing of the museum. The museum would cease to operate immediately after the event occurred
4	Very serious. The loss would not be disastrous, but the museum would have to suspend at least part of its operations immediately and temporarily. Reopening the museum might require significant monetary investments
3	Moderately serious. The loss would have noticeable impact on the museum. It might have to suspend some operations briefly. Some monetary investments might be necessary to return to full operation
2	Relatively unimportant. The loss would not cause any curtailment of operations or require any significant monetary investment to restore full operations. The loss would be covered by normal contingency planning
1	No effect. The impact of the loss would be so minor that it would have no discernible effect on the museum or its operations
0	Not applicable. This rating to be used when the relevant probability is zero

probability of 25%, ranked as '2, Improbable'. The once-a-decade storm would be ranked as '5, Virtually certain'. There is an approximately linear correlation between the number used to represent the probability and the actual probability.

The Loss Event Criticality is a measure of the impact of the disaster. This takes a holistic view of the museum as an organization, as well as an accumulation of objects. It accepts that the loss of people and resources could have as devastating an effect on the future of the museum as the loss of the collection.

Each of a list of about 100 hazardous events or agents is assessed using these criteria, leading to an array similar to that shown in Figure 16.7. By inspection, hazards that have a high rating for both probability and criticality will achieve a high rank. This will give priority to preventive and mitigation measures relevant to that hazard. It will also put the risk of some other imagined disasters into perspective.

The use of numbers rather than letters for ratings should be approached with caution. If the ratings are purely symbolic they can still be used as coordinates on a grid. The 0–5 ranking used in the CCI disaster risk assessment could lead to a 6×6 matrix with 36 possible distinguishable cells, each with its own defining pair of coordinates. As

Hazard	History	Probability	Criticality	Rank
Rainstorm				
Hurricane				
Lightning				
Hailstorm				
Blizzard				
Flash flood				
Slow rising flood				
Earthquake				
Landslide				
______				
Explosion				
______				

Figure 16.7 *Matrix for assessing and ranking risk of disaster (after Stewart and Tremain)*

we have seen, this grid can be divided up into any smaller number of areas, depending on how many different priority levels are desired. The consequence of an assessment leading to one particular set of coordinates or in one particular area can be made to have any outcome, all depending on institutional policy. (To that extent the grid is like a 'snakes and ladders' board.)

However, numbers automatically suggest relative quantities in a way that letters do not. Numbers also invite mathematical combination. The properties of probability and criticality, if quantified, could be multiplied together to arrive at an absolute figure for risk. If the rankings are representative of equally spaced points on a continuum of value (whether linear or logarithmic) they can be combined mathematically to arrive at

Add

	0	1	2	3
0	0	1	2	3
1	1	2	3	4
2	2	3	4	5
3	3	4	5	6

Multiply

	0	1	2	3
0	0	0	0	0
1	0	1	2	3
2	0	2	4	6
3	0	3	6	9

Figure 16.8 *Effects of combining two sets of ranking using either addition or multiplication*

quantitatively distinct and meaningful scores. As already mentioned, if the ranks approximate to a logarithmic scale they can be added, if they are linear they can be multiplied. Two 4 × 4 matrices are shown in Figure 16.8. Note that the number of possible scores is always smaller than the total number of cells in the grid and note the different symmetries resulting from the different methods of combination. Note also the immense power of including zero (check for yourself the different symmetry of the array if the lowest rating is 1). If the symbol zero is used as a ranking it should only be used to represent the quantity zero, as is the case with probability in the CCI example.

Benchmarks

The techniques described in this chapter are used to determine an order or ranking of risk, which in turn is used to suggest an order of priority for preservation action. Any decision can be seen as a choice of one from a series of options. Ranking the options may be all that is necessary to make the choice. You may not need to know absolute numbers for benefits, value, probability or rate of deterioration. The rank order may be sufficient. However, if you want to compare one decision with another, or one institution's behaviour with another, or make comparisons with monetary costs and incomes, it may become necessary to seek absolute values. As suggested at the beginning of this chapter, not all decisions are made using the desirable information about risk or benefit. However, when qualitative, arbitrary or intuitive decisions are made, they suggest the existence and acceptance of certain values.

As an example, a board of trustees may be asked to approve loans of objects on a regular basis. The only information they have is a monetary valuation of the object and, with luck, a conservation condition report. They may make qualitative judgements of the importance of the proposed exhibition or the status of the borrowing institution. In some cases the perceived benefits may over-ride an adverse conservation report. The decisions might seem more sound if they were taken using numerical estimates of risk and of net benefits. However, some of the properties needed for those assessments are not easy to quantify. Some, such as value and benefit, have a circular relationship. Value is a function of benefit and benefit is a function of value. You have to pin one down to get a fix on the other. However, the fact that the decisions have been made indicates that there is a level of risk the trustees are willing to accept and a level of benefits that they consider sufficient to outweigh the risks. In effect their decision amounts to another measurement of value based on willingness to pay.

The risks that have been taken in the recent past can be reasonably closely assessed. The quantified risk could serve as a benchmark for future decision-making. It would be a matter of local policy whether this benchmark represented the norm or an absolute minimum to be reviewed annually with a view to reducing it. The benchmark could be a proportionate risk figure or this could be combined with a valuation of the consignment to provide an absolute risk. 'We never accept risks greater than £*x*!'

An array of the type suggested in Figure 16.9 could be used to estimate the risk of sending an object or collection to another venue. If this is set up on a computer spreadsheet, the calculations will be done automatically, and it will be easy to test the effect of changing various estimates. Since there will be uncertainty about the degree of damage and the probability of accident, it is suggested that two estimates should be included for value loss. One should be close to the maximum possible proportionate loss and one somewhat lower than this. The appropriate probabilities should then be estimated. The risk can then be calculated from the products of the losses and probabilities (or extents). If the relationship between frequency and severity is linear then the two estimates should be close. A cautious person would always work with the larger value.

I have not included numbers in the array because they are very dependent on specifics such as the journey and the difference between the lender's and borrower's environment. I have, however, done some

Hazard	Value loss		Probability		Risk	
	max.	min.	max.	min.	max.	min.
Plane crash						
Road crash						
Vibration						
Case drop						
Object drop						
Light						
Pollution						
Humidity variation						
——	——					
Humidity extreme						
Temperature extreme						
Fire						
Theft						
			Total marginal risk			

Figure 16.9 *Possible spreadsheet layout for calculation of marginal risk of lending objects to another institution*

calculations for recent loans with which I am familiar. In general the marginal risks associated with loaning objects to other institutions were closer to 10^{-4} than my theoretical recommendation of 10^{-5}. More disturbing is that total risk which relates to the normal annual risk of keeping objects in their stores and galleries is a bit greater than 10^{-4}. If you accept the application of risk–benefit compromise then this risk figure would have to be set against the benefits that the objects generated while at the museum. Whether you do or not, this figure serves as a benchmark from which improvements are possible. This is why, for instance, it is an agreed policy at the V&A that any new building project must result in an improved environment for the objects.

Benchmarks for ethical intervention

When it is proposed that an object should be treated, there will be some qualitative or intuitive assessment of the increases in the aesthetic and potential values and the possible decreases in others, especially informational value. It is helpful to know what other people think and what they would do if they were in your place. Decisions about past interventions or proposals for new ones could be analysed using an array such as that shown in Figure 16.10. Again a computer spreadsheet is sensible, because calculations using formulae mentioned elsewhere in this book can be done automatically. Spreadsheets also ease toying about with figures, to test the sensitivity of the final answer to changes in what are very uncertain quantities.

It is important to know the relative weight that people put on changes in the different types of value. The rise of technological investigation of evidence is increasing the weighting given to informational value. A very good review of the qualitative weighing up of different types of value has been published by staff from the Textiles Conservation Centre (Eastop and Brooks, 1996). In one example quoted, soils from a Fifth Dynasty Egyptian funerary dress were not removed, despite 'potential continuing degrading effect of the soilings', as they could provide evidence of burial rituals. Soiling was not removed from the inside of the veil worn by Joseph Merrick, the 'Elephant Man', so that it can be subjected to forensic

Value type	Weighting	Maximum potential change	Probability extent	Risk	Net benefit
Informational					
Contextual					
Potential					
Aesthetic					
———	———				
			Total risk/benefit		

Figure 16.10 *Possible spreadsheet layout for calculation of risk of practical intervention*

tests 'when resources and technology allow'. In this latter case there is an obvious link between values relating to history and identity and the possible value of information not yet interpreted.

Benchmarks for different value weightings would eventually lead to better assessments of absolute values of future information.

Something to think about

What other types of museum decision would benefit from quantitative benchmarking?

Does the manipulation of uncertain numbers actually lead to any better conclusion than the intuition of someone with experience?

How likely and how important is a study of biological stains in nineteenth-century undergarments?

References

Ashley-Smith, J. (1986) *Environmental Monitoring and Control.* Geological Curators Group, London.

Canadian Museum of Nature (1995) Assessing and Managing Risks to Your Collections. UKIC Natural Sciences Section. Museums Association Annual Conference, Leicester.

Eastop, Dinah and Brooks, Mary. To Clean or Not to Clean: The Value of Soils and Creases. ICOM-CC. 11th Triennial Meeting, Edinburgh, 1–6 September. ISBN 1-873396-50-8, pp. 687–691.

Kantzenbach, Birgit (1996) Stepwise Approach to the Conservation and Restoration of a Diverse Collection. Paper distributed at ICOM-CC, Edinburgh. From National Museum of Ethnology, Steenstraat 1, PO Box 212. NL-2300 AE Leiden.

Krikken, J. (1997) A Dutch Exercise in the Valuation of Natural History Collections. The Value and Valuation of Natural History Collections. Proceedings of the International Conference, Manchester, 1995, edited by J.R. Nudds and C.W. Pettitt. Geological Society, London. ISBN 1-897799-76-4, pp. 123–126.

Marcon, Paul (1997) Decision Support Models for Preventive Conservation. The Interface Between Science and Conservation. British Museum Occasional Paper, No. 116. ISBN 0-86159-116-X, pp. 143–152.

Michalski, Stefan (1992) A Systematic Approach to the Conservation (Care) of Museum Collections. Canadian Conservation Institute.

Michalski, S. (1994) A Systematic Approach to Preservation: Description and Integration with Other Museum Activities. Preventive Conservation: Practice, Theory and Research. Preprints to the Ottawa Congress, 12–16 September. IIC, pp. 8–11.

Ministry of Welfare, Health and Cultural Affairs (1992) Plan for the Preservation of Cultural Heritage. Fact Sheet C-1-E, PO Box 5406, 2280 HK Rijswik, Netherlands.

Price, Judith C. and Fitzgerald, Gerald R. (1995) Categories of Specimens: A Collection Management Tool.

Research Libraries Group, Inc. (1993) Guide to the RLG Preservation Needs Assessment Package. Research Libraries Group, Inc. Mountain View, California.

Stewart, Deborah and Tremain, David (1994) Workshop Notes. Emergency and Disaster Preparedness for Museums. Canadian Conservation Institute, Ottawa K1A OM5.

Tennison, Heather, Van der Reyden, Dianne and Fei Wen Tsai (1996) Publish, Then Perish: The Reclamation of a Collection of Scientific Illustrations. *Restaurator,* Vol. 17, pp. 104–115.

Tennison, Heather, Van der Reyden, Dianne, Fei Wen Tsai and Parrish, Mary (1996) *AIC The Book and Paper Annual,* No. 15, pp. 145–159.

van Veek, Anneke (1995) In Quest of Hidden Riches: The Dutch Photographic Survey Project. *Rundbrief Fotografie,* 15 March. ISSN 0945–0327, pp. 32–34.

Waller, Robert (1994) Conservation Risk Assessment: A Strategy for Managing Resources for Preventive Conservation. Preventive Conservation: Practice, Theory and Research. Preprints to the Ottawa Congress, 12–16 September. IIC pp. 12–17.

17 Expert advice

In this final chapter the processes of decision-making are examined in more detail. The reasons why experts may not agree are discussed and means of overcoming that disagreement are suggested. The need for greater sharing of information is explained and directions for research that would complement some of themes in this book are indicated.

The complexity of selection

Throughout this book the analysis of risk has been seen as a part of decision-making. A risk analysis may lead to a decision to reduce the risk, or it may form part of the evaluation of options for a proposed venture. A risk analysis may be used to justify a past decision which will act as a benchmark for decisions in the future.

Throughout the book there has been an underlying conceit that given the right tools and enough information, it would be possible to make a succession of consistent and rational judgements. Any two people given the same tools and information would automatically make the same decision. The museum world is obviously not yet in this ideal state. We can continue this conceit a little longer by further analysing the decision-making process and seeing what could be done to move towards greater consistency and rationality. There have been several studies of rationality in decision-making (briefly reviewed in Watson and Buede, 1987).

In Figure 17.1 the preparation for the final selection of one option is broken down into four stages (Moore and Thomas, 1988). The factors that add complexity at each stage are listed. The process becomes more complex as you identify more people that you have to please and more people who should be involved in the decision.

Step 2 involves those questions that have been the main substance of this book: how likely is an unwanted outcome and does it really matter anyway? One of the contributions to complexity, one of the major problems in museums and conservation, is the multidisciplinarity of the subject. The information necessary to make a decision comes from a variety of professional disciplines. The relevant information is difficult to

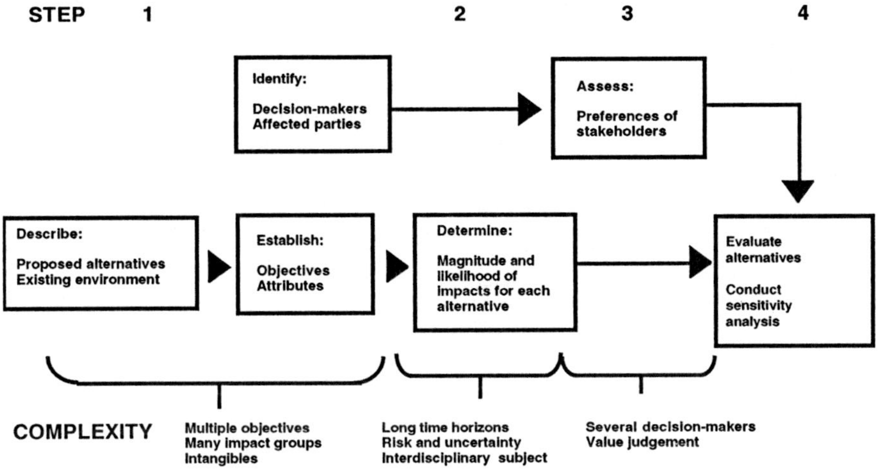

Figure 17.1 *The process of decision-making involving consideration of the preferences of all affected by the decision. The factors that complicate the process at each stage are listed*

find because it appears in so many different places. It is difficult to interpret because workers in different disciplines use the same words to speak different languages. Even if there were a will to consult and cooperate, the lack of a common language makes interdisciplinary collaboration difficult. Even within one discipline experts do not agree.

Step 3 involves looking at what the decision-makers and other affected parties actually want as an outcome. A word that has been frequently used in recent years to describe a member of this collective is 'stakeholder'. Part of the decision-making process must be deciding how much weight to give to the preferences of different groups. Do art historians have more right to be heard than conservators? Are the needs of scholars more important than those of the general public?

The literature about decisions in an uncertain world presupposes the existence of three people: the decision-maker, the analyst and the expert (French, 1997). The decision-maker is assumed to be a major stakeholder or the representative of stakeholders, and is the person who will make the final choice. Because of the complexity of the problem, the decision-maker is not yet able to make that choice. The analyst is a neutral consultant who aids the decision-maker by eliciting options and preferences, and evaluating possible outcomes. The expert is someone distant from the problem but who has relevant expertise. One or more experts may be consulted. Their opinions are sought on the validity of the data and the assumptions that are built into the analyst's model. When experts disagree, the analyst may have to use various techniques

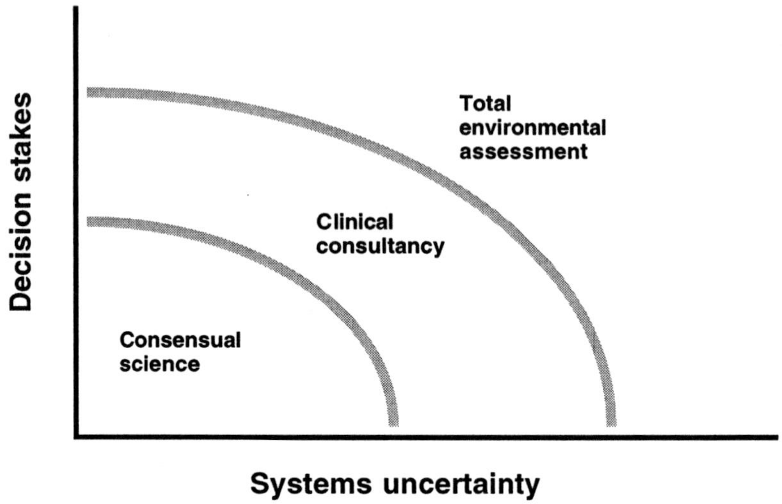

Figure 17.2 *Three types of risk assessment determined by the state of knowledge and the personal or societal rewards of a particular viewpoint (after Funtowicz and Ravetz)*

to elicit grudging moves toward consensus. In the real world these three ideal types will be combined to different degrees in one or more real people.

In other more mature areas of the study of risk, such as the impact of industry on the environment, it has been noted that there are three stages in the dissemination and acceptance of risk assessments (Funtowicz and Ravetz, 1985). As indicated in Figure 17.2 the boundaries between the three are determined by degrees of uncertainty about information on mechanisms and rates (systems uncertainty) and the importance of the outcome of decisions (decision stakes). At one end is 'consensual science' where there are reliable databases and there is agreement because there is no advantage in disagreement. At the other end is a system (Total Environmental Assessment or, more generally. Post-Normal Science) which is permeated by qualitative judgements and value commitments. Anyone has the right to an opinion and to be involved in the decision. In the middle is an area termed 'clinical consultancy'. This combines the roles of expert and analyst. The 'consultant' makes use of quantitative tools supplemented explicitly by qualitative judgement based on experience. This reliance on personal judgement tends to accentuate differences of interpretation arising from competing institutional, educational and disciplinary cultures. It also leads to an unbalanced state where views on risk can oscillate wildly. The development over the past three decades of these theories and observations has recently been reviewed by pioneers

Jerry Ravetz and Silvio Funtowitcz in the first volume of a new periodical, the *Journal of Risk Research* (Ravetz and Funtowitcz, 1998).

Something similar to this could be observed in the museum world, between 1993 and 1997, in attitudes to risk and fluctuating relative humidity. Because of the range of materials and constructions in museum objects, and the lack of well-recorded observations, consensual science has not been achieved. However, it has more or less been agreed that this is not just anyone's problem. The major protagonists are conservators and scientists. The analyst/experts that advise owners of collections are clinical consultants who by their actions declare whether they are from the Smithsonian, Michalski or Garry Thomson school of fluctuation damage.

When experts disagree

You may be the decision-maker and analyst all in one. You search the literature for consensus on risks and find conflicting expert opinion. How is it that experts can disagree? One reason that they may *appear* to disagree is that they are not all talking about the same thing. In scientific experiments it is necessary to limit the number of variables so that interpretable and reproducible data can be collected. What has been studied is not directly related to the real world. This situation is shown schematically in Figure 17.3. Experiments carried out by con-

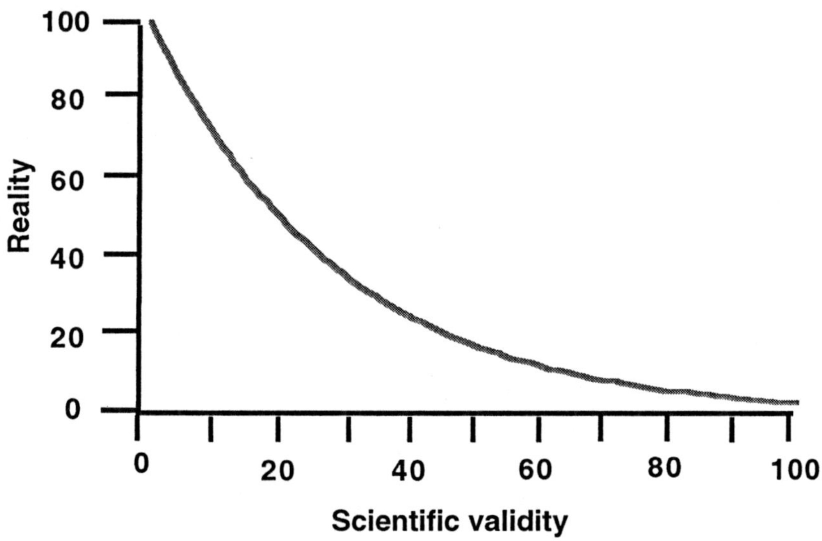

Figure 17.3 *The more a scientific experiment is designed to be reproducible and scientifically valid, the less it resembles what is observed in the real world*

servators will be toward the left-hand side, experiments by university scientists will be well over to the right. Conservation scientists work uneasily in the region between. When two scientists disagree this does not mean that either or both are wrong, but merely that their experiments were different. They were conducted at different points along this curve. If there is no disagreement this may be an indication that not enough experiments have been done.

The Sufi tale of the three blind men and the elephant is relevant. One held a leg, one the tail and the third held the trunk. Each was sure that his description of an elephant was correct and that the other two must be in error (Shah, 1973).

Scientists may forget that they have limited the variables in their experiments and their observations. They may start to feel that the factors they are investigating are the only ones that matter. I have observed this in the discussions about the deterioration of outdoor stone. A lot of breath has been wasted in claiming the dominance of one particular mechanism: pollution, frost, salt action, biodeterioration. Investigators who work in regions where frosts are rare cannot understand why other researchers even mention it as a possible cause.

Experts may be uncertain but feel forced into declaring certainty. It is quite difficult to maintain the pose of an expert while explaining that you don't really know enough. Risk involves subjective probability, which takes it a long way from the rigid certainty of cause and effect that afflicts some scientists, many conservators and most young people. They don't have the strength of will to remain uncertain themselves and cannot believe that, in their wisdom, experts want to be uncertain. From time to time experts will succumb to the pressure to commit themselves. In these circumstances two people that agree, and share the same uncertainty, may appear to hold different opinions.

Consensus

It falls to the analyst (which may be you) to seek some sort of consensus. In everyday life majority voting is often used to reach a single view in a short time. The assumption is that the majority must be right. However, there are circumstances where the process may not achieve a clear-cut group preference. It can be shown logically that, even if every member of a committee displays consistent views, it is perfectly possible for the decisions of the committee to be inconsistent (Watson and Buede, 1987, p. 107). You may not need the logical proof to be convinced of this! When studying the literature, the fact that a number of different authors make the same statement does not necessarily indicate a majority view. A large number of conservation papers merely repeat views from one or two sources, which may themselves be secondary.

In risk analysis the analyst/decision-maker needs to know the likelihood of an occurrence. For instance, what is the probability that continuing fluctuations of ±10% RH will cause damage to veneered furniture within a decade? Informed experts for such a question might come from a range of backgrounds; wood scientists, furniture curators, objects conservators. Their estimates might be very different. A possible approach is to combine the opinions of experts using weightings (Morgan and Henrion, 1990). A variety of approaches can be adopted to assign the weights. The experts may be asked to rate themselves, or they may be asked to rate each other. The analyst may weight the views based on the maturity of the experts or their track record for getting things right. The track record of an expert is called calibration. A well-calibrated person gets it right most of the time.

The fact that there are differences of opinion is a useful piece of information and the analyst should spend some time looking at the reasons for those differences. We have looked at some of them when discussing risk perception (Chapters 14 and 15). If an expert who is unused to estimating probabilities is asked to express a view about likelihood, there are several traps into which they can fall (French, 1997).

1. Overweighting evidence. When presented with new data they forget all they knew before. They do not combine the new data with their prior knowledge. If you learn that a medical test indicates you have a rare disease, you will believe that you have that illness, even though you may have been told that this test can produce false positives.
2. Misconceptions of randomness. Individuals expect random events to *look* random. The results of tossing a coin 10 times might be HHHHHTTTTT or HHTTTHTHHT. The first sequence would appear more miraculous even though the probabilities are equal.
3. Availability. In trying to estimate a probability the person may recall a set of similar circumstances and ask themselves what the frequency of the event was then. The 'similar circumstances' may actually be very atypical, and if the event caused distress may greatly increase the estimate of likelihood. Practical conservators spend their lives inspecting and mending damaged objects. Their curatorial colleagues spend time with the much greater number that are not damaged.
4. Anchoring. People tend to anchor on the first value they hear or estimate. The analyst must be very careful not to suggest an answer (unless that is the one they want!).

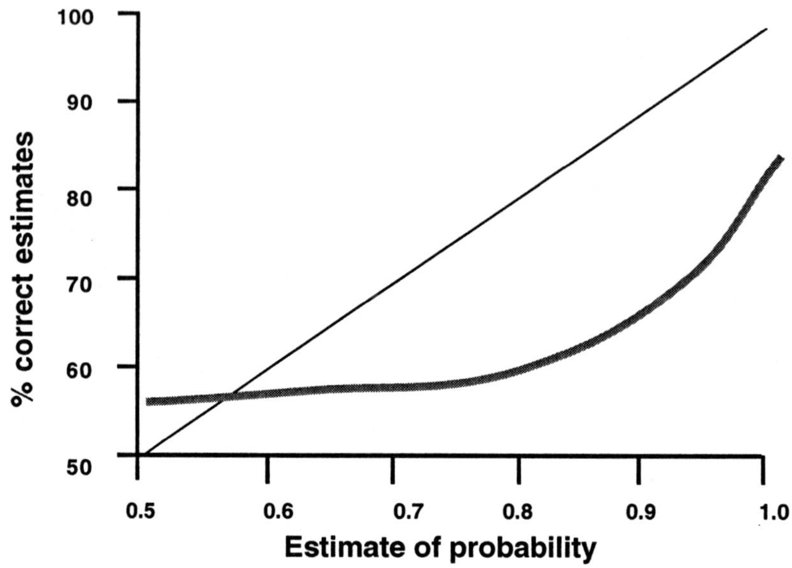

Figure 17.4 *Ability to estimate probabilities. Experiments show that people tend to be overconfident in their ability to predict. That is they underestimate the risk of their failure even when it is quite high. The diagonal line represents good calibration – getting it right all the time.*

The results of an experiment to see how good people are at estimating probabilities is shown in Figure 17.4. They are in line with other observations about risk perception. High probabilities are underestimated, low probabilities are overestimated.

There are a number of techniques for reaching agreement among experts. At one end of the spectrum the group meets face to face and has unrestricted discussion until a consensus is reached, as with a trial jury. There are benefits to working together but there can also be destructive pressures. The most dominant individual may not have the best calibration. At the other end of the spectrum is the Delphi technique, in which the participants do not meet initially and interaction is restricted to the exchange of anonymous assessments. Some summary measure of the degree of agreement such as standard deviation is fed back to the individuals. The feedback process is repeated until the degree of agreement is acceptably tight. At this point the group must meet to reconcile remaining differences. Stefan Michalski quotes an instance of the use of the Delphi method to bridge the gap between the precise data on fire occurrence and the lack of data on the influence of design factors on the probability of ignition or spread (Michalski, 1994). He proposes the use of the technique to establish expert opinion across the agents of deterioration in museum collections.

Variations of these 'normative' techniques are used to arrive at the standards published by institutions such as the International Standards Organization (ISO) and the American National Standards Institute (ANSI). If you see the interim assessments or drafts of the working parties, as they struggle to reach agreement, you can see quite wide swings in the apparent consensus view and begin to appreciate the effect of dominant members of the group.

Giving weight to stakeholders

Giving different weights to the opinions of experts may be necessary in order to arrive at an estimate of risk. To arrive at an estimate of the expected value of a decision you may have to attribute weights to the opinions of different stakeholders. In Chapter 15 it was stated that treatment proposals had very little effect on the public's willingness to pay to see an object. However, if a large weighting were given to an art historian's willingness to accept the object in a new state or a conservator's concern for professional standards, this might alter the decision.

Giving a weighting to the opinion of experts, rather than residents or users, often plays a significant part in cost–benefit exercises. This prior allocation of rights to the few may seem undemocratic but is accepted in our society if the few are landowners or industrial entrepreneurs. Giving prior rights to people with an intellectual interest might be an equally acceptable form of capitalism. Discussions about questions of rights and values can be found in most books on cost–benefit analysis (e.g. Zerbe and Dively, 1994; Hanley and Spash, 1993).

The most difficult case is probably when the view of an expert (however well calibrated) is in opposition to public perceptions or opinions. In this case the analyst is advised to present two different assessments.

The cost of information

> 'Those who use expert judgement have an obligation to link its use continually to the need for research.' (Morgan and Henrion, 1990, p. 168)

In a complex field such as museum preservation, decisions are always going to be made with incomplete information. The conservation field

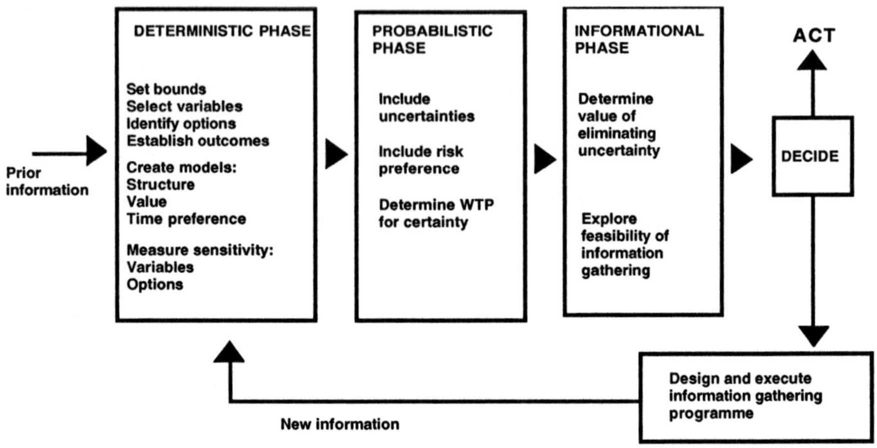

Figure 17.5 *Three phases of decision-making including the assessment of the need for more information and the cost of obtaining it*

relies on major national institutions to carry out research and on the publication of research findings. There are costs associated with research, the employment of expert consultants or even just talking to colleagues or going to the library. How much extra information do you really need to improve your decision-making?

A further model of decision-making is shown in Figure 17.5. It is a Bayesian model in that it assumes that the decision-maker is constantly adding new information to prior information to reduce uncertainty. The third 'informational' phase involves an assessment of how much more information is needed and whether the costs can be justified. The cost and value of new information are plotted in Figure 17.6. There are diminishing returns in the value of new information whereas the cost slowly accumulates. The optimum point is reached long before the costs exceed the value.

It is wise to test the sensitivity of your predicted outcomes to the existence of new information. Will doing more tests change your treatment proposal?

What new information is really needed?

There is a constant cry in conservation that more research is needed, and a constant moan that no one will provide the money to do it. If research means playing with expensive equipment in a scientific laboratory, we may need to ask whether this is in fact our top priority. The first step must

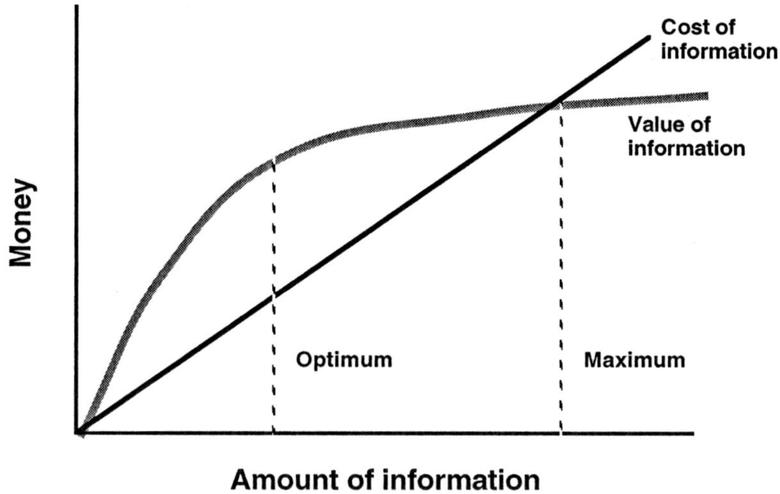

Figure 17.6 *If you keep gathering more information on a particular subject the cost keeps rising but the value of the information doesn't*

be to find out what questions we need answered in order to go about our business. A model such as I developed in Chapter 4 is designed to promote questions.

The information you need to answer these questions will be of two sorts: that which is universally applicable and that which relates only to your location and type of business. In either case you can be sure of one thing: the truth is out there. Or at least a substantial amount of it.

The American Institute for Conservation has conducted surveys of research needs in conservation. The large number of suggestions collated tend to indicate the poor spread of knowledge rather than its total absence. The problem is not that the work needs doing, but that knowledge of it has run aground somewhere. It needs to be rescued. The problem is one of the initial training of museum professionals and their continuing self-development. It is about the willingness to share information and the ability to select from the immense amount that is available. The answer almost certainly rests with the Internet and access to a greater range of bibliographic databases.

Relatively few researchers in conservation delve into the specialist literature of other disciplines. The physical properties of many of the materials we have to deal with have been studied, measured and published by the industries that make money from their use or manufacture. Yet we insist on studying and measuring them again. It is the role of the 'analyst' or 'clinical consultant' to act as selector and interpreter of this foreign information.

Conservators and curators are spending large amounts of time surveying their collections, to assess their condition and to make sure the objects are still where they last left them. The observations made during such surveys are not made widely known which makes any epidemiological studies of the effects of different types of care or treatment very difficult.

The spread of information would probably be accelerated if there was a clear distinction between the types of meetings that were held by the profession. There is a need for one type where 'analysts' and researchers meet to exchange views and reach consensus on the present state of knowledge. There is a second type where people come solely to learn about these developments and consensus views. On humanitarian grounds there is probably still room for the familiar third type, where nice people go and talk about anything they fancy and meet lots of other nice people. However, the opportunity to gain benchmarks for values should be used. At the 1994 IIC conference Miriam Clavir asked the participants to vote on a number of treatment options that involved consideration of the views of native peoples about the spiritual values of the objects. The voting indicated a movement toward acceptance that groups outside the museum should be allowed to influence treatment of museum objects.

Research and consensus

In the next section I will look at areas where I have been unable to find all the necessary information or where there seems to be a need for greater consensus in museum-related professions.

Environmental control

Following a survey of photographic archives Jesper Johnsen remarks that the rate of deterioration of photographs is very variable, depending as much on the quality of the processing as in the inherent stability of the materials. The standard recommended storage climate is both too lax, in that it does not prevent the deterioration of unstable images, and too strict in that it imposes the technical and cost burden of full air-conditioning, wherever in the world the archive is situated (Padfield and Johnsen, 1995).

Following a survey of ethnographic material Tom Stone remarks that no correlation could be made between the frequency of damage to objects in environmentally controlled collections and to those without environmental control (Stone, 1996).

The work from the Canadian Conservation Institute and the Smithsonian Institute suggests that tight environmental control to prevent temperature and humidity fluctuations may not be necessary (Chapter 11).

Studies show that installing air-conditioning in historic buildings may not always provide improved or stable conditions for objects (Oreszczyn, Cassar and Fernandez, 1994).

Given these observations, in what circumstances is the investment in plant and running costs of air-conditioning actually justified? In Chapter 5 we looked at model decision trees that could be used to answer that question. To use them we need damage functions that link the different sets of environmental conditions with rates of damage. We need consensus on the maximum potential loss in value for different object types. We need local information about the capital, running, maintenance and replacement costs of plant working to different specifications and in different locations.

The same sort of information is needed to give guidance in arguments about delicate objects on open display. What are the relative rates of damage due to soiling and cleaning?

Some of this information is out there, some of it needs new and systematic work. Some of it needs collaboration between different disciplines globally and within individual museums. Some is a matter of record and some is amenable to modelling using computer simulations. We also need guidance about the sensitivity of the answer to uncertainty about these relationships. There should be an assessment of whether different decisions would be made if this new information were available. All this is possible, it just needs a few people to give it a try and then talk to each other.

Decision theory, economics and the philosophy of value

The research that is indicated falls into the two types which have sometimes been described as 'hard' and 'soft' science. The hard science involves the study of objects, materials and constructions and their relationship to use and environment. The softer work is probably more important since so little of it has been done in the area of conservation.

The value of real objects in real museums is affected by the increasing ease of access to virtual objects in virtual museums. David Bearman asserts 'People do not want the things in themselves, they want the meanings they convey' (Rennie, 1998). There are probably now enough examples available to carry out an analysis of this relationship between information, object, image and value, and to predict its effect on future conservation.

Approaches to combining multiple value types need to be refined as do methods of constructing multi-attribute utility functions for conservation decisions. Analysis of decision-making and its locus in the museum management structure needs to be carried out. There needs to be consensus about the calculation of present value so that we can agree a sensible discount rate that reflects the reality of the museum world rather than that of commercial business.

Many of the quantities that are needed for calculating risks, costs and benefits are uncertain or cover ranges of value. Fuzzy logic allows calculations which can accommodate some of these uncertainties. Computer programs which include uncertainty by using simple frequency distributions are available to calculate risk for project planning and financial decision-making. Suitable frequency distributions of damaging events in museums should be derived for use in Extreme Value Theory to estimate what the real 'worst case scenarios' actually are.

The value of human life and limb could be incorporated into some risk–benefit calculations. Consideration of health and safety at work is limiting the options open for interventive treatments and adding to the cost of planning time. History has never shown that the value of human life was considered greater than the value of physical possessions, yet modern risk assessments for the workplace seem to imply that attitudes are changing. However, some artworks still have market values much greater than any calculation for the value of a human life.

The construction of condition surveys could also include a move towards definitions of condition that used utility rather than state. As suggested at the end of Chapter 7 there has been some good work in the field of health studies ascribing distinct 'health states' to humans with increasing degrees of disability or illness. Different health states can be ranked to give a type of value that can be used in cost–benefit analysis. One of the systems that has been used by the UK National Health Service is the QUALY, Quality Adjusted Life Year. This combines information about health state and life expectancy (Soby and Ball, 1991). When applied to objects these are both parameters of concern to museums, so some development of this system might be beneficial. Suzanne Keene has recognized both the potential and drawbacks of QUALYs (Keene, 1996) but, as yet no one has taken the idea forward in the field of cultural heritage.

Damage functions and prediction

Hard science could provide much more information about susceptibilities and rates of damage.

For specific object types such as photographic material the accurate scientific investigation of rates of deterioration may be possible. Given the supposed drawbacks of both historic surveys and of accelerated ageing, one way forward may be real time observation of very small changes. These could involve the detection and accurate measurement of very low concentrations of gaseous degradation products (Edge, 1996). The measurement of small changes requires a sound understanding of the mechanism of reaction if it is to be used in prediction of lifetime. Small changes *are* small and without certainty about the process it is dangerous to extrapolate too far into the future. Unfortunately the study of deterioration mechanisms is often seen as frivolous and an unnecessary expense.

Because of the complexity of many collections and the complexity of their environments it may never be possible to have anything other than a general view of rates of change. An area where scientists and conservators could work together for mutual benefit would be in the design and interpretation of collection condition surveys. Full conservation surveys to a standard format are the potential basis for epidemiological studies of deterioration. If there are enough similar objects with the same environmental history then information about susceptibilities to particular agents can be derived from the survey data. If objects have entered a specific environment at known times there is the possibility of using survey data to derive a form of damage function. This can be used to predict future states of the collection. In the field of stone deterioration the study of graveyards has been useful. Roughly similar objects inscribed with the date of entry remain in approximately the same environment for considerable periods (e.g. Mirwald and Buschmann, 1991).

A survey places each object in a condition category. The percentage of objects in each category is plotted against the year of acquisition. The percentage of objects in the worst state will increase the older the objects are, as shown by the solid black line in Figure 17.7. To predict the state of the collection in, say, 50 years' time, the line can be shifted horizontally to the right by 50 years. To predict the effect of improving the environmental factors the new line can be shifted vertically downwards. The damage function derived from the survey only includes the variables time and damage. To determine future states in future environments requires damage functions that include variables such as pollution levels. These could possibly be obtained by comparison with other surveys in other locations. The difference between rates of decay of paper in libraries has been ascribed to differences in pollution levels, but there has not been any attempt to turn this into even the crudest of damage functions.

The analysis of survey data must be interpreted with caution. Although the graphs shown in Figure 17.8 contain information about one type of material 'paper' there are two very different types of paper present (Palm and Cullhed, 1988). The hump in the middle is due to acidic nineteenth-

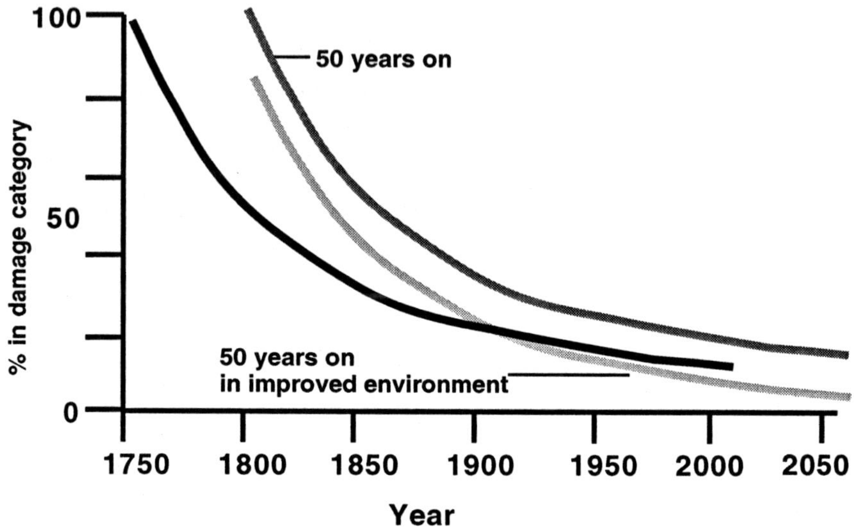

Figure 17.7 *Data from a condition survey about categories of damage is plotted against the year that each object entered the specific environment. The resulting curve can be manipulated to give predictions about future states of the collection (after Mirwald)*

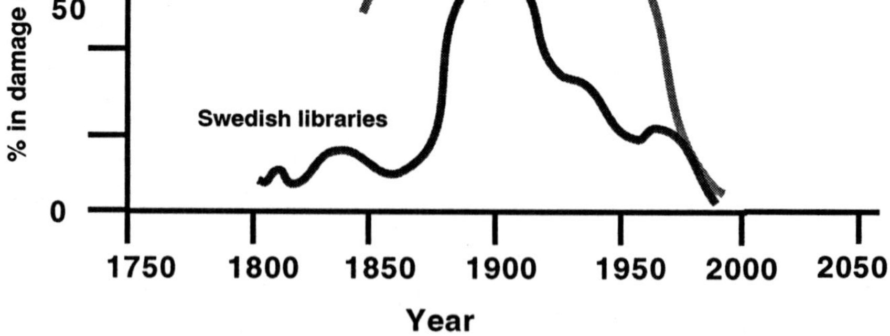

Figure 17.8 *The state of two library collections, one in Sweden and the other in the United States. The vertical axis represents the percentage of the collection in the poorest category*

century paper whereas the tail downwards to the left seems to indicate the very high stability of older paper, even under current conditions of pollution and use. Shifting the right-hand side of the curve further to the right will give a glimpse of the future. It may be a bit exaggerated but it is certainly depressing.

Another idea from the study of risk in health combines the damage function derived from survey with the separation into distinct health states. This methodology is slightly different from that used to create Figure 17.7. In the gravestone studies, the difference in state between assumed good health at the start through to the present poor state is used to predict the future for the same group of objects. For the health studies, the states of people were studied as they went from ill health to death. Previous behaviour of one group of subjects is used to predict the future for other individuals.

This leads to a plot of the type shown in Figure 17.9 (Stanley, 1983). In the case of human beings it represents one of those models that tell you what you already know. Fit people have a high probability of survival which declines gracefully. Very ill people have a probability of survival that sinks to zero very rapidly. If it is based on sound observations of large numbers of subjects (objects) it can provide a tool for accurate prediction based on a classification of condition. That is to say it validates the use of a single observation in the prediction of the future, and so justifies current conservation practice.

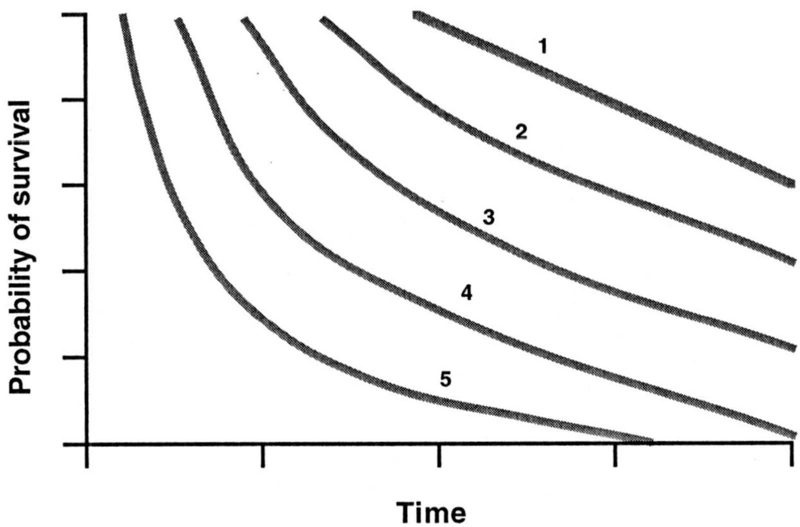

Figure 17.9 *The probability of survival as it decreases with time for five different health states*

Conclusion

In Chapter 1 I warned that objects were inanimate and there were dangers in drawing analogies with humans. Yet because of the huge expenditure in medical research there is a wealth of analytical, economic and philosophical methodologies that could be transferred to the study of conservation of museum collections.

It is true that museum objects are not human and do not have the same predictable probability of death. We know that there are many different object types and a range of possible agents of deterioration. We know that museum records do not encourage epidemiological study. We know it will be difficult. Think of the possibilities, look at Figure 17.9, the beautiful simplicity of the graph, the elegance of those curves – don't they inspire you to have a try!

Something to think about

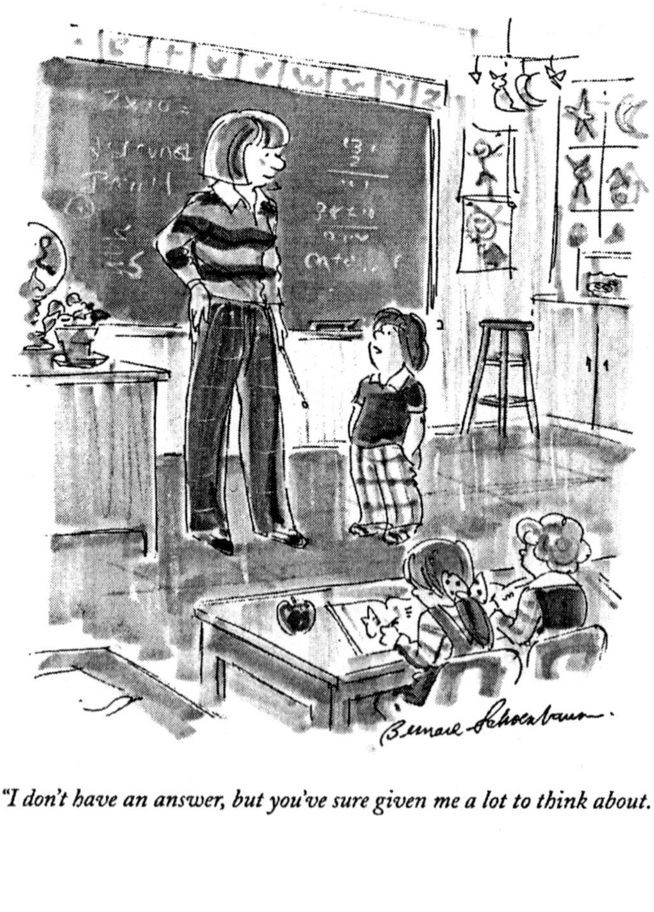

"I don't have an answer, but you've sure given me a lot to think about."

References

Edge, Michelle (1996) Lifetime Prediction: Fact or Fantasy? Research Techniques in Photographic Conservation. Proceedings of the Copenhagen Conference, 14–19 May 1995. ISBN 87-89730-18-6, pp. 97–100.

French, Simon (1997). Representations of Uncertainty, 1. Dependence Modelling and Risk Management: Practical Approaches to Correlated Uncertainties. Notes for a course organized for the University of Cambridge Programme for Industry, 9–11 April, pp. 1–9.

Funtowicz and Ravetz (1985) *Three Types of Risk Assessment. A Methodological Analysis*. Plenum Press. Quoted in Steve Rayner, *Risk and Relativism in Science for Policy. The Social and Cultural Construction of Risk*, edited by Covello and Johnson, pp. 5–23, 1987.

Hanley, N. and Spash, C.L. (1993) *Cost–Benefit Analysis and the Environment*. Edward Elgar Publishing. ISBN 1-85278-947-6.

Keene, Suzanne (1996) *Managing Conservation in Museums*. Butterworth-Heinemann in Association with Science Museum, London. ISBN 0-7506-2384-5, p. 58.

Michalski, Stefan (1994) A Systematic Approach to Preservation: Description and Integration with Other Museum Activities. Preventive Conservation: Practice, Theory and Research. Preprints to the Ottawa Congress, 12–16 September. IIC, pp. 8–11.

Mirwald, P.W. and Buschmann, H. (1991) Assessment of the Stone Inventory and Weathering State of the Tombstones of the Old Cemetery of Bonn FRG as a Constraint for Urban Planning. Science, Technology and European Cultural Heritage. Proceedings of the European Symposium, Bologna, Italy, 13–16 June 1989. Butterworth-Heinemann for the Commission of the European Communities.

Moore, P.G. and Thomas, H. (1988) *The Anatomy of Decisions*. 2nd edn. Penguin Books. ISBN 0-14-009120-3.

Morgan, M. Granger and Henrion, Max. (1990) *Uncertainty: A Guide to Dealing with Uncertainty in Quantitative Risk and Policy Analysis*. Cambridge University Press. ISBN 0-521-36542-2, p. 168.

Oreszczyn, T., Casar, M. and Fernandez, K. (1994) Preventive Conservation: Practice, Theory and Research. Preprints to the Ottawa Congress, 12–16 September. IIC, pp. 145–148.

Padfield, Tim and Johnsen, Jesper Stub (1995) The Breath of Arrhenius: Airconditioning in Photographic Archives. Research Techniques in Photographic Conservation. Proceedings of the Copenhagen Conference, 14–19 May. ISBN 87-89730-18-6, pp. 59–64.

Palm, Jonas and Cullhed, Per (1988) Deteriorating Paper in Sweden. Report No. 3 FoU-projektet för papperkonservering. Stockholm. ISSN 0284–5636, p. 16.

Ravetz, Jerry andFuntowitcz, Silvio Commentary. *Journal of Risk Research*, Vol. 1. ISSN 1366–9877, pp. 45–49.

Rennie, John (1998) Quoting David Beardman in Collector's Item. *Personal Computer World*, April, pp. 134–138.

Shah, Idries (1973) *Tales of the Dervishes*. Panther Books. St. Albans.

Soby, B.A. and Ball, D.J. (1991) *Consumer Safety and the Valuation of Life and Injury*. Environmental Risk Assessment Unit. School of Environmental Sciences, Norwich. ISBN 1-873933-00-2.

Stanley, Kenneth (1983) The Role of Risk in Treating Advanced Lung Cancer, in *The Analysis of Actual versus Perceived Risks*, edited by Vincent T. Covello, W. Gary Flamm, Joseph V. Rodricks and Robert G. Tardiff. Plenum Press, p. 157.

Stone, Thomas G. (1996) Artifacts Revisited: The Evaluation of Old Treatments. ICOM-CC. 11th Triennial Meeting, Edinburgh, 1–6 September. ISBN 1-873396-50-8, pp. 643–649.

Watson, Stephen R. and Buede, Dennis M. (1987) *Decision Synthesis: The Principles and Practice of Decision Analysis*. Cambrige University Press. ISBN 0-521-31078-4, p. 11–13.

Zerbe Jr, R.O. and Dively, D.D. (1994) *Benefit–Cost Analysis in Theory and Practice*. Harper Collins, New York. ISBN-0-673-18066-2, p. 270.

Index

Printed in the United Kingdom
by Lightning Source UK Ltd.
104155UKS00002B/8